PLANNING AND TRANSFORMATION

Planning and Transformation provides a comprehensive view of planning under political transition in South Africa, offering an accessible resource for both students and researchers from international and local audiences.

In the years after the 1994 transition to democracy in South Africa, planners believed they would be able to promote successfully a vision of integrated, equitable and sustainable cities, and counter the spatial distortions created by apartheid. This book covers the experience of the planning community, the extent to which their aims were achieved, and the hindering factors.

The book is organized into sections reflecting the main themes in international planning debates: Planning and governance; Discourses of planning; Planning and society.

Although some of the factors affecting planning have been context-specific, the nature of South Africa's transition and its relationship to global dynamics have meant that many of the issues confronting planners in other parts of the world are echoed here. Issues of governance, integration, market competitiveness, sustainability, democracy and values are significant and the particular nature of the South African experience lends new insights to thinking on these questions, exploring the possibilities of achievement in the planning field.

Philip Harrison is Executive Director of Development Planning and Urban Management in the City of Johannesburg and an honorary professor at the University of the Witwatersrand where he was previously Professor of Urban and Regional Planning in the School of Architecture and Planning.

Alison Todes is Professor of Urban and Regional Planning at the University of the Witwatersrand. She was previously a Research Director at the Human Sciences Research Council, and Professor of Planning at the University of KwaZulu-Natal.

Vanessa Watson is Professor in the City and Regional Planning Programme in the School of Architecture, Planning and Geomatics, University of Cape Town.

THE RTPI Library Series

Editors: **Robert Upton**, RTPI, London, UK
Cliff Hague, Commonwealth Association of Planners
Tim Richardson, Aalborg University, Denmark

Published by Routledge in conjunction with The Royal Town Planning Institute, this series of leading-edge texts looks at all aspects of spatial planning theory and practice from a comparative and international perspective.

PLANNING AND TRANSFORMATION

LEARNING FROM THE POST-APARTHEID EXPERIENCE

PHILIP HARRISON, ALISON TODES
AND VANESSA WATSON

Routledge
Taylor & Francis Group

LONDON AND NEW YORK

First published 2008 by Routledge
2 Park Square, Milton Park, Abingdon, OX14 4RN

Simultaneously published in the USA and Canada
by Routledge
270 Madison Avenue, New York, NY10016

Routledge is an imprint of the Taylor & Francis Group, an informa business

© 2008 Philip Harrison, Alison Todes and Vanessa Watson

Typeset in Akzidenz Grotesk by
GreenGate Publishing Services, Tonbridge, Kent
Printed and bound in Great Britain by
TJ International Ltd, Padstow, Cornwall

British Library Cataloguing in Publication Data
A catalogue record for this book is available from the British Library

Library of Congress Cataloging in Publication Data
Harrison, Philip, 1964–
Planning and transformation: learning from the post-apartheid experience / Philip Harrison, Alison Todes and
Vanessa Watson
p. cm – (The RTPI library series)
Includes bibliographical references and index.
ISBN 978-0-415-36033-3 (hbk: alk. paper) – ISBN 978-0-415-36031-9 (pbk alk. paper)
1. Planning – South Africa. 2. Political Planning – South Africa. 3. Policy Sciences. I. Todes, A. II. Watson,
Vanessa. III. Title.
JQ1929.P64H37 2007
320.60968–dc22

2007005464

ISBN-10: 0-415-36033-1 (hbk)
ISBN-10: 0-415-36031-5 (pbk)
ISBN-10: 0-203-00798-0 (ebk)

ISBN-13: 978-0-415-36033-3 (hbk)
ISBN-13: 978-0-415-36031-9 (pbk)
ISBN-13: 978-0-203-00798-3 (ebk)

CONTENTS

PART 4
PLANNING AND SOCIETY

LIST OF ILLUSTRATIONS

FIGURES

TABLES

PREFACE

There are few countries in the world that have been through the kind of political transformation that South Africa has experienced in the last decade. In the late 1980s, with the country in the grip of apartheid and civil war, descent into chaos and ruin seemed almost inevitable. For planners, these were dark days indeed: some had committed both their work and their daily lives to the apartheid project; others in the bureaucracies, NGOs and universities did what they could, often risking personal freedom, to provide critique and strengthen resistance to apartheid planning. The relatively peaceful transition to democracy in 1994, under the leadership of Nelson Mandela, was in many ways a political miracle. So too was the nature of the reconstruction and development programme and the new constitution put in place post-1994. National commitments to democracy, redistribution, equity and integration, and to replanning apartheid cities and regions, inspired planners to tackle the ambitious task of visioning alternative futures. The unique opportunity to sweep away apartheid planning legislation and design the country's planning system from scratch appeared to make these ambitions possible.

This book tells the story of the first ten years of South Africa's planning transition. A decade on, we believe that we have sufficient perspective to begin a process of critical appraisal of post-apartheid planning, although the transition itself continues. But it also offers a learning experience which we believe will speak to planners in other parts of the world. It allows us to pose questions about the ethical values that should guide planning, and how universal or particular these should be; its role and scope in relation to particular contextual issues; its relationship to related professions and policy streams and ways of integrating with these; its location within changing structures of governance and its relationship with other stakeholders involved in the built environment; and the nature of the tools, techniques and processes that it deploys in order to be effective. It allows the testing and evaluation of new planning and policy ideas which are also currently being tried elsewhere, integrated development planning being particularly significant here. It allows us to examine the process of change itself: the interplay of change and continuity in planning systems is a theme that has been explored in other parts of the world as well. And it allows us to explore the important issue of the international transferability of planning ideas, as South Africa's many imported policy and planning ideas continue to articulate, sometimes uncomfortably, with the realities of the local context.

It would be incorrect, however, to overstate the similarities between the planning experience in South Africa and in other parts of the world. The uniqueness of its historical and geographical context, its colonial and apartheid past together with its location on the southern tip of the world's poorest continent, and its very particular cultural influences, make South Africa very different from elsewhere. Moreover the transition has fashioned a planning system that is largely state-led, even in a context in which the rhetoric of governance and inclusiveness is very strong. Thus the relative absence of voice from organized business and from community groups in planning decision-making post-1994 may appear strange in some parts of the world where this has become the norm. We do not believe that these differences detract from our overall task: all regions of the world are unique and exploring both similarities and differences is in itself a useful learning experience.

Above all, this book has allowed us to explore the relative power of planning, and the limits to its power. We discuss the ways in which the current government has accepted planning as an important instrument of transformation, and has incorporated planning within its new policy and legislative frameworks, and the ways in which the ideas and methods of planning (forward-thinking, visioning, linking analysis and ideas to implementation, participation and networking) have become central to the very concept of developmental government. But while the discourse of planning has begun to permeate the work of a wide range of professionals and political representatives, and the concept of planning is perhaps more influential now than it ever was before, the spatial imprint of apartheid remains entrenched in cities and regions, and the ambitious plans to transform South African cities are, as yet, showing little impact.

Understanding why this should be the case, and the limits of planning power, become particularly important in the light of recent calls from organizations, such as UN-Habitat, for planning to play a leading role in addressing issues of rapid urbanization and slum formation. As international interest increases in the possibilities of planning to address not only urbanization, but also the threats of climate change and oil depletion come to the fore, we need to be particularly clear about what planning can, but even more importantly, can't, achieve within the current political and economic global order.

The three authors have worked for long periods in the academic sector, and have participated in national and international debates around planning within transforming societies. They have, however, also had strong connections with practice, including acting as policy advisers to the various spheres of government, and are thus able to provide a perspective that bridges the still entrenched theory–practice divide. Finally, each of the three authors is located in a different part of the country, and so this book is sensitive to the significant regional differences in practice and perception.

ACKNOWLEDGEMENTS

We would like to thank Robert Upton of the RTPI, series editor, for his thoughtful review of the manuscript, Georgina Johnson of Taylor & Francis for her patience and help, Kathy Forbes for editing work and Jacques Oberholzer and S'bo Zama (Knowledge Systems, Human Sciences Research Council) for maps and graphics. We would particularly like to acknowledge the early inputs and ideas of Mark Oranje who was unable to make the journey with us to the end of the production process due to a series of unfortunate mishaps including the theft of two laptops. We would also like to thank Mark for his comments on the first draft of the book.

The following illustration credits are due:

Figure 1.2: The model apartheid city. Adapted from Western, J. (1981) *Outcast Cape Town*, Cape Town, Pretoria and Johannesburg: Human & Rousseau, by J. Oberholzer.

Figure 1.5: Demolition of Crossroads informal settlement, Cape Town. Originally in Cole, J. (1987) *Crossroads: The Politics of Reform and Repression 1976–1986*, Johannesburg: Ravan Press. Also used in Watson, V. (2002a) *Change and Continuity in Spatial Planning*, London and New York: Routledge.

Figure 3.2: Cato Manor, Durban. Supplied by the Cato Manor Development Association, Durban.

Figure 5.2: Areas of population growth and decline. Adapted from Pillay *et al.* (2006) *Democracy and Delivery*, Pretoria: HSRC Press.

TERMS AND MEASUREMENTS

AAPS	Association of African Planning Schools
ANC	African National Congress
ARP	Alexandra Renewal Project
ASGI-SA	Accelerated and Shared Growth Initiative for South Africa
BDS	business development services
BEE	black economic empowerment
BESG	Built Environment Support Group
BID	Business Improvement District
BLA	black local authority
BP	before present
CBD	Central Business District
CDE	Centre for Development and Enterprise
CDS	City Development Strategy
CIAM	Congrès International du Architecture Moderne
CID	City Improvement District
CJP	Central Johannesburg Partnership
CODESA	Convention for a Democratic South Africa
COSATU	Congress of South African Trade Unions
CPD	continuing professional development
CSIR	Council for Scientific and Industrial Research
DAG	Development Action Group
DBSA	Development Bank of Southern Africa
DCD	Department of Constitutional Development
DDP	Decentralised Development Planning
DFA	Development Facilitation Act
DLA	Department of Land Affairs
DPASA	Development Planning Association of South Africa
DPLG	Department of Provincial and Local Government
DTI	Department of Trade and Industry
EIA	Environmental Impact Assessment
FEPD	Forum for Effective Planning and Development
FIFA	Fédération Internationale de Football Association
GAA	Group Areas Act
GDS	Growth and Development Strategy

GEAR   Growth, Employment and Redistribution
GGP   gross geographic product
GNU   Government of National Unity
GPEAN   Global Planning Education Association Network
GTZ   Gesellschaft für Technische Zusammenarbeit
GVA   geographic value added
IDP   integrated development plan
IDT   Independent Development Trust
IDZ   Industrial Development Zone
ILO   International Labour Organization
INK   Inanda–Ntunzuma–Kwamashu
ISRDP   Integrated Sustainable Rural Development Programme
ISRDS   Integrated Sustainable Rural Development Strategy
iTRUMP   Inner City eThekwini Regeneration and Urban Management Programme
JDA   Johannesburg Development Agency
JIPSA   Joint Initiative on Priority Skills Acquisition
LDO   Land Development Objective
LED   local economic development
LGNF   Local Government Negotiating Forum
LTAB   Land Tenure Advisory Board
MSDF   Metropolitan Spatial Development Framework
MTEF   Medium Term Expenditure Framework
MTSF   Medium Term Strategic Framework
NBRI   National Building Research Institute
NEMA   National Environmental Management Act
NGO   non-governmental organization
NPM   new public management
NRDC   National Resources Development Council
NSDP   National Spatial Development Perspective
NSMS   National Security Management System
NTRPC   Natal Town and Regional Planning Commission
PADA   Planning and Development Association
PCAS   Policy Coordination and Advisory Services
PGDS   Provincial Growth and Development Strategy
PIMS   Planning, Implementation and Management Support
PPP   public–private partnership
PWV   Pretoria–Witwatersrand–Vereeniging
RDAC   Regional Development Advisory Committee
RDP   Reconstruction and Development Programme
RIDS   Regional Industrial Development Strategy

RSC   Regional Services Council
RSDF   Regional Spatial Development Framework
RTPI   Royal Town Planning Institute
RUMP   Regional Urban Management Plan
SACN   South African Cities Network
SACP   South African Communist Party
SACPLAN   South African Council for Planners
SACTRP   South African Council for Town and Regional Planners
SAITRP   South African Institute of Town and Regional Planning
SAPI   South African Planning Institution
SDF   spatial development framework
SDI   Spatial Development Initiative
SEA   Strategic Environmental Assessment
SEPC   Social and Economic Planning Council
SGB   Standards Generating Body
SIPPs   Special Integrated Presidential Projects
SMME   small, medium and micro enterprise
TND   traditional neighbourhood design
TOD   transit-oriented development
TVA   Tennessee Valley Authority
UCT   University of Cape Town
UDF   United Democratic Front
UDS   Urban Development Strategy
UDZ   Urban Development Zone
UF   Urban Foundation
UIIF   Urban Infrastructure Investment Framework
UNODC   United Nations Office on Drugs and Crime
URP   Urban Renewal Programme
Wits   University of the Witwatersrand
WSSD   World Summit on Sustainable Development

CURRENCY

One hundred South African rand = 7.11 GBP (UK) and 14.33 USD
(10 July 2007)

PART 1

SETTING THE SCENE

INTRODUCTION

PURPOSE OF THE BOOK

Change within planning systems in most parts of the world is incremental. As the demands of context change, as new development pressures emerge, and as existing planning systems increasingly appear to be out of step with reality, so adjustments are made which usually take the form of modifications to what has gone before. Rarely, if ever, do nations consider that they could be faced with a moment at which they could design a planning system, or any other aspect of policy for that matter, from scratch. Such opportunities usually present themselves only at times of cataclysmic change, after war or revolution, and in the past few decades it has been primarily those countries in transition from socialism (Eastern European countries, China, and Tanzania and Ethiopia in Africa) that have been faced with this task.

It was this situation that also faced the new democratic government of South Africa in April of 1994 as it emerged from a political system based on racial segregation. Confronted with a full array of policies, at all levels of government, which had been crafted under apartheid and which for the most part had been designed to support or at least fit in with the aims of racial segregation, the new Government of National Unity as it was called at the time could quite legitimately argue that all aspects of South African policy, along with supporting legislation, regulations and bureaucratic structures, would require review and renewal. And given the central role that planning – both in the forms of 'forward' planning and land-use control – had played in the spatial segregation of races in South Africa, the planning system was marked as a target for thorough change.

While the complete transformation of a country's planning system may be a rare event in most parts of the world, we would nonetheless argue that it presents a significant learning opportunity for planners in all contexts. There are four central aspects to this. First, it presents the opportunity to pose fundamental questions about the nature and purpose of planning: the ethical values that should guide it, and how universal or particular these should be; its role and scope in relation to particular contextual issues; its relationship to related professions and policy streams and ways of integrating with these; its location within changing structures of governance and its relationship with other stakeholders involved in the built environment; and the nature of the tools, techniques and processes that it deploys in order to be effective. Second, it allows the testing and evaluation of new policies and new ways of acting. A good example of this is the problem of achieving integrated policies and action in government, an issue that confronts governments in most parts of the world today. In South Africa the process of integrated development planning, as a tool for municipal management, was designed as a new policy initiative in the mid-1990s, has subsequently been monitored and revised, and potentially provides a testing ground for integration in other parts of the world. Third, it allows an examination of the possibilities of the process of change itself. While there may be acceptance of profound change at the national level (in terms of adopting new economic and political systems), there will always be the problem of bureaucracies peopled with individuals who are likely to be resistant to change, perhaps for political reasons, for reasons related to a desire to maintain particular positions of power and influence, or perhaps due to ignorance and a lack of understanding of alternatives. The problem of historical inertia in bureaucracies and in organizational structures of all kinds is one which is confronted whether changes are incremental or fundamental. Fourth, a situation of transformation opens up an important debate on the transferability of knowledge and ideas. Many of the new policy and planning ideas put in place in South Africa after 1994 were not 'home-grown', but were introduced by international aid and development agencies and first-world policy think-tanks. The concept of three spheres of government (national, regional and local) as opposed to hierarchical tiers of government was one of these ideas, as was South Africa's new housing policy. While these policies were to some extent shaped to fit local conditions, the assumptions on which they were based remain, opening up an important avenue of inquiry regarding the articulation between imported policy ideas and the materially and socially situated nature of citizens at whom they are targeted.

In a sense transformation in South Africa has been more limited in scope than in those countries that confronted economic as well as political change – the countries of Eastern Europe are of relevance here and they, as well, offer significant insights into planning and change. The South African case offers other particular attributes, however. Important here is the juxtaposition of a modern, developed economy with large-scale informality; and great wealth adjacent to extensive poverty, which also shapes and is shaped by the form of South African cities and rural areas. South African planners thus confront issues that will be familiar to those working in both the global North and global South. South African planners also face an issue that is emerging as a central concern in many parts of the world – that of multiculturalism – and the problem of dealing with planning issues in places increasingly characterized by social and cultural conflict. As Bollens (2004: 121), in an analysis which includes Johannesburg (South Africa), correctly argues: 'differing value systems are a defining characteristic of ethnically polarized cities and also appear to be an increasing attribute of planning and resource allocation debates in North America and western European cities'. There may be no clear answers yet emerging from the South African experience of multiculturalism, but the sharpness of the divides in this society certainly allows a questioning of some of the assumptions embedded in mainstream planning thought.

This book thus in part speaks to an international audience, arguing that South Africa is an instructive case of political and planning transformation, which raises questions for planners elsewhere who are concerned with change. Linked to this aim, we realize that some readers may not be familiar with South Africa, and this assumption informs our explanation of events and concepts. The book also speaks to a South African audience. Planning (and related) professionals in this country have lived through tumultuous times. Some have been excited and energized by the potentials and possibilities that transformation has opened up; others feel marginalized and resentful. A good number have left the planning profession entirely while new recruits, increasingly black and female products of the tertiary education institutions, bring their own ambitions and concerns into play. It is an appropriate moment to reflect comprehensively on the successes and failures of the South African planning system during the last decade, so that we can be conscious of the road travelled thus far, build on this experience, and confront the future with a greater sense of purpose.

The remainder of the introduction gives an overview of the position taken in this book with regard to political transformation and changes in the planning arena, the theoretical perspective that has informed this account, and an explanation of the organization of the subsequent sections and chapters.

POLITICAL TRANSFORMATION IN SOUTH AFRICA: AN OVERVIEW

The territory that ultimately came to be called South Africa has been settled for many thousands of years. The ancestors of the nomadic Khoe-San people were probably responsible for the engravings found in the Blombos Cave on the Cape South Coast which have been dated at 70,000 Before Present (BP). Archaeologists now believe that the first Iron Age farmers moved into South Africa about 1700 BP, although they came in larger numbers in a substantial southwards migration of Bantu-speaking people about 900 BP. The Iron Age settlements were generally small and clan-based and so South Africa does not have the sort of pre-colonial settlements that West Africa has, for example, but there are some notable exceptions. Most important is the thirteenth-century capital of the Mapungubwe kingdom located on a striking hilltop in the Limpopo River Valley, which has been excavated since the 1930s, and which has become a potent symbol of the 'African renaissance'.

In 1488 Portuguese navigators first rounded the Cape, opening up a sea route from Europe to the East, and in 1652 the Dutch East India Company established a permanent refreshment station at what is now the city of Cape Town. Dutch control of the territory came to an end in 1795 when Britain occupied the Cape in order to secure its trading route, although British rule only became permanent in 1814 when the Dutch formally ceded the Cape to Britain. In 1910 South Africa was granted the status of a self-governing colony, this lasting until 1961 when the country declared itself a republic and withdrew from the Commonwealth. As a result of these early Dutch and British influences, current South African common law still contains many elements of Roman Dutch law and English law, although the system of administrative law – and to a large extent the inherited planning system – is strongly British.

The concept of racial segregation, a defining characteristic of the pre-1994 apartheid government, in fact had its roots in nineteenth-century British rule.[1] The first specific allocation of urban land for people other than whites can be traced to the city of Port Elizabeth in the 1850s (Mabin and Smit 1997) and became common towards the end of the century as 'native locations' were established in and around the larger urban settlements, with the right of Africans to own or rent any land outside of defined rural 'reserves' (or homelands) finally withdrawn by the 1913 Natives Land Act. It was not until 1948, however, and the succession of the National Party in government, that the full apparatus of the apartheid project came into being.

In the post-1948 period, apartheid (meaning 'apartness') involved the extension of various forms of segregation, which previously applied to Africans, to Indian and coloured people as well. By the 1960s it involved racial discrimination in almost every area of life, with spatial separation in place at the local urban scale (in the form of planned segregated residential areas) and at the regional scale (in the form of demarcated African homelands). In essence it was a policy that allowed white, and particularly Afrikaner, supremacy to survive in the face of growing African nationalism through the division and repression of people of colour. At no time, however, was apartheid unchallenged. By the end of the 1980s, increasingly organized resistance, largely orchestrated by the African National Congress (ANC), succeeded in bringing the apartheid government to the negotiating table and to the country's first democratic elections in 1994.

Political transition in South Africa can be described as transition to a liberal democracy, but this was coupled with the increasing insertion of the economy into a globalized international economy, giving rise to what may be considered as a double transition. The magnitude of these transitions may not equate to those experienced by countries undergoing a shift from communist and totalitarian regimes but nonetheless, compared with the relatively stable political economies of most developed and even many developing countries, change in South Africa in the 1990s was dramatic. Significantly, the apartheid government entered negotiations with the ANC in the early 1990s from a political position which was severely challenged, but not defeated. The ruling National Party had been able to maintain an effective system of administration, security and defence (strongly challenged in the black urban townships, however), a highly developed, if regionally uneven, system of infrastructure and communication, and operational systems of tax collection and welfare for at least part of the population. The National Party also retained cautious support from elements of capital, and, in the first democratic elections, showed that it had retained 20.4 per cent of the support of the total electorate. It retained the ability, therefore, to be a powerful player in the negotiation process and to influence the path of reform significantly.

The opposition movement, in the form of the ANC and its alliance partners, the powerful labour movement Congress of South African Trade Unions (COSATU) and the South African Communist Party (SACP), historically had strong socialist leanings. However, negotiations were occurring at a time when the collapse of the Soviet Union and the Eastern Bloc discredited left-wing economic policy, and ensured that the prime international players in the transition were the United States and its allies. Inevitably, 'the price these powers demanded for disciplining the apartheid government and extending promises of material aid to the ANC was a commitment by the ANC to embrace western-style free-market principles' (Webster and Adler 1999: 369).

Analysts of the South African political transition debate the extent to which the process was shaped by elite negotiators or by the extensive mass action that was occurring outside the negotiating chambers (Saul 1991). The negotiations were highly conflictual and repeatedly threatened to derail, but in the end compromises were made on both sides. The ANC's original draft politico-economic policy was revised to the extent that when it finally emerged, in the form of the Reconstruction and Development Programme, it was eagerly adopted by all political parties and by business. And in the negotiation process, the ANC conceded to the important 'sunset clause' which safeguarded the positions of existing civil servants. The possibility of both economic and administrative continuity was thereby greatly strengthened. Clearly a break with the past of some significance was made in 1994. The obtaining of full political rights by people of colour was not without importance, and it is also possible to point to a new constitution regarded as progressive in world terms, new policies in almost every field of government, major institutional reorganization, and important new legislation, particularly in the field of labour. But the continuities (particularly in terms of the economy) are there as well. In fact in the years following the 1994 election, macro-economic policy shifted closer to a neo-liberal position, and an emphasis on economic growth replaced the previous concern with redistribution. In the very recent period there has been a further shift: some individuals in government believe that there is a need for a stronger state (a 'developmental state') to ensure service delivery and administrative efficiency.

Institutional and legislative reforms were primary items on the agenda of the new government, given that all had been previously framed by racial categories. The extent of planned governmental reorganization was hugely ambitious, with South Africa unique among those countries undergoing political transition in its attempts to reform both national and subnational levels at the same time (Swilling 1997). As was the case with economic reform, institutional reform was strongly influenced by international (and particularly Anglo-American) thinking on new forms of government. Concepts of decentralization, integration, facilitative and entrepreneurial government, and various aspects of new public management, found their way into the policy documents on institutional reform. The previous system of hierarchical 'tiers' of government was replaced with 'spheres' of government in which three levels are intended to function together cooperatively. At the local level all racially defined units of government were scrapped and transition took place in three phases, the last of which saw a system of metropolitan, district and local councils put in place in 2000. In reality, however, imported concepts of public management have fitted uncomfortably into an inevitably messy context shaped by resistance to change and political tensions.

A process of devolution of powers and functions has been under way over recent years, which can be captured by the contradictory term 'decentralized centralism'. On the one hand there has been a very substantial devolution of functions, and of some power, to municipalities and to the nine provincial governments. At the same time there has been a concentration of power in terms of policy-making and coordination in the President's Office, the Treasury and other key national agencies. The outcome of these contradictory processes has been undercapacitated and cash-strapped local governments which have found it very difficult to implement a phalanx of new national policies and to change their orientation from service administration to development. Poor performances, a failure to deliver services and corruption have been the inevitable consequences in some parts of the country. Attempts at the privatization of public services and functions have come up against strong resistance from the still powerful organized labour movement and implementation of this idea has been limited.

At the current time the ANC has successfully gained control of the middle ground in parliament, its voter support continues to rise and political opposition parties are weak. A period of stronger economic growth, together with low interest rates and inflation, has certainly brought material benefit to a section of the population with the latter including a rapidly emerging black elite. However tensions remain. Income inequalities are now greater than under apartheid (although increasingly defined by class rather than race), and there is a growing sense of discontent among those who remain marginalized in the spreading shack settlements and the informal economy. Problems such as a high crime rate and a rampant HIV/AIDS pandemic tend to further disadvantage the poor, and ultimately threaten the foundations of economic growth itself. In policy terms there is a realization (at least at the level of rhetoric) on the part of government that service delivery and job creation are essential if popular support is to continue, but the structural constraints to implementing this as the country articulates ever more closely with the global economy make this difficult.

THE TRANSFORMATION OF PLANNING IN SOUTH AFRICA: AN OVERVIEW

Planning, as a function of government, has long been used in South Africa to play both a managing role in relation to the spatial separation of racial groups, and a welfare (and modernizing) role in relation to the planning of housing and facilities for those of the African and coloured population deemed necessary for the urban economy. The former role, that of racial segregation, manifested itself in an ad hoc manner prior to the election of the apartheid government in 1948, and was an outcome, primarily, of efforts to remove slum and 'unsanitary' areas, and to provide public housing for those so displaced. In the post-1948 years, however, urban racial segregation became an explicit policy of government, and town planning was viewed as the prime tool through which the new urban landscape could be fashioned (Mabin and Smit 1997). The latter role, that of providing healthier and more 'modern' environments, was formally proposed as a role for planning by a non-statutory, advisory body to government in 1944. The terms of reference of the Social and Economic Planning Council required it to 'suggest plans which are objectively well thought out on their merits, apart from purely political considerations ... following as much as possible scientific lines ...' (Mabin and Smit 1997; Wilkinson 1996: 154). The proposals of the Council included introducing a planning function at the level of national government, the adoption of a broader regional view on settlement patterns, and, in relation to the urbanized 'non-European population', the following of international planning principles of planned neighbourhoods separated by green belts (Wilkinson 1996). Throughout the apartheid years these two planning discourses co-existed in ways which at times appeared to be mutually reinforcing. In particular, planners involved in the layout of new, racially segregated townships were able to justify the design of discrete residential neighbourhoods, surrounded by green belts (or buffer zones, as they were locally known) and with few access routes (which in turn allowed more effective policing and control), by citing their compatibility with international practice and contemporary scientific principles of planning.

At an urban level the application of principles of apartheid resulted in cities and towns with very distinctive spatial forms. They were, of course, highly segregated by race and consequently also by income. The new townships (as the apartheid-created areas for people of colour were called) were without exception on

or beyond the boundaries of the 'white' urban areas and usually contained only residential land uses and some local facilities. The result was large-scale daily
commuting on the part of township residents from impoverished and poorly serviced
'dormitory' areas to the 'white' sections of the city or town where the main areas of
economic opportunity and higher-order social facilities were located. They were
urban areas, it was often argued, which not only reflected disadvantage, but
entrenched it: the poor were forced into long and expensive daily trips to work and
shops, or were physically trapped in areas where there was little possibility of generating an income; forced removals to the townships broke up communities and
social networks resulting in social breakdown and the escalation of crime; and barriers to land ownership prevented its use as a capital asset.

At a national and regional level the principle of spatial separation was replicated. Thirteen per cent of the national land was set aside for occupation by African
people, although they comprised over 70 per cent of the total population. It was in
these largely rural and undeveloped 'Bantustan' areas[2] that they were expected to
exercise their political rights and any travel outside of these areas to 'white' South
Africa required the possession of a valid 'pass' document, legitimating a temporary
stay. At this scale, international principles of regional planning, in particular the concepts of growth poles and deconcentration points, were deployed in an attempt to
prop up the ailing Bantustan economies and reduce urbanization, but also to provide cheap labour destinations for white-owned and later foreign industry.

The use of planning as a tool to implement the apartheid project impacted on
planning professionals in various ways. There is no doubt that a proportion of working planners supported the concept of segregation and used their skills to this end.
Other planners may have felt more ambiguous about it, but justified their continued
role in government bureaucracies and consultancies as being 'just a job', or perhaps
hoped that they could help to soften the worst effects of the policy. Still other planners, however, openly resisted apartheid planning: in the mid-1980s a number of
planning non-governmental organizations (NGOs) were established to work with
affected communities; planners engaged in an ongoing critique of government policy, pointing to the disastrous effects of apartheid planning, and attempts were
made to develop an alternative vision for what came to be called the 'post-apartheid
city'. The latter efforts in essence represented an attempt to replace the prevailing
apartheid-related discourse, which cast South African cities as too large and con-
gested, and thus requiring decentralization, deconcentration and de-densifying to
racially defined townships and satellite urban centres. The alternative and emerging
discourse of the late 1980s proposed instead that South African cities required
internal restructuring to achieve compact, higher-density, public-transport-based
and spatially integrated cities (Dewar and Uytenbogaardt 1991). There were clear
parallels here with international efforts in cities such as Toronto to use the 'compact

city' approach to achieve 'environmentally sustainable' urban environments. In South Africa, terms used by those promoting the new urban vision – such as 'integration', 'one city' and 'redistribution' – resonated closely with the rhetoric of the political opposition movements of the time, giving an appearance of unity between political and urban reform, and allowing a strategic political positioning of those planners who chose to adopt the new discourse. Significantly, however, there were also important commonalities between the older and new planning discourses: both were essentially modernist, based on the assumption that it is possible to envision an alternative and more desirable future and to achieve this; and both conceptualized space as an element of reality that can be objectified and manipulated to particular social and economic ends.

Nonetheless, the years leading up to, and after, the 1994 democratic elections, were a period experienced as a renaissance by many planners in South Africa. For those who had opposed the apartheid state and its policies, the transition to democracy seemed to present itself as a unique opportunity to demonstrate the positive role of planning in tackling the inherited problems of the apartheid cities and towns, and championing democracy at the local level. In local authorities that were being asked to transform themselves from bureaucratic service providers to developmental, democratic and forward-thinking organs of government, it was the planning professionals who had the expertise to think ahead, who had some experience of participation, and who could present, at least at the urban level, a coherent spatial vision based on concepts of equity, justice and sustainability which was also in tune with the goals of the new democratic government. In these early years of the new democracy planners found that they had an important new role to play, and many used this opportunity to move into central positions in government.

One of the central issues explored in this book has to do with the outcome of this window of opportunity for planning and it is this issue that, we believe, will be of interest to a wider audience. What the transformation of planning in South Africa demonstrates is that despite variation in local contexts, forces which appear to be international in their impact are fundamentally changing the role which planners and planning can play.

Thus at one level it would be possible to argue that planning has failed in its early 1990s mission to transform apartheid cities and to establish itself at the forefront of efforts to create integrated and developmental institutions of government. South African towns and cities today are possibly more spatially divided than they were in the days of apartheid, but for reasons no longer traceable to segregating legislation but rather to the operation of the market and to growing economic inequalities. Many of the larger cities have been experiencing new investment, but much of this is located in the historically wealthier (and previously 'white') parts of cities. Rapidly growing informal settlements as well as new public low-income housing projects are invariably found on cheaper land on the urban edge or in areas previously classified for racial groups other than white. The shift of middle- and upper-income black households into previously 'white' areas is occurring slowly, but the numbers are not large. The pattern of socially, economically and spatially segregated cities remains, with its attendant problems of lengthy and expensive commutes for the poor, and growing areas suffering from social exclusion, growing poverty, ill health and crime. Efforts in most of the metropolitan areas to draw up alternative spatial visions, aimed at creating integrated, equitable and sustainable cities, have largely remained on paper.

Within the bureaucracies, planning has faced a more complex and fragmented decision-making environment. Efforts to create transformed, integrated and developmental government, particularly at the local level, have not necessarily favoured spatial planning. New local government departments, particularly in the policy fields of environmental management and economic development, have tended to encroach on the historical areas of concern of planning, with the adopted definition of environment as including both natural and built areas presenting particular problems for planning. Further, new departments such as these, along with departments dealing with transport, housing and service delivery, have responded to national government policy directives to take a developmental and forward-thinking approach and as a result such departments have also tended to become involved in planning, but not always in a coordinated way with spatial planning. The 'silo mentality' remains strong in local government, despite efforts to overcome it.

Significantly, a new legislative and policy system for planning has not yet been put in place by the national department charged with doing this and planning remains one of the last policy arenas still to be fully reformed. As a result other national departments and certain provincial governments as well have, from time to time, produced laws and policies on aspects of the planning system and there has been a range of local initiatives. The current system is thus interim, regionally varied and partial and because of this it remains more open, fluid and potentially innovative than it might otherwise have been. However, this has also allowed older embedded practices and discourses to continue.

Forward or indicative spatial planning has been given some recognition through its incorporation, by the Department of Provincial and Local Government, into the new system of five-year integrated development plans (IDPs) at the local level. But the key coordinating mechanism in the IDPs is the municipal budget rather than the spatial plan, and the spatial development frameworks (SDFs) play a weaker role as a mechanism for spatially coordinating the outputs of other line-function departments, rather than giving spatial direction or input to the plans of other departments. A similar tendency has been noted in the UK (Vigar and Healey 1999) where vertically integrated sectoral policies forced land-use planning to take on the role of a functional policy sector and weakened its ability to integrate the impact of policy sectors on territories. The SDFs themselves are continually evolving, but as we discuss in Chapter 6, they remain dominated by a particular set of spatial concepts (edge, corridor, node) and by the goal of producing paper plans for institutional approval. Their prime implementational mechanism is still, potentially, the development control system, which itself has been evolving with some regional variation, and often in isolation from the process of constructing IDPs and SDFs.

A central question then could be whether or not South African planning is likely to follow in the footsteps of planning elsewhere in the world, as it has so often done (problematically, we will suggest) in the past. At a regional level and in the context of the spatialization of European policy, the spatial concepts of polycentric urban development, underpinned by the notions of frictionless mobility and balanced regional development (Dabinett and Richardson 2005) have been gaining prominence in South Africa, while concepts of urban renaissance and regeneration projects especially within inner-city areas (Hutton 2004), mega-projects linked to the promotion of economic growth and enhancing urban place identity (Beriatos and Gospodini 2004) and 'new urbanist' residential developments, occupy planners at the urban scale. More fundamentally, however, planning theorists such as Healey point to the growing critique of an approach to planning which assumes that it can '"order" the dynamic and inherently disorderly development of cities and regions' (Healey 2004: 47), and she questions the continued use of an essentialist and Euclidean understanding of space which in the past has lent support to the use of fixed spatial concepts for strategic purposes. While planning theorists in South Africa are using frames such as these to understand what is happening in urban areas and the implications of this for planning (Harrison 2006a; Watson 2003a), there is little indication at the present time that these sensitivities are impacting on the world of practice. This may change in the wake of the call to planners by UN-Habitat at the World Urban Forum in Vancouver (Tibaijuka 2006) to place the issues of rapid urbanization and slums firmly at the top of their agendas. At the same time, however, UN-Habitat Executive Director Anna Tibaijuka cautioned planners that conventional approaches to planning in the cities of the global South, based largely on laws and tools developed in the global North, had often done more harm than good. Tibaijuka called on planning practitioners to develop a different approach that is pro-poor and inclusive, that balances the 'green' and 'brown' agendas, and that places the creation of livelihoods at the centre of planning efforts.

In South Africa the shape of a new formal planning system is still being contested and planners in the public sector often find themselves engaged in a battle for legitimacy. However, we argue that there has been a transformation in terms of how the practice of planning is taking place in government. As the ideas and methods of planning (forward-thinking, visioning, linking analysis and ideas to implementation, participation and networking) have become central to the very concept of developmental government, so the discourse of planning has begun to permeate the work of a wide range of professionals and political representatives. At the same time, those trained as planners have found that their skills and methods are of value in areas outside of traditional planning departments and in other areas of work in the private sector as well. Thus it is no longer unusual to find people with a planning background in other public sector departments, or working as IDP or organizational managers. In some regions of the country the IDP manager is invariably a planner. Outside of government, planners are acting as consultants in a wide range of development fields: as project managers, as facilitators and as investment advisors. This trend is not unique to South Africa. Thomas (2004: 191) makes the point in relation to the UK that as local councils have changed from service providers to orchestrators of strategies to improve places, so departmental and professional boundaries are being destroyed, and planning functions are being unbundled into various locations within and also outside of government. While this certainly raises questions for the organized profession of planning, and for the education of planners, what it also suggests is that the diffusion of planning across disciplines and departments is making it more effective than it ever was before. It is certainly opening up a wider and more challenging range of employment opportunities for planning graduates. This is perhaps a rather more postmodern view of planning which will undoubtedly be a contentious one, but it lends weight to the argument that planning, like most other professions, is fundamentally affected by the context within which it operates and needs to be responsive to an increasingly changing and unpredictable world.

It is this understanding of the role of planning that has emerged in post-apartheid South Africa that, in part, informs the definition of planning adopted in this book. It leads us to believe that it is impossibly limiting to work within the post-war conception of 'town and regional planning' which saw the discipline as concerned solely with land-use planning and the design of human settlements (although this remains a central and important part of what many planners do). In a context of poverty and inequality planning has to be about more than this. It also has to concern itself with the development of people (sustainably) in particular places or localities and the distribution of developmental actions across space. We need to bear in mind as well that understandings of what development might mean are likely to be diverse.

Linked to this point is our understanding of planning as an activity which, in many parts of the world, is no longer seen as the sole preserve of the state. Ironically, in the case of South Africa, it was the apartheid era that inspired a strong interest in planning from political opposition movements and business, as they attempted to construct alternatives to the apartheid city. In the post-apartheid era it appears that planning has become far more of a state-led activity, with no clear evidence of competing visions being promoted by organized, civil-society-based stakeholders. We suspect that this might be because business has discovered that it can easily thwart the planning system in its own interests, or that it is still well served by the outdated planning regulations and discourses that are still dominant in land-use decision-making in various realms. Where planning interventions work against the interests of the poor, the response has largely been in the form of quiet and fragmented subversion although there are instances of protest or resistance to the way planning solutions come to ground in particular contexts. It is possible to argue however that the poor have been marginalized less by planning visions, than by the failure to implement them.

THEORETICAL PERSPECTIVES

Our understanding of the transformation of planning in South Africa has inevitably been coloured by particular theoretical perspectives: what we present in this book is not neutral description and analysis. It is important, therefore, to clarify the nature of the theoretical 'lens' through which we have approached this task, as well as our own normative perspective on planning.

We align ourselves (at a broad level) with the approach termed 'critical policy analysis' outlined and consolidated in a recent book by Maarten Hajer and Hendrik Wagenaar (2003). As the authors point out, this is not a new approach, but a tradition with roots in the 1980s which emerged as a critique of positivist and technocratic policy science. In the planning field Fischer and Forester (1993), Schön and Rein (1994) and Forester (1999) advocated an 'argumentative turn' in policy analysis to better describe what social scientists and policy actors do. What they were suggesting was a shift from an emphasis on 'rigorous empirical proof and verification to a discursive, contextual understanding of social knowledge and the interpretative methods basic to acquiring it' (Fischer 2003: 211). The understanding of planning transformation in South Africa that we present here is 'interpretive' in the sense in which the term has been used by Fischer and Forester, and subsequently Hajer and Wagenaar. It is not an assembly of scientifically verifiable facts. It reflects our perspective on events at a particular moment in time, and allows for the possibility that other perspectives may view the situation differently. It draws on the concrete experiences in planning of the authors, each located in a different part of the country, and we have (following Fischer and Forester's *Argumentative Turn*) created our own meanings out of our submersion in these experiences and practices. Inevitably, our individual experiences and perspectives differ, but we feel that we have enough of a common view to produce a coherent account, and that our differences will enrich the final product.

Hajer and Wagenaar (2003: xiv) argue that the critical approach to policy analysis is particularly appropriate for today's 'decentred world of governance':

assumptions about the 'inherently contextual nature of knowledge' on which critical policy analysis is based are in tune with the trend to more dispersed forms of governing; complex, fluid and sometimes informal decision-making processes; the networked nature of society; diminishing trust; and growing transnational influences. They complain, however, about the way in which these macrosociological concepts are often used to describe particular policy contexts, without demonstrating exactly what is new and how the activity of policy-making and politics is really different on the ground. They thus identify the need 'to trace telling experiments with governance and to conceptualize the new settings in which politics and policymaking take place as well as the way in which this changes the character of the political game' (Hajer and Wagenaar 2003: 5). Our book is an overview of policy shifts and their relationship with macro trends in a country which itself is highly diverse. It deals with changes in the realm of one policy arena, planning, at a level which may be too generalized to meet fully the needs identified by Hajer and Wagenaar. It does, however, begin to examine how these macro shifts have articulated with local specificities at the level of the nation state, explaining where necessary how questions of regional variation may be important. Our approach is not to take a starting point in these macrosociological theories with the intention of seeing how they can apply in the context of South Africa. Our approach is rather a 'bottom-up' one: where our understanding of contextual realities indicates similarities with, or the influence of, wider forces and trends, we have drawn attention to this and tried to explain it.

We align ourselves as well to the conception of society which underlies critical policy analysis. We understand this to be a conception which accepts that conflict is intrinsic to human communities and that policy and planning issues are inevitably contested (Hajer and Wagenaar 2003). It is moreover an understanding that societies are made up of people and groups with different and often conflicting world views and value systems, and it is erroneous to assume that we can identify, or hope for, a set of universal values that accommodate everyone. The implication of this is that there cannot be universal planning and policy solutions which can be used in any part of the world: the imposition in South Africa of planning ideas which have been generated in an Anglo-American context is a theme to which we return often in this book.

This approach also influences what we pay attention to as we examine the changing planning system in South Africa. In line with the 'sociological institutional' perspective which has come to occupy centre-field in planning theory (and which informs the work of Hajer and Wagenaar as well), our understanding of the transformation of planning in South Africa emphasizes not only the 'hard infrastructure', or formal elements of the planning system (the tools of the system such as laws, financial measures, state powers and plan requirements, the purpose of the system and the allocation of institutional responsibilities), but also the 'soft infrastructure' (Healey 1997) which includes the 'practices and relationships through which the system comes alive ... the actors and networks ... the policy communities ... and the policy discourses which shape specific agendas' (Vigar *et al.* 2000: 7). Thus both the 'structures' in place and the 'softer' elements, such as the role of agency, power, practices and discourses, are of importance in shaping the way in which planning operates. In a context of change, such as that of South Africa, the role of past practices and discourses, the effect of history and of changing approaches also need to be taken into account. While policy change is generally directed at changing the 'hard infrastructure' of policy, the effect of historically built-up practices and discourses all play a role in the way in which policy is implemented and how it is reshaped in practice (Gonzalez and Healey 2005; Vigar *et al.* 2000).

On a more personal note, as planners we share a belief that the purpose of planning is to contribute to the realization of socially just and sustainable cities and regions, although we recognize that there are different interpretations of what these concepts may mean. To this end we believe that both the process and products of planning are important and that they cannot be considered separately from each other. Hence the book speaks to a number of current international planning debates: on communication processes in planning, on the workings of power and rationality in such processes, on the institutional settings through which planning decisions occur, and on the products and plans that emerge from these processes.

ORGANIZATION OF THE BOOK

The remainder of Part 1 of this book details the nature and products of colonial and apartheid planning in South Africa (Chapter 1) as well as the growing resistance to this planning and the beginnings of an alternative planning vision for South Africa (Chapter 2). Chapter 3 deals with the transformation of planning in the post-apartheid years, the new roles that planners have taken on, and the new forms of planning that have emerged.

The rest of the book is divided into a number of themes or issues which we believe have been important in the recent history of planning in South Africa. Each section is preceded by an introduction in which we have drawn on more general theoretical and international debates on these issues to help situate the South African case. Part 2 deals with the relationship between planning and governance and we consider (Chapter 4) how this has played itself out at the level of local government and (Chapter 5) at the broader regional and national scales. Part 3 deals with the discourses of planning: the key concepts and arguments that have shaped or 'framed' the debate on planning in South Africa. Prominent here (Chapter 6) have been understandings of space and the ability of planners to direct spatial change; discourses around questions of institutional integration and social transformation (Chapter 7); the issue of the economy and the market in relation to planning (Chapter 8) and the incorporation of questions of the environment and sustainability into planning discourses (Chapter 9). Part 4 focuses on the relationship between planning and society in South Africa. The first two chapters deal with the production and organization of planning professionals: Chapter 10 examines the changing nature of the planning profession in South Africa, and Chapter 11, the transforming education of planners. The remaining chapters in this section consider how planners have responded to some of the key social issues of the time: value diversity (Chapter 12), cultural and social difference (Chapter 13), and informality (Chapter 14). The conclusion (Chapter 15) is a reflection on the outcome of the transformation of planning and what we believe are the emerging strengths and limitations to the power of planning in this context.

CHAPTER 1

PLANNING THE SPACES OF COLONIALISM AND APARTHEID

INTRODUCTION

In 1994, when South Africa finally emerged from a long history of colonialism and apartheid, urban and regional planning was deeply compromised as it had played a significant – although sometimes complex and ambiguous – role in creating spaces of inequality and division. This chapter explores the development of planning in South Africa prior to 1994, with specific attention to the relationship between planning, colonial segregation and apartheid. The chapter emphasizes what Robinson referred to as the 'importance of spatiality in the construction of state power' (1997: 365). The chapter traces the story of planning in terms of five broad periods: pre- and early modernity (until the 1880s); the rise of modern South Africa (1880s to the 1940s); a 'peculiar form of modernism' (i.e. high apartheid) (from the late 1940s to the early 1970s); apartheid in decay (from the mid-1970s to 1990); and the final transition (from 1990 to 1994). The chapter draws largely on the work of writers who have written from a 'critical radical tradition' that has brought together the insights of a political economy approach with the specificity of historical research.

PRE- AND EARLY MODERNITY: C.700 TO THE 1880S

The first settlements of significant size in Southern Africa emerged around 700 AD. as nodes within a trading network that extended from what is now eastern Botswana, along the Limpopo River Valley, to the Indian Ocean coastline (and from there as far as India and China). The greatest of these settlements was Great Zimbabwe, north of the Limpopo, which survived until about 1450, but it was preceded by Mapungubwe which occupied a hilltop citadel in the far north of South Africa's present-day Limpopo province from 1220–90 (Hall 1987).

The arrival of the Portuguese traders along the African coast from the late fifteenth century severely disrupted African trading networks, and settlements such as Great Zimbabwe went into decline. In the eighteenth century, however, large stone-walled Sotho and Tswana towns emerged in the western and central parts of South Africa, with the Hurutshe capital of Kaditshwene, for example, reaching a population of about 18,000 by 1815. All these settlements were, however, destroyed in a violent disruption of social life in the 1820s known as the *Difaqane* or *Mfecane*. In

KwaZulu-Natal, the Zulu royal kraals of the nineteenth century typically had a population of 5000 or more, but the last of the Zulu capitals was destroyed by the British in 1879 during the Anglo-Zulu War (Hall 1987).

Laburn-Peart reminded us that these pre-colonial settlements were 'highly organized, functional and ordered settlements expressing a variety of spatial and social principles, notably those of power relationships, which can be identified and studied' (1993: 231). Although there was variation, the basic morphology of these traditional pre-colonial settlements was a circular form, with tradition and social organization determining the placement of the various elements.

By the late nineteenth century, it was colonial settlement that dominated the landscape. The Dutch East India Company had established Cape Town in 1652 which developed gradually as a company town – with layout organized along a gridiron pattern – reaching a population of only 5000 in the 1760s, a century after its founding, and 20,000 in 1840 when it was proclaimed a municipality (Western 1981). Through the late seventeenth and eighteenth centuries, colonial settlement expanded into the interior – Stellenbosch was founded in 1679 followed by Swellendam in 1743 and Graaff Reinet in 1786.

The British occupied Cape Town in 1795 to prevent it from falling into the hands of Napoleon and formally annexed the colony in 1814 after the Battle of Waterloo. In 1820, the arrival of 4000 British settlers in the Eastern Cape led to the development of urban centres such as Port Elizabeth and Grahamstown (the latter of which had initially been established as military headquarters on the contested frontier). In the 1830s the Dutch settlers began their northwards trek to escape British rule, and a network of small towns – or *dorpe* – developed in the Transvaal and Orange Free State Republics, and in Natal, before the Boers retreated back across the Drakensberg mountains leaving the British to establish a new colony.

Although there were subtle differences in the layout patterns for British and Boer settlement, the functional gridiron pattern was the dominant feature. In the case of the Boer settlements, the church played a key role in the initial settlement formation, but in the British colonies, the colonial land surveyor had enormous power in determining the siting and layout of towns. The British and Boer settlements generally grew very slowly, supported by a mainly agrarian economic base, but the hierarchy and network of settlements established by the end of the nineteenth century were hugely important in securing Dutch settler and British domination across South Africa.

The origins of urban segregation can be found in this period, although the trend towards segregation was very diverse regionally (and even locally), with the colonies and republics (and even the different municipalities) following different policies towards race. Policies in the Cape were theoretically colour-blind but in the Eastern

Cape there were regulations for racially separate municipal settlement from as early as 1847, with formal residential segregation in Port Elizabeth and East London from the 1850s (Maylam 1995). The Colony of Natal was even more conservative in its racial policies and Africans were generally only permitted in urban areas as single workers, and were housed mainly in municipal or private barracks (Christopher 1990). The Boer republics had tough racial policies, although they did not always have the resources to implement them. Africans were housed by employers or in separate 'locations' outside the 'white' towns. The Indian population was also a concern to the republican governments, with the Transvaal government passing legislation to create segregated 'Indian bazaars' in 1885 and the Free State imposing a wholesale ban on Indians from its territory in 1891 (Western 1981; Maylam 1995).

Although pressures for urban growth, and therefore for urban planning, were very limited through this period, dramatic changes were on the horizon. In 1867, diamonds were discovered in Griqualand West and by 1870 thousands of fortune-seekers had flocked to a ramshackle mining camp that was to become the city of Kimberley. It was here that a new black working class developed, and also here that another strand was added to the evolving practice of urban segregation – it was in Kimberley that the system of single-sex compounds for housing African labour was first designed. It was a system that was later adapted on the Witwatersrand (the region around Johannesburg) to provide mine-owners with a reliable, well-controlled and easily accessible supply of labour (Mabin 1986).

THE RISE OF MODERN SOUTH AFRICA: 1880S TO THE 1940S

In this period, South Africa's economy transformed from its agrarian base into a modern mining and industrial complex. The process was, however, not without considerable disruption and deep trauma. The discovery of gold on the Witwatersrand in the 1880s provoked a bitter contest between Boer and Briton that culminated in the agonies of the South African War (1899–1902). The displacement of war, and the expansion of the mining and industrial sectors in the years that followed, brought a flood of poor whites and Africans into the cities.

In 1910, the four colonies came together to form the Union of South Africa but the political arrangements for Union excluded the majority black population, an affront which prompted the formation of the ANC, and the beginning of a prolonged resistance struggle that spanned almost the entire century. The Land Act of 1913 imposed further restrictions on the African population by confining their right to land ownership to the so-called Native Reserves that comprised about 13 per cent of South Africa's land area. Although the black majority was largely ignored, the Boer generals, Louis Botha and Jan Smuts, who served as the first prime ministers of the Union, worked hard to reconcile English- and Afrikaans-speaking white South Africans. In the process, however, they offended their fellow Afrikaners, still bitter from defeat by the British, and thus provoked the rise of an Afrikaner nationalism. In the 1930s, Smuts reconciled with the nationalist General Hertzog but when Smuts led South Africa into war on the side of the British in 1939, the rift reopened. In 1948, Smuts suffered a shock defeat when Dr D.F. Malan led his Purified Nationalist Party to a victory in the 'whites'-only election under the banner of *apartheid.*

The controversies in the literature on South Africa's transition to modernity have largely taken the form of a dispute between liberal and radical materialist traditions of historiography. In the liberal interpretation, South Africa's recent history was primarily a conflict between races, and the sin of apartheid was its interference with the natural progression of economic development (see, for example, works by R. Davenport, H. Houghton and W.M. Macmillan) but the radical or materialist view focused on the close, mutually supportive relationship between apartheid and capitalism (see, for example, works by H. Wolpe, M. Leggasick and C. Bundy). The radicals argued, for example, that the migrant labour system ensured that capitalists enjoyed a ready supply of cheap labour, with the homelands taking care of the reproduction costs of labour.

The history of urban planning in this period has two strands. The first is the relatively uncomplicated story of the transfer of a mainly British system of town planning to the Union of South Africa. The second has to do with the rise of a nationwide system to control and regulate the urbanization of black South Africans.

The first part of the story begins in the 1880s with the increased pressures for urban development following the opening of the goldfields on the Witwatersrand. Between 1881 and 1885, the Colony of Natal, and the Free State and Transvaal Republics, introduced procedures to regulate the subdivision of land. A further impetus for regulation came in the aftermath of the South African War during a period of reconstruction (Mabin and Smit 1997; Oranje 1998). The governor of the Transvaal, Lord Milner, brought a coterie of young men to South Africa who were familiar with the then avant-garde ideas on local government and town planning in Great Britain, and elsewhere in the British Empire. Some of these ideas were implemented in the Transvaal through legislation such as the Johannesburg Municipal Proclamation Act of 1901 and the Transvaal Proclamation of Township Ordinance of 1905, although these measures were concerned with further regulation of subdivisions and of building, rather than with land-use management (Parnell and Mabin 1995). This interest was, however, not sustained, and the period from 1906 until at least the late 1920s represented a long struggle to gain proper recognition for town planning, although an interesting, but limited, development at the time was the construction of Pinelands, outside Cape Town, in 1919, as South Africa's first 'Garden City' (Oranje 1998).

In Great Britain, town planning schemes had been introduced with the Town Planning and Housing Act of 1909, but in South Africa there was a long delay in establishing appropriate legislation. A major cause of this tardiness was a dispute between national and provincial governments over powers for planning and land management, with English-speaking Natal, especially, insisting on provincial control over these matters. The matter was only resolved in 1925 when provinces were allocated these powers and, over the following decade, the provinces put in place Town Planning Ordinances which allowed for the creation of township boards and town planning schemes. These Ordinances were not racially based but this was because town planning was simply never envisaged as an instrument to benefit the black population (Parnell 1993).

By the 1930s, town planning in South Africa was a relatively minor and technocratic concern, hardly a reflection of the avant-garde ideals of previous decades, with Mabin and Smit referring to the 'disappointing narrowness of the "town planning" which emerged in the South Africa of the thirties' (1997: 202). However, the arrival of an avant-garde modernism – inspired by the thinking of Le Corbusier and the Congrès International du Architecture Moderne (CIAM) – reached South Africa in the late 1930s, and provided planning with new inspiration. This modernism found its expression, for example, in the plan for the reclamation and development of the Cape Town foreshore.

During the Second World War ideas of modernism meshed with the ideal of post-war reconstruction despite South Africa being far from the theatre of war. Smuts appointed the Social and Economic Planning Council (SEPC) to prepare for a post-war South Africa, and it was the Fifth Report of the SEPC on Regional and Town Planning that made recommendations for a strong central planning agency. In the final event, the Smuts government was reluctant to set up a national department of planning but did establish the National Resources Development Council (NRDC) with powers to plan within specially designated areas, such as the then newly developing goldfields of the northern Orange Free State (Wilkinson 1996). The NRDC was also involved in the planning of New Towns – such as Vanderbijlpark and Sasolburg – to house the workers of major new state-owned iron-and-steel and oil-from-coal plants (Oranje 1998). There were some regional variations in planning, with Natal, for example, drawing more heavily on the British connection than elsewhere, and establishing its own Town and Regional Planning Commission, in partial competition to the NRDC (Harrison and Mabin 1997).

Parnell (1993) argued that town planning was largely introduced within South Africa to improve the conditions of the white working class, and affected the black population mainly by omission. There was, however, a set of other measures – which had to do with public health, slum control and racial segregation – that had more direct implications for black South Africans. In the early twentieth century there was a renewed concern for segregation inspired by the fears of middle-class whites who identified racial mixing and slum conditions with health hazards – a phenomenon referred to by Swanson (1976) as the 'sanitation syndrome'. The bubonic plague which swept through South Africa in the early years of the century (1901–04), beginning in the port cities and then moving into the interior, was associated with destruction of racially mixed slums, and the movement of Africans to townships on what was then the urban periphery (e.g. Ndabeni in Cape Town, Klipspruit in Johannesburg and New Brighton in Port Elizabeth). The influenza epidemic of 1918–19 had a similar effect with the Johannesburg City Council, for example, creating the Western Areas Native Township which survived until the late 1950s when it was removed by the nationalist government (Maylam 1995; Beavon 2004).

Concerns for public health were also behind the introduction of the provisions for regulating density and land usage in the Public Health Act of 1919 (although these 'town planning' instruments were never implemented because of the ongoing dispute over provincial and national powers). The Housing Act of 1920 also assisted with the segregation process. Although the Act was racially neutral, its provisions were used by municipalities to construct subsidized housing estates for poor whites, especially in Johannesburg where the Labour Party had taken control of the local council in 1919 (Parnell 1993). Likewise, the Slums Act of 1934 was racially neutral but was also used as a cover for segregationist measures. In Cape Town, for example, it was employed to remove city slums and develop the first housing schemes on the Cape Flats, while in Johannesburg, places like Vrededorp and Bertrams were cleared of multiracial slums and redeveloped as subeconomic housing for whites (Mabin 1992; Maylam 1995).

It was, however, the Native (Urban Areas) Act of 1923 that was most directly concerned with segregation. It was an Act that empowered municipalities to proclaim 'white'-only areas, and then move black residents to segregated 'locations'. The significance of the Act was not in its short-term effects – which were limited as relatively few municipalities implemented it – but rather in its long-term implications. The 1923 Act began a process of greater state intervention in the regulation of the urbanization process, which was gradually extended through the 1930s and 1940s. The Act also provided the framework for a later piece of legislation, the Group Areas Act of 1950, which *compelled* municipalities to enforce racial zoning, and which was to be implemented with far grander design and with more draconian measures (Maylam 1990). Interestingly, Johannesburg was one of the few places where the 1923 Act was applied – the whole city, with the exception of Sophiatown and surrounding areas, was designated as 'white' in 1933 leaving almost 50,000 Africans with no right of residence. This forced many Africans to move to the newly constructed 'model' township known as Orlando (now part of the Soweto complex), which as Beavon explained, may have been designed with 'a Garden City flavour', but in reality was 'little more than a bleak residential outpost in the veld' (2004: 121).

Although the 1923 Act was targeted only at Africans, the government also moved to tighten control over the Indian population through legislation such as the Asiatic Land Tenure and Representation Act of 1946. When the Purified National Party came to power, it was to take these anti-Indian measures and extend them to the African and coloured communities (Christopher 1990).

In this period, planning was generally not seen as something that applied to rural areas. An exception was the practice of 'betterment planning', within the so-called Native Reserves, which was about the concentration of the scattered rural settlement in order to combat erosion and release consolidated land for agriculture. However, these measures generally failed as growing numbers of rural dwellers were crowded into the increasingly degraded homelands. Hertzog's 1936 Land Act did little to increase the available space.

In the 1940s, the Smuts administration failed to manage urbanization processes. With its focus on the war effort it produced no coherent urban policy at a time when industrialization and urbanization were rapidly accelerating. One of the visible consequences was the proliferation of informal settlement at a scale not to be seen again until the late 1970s (Beavon 2004). After the war there was an indication of a liberalization of urbanization policy, with the Smuts-appointed Fagan Commission recommending permanent African settlement in urban areas – a far cry from the findings of the now infamous (Transvaal) Stallard Commission report in the early 1920s that Africans should be permitted in urban areas only to serve the needs of white citizens. However, this new pragmatism was never implemented as the Purified National Party came to power in 1948, on the basis of the doctrine of apartheid, spelt out by its own Sauer Commission of 1947, which drew heavily on the thinking of the Stallard Commission more than 20 years previously.

A PECULIAR FORM OF MODERNISM:
LATE 1940S TO EARLY 1970S

The late 1940s to the early 1970s was the era of high apartheid. In the 1950s, under prime ministers D.F. Malan and J.G. Strijdom, apartheid was associated with a crude notion of *baaskap*, or white domination, but when H.F. Verwoerd, the grand architect of apartheid, became prime minister in 1958, a more sophisticated version of 'separate development' evolved, which included the creation of ten ethnic states where South Africans would exercise their political rights. Verwoerd was, however, assassinated in 1966 and from then on the 'purity' of the apartheid ideal was gradually compromised under the conservative but pragmatic leadership of B.J.Vorster and the reformism of P.W. Botha.

In the 1950s, apartheid faced the challenge of the ANC-led Defiance Campaign but in 1960 opposition to influx control and the pass system culminated in the shootings at Sharpeville and the imposition of a state of emergency. Verwoerd's government was able to reimpose control, and force the liberation movements into exile. The 1960s was a period of relative stability and rapid economic growth, which enabled the apartheid regime to implement many of its policies.

In liberal mythology, 1948 represents a dramatic break from the moderate policies of the previous government. However, the apartheid government was able to build on the earlier practices of segregation, and also on modernist planning approaches. Apartheid did, however, represent a far more extreme and systematized approach to segregation than in the past, and was referred to by Parnell and Mabin (1995) as a 'peculiar form of modernism'.

The most powerful instrument of racial restructuring was the Group Areas Act (GAA) of 1950 which, as indicated, was modelled on the Native (Urban Areas) Act of 1923, while the instrument used to plan and implement Group Areas was the Land Tenure Advisory Board (LTAB) which Smuts had initially set up to address the segregation of the Indian community. The GAA and the LTAB brought town planning schemes into a direct relationship with segregationist measures – although racial reservation did not happen under the town planning schemes, the adoption of these schemes could only happen once the Group Area designations had been approved (Mabin 1992).

The implementation of the GAA led to large-scale forced removals. From the late 1950s bulldozers moved in to flatten settlements in places such as Sophiatown (Johannesburg), District Six (Cape Town), Cato Manor (Durban), Lady Selborne (Pretoria), South End (Port Elizabeth) and Duncan's Village (East London). At the beginning of the 1950s, many Africans and coloureds lived in the relative freedom of racially mixed inner-city slums, that were known for their gangsterism and crime, but which also inspired extraordinary music, theatre, visual art and literature. By the 1970s, after the removals, these places no longer existed (Western 1981).

The removals happened in tandem with massive township development that has left an enduring imprint on South Africa's urban form. Planning for this development began in the early 1950s; in 1952, for example, the Mentz Committee, with the support of planners working for the NRDC, decided on the location of townships in the Pretoria–Witwatersrand–Vereeniging (PWV) region. In the years that followed, township construction happened on a grand scale, with places like Soweto, Kathorus, Daveyton, KwaMashu, Mamelodi and Gugulethu literally rising from the veld. In support of township construction, which reached a peak of over 11,000 units per year in the late 1950s, the National Building Research Institute (NBRI) developed standardized layouts and housing designs (the so-called 51/6 and 51/9 houses[1]) (Mabin 1993). The townships were surrounded by buffer zones

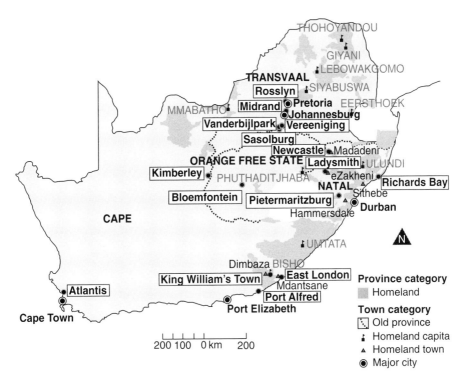

Figure 1.1 Apartheid South Africa

which included natural features, industrial areas and vacant land, and were care-fully designed to ensure maximum control, leading Robinson (1997), for example, to compare the apartheid city with Michel Foucault's carceral and panoptic spaces. This township construction arguably marked the pinnacle of South Africa's peculiar version of high modernity but, by the late 1960s, this development around South Africa's major urban areas halted as the focus shifted to the construction of towns in the African Reserves (places like Madadeni, Mdantsane, Bisho and Mmabatho).

While apartheid reconstructed South Africa's urban space, it also involved an ambitious programme of regional reconfiguration. Although the idea of African Reserves goes back at least to colonial administration in Natal in the nineteenth cen-tury, it was given a grand philosophical foundation by H.F. Verwoerd (Minister of Native Affairs from 1951). A plethora of Acts was introduced to give effect to an emerging vision of a balkanized South Africa where Africans would have their political rights confined to ethnically defined homelands.[2]

One of the most pernicious aspects of the system was the large-scale removal and relocation of communities in an attempt to consolidate the African population within the confines of the homelands. It was estimated that more than two million

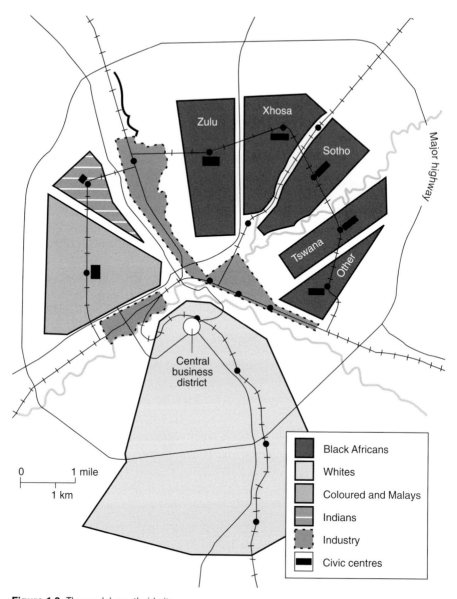

Figure 1.2 The model apartheid city

people had been forcibly relocated through either the elimination of the so-called 'Black Spots' or through legislation abolishing labour tenancies and eliminating 'squatting' on white-owned farms (SPP 1983). Some cases of removal and resettlement, such as Limehill in Natal and Dimbaza in the Eastern Cape, attracted international attention and condemnation but much of this planned destruction happened far from the glare of the media.

Key to the success of Verwoerd's vision was the economic viability of what were planned to be independent ethnic homelands. To this end – and also to help stem the flow of Africans into the cities – the government introduced a programme of industrial decentralization, supported by a combination of incentives to draw industry to the rural periphery and controls over the employment of Africans in urban areas. This politically inspired drive resonated with international views on regional planning at the time, and the government was thus able to offer a technical rationale for its programme. Debates have raged over the impact and merits of decentralization. The liberal view, most strongly represented by the Urban Foundation, was that the decentralization programme ran counter to natural processes of economic development. However, writers from a critical radical tradition argued that the government's programme reinforced a market-led process in which industrial capital sought reservoirs of cheap non-unionized labour in the rural periphery (see contributions in Tomlinson and Addleson 1987).

Industrial decentralization has left a spatial imprint in places such as Atlantis, Hammarsdale, Rosslyn, Ezakheni, Isithebe, Dimbaza and Richard's Bay. Although some of its local impacts were significant, the overall impact of industrial decentralization was modest, and did little to achieve the state's objective of reducing the flow of black labour to the cities, although it may have bolstered the position of homeland governments including KwaZulu and Bophutatswana.

Through the 1950s and 1960s, national government worked to centralize control over local planning processes that related to African urbanization. The provinces were never given powers to undertake regional planning, although the Natal Town and Regional Planning Commission (NTRPC) partially circumvented this restraint through its regional surveys, most famously for the Tugela River Basin (Mabin and Harrison 1996).

Box 1.1 Regional variation: the case of planning in the province of Natal

Natal, with its largely English-speaking white population, retained stronger links with the UK than the other provinces, and agitated for greater provincial autonomy. There were even influential groupings within the province arguing for secession. The link with the UK was very evident in the field of planning. In 1946, Natal recruited its first professional town planner, Eric Thorrington-Smith, from the UK, and his experience in planning for Greater London during the war was influential in shaping planning discourse in Natal from the late 1940s until at least the 1970s. Thorrington-Smith was, however, also influenced by his reading of the achievements of the Tennessee Valley Authority (TVA) in the USA, and he attempted to replicate the TVA approach in his planning for the Tugela Basin through the 1950s and 1960s.

Natal was also the only province where a planning commission was established. The Natal Town and Regional Planning Commission, set up in 1951, and at least partially free of the provincial bureaucracy, was concerned with providing research, advice and policy guidance. The existence of the Commission meant that planning in Natal had a broader scope, and was more research-informed, than elsewhere in South Africa. It was only in Natal, for example, that provincial authorities were engaged in some form of regional planning. The Commission was famous for its work on the Tugela Basin, although relatively little of the planning for this deep rural area was ever implemented. In the 1970s the work of the Commission shifted to planning for the Durban–Pietermaritzburg Metropolitan Area although, again, the planning was more striking than the implementation. The Commission also pioneered work on the natural environment, with a very strong biophysical emphasis.

The relationship between the Commission's work and apartheid was complex. Harrison and Mabin (1997) concluded that the Commission's general attitude towards apartheid could be summarized as one of some distaste, but lacking overt hostility, given the extent to which a racially segregated model of the use of space underlay almost all planning throughout the apartheid period. The Commission never directly confronted apartheid but rather found its way around apartheid; sometimes quietly ignoring or at least diluting the more extreme provisions for racial ordering but more often than not accommodating itself with the system.

Source: Mabin and Harrison (1996) and Harrison and Mabin (1997)

The creation of a national Department of Planning in 1964 (which replaced the NRDC and LTAB) furthered the centralization of control, as did the Physical Planning Act of 1967 which gave national government new powers to dictate local planning through the preparation of Guide Plans for local areas. In 1972, in one of the final acts of high apartheid, the control of black townships was shifted from municipalities to central government-controlled Administration Boards (which were financed largely through the State's monopoly over the production and selling of sorghum beer to the African population, a system devised in Durban in the early twentieth century).

Although apartheid planning was imposing unique burdens and controls on the black population, the trends in planning (and in spatial form) in increasingly sanitized 'white South Africa' were not much different from those of Europe or North America. This was the era of low-density suburbanization abetted by large-scale investment in freeways, the rise of multicentred metropolitan cities, the decentralization of commercial and office activity, the separation of land uses through the application of zoning schemes, and high-rise modernist architecture (Oranje 1998). These developments were supported through the 1960s and early 1970s by rapid, sustained economic growth that benefitted mainly the white working and middle classes. The town planning schemes, provided for in the provincial ordinances, regulated planning and land-use control in 'white' areas, and provincial administrations played the key role in administering the system. It was a system

Figure 1.3 Soweto township, Johannesburg

that protected residential properties and local business interests, and supported the property market by maintaining the relative scarcity of land.

During this period of high modernism, planning had a close but uneven relationship with apartheid. There was a large group of planners working for various tiers of government, and for the private sector in support of government, whose work was directly focused on planning for apartheid. However, as Mabin and Smit pointed out, there were also many planners, working for local authorities and the private sector, whose work was 'not markedly dissimilar to those being pursued by their professional counterparts in other national contexts, even if they occurred within the overall framework of apartheid' (1997: 208). In the next era, the relationship between planning and apartheid became increasingly complex as apartheid entered a period of crisis and eventual decay.

APARTHEID IN DECAY: THE MID-1970S TO 1990

Even as apartheid was achieving apparent success in the reorganization of urban space, it was creating enormous contradictions that would ultimately be its undoing.

Figure 1.4 Township houses under apartheid

The greatest of these was the desire to remove blacks from white-occupied space at the same time as needing blacks in close proximity to provide labour for the white-owned economy. Other spatial contradictions of apartheid were also magnified as the economic boom of the 1960s and early 1970s came to an end; for example, the movement of Africans further and further away from the urban core was leading to huge transportation costs which government was forced to subsidize (Maylam 1990).

By 1973, more than a decade of political quiet was ended when black labour engaged in a series of illegal strikes and, more seriously, in 1976, when African youth in Soweto rose up in mass defiance against the government's attempt to impose Afrikaans as a medium of learning in the schools. As Maylam put it, 'there can be little doubt that the township uprising of 1976 was a shattering blow to an urban apartheid system already weakened by its own contradictions' (1990: 83). In 1978, in the context of a deepening crisis of legitimacy, P.W. Botha replaced the disgraced B.J. Vorster as prime minister, and introduced a programme of reforms which attempted to mollify and co-opt the Indian, coloured, and African middle class, while keeping the fundamentals of apartheid intact.

A key political dilemma was how to handle the growing black urban population. The outline of a new urbanization strategy was sketched out by the Riekert Commission Report of 1979: the idea was to stabilize an urban black middle class in the city by accepting its permanence and providing secure tenure rights. These 'insiders' were to be protected from the poor migrants from rural areas through an intensified system of influx control. Also important to the strategy was the creation of black local authorities (BLAs) that would give the urban insiders a limited degree of self-government. The strategy was, however, a failure, as floods of migrants defied influx control and settled in mushrooming squatter settlements, while the BLAs collapsed in the face of grassroots resistance and financial crisis.

The government was forced to accept far larger numbers of Africans in urban areas than initially desired, with a 1985 Report of the President's Council calling for the abolition of influx controls and the replacement of racially defined controls over settlement with racially neutral measures such as slum, squatter and health laws (Hindson 1987: 74–106). These proposals were largely accepted in the 1986 White Paper on Urbanization, although the Group Areas Act was retained, and provision of new housing for Africans was to happen on the urban periphery. The central concept in the White Paper was 'orderly urbanization' which meant an acceptance that the urbanization of black South Africans was inevitable but also the introduction of measures to ensure that this urbanization happened in a planned and controlled way in parts of the city designated for black settlement. 'Orderly urbanization' was, however, a failure, as the State's squatter, health and trespass laws did not prevent land invasions or the continued growth of informal development. Also, the Group Areas Act was fast failing, with a growing infiltration of other races into

Figure 1.5 Demolition of Crossroads informal settlement, Cape Town

'white' group areas such as Hillbrow, Mayfair and Yeoville in Johannesburg, and Albert Park in Durban. Although 'orderly urbanization' did not succeed and may even have accelerated the final collapse of apartheid's spatial order, it did leave its imprint on the urban landscape with the creation of 'semi-formal' settlements on the urban periphery including Orange Farm (Johannesburg), Ivory Park (Midrand), Khayelitsha (Cape Town) and Motherwell (Port Elizabeth) (Hindson 1987).

There were also attempts at regional restructuring. In 1981 P.W. Botha met business leaders at the Good Hope Conference where he spelt out a new regional strategy which involved the creation of eight (later nine) Development Regions that cross-cut homeland and provincial boundaries. New forms of technical coordination, including cross-border planning and delivery of bulk infrastructure, were now possible, supported by the newly created Development Bank of Southern Africa (DBSA), the Regional Development Advisory Committees (RDACs) and Regional Services Councils (RSCs), but political structures were to remain largely separate and racially defined. The Development Regions were an implicit recognition that homelands had failed to develop as viable economic units, with some observers seeing in the Development Regions the outlines of a future federal system of government (e.g. Glaser 1987: 28–54). The link between spatial policy and Botha's reform strategy was emphasized by the institutional location of planning in national government: between 1980 and 1984 the functions previously performed by the Department of Planning were located within the office of the prime minister, and between 1984 and 1989 in the hugely influential Department of Constitutional Development and Planning. It was only in 1989, when de Klerk came to power, that planning was demoted to a junior ministry. In the final event, however, Botha's constitutional reforms degenerated into a muddled and seemingly ad hoc process.

Botha's reforms arguably did little more than provoke further opposition. The catalyst for a nationwide uprising was the introduction of the so-called Tricameral Parliament in 1983, which included the participation of coloured and Indian groups but excluded Africans. There was massive popular rejection of this constitutional change, which spurred the formation of the United Democratic Front (UDF), an umbrella organization for local civic structures that had emerged from the late 1970s. 1983 marked the consolidation of a new era of struggle associated with grassroots mobilization and ideas such as 'popular democracy', 'people's power', and 'democracy from below' (Suttner 2004). Instead of decisions being transmitted downwards from leaders-in-exile, 'people on the ground were more than mere instruments, implementing what others advised or instructed. They were direct actors, who decided what should be done, and in so doing, they exercised considerable creativity' (Suttner 2004: 696). The civic struggles of the 1980s focused mainly on local politics and the living environment including, for example, on such issues as housing rentals and bus fares. The struggles thus connected with the concerns of local planning and, from the mid- to late 1980s, progressive planners were working directly in support of the civic movement through organizations such as the Built Environment Support Group (BESG) in Durban, Planact in Johannesburg, and the Development Action Group (DAG) in Cape Town (see Chapter 2).

The township uprisings of 1984 meant the end of Botha's attempts to establish viable BLAs, and the beleaguered state resorted increasingly to repression. Botha's disastrous 'Rubicon speech'[3] in August 1985 ended speculation that he would make a bold move to accommodate black aspirations and, in May 1986, Botha once again dashed hopes for change when the South African military raided Lesotho, Botswana and Zambia on the eve of a key meeting set up by the Commonwealth heads of state to break the logjam in South Africa. On 12 June 1986, Botha declared a nationwide state of emergency, and his troops moved into the townships. Although the state responded ruthlessly to the uprising, resistance could not be contained for long. There were also cracks opening in the edifice of white rule; in September 1985, for example, leading white business leaders and opposition parliamentarians met with the ANC in Lusaka and these engagements, including with prominent Afrikaners, continued through the late 1980s.

With an insurrectionary people's war in the townships, economic sanctions and a declining economy, Botha had few options, but he stubbornly persisted in defying the world. He attempted to re-establish control through a parallel system of government known as the National Security Management System (NSMS) which was dominated by national intelligence and the military. One of the key objectives of the NSMS was to 'win the hearts and minds of the people' and, through the NSMS, military leaders became closely involved in initiatives such as township upgrading (the full story of which may never be told as it was known only to Botha himself, who died in 2006, and a handful of his closest acolytes).

In 'white' local authorities, planning continued to evolve in line with international trends, although it was increasingly difficult for planners in this sphere to remain isolated from the wider political context. Significant trends included the shift towards strategic and forward planning, and the devolution of planning powers to municipalities. In the Transvaal a new ordinance was introduced which allowed for devolved powers and, in Natal, municipalities that completed a 'package of plans' (structure plans, development plans and town planning schemes) could approve their own development applications. This was, however, merely tinkering at the end of an era. In some localities, such as Pietermaritzburg, Port Alfred, Cape Town and Port Elizabeth, this was understood, and there were local planning and development initiatives that involved genuine negotiations between municipal authorities and the civic movement, but without the support of provincial and national government, the initiatives were short-lived. By the end of the 1980s, Botha's reform agenda was in tatters and South Africa's future (and the future of planning) was bleak indeed.

THE FINAL TRANSITION: 1990–94

In 1989, P.W. Botha suffered a mild stroke, and in his absence there was a 'palace coup'. Faced with political stalemate the new State President, F.W. de Klerk, made a bold decision. On 2 February 1990 he announced in parliament the unbanning of the ANC and other liberation movements, and also the release of Nelson Mandela from imprisonment. The ANC, which had been in secret contact with the South African government for a while, responded pragmatically and, in December 1991, 23 political parties convened for the Convention for a Democratic South Africa (CODESA). The negotiating process was, however, complex and conflict-ridden and surrounded by deep social and political trauma. The civil war in KwaZulu-Natal and in the townships of the Witwatersrand intensified, with almost 15,000 people dying violently in the period 1990–94. South Africa hovered on the brink of chaos and civil war following the assassination of Communist Party boss, Chris Hani, in May 1993, and also after horrific killings in places like Sebokeng, Bisho and central Johannesburg, but strong political leadership prevailed. Mercifully, the negotiations were successfully concluded and, despite a threat of carnage in KwaZulu-Natal, the April 1994 elections proceeded peacefully. The ANC won the elections and took office as the senior partner in a Government of National Unity, with Nelson Mandela being inaugurated as the first president of a democratic South Africa.

The ending of apartheid came through negotiation and compromise, rather than through military defeat or the collapse of the state. It was a classic example of what Huntington (1991) called 'transplacement' (also described as 'elite-pacting') – a form of transition that happens when a mutually perceived stalemate prompts negotiations between reformers in the state and democratic elements in the opposition. The significance of transplacement is that there are important elements of continuity between the old and new orders, and that policies often represent forms of consensus rather than radical departures.

The story of planning and urban policy in the period 1990–94 is largely one of consensus-making, but first F.W. de Klerk's government had to remove the final legislated instruments of apartheid. The Abolition of Racially Based Land Measures Act of 1991 scrapped the Group Areas Act, the Land Acts of 1913 and 1936, and the Black Communities Development Act of 1984. This was followed by measures to accelerate urban land development for low-income groups through the Less Formal Township Establishment Act of 1991, and the establishment of the Independent Development Trust (IDT) which pioneered the housing subsidies, that were eventually adopted by the post-apartheid government.

New policies for local government, and for urban policy and planning, were negotiated in multiparty chambers such as the National Housing Forum and the Local Government Negotiating Forum. There were also significant local and regional forums including the Natal Hostels Steering Committee and the Cato Manor Steering Committee in Durban (Mabin and Smit 1997). One of the most significant local initiatives was the formation of the Central Witwatersrand Metropolitan Chamber which followed the Greater Soweto Accord in 1990 that ended the long-standing rent boycott, and prompted a series of negotiations which were to provide the basis for the present-day system of metropolitan government (Beavon 2004). For Horwitz, these negotiating chambers or stakeholder forums

> appeared in the nether-world of the period between the disintegration of the
> *ancien régime* and the emergence of a new political dispensation, in which the
> National Party still held the reins of power after 1990 and continued to function
> as government, but now possessed little legitimacy.
>
> (1991: 14)

See Chapter 2 for a further discussion of these forums.

Conclusion

1994 marked a significant rupture in the history of planning in South Africa, but it is a rupture that can only be explained in terms of what came before. Planning post-apartheid cannot be properly understood without reference to the preceding history of struggle against a system of racially and ethnically based spatial ordering that had its roots deep in the colonial era, and was applied most ruthlessly and systematically after 1948. However, as significant as the discontinuities were before and after 1994, there were also important continuities in policy and apartheid that need to be understood against the post-1976 story of the reform and decay of apartheid, and the short but key period of negotiation and transition in the early 1990s.

By 1994, the form of planning practised by the apartheid state had run its full course – it had been in decay for at least two long decades. However, despite the long association of planning with apartheid, the sentiment was not necessarily anti-planning. There was rather an aspiration to another form of planning, and for planning to play a strong role in delivering the ANC's new vision articulated in the Reconstruction and Development Programme. Part of the persisting faith in planning had to do with the new visions for a post-apartheid planning that had emerged during the late apartheid era, and which are the subject of the next chapter.

CHAPTER 2

NEW PLANNING VISIONS

INTRODUCTION

As Chapter 1 has demonstrated, planning under apartheid focused largely on physical planning and land-use management. It was used to support the creation of apartheid cities and regions. From the 1970s, however, and in the context of rising resistance to apartheid, alternative planning movements and new visions of planning began to emerge. This chapter documents these movements and shows how they contributed to the reshaping of the 'soft infrastructure' of planning in the post-apartheid era – its purpose, domain and meaning, its dominant discourses and practices.

As explained previously, the two decades from the early 1970s to the early 1990s were a time of considerable political ferment. After the repression of the 1960s, when the state banned several oppositional political organizations and jailed key leaders, new oppositional movements began to emerge. The 1973 union strikes and the 1976 Soweto uprising marked growing discontent with apartheid policies. New political movements developed, most importantly the United Democratic Front (UDF), which had links to the external African National Congress (ANC). The UDF was a broad front for a wide range of organizations, including women, churches, unions and civics, among others. Civic organizations protested about the urban conditions created for black people under apartheid, such as limited access to cities, forced removals, racial segregation, high rent and transport costs, poor housing and services.

Planners responded to the challenge to the state in various ways. While the organized planning profession (see Chapter 10) argued that their work was not political, and refused to challenge apartheid (Smit 1988), other planners mounted a sustained critique of apartheid planning practice and posited alternatives, sometimes in concert with NGOs and oppositional political organizations. Several planners saw themselves as 'guerrillas in the bureaucracy',[1] and attempted to work towards change within the system, especially in the larger, English-speaking municipalities in the cities, which were under the control of the political opposition.

There were two main strands to the alternative planning movement. The first, a more liberal grouping, comprised academics and practitioners, who critiqued the apartheid style of planning, its state-centred approach, and its strong regulatory thrust. Some academics within this grouping focused on social justice, while others developed an alternative spatial vision of the city. Liberal academics called attention to the negative effects of influx control, industrial decentralization, state housing policy and racial segregation. These ideas accorded with the business-oriented Urban Foundation (UF), itself staffed by several planners, which piloted new approaches to low-cost housing and attempted to steer the state towards more laissez-faire approaches to housing and urban development as the crisis deepened.

A second main strand comprised the self-styled 'progressive[2] planners', often with a socialist orientation and a background in anti-apartheid organizations linked to the African National Congress (ANC), who worked actively with oppositional civic organizations around, for example, resistance to public housing rate and rent increases, poor housing quality, informal settlement removals, influx control, and in campaigns for a unified city. These planners worked with other urban development professionals and academics to put in place progressive urban 'service organiza-tions' which operated as advocates for the urban poor. While beginning as voluntary organizations, most later became fully staffed NGOs, which worked with civic orga-nizations and communities in pioneering new forms of urban development practice.

In practice, the work of the two groupings converged in several ways, and both people and ideas moved between the two. Both were influential in the urban develop-ment negotiating forums of the early 1990s, which experimented with the new approaches, and in the early policy thinking of the new government. Although planners in both of these contexts worked alongside other urban development professionals and the nature and role of planning were rarely preoccupations in their own terms, the discourses of the time were critical in rethinking planning in the post-apartheid era.

The late 1980s and early 1990s might be seen as a heyday for planning, when planning offered hope of social transformation. Planning came to be seen as a development practice contributing to urban social transformation, and to altering the position of the poor. This position was in line with the international radical planning (e.g. Fainstein and Fainstein 1979) and development planning movements of the time. The development planning movement in particular was highly critical of plan-ning as regulation in developing countries, and argued for a community-centred, developmental approach (Devas and Rakodi 1993). These perspectives were influ-ential in moving planning away from its earlier focus on physical planning and land-use management towards a broader developmental approach in the post-apartheid period.

EARLY VISIONS: THE LIBERALS

Despite the predominant compliance of planners with apartheid, some liberal plan-ners railed against apartheid planning practice (see Muller 2003). The professor of town and regional planning at the University of the Witwatersrand (Wits), John Muller, developed a strong liberal critique of apartheid planning, and argued for a theoretical approach that was both process-focused and overtly committed to the pursuit of social justice. Muller was head of the department from 1979 to 2000 and generations of students were influenced by his approach. During the early years of his headship, a postgraduate development planning programme was introduced with the explicit intention of attracting black students into what was at the time a predominantly white profession. The development planning programme also moved away from a predominantly physical approach to planning, and drew from the international development planning movement in its thinking.

A small group of planning academics at the University of Cape Town (UCT), particularly David Dewar and Roelof Uytenbogaardt, developed an alternative urban vision and approach to planning, which proved to be highly influential in the post-apartheid era. Beginning in the 1970s, they developed systematic critiques of the apartheid urban form and the modernist design ideas through which it had been planned. They offered a view of cities as far more mixed and integrated than the typical apartheid city which was divided on land use, race and class lines. Their spatial visions, which lent themselves to more radical ideas of urban spatial restructuring and urban transformation, were critical in giving planners a sense of mission and a potential role in redressing the apartheid city. The spatial ideas of this grouping, and their links to international discourses on urban compaction and new urbanist design, are discussed more fully in Chapter 6.

The form of planning they advocated was also significant in redefining the nature and domain of planning in the post-apartheid era. They eschewed the control-oriented 'blueprint' approach to planning in use at the time, and argued instead for a minimalist approach to planning based on defining only key structural elements and the use of a set of normative principles to guide land-use planning and decision-making. The UCT ideas were important in marginalizing the significance of land-use regulation as a field of planning in the thinking of the time, and in post-apartheid planning discourse. The UCT school was also important in elevating a design-based 'framework' approach to spatial planning, which gained prominence in the post-apartheid era (Chapter 6).

The political resurgence and protests of the early 1970s were largely concentrated in urban areas. While protests initially focused on education and worker rights, the crisis of urban apartheid soon became a critical focus in its own right (Swilling 1995). State influx control policies denied the reality of growing urbanization – the consequence of both economic growth and the declining productive base of rural areas – and the growing demand for a more skilled and stable urban labour force. The relegation of black people to peripheral parts of cities and urban areas put pressure on transport costs and thus wages, while urban administrative apartheid meant that townships reserved for black people had to be self-financing. With economic recession, these conditions were felt more sharply, resulting in a series of boycotts and protests, particularly around transport and rents (Mabin and Smit 1997). One response to crisis was the establishment in 1976 of the Urban Foundation – a private-sector think-tank to develop solutions to the urban crisis and to encourage government to shift its thinking towards more market-oriented principles. The Urban Foundation employed several planners who, like some of the planning academics, were critical of conventional planning practice at the time. Key figures included Anne Bernstein, a graduate of planning from the University of California, while Jill Strelitz and Matthew Nel had passed through the planning programme at Wits.

While the Urban Foundation had strong informal ties to the parliamentary liberal opposition party, the Progressive Party, it attempted to encourage the state to adopt reformist solutions. The Urban Foundation's work had two main thrusts. The first, which was developed through both policy work and through urban development projects, was on low-cost housing. The Foundation urged the state to accept the reality of urbanization and argued for the promotion of individual ownership of housing, self-help housing, and informal settlement upgrading. The Foundation worked with several academics in various built-environment professions in developing solutions along these lines. Its market-oriented approach to housing, in particular its critique of state rental housing, and its advocacy of a Chilean-style capital subsidy system in which beneficiaries qualified for ownership of a plot or house, was highly influential in post-apartheid housing policy. In the early 1980s as influx control began to break down, the Urban Foundation was instrumental in assisting the state to develop new legislation for rapid land release for urban development, which included a simplified system of land-use regulation based on an acceptance of land-use mix as a starting point. Its later work included investigations into planning systems – although this was weakly developed – and mechanisms for access to land by the urban poor. The focus of the housing section of the Urban Foundation, although not self-consciously about planning, was important in redefining South African planning to include concerns about the living conditions and housing needs of the urban poor. In this their influence was similar to that of the progressive urban service organizations although the orientations of the two groupings were somewhat different.

The second Urban Foundation thrust was to counter the gamut of anti-urban state policies, particularly influx control and the regional industrial decentralization policy. Drawing on a wider literature by planners and other academics, it put together arguments for an acceptance of urbanization and big city growth, and critiqued initiatives to direct 'unsustainable' growth to peripheral areas. The policy of industrial decentralization was a significant focus of its critique. Drawing on an emergent literature on 'bottom-up' regional development and local economic development, the Urban Foundation and academics such as Richard Tomlinson argued for alternative approaches based on locally generated economic activity and notions of competitive and comparative advantage. These ideas have been influential in planning post-apartheid (see Chapter 5) and in defining the domain of planning, although they were never seen as solely the preserve of planning.

PROGRESSIVE PLANNING

From the mid-1970s, the apartheid state initiated a series of rolling reforms to address popular discontent. These included an attempt to divide the African population into a secure urban skilled labour force living in their own homes and governed by their own self-financed local authorities, and a second grouping whose political and economic aspirations would be accommodated in 'homeland' areas. Continuing movement of people to cities however led to the declining effectiveness of influx control and the rapid growth of informal settlements. The sprawling nature of towns and cities – particularly where these cross-cut homeland boundaries – resulted in high transport costs. Attempts to establish independent black local authorities confronted the limited revenue base of township areas, and political resistance to the system. Protests and struggles began to occur over a number of terrains in townships, and civic organizations linked to broader political organizations emerged to contest forced removals of informal settlements, rising transport and rent costs, and initiatives to establish self-governing black local authorities, *inter alia.*

From the early 1980s a group of mainly young white middle-class planners who identified themselves with the struggle against apartheid began to work with emerging civic organizations and to form planning advocacy organizations (Smit 1988). Although liberal planners were involved in these activities, many participants had visions of wide-ranging social transformation, and saw themselves as 'progressive' planners. Planners were not alone in this activity – they worked with other built-environment professionals and with academics interested in the urban terrain. Like the Urban Foundation, the focus for the most part was not on planning per se, and disciplinary boundaries and the organized profession were largely ignored. Nevertheless, some planners involved in these activities were actively exploring how planners and planning could contribute to social change.

While several planning academics at English-speaking universities were finding ways to link to civic organizations and to make their skills available to oppressed communities, the then University of Natal's planning school, and particularly the academic Dan Smit, led initiatives to develop a self-consciously progressive planning practice. Frustrated with the predominantly negative and analytical tone of much Marxian theory, Smit (1984: 2) explored how 'Marxian analysis in planning theory both can and must be made relevant to the everyday policy considerations of practicing planners'. He drew on the work of international planning theorists of the time such as Fainstein and Fainstein (1979) and Roweis (1983), as well as from literature on urban political economy (Castells 1977) and urban social movements (Castells 1983).

Translation of analysis into action was influenced by the work of the advocacy planning movement internationally and by organizations such as the self-styled Radical Institute Group of the Royal Town Planning Institute. The first urban 'progressive service organization' (Beauregard 1995), the Built Environment Support Group (BESG), was established at the University of Natal in 1982. It included planning academics Dan Smit, Michael Sutcliffe and Mike Kahn, architectural academics Errol Haarhoff and Rodney Harber, and the geographer Jeff McCarthy. Although Smit, Sutcliffe and McCarthy were trained in the USA and were influenced by their studies on Marxist urban and planning theory there, they were also drawn into this work through the efforts of a particularly active and well-organized civic movement. At a recent memorial for the civic activist Vish Supersad, Michael Sutcliffe (now municipal manager of eThekwini municipality in KwaZulu-Natal) commented on how in the early 1980s, Vish, then with the Community Research Unit, and the Durban Housing Action Civic, had approached him to work with them on various campaigns and to use his skills in the interests of the broader struggle for social transformation. Others were drawn in through the efforts of Vish, his wife Vidhu Vedalankar, who later trained as a planner, and Pravin Gordhan, now head of the highly effective South African Revenue Service.

BESG worked with civic organizations on 'community defence' (assistance to communities in their struggles against forced removals, rent increases, incorporation into homelands, etc.) and on the upgrading of informal settlements and community development, policy aid, training and education, technical assistance on housing and community buildings, and negotiation and mediation (Smit 1988). Some of its earlier projects included the St Wendolins and Clairwood projects in Durban. Both St Wendolins and Clairwood were areas facing forced removals, and BESG worked with community organizations in these areas to fight against this by developing plans that would show that an alternative development path was possible. While St Wendolins was classified as a 'black spot' to be removed in terms of Group Areas legislation (Box 2.1), Clairwood was an area that had been zoned for industrial use. Its contested and uncertain status and the dominance of absentee landlords in the area had enabled uses such as informal dump sites and parking of large trucks to encroach into the area, and the position of its marginalized tenants was threatened.

Box 2.1 The development of St Wendolins

St Wendolins is an area in Southern Pinetown, about 10 km from the Pinetown central business district (CBD) in the greater Durban area. The St Wendolins community occupied land owned by individual African landowners, the state and the Roman Catholic Missionary Congregation of Marianhill. Land was sold to African owners or leased by the Mission Institute to African tenants until the 1950s, when the state warned the church against selling further land to Africans. In 1966, the Group Areas Board zoned the area for use by non-Africans (mainly Indians) and industry, and removals to townships within the KwaZulu homeland began in a piecemeal fashion in the late 1970s. More concerted removals began in 1979 and the St Wendolins Welfare Committee and the Save St Wendolins Association were established to contest removals. In response to pressure, the Group Areas Board agreed to review the situation in 1992, and 99-year leasehold rights were granted, subject to development and upgrading of the area, although the larger Savanna Park area remained under threat. Community initiatives to begin the development process resulted in the formation of the Isolumusi (a committee of 15) in 1984. Isolumusi and Save St Wendolins approached BESG to help to coordinate the upgrading and development programme. Until 1986 however the state wavered on the development of the area. BESG's early efforts therefore centred on supporting arguments against removals and for in situ upgrading. BESG worked with community organizations to develop a set of planning proposals for the development of the area, bringing architectural and planning students into the project. Proposals included guidance on the physical development of the area, but also emphasized the importance of a process approach, and the development of strong local community organization, empowered to have control over development in the area (BESG 1986). In later years, as the idea of development was accepted, BESG worked with community organizations to develop acceptable forms of housing and development which did not exclude the poor. Development on Mission Institute land was handed over to an Urban Foundation housing utility company, Innova. BESG's role shifted from one of advocacy to advising organizations on the mode of development. A key concern was affordability, since Innova's initial model was focused on greenfields development and loan finance that would be accessible only to the better-off groupings. At this stage, Innova was unable to raise cheap finance. In addition, in situ upgrading was ignored. Proposals for another part of the area by another utility company, Comhousing, had similar problems. BESG spent considerable time on these issues and they were resolved by 1989. In later years, BESG moved away from the advisory model to actually undertaking development, including in some of the areas linked to St Wendolins, such as Luganda. Its efforts here were in part to show that alternative development models to the standard path were feasible (Forster 2006; BESG 1988; BESG 1986).

ST. WENDOLINS:

BUILDING THE COMMUNITY

UNIVERSITY OF NATAL, DURBAN
BUILT ENVIRONMENT SUPPORT GROUP

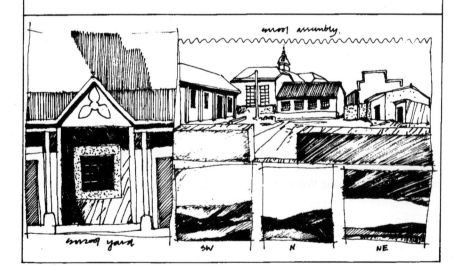

Figure 2.1 St Wendolins, KwaZulu-Natal: the BESG report

Progressive urban service organizations soon emerged in other parts of the country too. Cape Town's Development Action Group (DAG) was set up in 1986 initially in response to government's attempted removal of the Crossroads informal settlement, which had developed as Africans moved to the city in defiance of influx control laws. Such laws were applied particularly strictly in the Western Cape which, under apartheid, was defined as a 'coloured labour preference'[3] area. DAG drew together planners and architects within academia, local authorities and the private sector who identified themselves with the anti-apartheid organization, the UDF. Many were already involved in UDF-linked organizations. It included planners such as Laurine Platzky, who ran the National Land Committee, had headed up a major campaign against rural forced removals, and was later key to the reformulation of planning at national level; Amanda Younge, a senior planner in local government; and UCT planning academics Vanessa Watson and Peter Wilkinson, both of whom had had previous direct links with civic organizations in Cape Town. Organizations also emerged in Port Elizabeth and East London.

Johannesburg's Planact, established in 1985, was perhaps the most important progressive urban service organization, and has recently celebrated its twentieth year. The Pretoria–Witwatersrand–Vereeniging region (or PWV as it was then known – now the Gauteng Province) was South Africa's economic heartland and the centre of white politics and political resistance, as well as being home to about half of the professional planners in the country. Planners in the PWV tended to be divided along linguistic lines. Afrikaans-speaking planners, trained mainly at the Universities of Pretoria and Potchefstroom, worked largely in national, provincial and local government, and English-speaking planners, trained mainly at the self-consciously anti-apartheid University of the Witwatersrand, were concentrated in the private sector and some of the 'white' local authorities. By the early 1980s, the number and size of private firms were significant – far larger than elsewhere in the country. The PWV was a region of political militancy where black local authorities were in crisis almost from their establishment, and the civic movement was radical and active. The scale and intensity of political resistance in the 1980s was considerably greater than in the Western Cape and Natal regions.

Yet despite the liberal influence of the Department of Town and Regional Planning at Wits, and the concentration of planners in the region, there was no coherent collective of planners which saw itself as an alternative to mainstream planning until late in the 1980s, and even then, the 'progressive planning movement' never came together in the same cohesive form as it did in Natal or even the Western Cape. The PWV region, however, contained a large network of individuals across a range of disciplines with a concern for urban and rural issues and problems from a liberal–radical perspective. For instance, the Black Sash had an urban advice centre and had established the Transvaal Rural Action Committee, while the Legal

Resource Centre and the Committee to Stop Eviction took up many urban injustices. At Wits there was an extraordinary collection of individuals across the
disciplines who provided intellectual and practical support for the urban struggle, for
instance, Billy Cobbett (later the first Director-General of Housing post-apartheid),
Mark Swilling, Daryl Glaser, Alan Mabin (later deputy head of the post-apartheid
Development and Planning Commission), Doug Hindson, Eddie Webster, Sue
Parnell and Phillip Bonner.

In the early 1980s, individuals such as Mark Swilling and Alan Mabin had been
providing ad hoc support to civic organizations in the PWV and the Eastern Cape.
However there was a need for a more structured form of support. The earlier formation of BESG in Natal provided inspiration and a model to a grouping of individuals
– Swilling, Mabin, Parnell, Hendler, Cobbett, Tomlinson, Abbot, Feldman and others
– who came together to found a voluntary association to respond to requests from
civic and other community-based organizations. Planact was established in 1985,
and its first major project was in Langa township in the Eastern Cape. Soon
Planact's work was increasing in volume and complexity. Box 2.2 provides an indication of some of the projects undertaken by Planact in the early period.

Common to all organizations was a commitment to democratization. For
some urban activists and academics, such as Swilling, urban civic struggles could
be seen as a new terrain of struggle distinct from national political struggles and

Box 2.2 Some Planact projects

- The National Union of Mineworkers requested Planact to assist with negotiations with management over mine accommodation. Planact workshopped
  housing concepts with the national negotiating team, and the proceedings of
  the workshop became a model for union engagements on this issue.
- Community organizations and unions in Langa, Uitenhage, requested Planact
  to prepare a proposal to upgrade Langa in defence against the white council's
  plan to remove the settlement. Planact worked with groups to formulate a
  response, including a plan to establish a free settlement area where all races
  could live.
- The South African Council of Churches requested Planact to assist with the
  design of a community resource/library centre.
- The Wattville Concerned Residents Association requested Planact to assist
  with housing and service delivery issues in the area. Planact helped the
  Association to negotiate with the Benoni Council for the right to retain and
  develop council-owned land that had been invaded by overcrowded residents.
  The negotiations were successful and black residents won the right to develop
  land previously reserved for whites – a first in South Africa.

Source: Development Works (2006)

worker organization. They were not merely an extension of political organizations or for material improvements, but could also be seen as a struggle for 'urban citizenship through the democratization of our cities' (Swilling 1995: 7). The work of the progressive urban service organizations can be seen partially in this context. They eschewed a technocratic approach in favour of community-centred processes in which the focus was on using skills to empower communities (Swilling 1995). Urban service organizations largely responded to requests for assistance by community organizations rather than seeking to create a development agenda. Furthermore, all organizations placed a strong emphasis on 'process' – on highly participatory forms of planning and decision-making in which the technical expertise of professionals was largely supportive. Beauregard (1995: 367) cites Planact's Mark Swilling as stating that its intent was 'to provide a resource, not a paradigm; to empower, not lead; to listen, not talk; to facilitate, not dictate'. Thus the progressive service organizations put professionals in a different position, one similar to conceptions of collaborative planning practice.

In its focus on 'process' and participation, and in its emphasis on a developmental approach, the work of the progressive urban service organization was formative in post-apartheid discourses on the appropriate orientation of planning. Similarly, the identification of the work of planners through the conditions and expressed needs of poor urban communities – rather than through an abstract definition of planning and its roles – was also critical in shaping the domain of planning post-apartheid. In contrast to many other contexts, planning was not split from implementation and planners had to confront the difficult realities of poor urban communities, ranging from their material conditions to the implications of shifting power bases and politics.

By the late 1980s, most progressive urban service organizations had moved from being voluntary organizations to becoming funded NGOs employing permanent staff. An Urban Sector Network linking NGOs in the field of urban development was set up, also including some research and training organizations. By the early 1990s, several organizations had staffs of around 30 people. At its height in 1993, Planact employed some 47 people (Development Works 2006). Organizations were involved in a number of proactive projects, as well as advocacy work, policy support, education and training. Planact's mission statement in 1992, for example, was 'to promote integrated, community-driven development to ensure an equitable distribution of resources and a democratic and sustainable urban environment' (Development Works 2006: 13).

Progressive urban NGOs were critical in campaigns to unify and democratize the city, and in the context of the negotiating forums of the early 1990s, played key roles in supporting civic and political organizations. In doing so, they engaged in a broader terrain of urban development from local economic development to urban spatial restructuring, as well as their more usual spheres of housing and local government. They also engaged in research and policy development in processes linked to the ANC's post-apartheid thinking. The progressive urban NGOs and urbanists linked to them brought to bear an agenda of social transformation: addressing race and class inequalities in urban development. The need to address inequalities based on gender within urban development was also raised by feminists within these organizations, but this emphasis was never taken through to the same extent as questions of race and class.

Swilling comments that some of the weaknesses of urban policy post-apartheid can be traced to the way the urban NGOs were organized:

> inevitably there was a team that included planners and engineers, who dealt
> with housing projects, and another that included people with social science and
> legal skills, who supported the local government negotiation processes. As a
> result … there was no coherent and authentic post-colonial sense of the city.
>
> (Swilling 1995: 7)

These divides mirror the predominant contemporary organization at national level of departments of housing and local government, with a weak and poorly located urban policy (Pieterse 2004a). The weak links between urban and rural-based NGOs (despite some initiatives to connect the two) are also mirrored in separated rural and urban discourses and policies.

None of the progressive urban service organizations was primarily about planning, but there were more planners in BESG and DAG than in Planact. In the early years of consolidation into NGOs, however, planners were often employed in key positions, such as Clive Foster and Norah Walker in BESG, Kim van Deventer in DAG, and Leila McKenna and Lauren Royston in Planact, but a mix of skills and experience was always important and work was not divided along occupational lines. Initially, the progressive urban service organizations were dominated by the 'white left', but black professionals arrived as they consolidated. Examples are BESG's Nolulamo GwaGwa, the first black woman planner, who later became Deputy Director-General for Public Works and head of the Independent Development Trust; Planact's Pascal Moloi, who was to become Johannesburg's Municipal Manager, and Blake Moseley, who was to hold a similar position in Tshwane.

In the post-apartheid period the Urban Sector Network and its NGOs have struggled with a difficult funding environment, the decline of urban social movements, an uneasy relationship with government, and the loss of staff to government and the private sector. Many organizations have struggled to find an identity and several have closed down or downscaled considerably. Few planners are now employed in these organizations and the voluntary base has long disappeared.

Although the focus of these organizations was not necessarily on planning, they played critical roles in shifting the orientation of planners and planning.

Political issues were debated for the first time at a 1985 conference of the South African Institute for Town and Regional Planners (see Chapter 10). While the conference refused to support a motion stating that apartheid was antithetical to planning principles, it became apparent that many planners were disillusioned with planning under apartheid and the technicist consensus was breaking down (Smit 1988). Mabin cites a community activist as stating that

> planners have an important choice ahead of them. The choice is one of either willingly being the functionaries of the apartheid system and all those unjust policies that go with it, or on the other hand, becoming participants in actively formulating a future approach.
>
> (Mabin 1995a: 6)

The progressive planning movement was an important step in the latter direction.

THE TRANSITIONAL PERIOD

In several respects the work of the Urban Foundation and the progressive urban service organizations covered similar ground and suggested a common broad domain for urban development practitioners. The Urban Foundation however was closely linked to business and to market-oriented ideas. It attempted to reform government policies and by 1994 had become a powerful influence on the reforming apartheid state. By contrast, the progressive service organizations were closely associated with the organizations of the United Democratic Front and the ANC, and much of their earlier work was located in resistance to the apartheid state and state reforms, and drew from socialist theory and a strongly community-centred approach. Several individuals within the progressive urban development movement defined themselves by their opposition to the Urban Foundation. However through the late 1980s and early 1990s, people and ideas moved between the two, and both groupings were influenced by dominant international urban development discourses associated with the United Nations Centre for Human Settlements and the World Bank. This influence was particularly strong as several planners had studied in overseas universities in the USA and the UK, and in institutions such as University College of London's Development Planning Unit, which had links to international agencies, and espoused a developmental approach to planning.

Notions of planning as that of managing cities, rather than controlling their growth, were accepted by all sides. The emphasis on urban management shifted the focus of planning away from a traditional preoccupation with regulating land and built environments, but there were several strands to 'managing the cities'. Some planners argued for new approaches to spatial planning, while others promoted broad ranging development strategies going beyond spatial planning at either a community or city level. Another strand saw planning as concerned 'with the effective functioning of local governments, in particular their financial performance and effective delivery of services to rapidly growing poorer populations' (Mabin 2002: 43). All of these elements were evident in the new forms of planning used within the negotiating forums of the early 1990s, and in the post-apartheid period.

By the late 1980s, cracks in the state's repressive regime were becoming increasingly apparent. Already in 1987 a group of leading Afrikaners had met the ANC in Dakar and, at a local level, tentative negotiations between civic organizations and local authorities had begun by 1989. The coming to power of de Klerk as leader of the National Party in 1989 and the opening up of the political terrain in 1990 laid the basis for a national transition characterized by negotiation, consensus and compromise. Since all pre-existing policy was seen as tainted in some way by apartheid ideology, new policies had to be developed in a range of arenas. As explained in Chapter 1, stakeholder-based policy forums, comprising representatives of the main stakeholder groupings (usually government, political parties, business, communities and NGOs), became the prime vehicle for negotiating new policies at national and local level. Policy forums emerged in a context where government lacked legitimacy, but was responsible for decision-making and implementation. At national level, forums were engaged in policy-making in the spheres of economic policy, housing, transport, water and sanitation, education, and local government, *inter alia*. These forums in many cases provided an important basis for post-apartheid policy. Forums at local level brought together local stakeholders to chart a development path and a set of priorities for cities. Forums were not merely places for debate but were intended to enable change. These forums followed campaigns to unite cities administratively and financially, in order to overcome the inequities associated with local government fragmentation of the past. Planners and other professionals from the Urban Foundation, the Development Bank of Southern Africa (with similar orientations to the Urban Foundation), the urban NGOs and several academics, were actively involved.

The earliest, and perhaps the most important of these local forums, was the Central Witwatersrand Negotiating Chamber, which was established in 1991 following the Soweto Accord of 1990. The accord followed years of campaigns for a 'one city' approach. Planact emerged as the technical arm for the civic movement in the negotiations. During 1992 and 1993, seven regional development forums developed in different parts of the country. Most were inclusive debating and policy-shaping forums. The Western Cape Economic Development Forum launched at the end of

1992 was seen as one of the more successful forums, and was used by local authorities as a vehicle for their metropolitan planning process (Watson 1998). Cape Town's Development Action Group played a critical role in this process.

Wide-ranging plans were prepared, drawing on the spatial ideas of the UCT school, but also the broader developmental orientations of both the Urban Foundation and the progressive urban NGOs. For instance, the Durban Interim Development Forum of 1993–4 developed a normative framework for assessing development expenditures, which included ideas ranging from service delivery needs, economic impacts, participation and process issues and gender, to effects in terms of spatial restructuring. A short-term strategic framework focused on critical needs and directions. The Central Witwatersrand Metropolitan Chamber developed an interim strategic framework (Turok 1994a), which embodied the UCT spatial ideas, but also went further to explore how access to land for the urban poor could be established. While several metropolitan forums explored economic and social issues, these received less attention than the traditional local government responsibilities of infrastructure and spatial development. These planning processes, nevertheless, were forms of development strategies that prefigured the intentions of later integrated development plans.

The work of the local negotiating forums contributed to an increasingly broad conception of the domain of planning and a focus on a developmental approach. The spatial component of planning nevertheless remained critical, but here the emphasis was on restructuring the city. Mabin (2002) comments that planning came to be seen as an important part of urban reconstruction. Both the National Housing Forum and the Local Government Negotiating Forum looked for ways to 'reshape the built environment' (Mabin 2002: 44). These led to an examination of planning systems, and the need to reform planning law and institutions, linking to work which was being undertaken through the ANC-associated Institute for Local Government and the Urban Sector Network.

By 1994, alternative[4] (liberal and progressive) planners and urbanists had begun to develop new visions of the spatial organization of the city and had started to redefine the scope and nature of planning. Although spatial planning continued to be important, the focus was on long-term strategic planning, with less attention given to land-use management. 'Settlement planning' continued to be of significance, but with a much greater focus on participatory and developmental processes. Planning as a form of generating development strategies was cast far more broadly, to include economic and social development and a range of interlinked policy thrusts beyond a purely spatial focus. These strands were to emerge as significant in the post-apartheid period.

The planning that was undertaken in the forums prefigures post-apartheid planning in another way; that is, in its distancing of planning processes from communities.

Although the progressive urban NGOs attempted to take forward their community-based approaches into decision-making within these forums, Watson (1998) questions the extent to which this occurred. Her research on the Western Cape Economic Development Forum suggests that it was far more limited than generally expected, resulting in the dominance of a planning discourse abstracted from community needs. Civic, labour and squatter organizations had little direct presence; the capacity of organized groups was limited and unable to keep up with the many demands of the process; and representation was dissipated by the many small task groups. Not all contributions were 'heard' in the planning process. Information was generally framed by planning consultants and would not necessarily have been understood by non-professionals. Similar comments have been made on integrated development and spatial planning processes post-apartheid (Watson 2002a), reflecting on the scale and style of planning processes.

INFLUENCING POST-APARTHEID PLANNING

The planning visions of the alternative planning movement were highly influential post-apartheid. Adapted versions of the spatial visions of the UCT planning school and the alternative planning movements, in particular the notions of urban compaction, urban restructuring and spatially integrated development, are all contained in policy and legislation (Chapters 3 and 6). Spatial planning has shifted away from planning as control towards a greater emphasis on strategic spatial planning, and the development of plans at a macrometropolitan and regional scale. This reflects the thinking of the UCT school, but is also the legacy of attempts to 'see' the city in a united 'integrated' way in contrast to the legacy of racial fragmentation and urban sprawl.

Similarly, the emphasis on participatory and community-based planning is contained in notions of 'social compacts' in housing projects, in which community groupings participate in the planning of housing and are expected to agree on the products; in many of the integrated area-based projects and programmes; and in legislation governing integrated development planning and land-use decision-making. Since the early post-apartheid period, however, levels of participation have been downscaled considerably, in part in response to the complexities and difficulties of participatory processes, but also to accelerate service delivery (see Chapter 12). Competing power bases within communities, particularly between local government councillors and other local actors, have also influenced declining levels of participation in some areas, with councillors arguing that they should be the sole voice of the community. Research indicates that local organizations feel alienated from local authorities (Williamson *et al.* 2005) and there are questions as to whether the scaling back of levels of participation has been counterproductive.

Multiple ideals of integrated development contained in various strands of the alternative planning movement are evident in post-apartheid policy on housing, spatial policy and integrated development planning: that planning should be multisectoral and not simply focused on physical development; that it should project a holistic vision for an area; that it should link and integrate the work of various departments within and between spheres of government; and that it should create settlements which contain the appropriate range of services and facilities, and are well linked to transport routes and employment opportunities.

A strong developmental approach, a sensitivity to poverty and unemployment, and to the reality of informality, were also important in the ideas and work of the alternative planning movement. Local economic development has become a significant component of developmental local government (see Chapter 8). Post-apartheid policy has embraced the notion of planning as developmental, and guides for integrated development plans require attention to gender, poverty, economy and the like. However, there is a real ambivalence towards the persistence of informal settlements and the reality of the informal sector, as Chapter 14 demonstrates. In both cases, sensitive policy tends to be localized and somewhat uneven, and there is a lack of sympathetic overarching policy at national level.

The alternative planning movement was also influential in reshaping the domain and nature of planning (see also Chapter 10). By the turn of the century, planning had shifted strongly away from its traditional base in physical planning and land-use management, towards development planning. A survey of planning skills in demand (Todes *et al.* 2003) found that fields such as strategic planning, integrated development planning, local economic development and the more developmental aspects of physical planning had grown, while traditional areas had declined, although they remained important mainstays of work for some planners.

While the alternative planning movement was important in reshaping the nature of state planning post-apartheid, the role of progressive planning in supporting communities resisting dominant state planning practices however declined. The weakening of both civic organizations and progressive urban NGOs has meant that this element of planning has become less prominent than it once was. Although some of the remaining progressive urban NGOs (and other new organizations) continue to provide this type of assistance, and a level of 'insurgent planning' by community organizations resisting dominant practices still occurs (Miraftab 2006), it is not on the scale of the period prior to 1994.

CONCLUSION

The alternative planning movement played critical roles in transforming the domain of planning, its dominant discourses and practices. Not all the influences of this movement were sustained in the post-apartheid era, but the new approaches developed in this period were significant in reshaping the image of planning as a hopeful profession, one concerned with social transformation. Although the 1980s was a period of repression, it was also one in which old discourses and approaches were challenged. The projects mounted by the urban NGOs and the forums of the early 1990s provided a space for exploring new forms of development. The alternative urban visions and development practices of the time were largely forged by a broad grouping of urban activists, academics and practitioners, with people from a variety of disciplinary backgrounds, including planners. Very little attention was paid specifically to planning per se. Nevertheless, these influences were taken through in the reconsideration of planning after 1994, as Chapter 3, and the following chapters demonstrate.

PLANNING POST-APARTHEID

INTRODUCTION

Chapters 1 and 2 provide the historical background to the development of planning post-1994. They show how deeply planning was implicated in various forms of domination during the eras of colonialism and apartheid, but also how new and alternative visions for cities and spatial planning emerged in the dying days of apartheid – visions which were to provide the basis for a new era of planning practice. This chapter provides a condensed account of the development of planning from 1994 onwards. It provides a frame for the more detailed, theme-specific chapters on post-apartheid planning that follow.

When the ANC came to power in 1994, planners were confronted with deep questions of legitimacy but, although planning had been profoundly implicated in the practice of apartheid, it had also been associated with a number of reformist and oppositional practices under late apartheid and, for the left-wing of the ANC-led alliance at least, the idea of planning had an association with socialist practice. Thus, despite the dishonourable history of much previous planning practice, South Africa's new Government of National Unity (GNU) had more enthusiasm for planning than the tired, outgoing regime that had long since abandoned its hopes for apartheid-based spatial order.

The question in 1994 was not whether the practice of planning would survive but what form it would take. Within the ANC-led alliance there was a diverse set of influences and ideologies at play, and questions around the appropriate role of the state, and of its various levels, in shaping the space-economy, were highly contested. The nature of the negotiated settlement also dissipated and constrained many of the more overtly socialist transformation agendas of the alliance. In the consensus-building processes of the early 1990s, many compromises were made, including in the area of planning and human settlement, where the new housing policy laid emphasis on developer-driven processes albeit within a framework of government-provided subsidies. Also, from the early 1990s a huge, interlinked global network of development agencies, major donors, governments in the global North, and international consultants, brought their influence to bear on the development of policy positions. Particularly influential in the development of urban policy, for example, were the World Bank's 'Urban Sector Missions'.

The chapter discusses post-apartheid planning in terms of four periods which coincide broadly with shifts in macroeconomic or development policy. The period 1994 until early 1996 was dominated by the Reconstruction and Development Programme (RDP). In July 1996, however, the government released its Growth, Employment and Redistribution (GEAR) Programme and government policy in the latter part of Mandela's presidency, 1996 to 1998, was strongly influenced by this new macro-framework. This was also the period in which the building blocks of South Africa's new planning system were put in place. The third period, between and including 1999 and 2003, represents the first part of Mbeki's presidency, a period in which considerable attention was paid to ensuring integrated and effective systems of governance. These themes continued in the period beginning 2004 but there was an important shift at this time from the 'neo-liberal' approach taken by GEAR towards the idea of the developmental state which is clearly represented in the new Accelerated and Shared Growth Initiative for South Africa (ASGI-SA).

RECONSTRUCTION AND DEVELOPMENT: 1994–96

The ANC's election manifesto, the RDP, was the key indicator of consensus positions within the new ruling alliance at the time it assumed power in 1994. The RDP was not overtly socialist but was rather a neo-Keynesian programme for state-led investment in infrastructure and basic services to address the backlogs and inequities of the past. It was, nevertheless, arguably, a radical document that defined a progressive agenda for the new government. It was eagerly accepted by many planners as it seemed to offer planning a key role in the reconstruction of South African society – the final chapter of the manifesto, for example, laid strong emphasis on the role of development planning in realizing the reconstructive vision.

After the elections the manifesto became known as the RDP Base Document, and it was this document that formed the basis of the RDP White Paper, which was released in November 1994 as the official policy of the GNU. There were, however, important differences between the Base Document and the White Paper which were indicative of a trend in ideology and policy that was to become far more obvious in subsequent years. In relation to planning, for example, there was a crucial shift from the language of 'national development planning' to that of 'strategic and business planning'. The radical feel of the manifesto was missing in the White Paper which was already showing the impact of the new public management, and of the sobering effects of a liberation movement now in power and confronting the challenges of governing a country in the context of an unstable global economy. For Adelzadeh and Padayachee (1994: 2) the White Paper represented 'a very significant compromise to the neo-liberal, "trickle down" economic preferences of the old regime'.

An RDP Office was established in 1994 in the Office of the President under the former General Secretary of COSATU Jay Naidoo. The office was tasked with coordinating and overseeing the implementation of the RDP, and was regarded by some at the time as the precursor to the creation of a powerful national development planning agency (similar to models provided by Malaysia or Singapore). This was, however, clearly not the intention of the White Paper, while the limited capacity and authority given to this office meant that it was unlikely to fulfil a meaningful role in coordinating and planning across and between tiers of government. In April 1996, at a time of capital flight when government was anxious to reassure international markets that its economic policies were orthodox, President Mandela closed off the RDP Office, ending this limited and largely unsuccessful experiment with a (very limited) form of nationally directed development planning. With the closure, the national coordinating role, and the management of RDP Funds, shifted into the hands of National Treasury, which pursued a fiscally driven and generally cautious approach to development policy.

While the RDP did not lead to the creation of a national development planning system, as many planners may have wished, it did provide a new impetus to planning and development. Most important were the creation of the RDP Fund and the launch of the Special Presidential Lead Projects. The fund – initially administered by the RDP Office but, after 1996, by the Treasury – provided the resources for a variety of special programmes including Land Reform and Restitution, Urban Renewal, Public Works, Primary School Nutrition and Rural Water Supply. Between 1994 and 1998, R18 billion was allocated to RDP projects (although, since then, funding for projects has been channelled through normal budgetary mechanisms). The availability of resources did play an important role in the broadening out of the ambit of planning, and, in the mid- to late 1990s, planners were drawn into areas including land reform and restitution, urban renewal, public works and rural development.

There were two areas that were particularly important for planning. The first was urban renewal. The RDP White Paper identified six urban renewal projects that were to kick-start development in major urban areas, focusing on violence-torn communities and communities in crisis. These included Kathorus (East Rand), Duncan Village (East London), Ibhayi (Port Elizabeth), Botshabelo (Bloemfontein) and serviced land on the Cape Flats, and were among the presidential lead projects and special integrated presidential projects announced in Mandela's first State of the Nation Address. In 1995, Cato Manor in Durban – the site of the largest inner-city urban renewal project in post-apartheid South Africa – was added to the list.

These projects were implemented in an extraordinarily difficult environment. Although funding was available through the RDP, the institutional mechanisms for planning and delivery were only in embryonic form, and projects were often highly contested at local level. There was wide variance in the levels of success. Kathorus

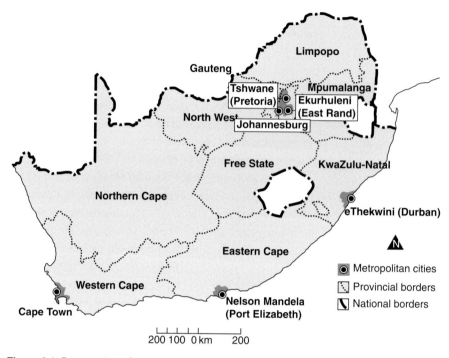

Figure 3.1 Post-apartheid South Africa

on the East Rand achieved high levels of success in terms of delivery targets at least (Silverman and Zach 2003), and the Cato Manor development programme, which also received substantial funding from the European Union, is now widely regarded as an international best practice (Robinson *et al.* 2004), but many other projects were disappointingly slow. Nevertheless, these early urban renewal programmes were critical in pioneering integrated area-based approaches to planning and development, and in generating the knowledge and experience for a new round of urban renewal after 2000 (Napier and Rust 2002).

The second area was housing policy. Post-apartheid policy was the product of consensus-building in the National Housing Forum in the early 1990s, which culminated in the October 1994 Botshabelo National Housing Summit, and the 1995 White Paper on Housing. Like many other policies, housing policy represented a compromise position – central to the new policy was the idea of a one-off capital subsidy paid by the state to developers for servicing land and constructing houses for low-income households. The outcome of this policy is the subject of considerable debate. Although a considerable number of housing units – more than a million-and-a-half – have been produced, there has been criticism of the quality of the housing produced, the sterile and peripheral nature of many of the new estates,

Figure 3.2 Cato Manor, Durban: newly built Bellair Road corridor

the focus on greenfield development at the expense of informal settlement upgrading, the orientation towards individual households rather than community-building
housing processes, and the lack of attention given to producing integrated, sustainable settlements (see, for example, Tomlinson 1999; Jones and Datta 2000;
Huchzermeyer 2001; Tomlinson *et al.* 2002; Charlton *et al.* 2003; Khan and Thring
2003). Significant contradictions emerged between the stated principles of post-
apartheid planning and development – including urban compaction and integration
– and the outcome of the mainly developer-driven approach (Todes 2000). Planners
were drawn into the housing delivery process, although the link between planning
and housing was inadequate in many respects – for example, projects were generally implemented in the absence of robust planning frameworks which may have
contributed to problems such as the poor location of many of the new estates.

Among the most severe constraints in addressing housing backlogs were
access to land and secure tenure. This prompted the drafting of the first post-
apartheid planning legislation, the Development Facilitation Act, No. 67 of 1995
(DFA). The Act did not provide a comprehensive framework for planning as it was
intended mainly to 'introduce extraordinary measures to facilitate and speed up the
implementation of reconstruction and development programmes and projects in
relation to land' (RSA 1995). These measures included special powers for tribunals

to make decisions on land development, simplified land development procedures, and provisions to upgrade informal tenure to full ownership rights. The Act did, however, also introduce a set of principles to guide planning practice in South Africa, and was thus instrumental in moving planning towards a more normative approach. It also made provision for a Development and Planning Commission to advise government on setting up a new planning system, and for the preparation of Land Development Objectives (LDOs), which were intended as development performance measures to guide land development.

The DFA is significant as the first piece of post-apartheid planning legislation, and does deserve some attention. The Act represents an uneasy juxtaposition of different influences on planning thought in the early to mid-1990s. The planning principles within the Act indicate the influence of the compact city approach, which was most strongly propounded at the time by the University of Cape Town (UCT) planning school, and it is no surprise that a number of UCT graduates played a key role in conceptualizing and drafting sections of the Act. However, the DFA also draws on the thinking and influence of key individuals from the Urban Foundation – and its successor, the Centre for Development and Enterprise (CDE) – which had played a key role in the National Housing Forum. These individuals emphasized aspects such as urban competitiveness and efficiency, rather than spatial form, and the role of the LDOs as performance management measures can be partially attributed to them.

There were other influences and discourses which were influencing planning thought at the time, an example being the concern with sustainable development, and with the Local Agenda 21 Programme introduced at the United Nations Conference on Environment and Development held in 1992 in Rio de Janeiro, although, in the context of post-apartheid reconstruction, sustainability concerns were often subservient to the demand for restitution and rapid delivery.

GEAR, LOCAL GOVERNMENT TRANSFORMATION, AND A NEW PLANNING SYSTEM: 1996–8

By 1996, the South African government's policies represented an uneasy and shifting mixture of objectives – the state clearly retained a concern with poverty alleviation, redistribution and participatory governance but was also concerned with pacifying global markets and ensuring competitiveness in an unstable global economy. In July 1996, three months after closing the RDP Office, government released its controversial GEAR programme. As Netshitenzhe explained, 'GEAR was a structural adjustment policy, self-imposed, to stabilize the macroeconomic situation [to deal with] the realities of an unmanageable budget deficit, high interest rates and weak local and foreign investor confidence' (cited in Gumede 2005: 88). Although

GEAR was presented as being 'in keeping with the goals set out in the Reconstruction and Development Programme' (Paragraph 1.1, RSA 1996a) it was perceived on the Left to be a replacement for the RDP, and an expression of neo-liberal economic and development policies (Adelzadeh 1996; Marais 1998; Bond 2000). The insistence of Trevor Manuel, the Minister of Finance, that GEAR was 'non-negotiable' may have pleased global investors but it created enormous resentment within the ANC, and between the ANC and its more left-leaning partners, COSATU and the South African Communist Party (SACP), and it remains one of the key sources of the current tensions within the ruling alliance.

The focus of GEAR was on macroeconomic stability and creating a 'competitive fast-growing economy' (RSA 2006), and it did lead to a refocusing of government attention away from some of the more progressive objectives of the RDP, but the relationship between GEAR and the RDP is more complex than some of the left-leaning critics of government suggest (Pieterse 2001). Also, many elements of GEAR were already present in the RDP White Paper.

GEAR's concern with creating a globally competitive, outward-oriented economy underpinned two significant spatial initiatives driven by the national Department of Trade and Industry (DTI). The first are the industrial development zones (IDZs), the most important of which is the new deepwater port and industrial estate at Coega outside Port Elizabeth. The second are the spatial development initiatives (SDIs), which were an attempt to identify, package and fast-track local and international investment within globally competitive sectors in targeted areas. The first SDI was the politically strategic Maputo Corridor that linked the greater Johannesburg region (now Gauteng) with the port in Mozambique, but, by 1999, there were 11 designated SDIs, many of which crossed national boundaries. The SDI programme eventually ran out of steam, although it still remains a vehicle for regional integration in Southern Africa (for a discussion see Chapter 5). Many of the SDIs took the form of interregional (and also international) corridor developments, aligned along major transportation routes. The link to transportation also brought the national Department of Transport into the broad area of planning and development. Apart from the SDI corridors the Department of Transport promoted integrated metropolitan-scale corridors to support both public transportation and urban spatial restructuring, such as the Baralink corridor in Johannesburg that linked the city with Soweto, and the Wetton–Landsdown Road corridor in Cape Town that joined the wealthy western suburbs of the city with the marginalized communities living in Khayelitsha.

The SDIs, IDZs and corridor programmes were driven mainly by national departments. However, by 1996, the attention of government was shifting very quickly to the role of local government. The new national constitution established local authority as one of the three 'distinctive, interrelated and interdependent spheres of government' and gave this sphere a broad developmental mandate (RSA 1996b). In the 1990s decentralization was a powerful, even hegemonic, global discourse and so it was no surprise that, despite the centralist tendencies of some segments of the ANC-alliance, local government would be prioritized within the national Constitution and development policy (Galvin and Habib 2003).

As a growing number of responsibilities were placed in the hands of local government so there was a need for mechanisms to assist local government in performing its functions. The integrated development plan (IDP) was introduced through a 1996 amendment to the Local Government Transition Act (1993) shortly after the elections for South Africa's transitional local councils, at a time when national government was deeply concerned that the newly established local authorities would be financially responsible, and would act to fulfil their constitutional mandate as agents of developmental local governance. Although IDPs were instruments to be used by local authorities, they were devised by national government as a way of directing local government towards certain nationally defined objectives. IDPs were to be mechanisms that would set out the vision and strategies of an elected local council and link the many sectoral plans and programmes that local councils were required to produce. The important story of the IDPs is told in some detail in Chapter 4 and so is not elaborated on here.

Together with the new focus on local government came the influence of the new public management (NPM). As early as 1994, the RDP White Paper directed attention to business planning, performance indicators and goal-directed budgeting. In 1995, the NPM was clearly apparent in the White Paper on the Transformation of the Public Service. It was also present in the Urban Infrastructure Investment Framework (UIIF), the Urban Development Strategy (UDS) and in the way the IDP was conceptualized (Tomlinson 2002; Pieterse 2003a).

The model of planning that emerged in South Africa during the late 1990s within the context of decentralization, local government transformation, and the influence of the NPM, may be termed 'institutionalist'. Its focus was primarily on supporting the decision-making and implementation processes of local government, and in linking and integrating the local activities of different agents of government. By 1998, this approach had eclipsed the previously mainly physical orientation of planning (Watson 2002a).

Institutional rivalries complicated the emergence of the new planning system. The Department of Constitutional Development and then its successor, the Department of Provincial and Local Government (DPLG), were responsible for managing and directing the new system of integrated development planning while the Department of Land Affairs (DLA) had responsibility for physical planning and land-use management. Initially, the DLA had a key role in planning as it administered the Development Facilitation Act, including the preparation of LDOs. However, with the introduction of IDPs in 1996, the initiative shifted to the DPLG. For four years, between 1996 and 2000, a parallel planning system operated with local authorities having to prepare both IDPs and LDOs although, after some time, it was agreed that an LDO would be a component of an IDP and, eventually, LDOs were dropped entirely. While this divide has been removed an overlap remains in the processing of development application which is, currently, a source of tension between municipal and provincial authorities. The DFA provided for a Development Tribunal to consider development applications whereas other legislation allows for municipalities to deal with these matters. In Gauteng, for example, the Development Tribunal has made decisions that are contrary to the City of Johannesburg's spatial development framework, and has provoked the metropolitan authority into legal action against the provincial government.

The Minister of Land Affairs was responsible for setting up a development and planning commission to advise on the new system of planning in South Africa. In 1999, this commission produced a Green Paper on Development and Planning which was followed by the White Paper on Spatial Planning and Land Use Management of 2001. These policy documents captured many of the evolving approaches to planning – the focus on spatial integration, the roles of the different spheres, a normative rather than regulative orientation – but it was released at a time when the focus was very strongly on the IDP process in the context of forthcoming local government elections. The impact of the commission was thus muted. The White Paper was to provide the basis for a land-use management Act, but there have been long delays in the promulgation of the Act (partly due to institutional conflict) and, at the time of writing (in 2006), it was not yet on the books. Land-use management, therefore, remains one of the least transformed and least developed areas of post-apartheid planning (see Chapters 6 and 9 for further discussion).

The other clear institutional divide was between the emerging system of development planning on the one hand and environmental management on the other. These integrally related areas were developed along quite different tracks and under the championship of different departments. The White Paper on Environmental Management (1997) preceded the White Paper on Local Government (1998). In 1998, the National Environmental Management Act (NEMA) was promulgated a year or two before the key pieces of legislation that framed post-2000 local government, and planning and environmental management systems have continued to evolve out of sync (see Chapter 9).

The other institutional complexity involved the overlapping roles of national and provincial government. The existence of nine provincial governments in post-apartheid South Africa was the product of a political compromise between the mainly centralist ANC and parties with a regional base that pushed for a federal system. Both national and provincial governments were given the powers to produce planning-related legislation, and KwaZulu-Natal and the Western Cape – the two provinces that fell outside the control of the ANC – took up the opportunity. Overlapping and sometimes divergent legislation, together with the political rivalry that underpinned this legislation, created complexity in the planning terrain but eventually compromise positions were found (Oranje 2002). Although the drive towards preparing planning legislation was led by provinces with political reason to do so, after 1994, all provinces prepared Provincial Growth and Development Strategies (PGDSs), to provide strategic vision and guidance for provincial activity. The PGDSs were, however, of variable quality, and the non-statutory status of a PGDS meant that players, even within provincial governments, often had little commitment to their implementation. It is only recently that the DPLG has paid attention to the PGDSs, and has provided guidelines for improving quality (see Chapter 5).

In 1999, when Mandela stepped down as president, South Africa had in place the outlines of a new planning system. To begin there were the provisions of the DFA, a piece of legislation that had shifted planning towards a more developmental and normative approach. Then there was the IDP, an instrument of governance that was closely tied with the transformation of local government. Instruments of provincial planning were, however, still poorly developed, while the closure of the RDP Office still left a void within national government. The weaknesses in the emerging system included the meagre capacity of many local (and provincial) authorities, the poor linkages between and within the spheres, and the fragmentation of processes such as environmental management and development planning.

1999–2003: INTEGRATED GOVERNANCE AND LOCAL PARTNERSHIPS

Mbeki brought a different style to leadership and governance. After the lively, sometimes disorganized, but engaging leadership of Mandela, Mbeki came across to many as an aloof managerialist. His ideology was a pragmatic, pro-business Africanism, which brought to the centre a concern for black economic empowerment (BEE), but also for effective, integrated governance and delivery.

Mbeki's style, and also the content of many of his policies, had much in common with those of 'third way' leaders like Tony Blair and Bill Clinton. Like Blair, Mbeki made 'integrated governance' a hallmark of his term in office, and developed increasingly elaborate mechanisms to ensure intergovernmental planning and coordination. Also, like Blair's, Mbeki's administration revealed the paradox of growing central coordination at the same time as the increased devolution or decentralization of responsibilities to the local level. This is an approach that has been referred to as 'top-down direction for bottom-up implementation' (Long and Franklin 2004: 309).

This paradox is apparent in almost all areas of planning and development. Chapter 4, for example, shows how the practice of local integrated development planning was strengthened and extended in this period, but how this development happened in terms of national legislation and nationally derived guidelines, and was increasingly tied into an evolving system of intergovernmental planning. The chapter also refers to other planning instruments at national level, such as the National Spatial Development Perspective (NSDP) and the Medium Term Strategic Framework (MTSF), which are increasingly important in providing the framework for local level planning.

Then there has been the launch of a number of nationally coordinated programmes that are implemented at a local scale. In 2001, for example, Mbeki launched the Urban Renewal Programme (URP) and Integrated Sustainable Rural Development Strategy (ISRDS). The ISRDS involved the designation of 13 nodes in marginalized parts of the country for special coordinated intervention in terms of rural development, and was in response to a belief that the limited impact of rural development programmes in the period 1994–2000 had to do with the fragmented, uncoordinated nature of anti-poverty and rural development programmes. The URP – which had as its antecedent Mandela's Special Integrated Presidential Projects (SIPPs) for urban renewal – had a similar rationale. It involved the selection of eight nodal points targeted for large-scale upgrading and development projects, which would serve as pilots for the implementation of a national urban renewal strategy. Unfortunately, however, both the URP and ISRDS are under severe stress, with their outcomes more disappointing than was initially hoped for.

The most well-known renewal initiative in South Africa is the multibillion rand Alexandra Renewal Programme which reports to an intergovernmental committee, and is jointly funded by the different spheres of government. The project – aimed at the radical transformation of the physical, social and economic environment of the township – illustrates the enormous political, institutional and technical challenges of achieving both integration and rapid implementation in the current context. The other major urban renewal project under way in South Africa is the Inanda–Ntuzuma–Kwamashu (INK) programme which covers an area that includes half a million of Durban's poorest citizens, and which draws closely on the experience generated through the Cato Manor initiative.

Not all area-based renewal programmes have been coordinated and directed from national government. One of the most significant features of city development in the early 2000s – in South Africa and internationally – has been the success of locally driven partnership-based approaches to urban regeneration. It is a process that was supported by the reinvention of local government in South Africa, and especially by the creation of powerful single-tier metropolitan authorities.

Box 3.1 The Alexandra Renewal Project

The Alexandra Renewal Project (ARP), launched in 2001, is one of the most ambitious of South Africa's post-apartheid urban interventions, and has high political profile and support. It is a joint urban regeneration project involving all three spheres of government, the private sector, NGOs and community organizations, and is aimed at fundamentally changing the social, economic and physical environment of Alexandra, one of South Africa's oldest and most famous townships. Situated close to the super-affluent suburbs and business centre of Sandton, Alexandra township – with its 350,000 mainly very poor people, squeezed into 800 hectares – has an extraordinary location.

The project has been the source of considerable controversy. In its early phases, for example, a de-densification programme resulted in the removal of over 7000 households from the banks of the Jukskei River in Alexandra to poorly located semi-formal settlements such as Diepsloot to the north of Johannesburg. This action was hugely disruptive of household livelihoods, and was an echo of apartheid-style forced removals. Community members have also complained of the slow pace of delivery, while project managers have struggled with the challenge of coordinating between and across spheres of government and other agencies. The ARP has, however, been a learning process and under energetic new leadership, and with the benefit of a newly established joint project office, the products of more than five years of planning and implementation are now increasingly visible. Major initiatives have included: the production of housing for owner-occupation and rental; engineering services including bulk water, roads and street lighting; local economic development initiatives; and social infrastructure, including world-class sport facilities, tourism and heritage programmes, schools and health facilities. The ARP in both its failures and successes provides a hugely important learning resource for urban regeneration into the future.

Current successes within the ARP are providing valuable lessons on such matters as how to: incorporate rental housing within housing programmes; reduce plot size and increase densities through innovative design; integrate township and hostel communities; redesign hostels to improve security and communal life; and, relocate residents of shack settlements into formal housing using temporary accommodation in a transit village.

For further information see www.alexandra.co.za

In Johannesburg, processes of spatial decentralization had undermined the economy of the inner city since the 1960s but, in the 1990s, the decay of the inner city accelerated in a context of rapidly rising crime levels and poor urban management. Johannesburg responded proactively (although sometimes controversially) with key players in the urban regeneration process including special agencies and partnership-based arrangements such as the Central Johannesburg Partnership (CJP), which pioneered the City Improvement District (CID) approach in South Africa (which partially privatizes the management of space); the Johannesburg Development Agency (JDA); Blue IQ, which is the funding arm of provincial government; and the Johannesburg Housing Company, which has delivered social housing in and near the inner city. There are currently strong indications of regeneration in inner-city Johannesburg, including rising property and rental prices and an upsurge in investment (especially in the housing sector). Most other major cities in South Africa also now have strategies and partnership-based institutions focused on inner-city regeneration. These include Inner City eThekwini Regeneration and Urban Management Programme (iTRUMP) for Durban, the Cape Town Partnership, and the Tshwane (previously Pretoria) Inner-City Urban Regeneration Programme. However, although local initiative and partnership have been central to the recent wave of inner-city regeneration initiatives, national government has provided an important stimulus through the designation of Urban Development Zones (UDZs), where investment is promoted in decaying areas through substantial tax deduction for renovation and new development, and through annual depreciation allowances. The partnership model for development also underlies the Treasury's new Neighbourhood Development Programme which provides funding for initiatives in the former black townships. This programme is likely to reinforce a recent pattern of increased public and private investment in townships. It is also likely to increase further the already expanded role of the Treasury in planning and development.

Figure 3.3 Decayed inner-city areas: Johannesburg

2004– : THE DEVELOPMENTAL STATE

The period since the 2004 national elections has been marked by a deep and growing divide between the pragmatic managerialists around Mbeki and the (ostensibly
left-leaning) populists who have mobilized around erstwhile Deputy President, Jacob
Zuma. The outcome of this struggle has enormous implications for a planning system that was largely shaped within a managerialist mode.

The institutional issues in this period are dealt with in Chapters 4 and 5.
These include the growing focus on intergovernmental coordination, illustrated, for
example, in the Intergovernmental Relations Framework Act of 2005; new debates
around the role and future of district and provincial authorities, with growing speculation that provincial government may be rationalized or even abolished; a crisis in
the performance of local government; and, the rise of new forms of networking and
institutional relationship, such as the Gauteng global city-region. These all have
significant implications for planning.

The growing focus on intergovernmental coordination may result in the IDP
being reconstituted as an instrument of cross-sphere engagement and agreement,
rather than as simply a mechanism of municipal planning. The future of provincial
authorities remains an area of uncertainty but the weakness of many municipalities
is, perhaps, the greatest threat to planning. Beginning in 2004 and continuing until
the 2006 local elections, the ANC was confronted with (sometimes violent) grassroots protests against the failure of local government to deliver services, and problems
of corruption and patronage. Places like Intabazwe outside Harrismith in the Free
State, and Delmas in Mpumalanga, where failure to purify water led to a typhoid epidemic, have become icons of a widespread dissatisfaction and disappointment. As
discussed in Chapter 4, the relationship between planning and service delivery is difficult to track, but it is clear that many municipalities do not even have the capacity to
prepare a basic IDP. The DPLG (2005a) reports, for example, that only 37 per cent of
municipalities have the independent capacity to prepare effective IDPs, while 35 per
cent have a basic institutional capacity but require continued support to deliver the
plans, and 28 per cent lack the most rudimentary capacity and, even with support, will
struggle to prepare a basic plan.

While capacity constraints in at least two-thirds of South Africa's municipalities have emerged as a key national concern, some of the larger, better-resourced
municipalities have responded creatively to the challenges of urban management.
For example, a number of metropolitan authorities, starting with Johannesburg, have
prepared City Development Strategies, which provide a long-term strategic perspective on development. The South African Cities Network (SACN), which links
together the largest nine urban local authorities in the country, has also emerged as
an important source of new ideas and creative networking, while the idea of

Gauteng as a 'polycentric global city-region' has offered new opportunities for inter-action and institutional collaboration (see Chapters 4 and 5).

Within national government, there has been some reassessment of policies. An example is South Africa's new housing policy, known as Breaking New Ground, which draws in UN-Habitat's concerns with 'sustainable human settlement', and promises a more holistic and integrative approach to housing and settlement than in the past. The trailblazer for the new policy is Cape Town's R3 billion N2 Gateway Project which is to provide housing for upwards of 20,000 people living in informal settlements and back-yard shacks along the major transportation corridor between the city and the international airport. The project represents both the promises and weakness of the new approach; at the time of writing it was mired in controversy and political conflict, with serious questions raised over its affordability for the poor (see Chapter 14).

The most significant discursive shift in the state's approach since 2004 has been the move from the 'neo-liberal' orthodoxies of GEAR to the notion of a 'devel-opmental state' which gives far more attention to building institutional capacity within government. It is a shift that has been associated with the strengthening of the policy and coordination functions of national government (although it has been contested within the ANC-led alliance as the developmental states of East Asia, which have informed the South African model, have been technocratic and weak on democracy).

The developmental state ideology is strongly represented in ASGI-SA which was announced in February 2006 as a new macro-framework for state policy. ASGI-SA's target is an annual GDP growth rate of at least 6 per cent, and the focus of the strategy is on eliminating the binding constraints on economic development through massive infrastructural development, the implementation of special programmes to support priority sectors, targeted education and skills development, eliminating the so-called second economy, and addressing institutional weaknesses (see Chapter 14 for a discussion on the second economy and Chapter 8 for the relationship between planning and economic development). ASGI-SA has significant points of connection with planning. To begin with, there are the proposals for infrastructural development which will require infrastructure planning, strong planning frameworks and project management skills. Among the major challenges is the 2010 FIFA World Cup which has enormous implications, not only for construction of stadiums, but also for transportation planning and urban regeneration. Then there is the R20 bil-lion Gauteng Rapid Transit Rail System (the so-called Gautrain) with its impacts not only on transportation and mobility, but also on property markets and urban form.

Planning and land-use management were identified within ASGI-SA as key areas requiring institutional reform. The concern was that 'many investment pro-jects are unnecessarily held up by the weakness of local or provincial planning and zoning systems or the cumbersome Environmental Impact Assessment sys-tem' (RSA 2006, Section 8). Planning will thus be under considerable pressure to respond by streamlining and strengthening systems of development regulation and approval, and the attention will shift again to the neglected area of land-use management. However, planning is also likely to benefit from the increased attention. It has, for example, been recognized by the JIPSA – a high-level committee chaired by the Deputy President – as a vital skill for the implementation of ASGI-SA (see Chapter 11).

CONCLUSION

Despite its legitimacy problems – its relationship with apartheid rule – planning as an activity of government survived the transition to democracy and was adopted as a key instrument for the implementation of the Reconstruction and Development Programmes (and later policies and initiatives). The post-apartheid planning system has evolved incrementally in line with shifting macropolicies and institutional developments, with key moments including the Development Facilitation Act in 1995, the introduction of IDPs in 1996, the White Paper on Local Government in 1998, the Municipal Systems Act of 2000 and, possibly, the launch of ASGI-SA in 2006.

The future direction of planning remains uncertain. Key trends include the growing focus on intergovernmental planning and the link between planning and major infrastructural development, but key questions remain. What, for example, will the capacity problems in local government mean for the future of planning? Will planning be able to deliver on the demands of ASGI-SA and the requirements of major initiatives such as the Gautrain development and the 2010 World Cup? Will planning take a more technocratic or more participatory direction, or will it simply, as current tendencies suggest, continue to evolve as a multiplicity of practices that will never be perfectly aligned? To a very large extent, as will be argued in Chapter 15, the future legitimacy of planning in post-apartheid South Africa will depend on the way these questions will be answered.

PART 2

PLANNING AND GOVERNANCE

INTRODUCTION: INTERNATIONAL DEBATES

In contemporary debate and practice, the idea of planning is being tied ever more closely with the theme of governance, and with variations on themes such as 'territorial governance', 'collaborative governance', 'spatial governance' and 'multilevel governance'. In South Africa, the discourse around governance and planning is informed by both the debate in the global North, and especially in Europe, where new forms of governance have been linked to the 'reconfiguration and re-scaling of forms of territorial organization' (Brenner 1999: 432), and shifting perspectives on governance in the South which are shaped largely by powerful multilateral institutions such as the World Bank.

Within the global North the notion of governance has captured a growing sense of the complexity of organizational forms. In Europe, but also elsewhere, there has been both an upscaling of territorial organization towards a supranational level, and a downscaling towards subnational levels such as city-regions, as well as a diffusion of power outwards from the state to a variety of non-state and quasi-state actors (Brenner 1999). It is within this context that a notion of governance emerged which refers to the networks of organization that cut across scales, and that transcend traditional administrative jurisdictions of the state by linking state and civil society together in 'complex, multi-actor configurations' (Bache and Flinders 2004).

In Europe there is now wide reference to ideas of 'multilevel', 'multiscalar' and 'meta' governance (e.g. Böhme *et al.* 2004; Shaw and Sykes 2004; Jessop 2005) while in the United States Michael Neuman and others are taking the discourse on to 'multiple large-scale institutional networks' (e.g. Neuman forthcoming). The increasing diffusion and complexity of governance has prompted a growing interest in ideas and mechanisms of coordination and integration. In the UK, New Labour has made 'joined-up government' one of its key concerns (Perri 6 2004) while the French notion of 'territorial cohesion' is now central to European Union social, spatial and economic policy (Faludi 2004).

The idea of governance – which was increasingly differentiated from the idea of *government* and which came to mean for some 'organization *beyond-the-state*' – arguably went too far in downplaying the role of the state which remains significant and pervasive (Jordan *et al.* 2005). Fortunately, as T. Weiss (2000: 803) shows, recent contributions to the debate have 'moved away from a visceral dismantling of the state' and are 'less about jettisoning state institutions than improving and reforming the functioning of democratic institutions'.

Institutionalists such as Patsy Healey have worked energetically to draw the links between planning and the new discourse on governance. The new institutionalism gives strong emphasis to the role that the formal and informal institutions of society have in shaping human behaviour, and to the norms, routines, social conventions and patterns of trust and reciprocity that underlie the operation of these institutions. Healey directs attention to the importance of finding ways to bring diverse actors together in networks of collaboration and mutual learning, and has expended considerable energy in showing how collaborative forms of planning may assist in doing this. In recent work she and others have made the link between new forms of governance and the rise of new ways of thinking about space and place, and producing spatial plans (Healey 2004). Planning theorists concerned primarily with *Realrationalität*, rather than with idealized normative conceptions, have also directed attention to the new discourse on governance. They have drawn on Foucault's notion of *governmentality* to explore the ways in which the new ideas around governance and territoriality are being translated into the programming of space (e.g. Böhme *et al.* 2004).

In the global South, the 1990s saw a significant discursive shift towards a normative conception of governance that was driven largely by multilateral institutions such as the World Bank and UN agencies. As early as 1976, the date of the Vancouver UN-Habitat conference, UN agencies were propagating an 'urban management perspective' that was to become influential in the early policy debates of post-apartheid South Africa (Mabin 2002: 40–54). However, during the 1980s, a mainly economic perspective dominated, with World Bank–IMF-sponsored structural adjustment programmes providing the framework for development across the global South. To the extent that there was a focus on institutions, the principle ideas were privatization, deregulation and decentralization. By the end of the 1980s, however, key World Bank officials had accepted that *good governance* was the key issue (Leftwich 1993) and, by 1997, the shift was firmly entrenched when the Bank's World Development Report emphasized the importance of strong and effective institutions, rather than on rolling back the state as in the past.

From the late 1990s 'good governance' became the mantra for development in the South and planning was supported to the extent that it promoted this ideal. There are, however, significant nuances in the meaning of good governance. The World Bank, for example, has been associated with a mainly administrative and managerialist interpretation of good governance while agencies such as the UNDP have emphasized democratic practice and human and civil rights. In the global South, as elsewhere, there is a tension between the participative and technocratic dimensions of new approaches to governance, and between performance-based and process-oriented approaches. Desai and Imrie recognized the extent to which the so-called new public management had permeated the global South, albeit in 'complex, uneven and contradictory ways', and warned against the 'narrowing of the framework for the evaluation of public services to their performance and efficiency as a business' (Desai and Imrie 1998: 635, 640).

While the newspeak around governance is still highly contested, there has, undeniably, been a profound shift in perspective over the past decade or so. Already, by 1998, the controversial ex-chief economist of the World Bank and author of *Globalization and its Discontents*, Joseph Stiglitz, identified the emergence of a 'post-Washington consensus', which challenges an earlier 'market fundamentalism', and which recognizes the role and importance of strong institutions in areas such as regulating the financial sector, supporting productive activities, providing public goods, and building infrastructure (Perales 2004). Part of the post-Washington consensus is a more pragmatic approach to ideals such as decentralization which were part of 1980s dogma. Kulipossa (2004: 768) reflects this pragmatism when he acknowledges that 'decentralization is a complex and multi-faceted phenomenon that may have both positive and negative effects'. There is an emerging consensus around the need to retain and build capacity in all spheres of government, and in civil society.

The recent shifts in the official thinking of major multilateral institutions connect at least partially with another key strand of development discourse, the so-called *developmental state approach* which is currently highly influential within South African government circles. The notion of the developmental state emerged from an analysis of the East Asian Tigers, and especially of Japan, which argued that their economic success had much to do with the role of the state in selecting and supporting strategic industrial sectors, targeting investments in areas such as education and infrastructure, and supporting this development through a more equitable distribution of the fruits of growth (L. Weiss 2000). The developmental state was popularized by Robert Wade's (1990) *Governing the Market* and was strongly supported in 1993 by Adrian Leftwich, who defined the developmental state as 'a state whose political and bureaucratic elite has the genuine developmental determination and autonomous capacity to define, pursue and implement developmental goals'. As Leftwich pointed out, 'such measures require not simply less government but both better government and stronger government' (Leftwich 1993: 620).

This state-oriented approach does, however, have to be balanced with a continued recognition of the role of non-state actors within the management of the public realm. Here the institutionalist perspective from the global North may be useful but also important is an emerging perspective from Africa that highlights the significant role of informal associational or self-initiated networks in the management of the public realm (e.g. Beall 2001; Simone 2001a). Simone (2001a: 104) acknowledges that these networks are highly mobile and often ephemeral, and 'do not necessarily replace the need for developments in formal institutional building and municipal governance', but his argument for the significance of relational webs in the urban arena is hugely important in African cities where familial and community networks are critical for both personal livelihood and social coherence.

The current debate around governance is complex and contested. However, it is possible to see the outlines of a new synthesis emerging – a synthesis that brings together a recognition of the associational networks of civil society with an acknowledgement of the continued role of the state, and the need to further strengthen the state at all levels. The outcome of the debate is critical for planning, a practice concerned primarily with the organization of activity in the public arena. How this organization happens and who may legitimately be involved in it will largely be determined by the outcome of the discursive practices that have been outlined above.

CHAPTER 4

PLANNING AND LOCAL GOVERNANCE

INTRODUCTION

The arrival of the integrated development plan (IDP) in 1996 cemented the relationship between planning and local governance. Prior to this, planning was linked primarily to one sector of local government activity, namely spatial development (and especially land-use management) but, with the IDP, planning became an integrative device connecting the many threads of local governance. The importance of this connection requires the story of planning in post-apartheid South Africa to be told together with the history of local governance. There is, fortunately, a growing corpus of work on South Africa's evolving system of local governance that recites the tale of an ambitious but flawed attempt to overcome the cruel legacies of the highly inequitable and fragmented system of local government under apartheid, and to create a system of *developmental local government* (see, for example, the contributions in edited volumes by Parnell *et al.* 2002; Mhone and Edigheji 2003).

This chapter does not provide a comprehensive account of this literature but does locate the arrival of South Africa's new system of municipal-scale planning within the evolution of post-apartheid local government more broadly, and local governance. The focus is largely on the IDP – as this is the centre-piece of the local planning system – but the chapter also deals with other instruments of planning such as the City Development Strategy (CDS) and the Land Use Management Plan.

TOWARDS DEMOCRATIC NON-RACIAL LOCAL GOVERNMENT

The framework for a new system of democratic non-racial local government was negotiated in the early 1990s within the all-party Local Government Negotiating Forum (LGNF) and laid out in the Local Government Transition Act, 1993. The LGNF accepted the immense complexity of undoing the effects of apartheid at the local level and proposed a phased process leading towards the full implementation of a new system. A pre-interim phase led up to South Africa's first democratic local elections in November 1995 (later for KwaZulu-Natal and the Western Cape) while the interim phase lasted from 1995/1996 until the local elections of December 2000 finally ushered in the new system. Key milestones along the way included: the 1996 National Constitution which established the autonomy of the local sphere of

government and laid out the mandate of developmental local government; the 1998
White Paper on Local Government which set out the principles and structures of the
post-2000 system; and key pieces of legislation such as the Municipal
Demarcations Act, the Municipal Structures Act, and the Municipal Systems Act.
There was a recognition that, even after 2000, a process of development would
continue. It was envisaged that the new system would consolidate in the period
2000 to 2005, with the focus in the period from 2005 to 2010 shifting to the interactions between local government and the other spheres.

A NEW FORM OF LOCAL PLANNING

South Africa's new system of local planning thus emerged at a time when local government was in a process of comprehensive restructuring. Before the new National
Constitution was promulgated in 1996 there was a level of uncertainty as to the status and role of local government within the post-apartheid era. Although the Interim
National Constitution of 1993 had recognized local government as an autonomous
sphere of authority with its own constitutionally guaranteed functions, there was
continued ambivalence towards decentralized government within some segments of
the ANC-led alliance. This was evident in the RDP Base Document, and even the
RDP White Paper, which had referred to the role of local government in reconstruction and development with vagueness and uncertainty (Parnell and Pieterse 2002).

In 1995 when the Development Facilitation Act (DFA) was introduced as
South Africa's first piece of 'planning' legislation (see Chapter 3), the role of new
forms of local government was still only beginning to take shape, and it was not surprising therefore that the Land Development Objectives (LDOs) introduced by the
Act had to be approved by provincial government, and that decisions on land development were to be made by provincial-level tribunals (Mabin 2002: 40–54; Oldfield
2002: 92–103). By 1996, however, the matter was settled – the vital role of local
government, and of its development mandate, was firmly established[1] (Parnell and
Pieterse 2002). The establishment of post-apartheid local government was strongly
influenced by the then prevailing international discourse on governance and decentralization. The decentralization process, so common internationally, happened in
South Africa through the creation of local government as an autonomous sphere of
authority, rather than through the incremental transfer of powers to the local tier, as
occurred in many other parts of the world.

The creation of the new transitional local authorities brought considerable fiscal and political risk, and the national agency responsible for overseeing the process
– the Department of Constitutional Development (DCD), later known as the
Department of Provincial and Local Government (DPLG) – was concerned with

introducing mechanisms that would encourage local government to act in a developmental and fiscally responsible manner. Senior officials in the DCD who had been transferred to the department from the RDP Office (which had been closed in April 1996) introduced the idea of integrated development planning, and used a planned amendment to the Local Government Transition Act to introduce a (rather sketchy) legal provision requiring all municipalities to prepare Integrated Development Plans (Harrison 2001). Mabin (2002: 45) identifies this as the moment when 'the development planning idea made its way into legislation', and pointed out that 'its brevity masked its radicalism'.

It is clear from the wording of the Local Government Transition Act Second Amendment Act, 1996, that the IDP was intended as an instrument to promote rational and developmentally oriented budgeting, and as a mechanism for performance management. In this conceptualization, the IDP had little in common with South Africa's more traditional instruments of planning – the town planning schemes, guide plans and structure plans, for example. However, the first set of IDPs was to be prepared mainly by planning consultants who were steeped in traditions of physical planning, and so the shift in the purpose and nature of planning was less evident than may otherwise have been the case. However, the IDP did have far-reaching effects on the way planning was understood and performed. Historically, for example, planning in South Africa's municipalities was an adjunct of the town or city engineer's department but, after 1996, it began to take on a strategic dimension, and was increasingly seen to be the responsibility of executive mayors and municipal managers (Mabin 2002).

The IDP did not only eclipse traditional forms of planning such as land-use management but also a first wave of post-apartheid spatial planning that had been rooted in the spatial logic of designer-planners (see, for example, the discussion on the Cape Town MSDF in Chapter 6). After 2000 when IDPs were required to include a spatial development framework, the spatial dimensions of planning were strengthened. The purpose of spatial planning had, however, shifted. It was now mainly about the spatial coordination of investment rather than the management of land use.

The IDP also emerged in competition to other forms of planning such as the LDOs introduced by the DFA (as explained in Chapter 3) and provincial planning instruments such as KwaZulu-Natal's Local Development Plans. Institutional rivalries between national departments complicated the terrain, as did the relationships between the then Inkatha Freedom Party-controlled KwaZulu-Natal provincial government, the National Party-dominated Western Cape administration and the ANC-led national government. In the final event, LDOs were dropped, and the IDP was secured as the chief instrument of local planning, while provincial governments relented and brought their planning systems in line with national legislation.

Some difficult points of connection remain. For example, while the strategic planning of municipalities was radically overhauled with the arrival of the IDP, very little progress was made with land-use management systems. At the time of writing, the Land Use Management Act, promised by the White Paper on Spatial Planning and Land Use Management (2001), was still to be finalized by the Department of Land Affairs, and was the subject of continued debate, and even contest, within national government. This was delaying the implementation of provincial planning and land-use management legislation, and seriously constraining the ability of municipalities to bring their land-use management plans (previously known as town planning schemes) in line with IDPs and SDFs. Land-use management plans were still being prepared under the old Provincial Ordinances that had been put in place under apartheid and before.

Although the IDP had a peculiarly South African genealogy, it was also shaped within an emergent international discourse on governance, planning and urban management. As Parnell and Pieterse (2002: 79–91) pointed out, 'the IDP process will be familiar to international development professionals who have followed the move towards a more management-driven local government process' (see page 87). The link between the IDP and themes that were to be associated with the 'third way' movement of Clinton, Blair *et al.* – including, for example, joined-up government, performance management, rational budgeting, service delivery partnerships and participatory governance – was evident in the 1996 Act but was more fully articulated in the 1998 White Paper. There is, for example, a close and interesting correspondence between South Africa's White Paper and New Labour's White Paper of the same year published in the UK under the title *Modern Local Government: In Touch with the People* (Harrison 2006b). The White Paper strengthened the role of planning within local governance but also sharpened the tensions that emerge from the ideologically hybrid third-way approach – tensions that have partly to do with balancing participatory governance with a largely technocratic approach to strategic budgeting, performance management and integration (Harrison 2006b). Mbeki's taking office as state president in 1999 arguably strengthened the managerialist and technocratic dimensions of policy-making and planning although participation remained at least a rhetorically important element of the IDP process.

Preparing the first IDPs was an enormous challenge for newly constituted transitional local authorities. After 1998, support was provided by the Decentralised Development Planning (DDP) unit, a semi-autonomous agency housed in the DPLG that had been set up in partnership with the German Gesellschaft für Technische Zusammenarbeit (GTZ). This support (which included the preparation of a detailed manual on IDP process) was important but limited, and most of these first IDPs were partial and inadequate documents prepared mainly by consultants who were struggling to adapt to a new mode of planning.

In 2000, the Municipal Systems Act elaborated on the purpose and require-ments of an IDP, and provided a strengthened basis for the second round of local planning subsequent to the local elections of December 2000. The elections marked the consolidation of 843 local authorities (over 1200 before 1995) into 284 municipalities, the linking of urban and rural areas into single authorities, and the cre-ation of six single-tier metropolitan authorities.[2] These were radical and important changes, but also changes which imposed an enormous burden of further restruc-turing on a fragile sphere of government.

The new municipalities were given until March 2002 to prepare their IDPs (with an earlier deadline for an interim IDP). The inadequacies of the previous round were highlighted in a performance review (see Harrison 2003a) and so the DPLG (through the DDP) put in place a comprehensive system of support for local gov-ernment. Using the services of the Council for Scientific and Industrial Research (CSIR), revised guide packs were prepared and distributed, an extensive training programme for local councillors and officials was rolled out, national government staff and other resources were deployed to Planning, Implementation and Management Support (PIMS) centres within district municipalities, and an elec-tronic information system was introduced. This support arguably assisted in improving the quality of the second round of IDPs, although municipalities struggled to meet target dates and there was still a high variability in performance.

CROSSING SCALES

Until 2000, the IDP was conceived of almost entirely as an instrument of local gov-ernance. However, from about 2000, it was gradually connected with an evolving system of intergovernmental planning and coordination. The 1996 constitution, with its principle of cooperative governance, and its complex formula for sharing power between national, provincial and local governments, made integrated governance a difficult task. The simple model of centralized coordination used by the RDP Office between 1994 and 1996 was not feasible within this constitutional set-up, and new mechanisms were required that related to what Oldfield (2002: 99) referred to as 'a web of structured, interrelated, multi-scaled strategies'.

As Chapter 3 explained, integrated governance has been a strong theme in the Mbeki era. In pursuing the goal of alignment and harmonization of policies and programmes across the spheres of government, national agencies, such as the Office of the President, the Treasury, and the DPLG, have become increasingly influ-ential in setting the parameters for planning. Processes of integration have included the strengthening of the policy-making and coordination role of the Policy Coordination and Advisory Services (PCAS) unit in the presidency; the creation of a network of intergovernmental forums which have been formalized in the Intergovernmental Relations Framework Act of 2005; and, the development of strategic instruments of coordination at national level (partly replicated at provincial level) such as the Medium Term Strategic Framework (MTSF), the Medium Term Expenditure Framework (MTEF) and the National Spatial Development Perspective (NSDP). The IDP has been identified as a key element within this evolving intergovernmental framework although the practical mechanisms for linking the IDP with planning in the other spheres of government have yet to be properly developed, and the national IDP hearings of 2005 pointed to many continued weaknesses in the linkage across the spheres.

The complex system of intergovernmental relations remains one of the greatest challenges for planning in South Africa. The DPLG may succeed in improving the linkage between the IDP and planning in the other spheres – perhaps through making district- and metropolitan-scale IDPs instruments of intergovernmental negotiation and agreement – but South Africa's highly complex, three-sphere constitutional arrangement will continue to make integrated planning a complicated process. One proposal for simplifying the system is to abolish the provincial sphere of government and, at the time of writing, there was media speculation that this was being considered within national government.

NETWORKING

Although integration and coordination have been driven mainly from the centre, there are instances in which a networked or collaborative approach has emerged from within the local sphere. In 2002, for example, the South African Cities Network (SACN) was formalized as a strategic partnership bringing together South Africa's nine largest cities. Through its bi-annual State of the Cities Report, and its other programmes, the SACN has proven to be highly influential in shaping a common understanding of urban development issues in South Africa, and in promoting approaches such as the City Development Strategy (see discussion in Chapter 3).

By 2004, the idea of city networking was taken further by an emerging discourse on *global city-regions*. In Gauteng, especially, the concept of the global city-region offered a means to conceptualize new forms of relationship between three metropolitan authorities (Johannesburg, Tshwane and Ekhuruleni), and between metropolitan, provincial and national governments. Although the global city-region was primarily about arrangements and relationships of governance, it also has a spatial dimension captured in the idea of urban polycentricity (see Chapter 5 for a more detailed discussion on the global city-region).

THE LONGER-TERM HORIZON

The IDP is a medium-term plan linked to a political cycle (although aspects of the plan, including the vision and the spatial development framework, have a longer-term horizon). Increasingly, however, the international trend for major cities, at least, has been towards longer-term strategic planning that focuses on such matters as major infrastructural investments, economic strategy, environmental sustainability and growth management. Since metropolitan areas are often highly fragmented institutionally, complex arrangements for joint planning often have to be created. In the South African case, however, the creation of single-tier metropolitan authorities created a strong institutional base for integrated, metropolitan-scale strategic planning.

The city of Johannesburg led the way with the Jo'burg 2030 strategy approved in late 2001 (which followed earlier plans to restructure the city on more businesslike lines), and the creation of a corporate planning unit in the office of the executive mayor to drive the implementation of the strategy. The strategy had a strong economic focus and was aimed at making Johannesburg a world-class city by 2030. Jo'burg 2030 was criticized for its overriding focus on the economy and on world city status and, in 2004, the city released a Human Development Strategy, followed, in 2006, by a new Growth and Development Strategy (GDS) which stressed the importance of inclusiveness and of addressing urban inequalities. The 'proactive absorption of the poor' is, for example, one of the key principles in the GDS.

The SACN (backed by the World Bank-funded international Cities Alliance Network) has also actively promoted the introduction of what are known internationally as City Development Strategies (CDSs). As conceptualized by the SACN, the CDS balances concerns with the 'productive city', the 'inclusive city', the 'sustainable city' and the 'well governed city'. Following from the example of Johannesburg, and prompted by the SACN, most of South Africa's large cities are embarking on the preparation of a CDS.

GOVERNMENT OR GOVERNANCE?

The IDP has helped planning shift from the domain of a profession to being a *societal* activity (albeit one strongly directed by the requirements of national government). While some planners have embraced the shift, others have become uneasy and uncertain in their role (see Chapter 10). The IDP has also brought higher levels of non-state participation into planning than ever before.

However, despite these positive shifts, the IDP falls largely within a contemporary managerialist mode of government. It is significant, for example, that in designing South Africa's post-apartheid planning system, mobilizing and participatory models of planning and development, such as the widely applauded Brazilian-style participatory local budgeting, were given only marginal attention, while more technocratic approaches to institutional linkage and coordination, such as those provided by the German and UK experience, received far closer scrutiny (Pieterse 2002: 1–17). The 'technocratic creep' within post-apartheid planning has been criticized by Heller (2001), Friedman (2001) and Pieterse (2004a), among others. Pieterse reminded us of how easily planning systems can be 'emptied of transformative political content', while Friedman criticized the structured processes of participation in the preparation of local plans, arguing that they 'are favoured because they are more amenable to frictionless administration than the robust and messy world of real public mobilization' (Pieterse 2004a: 85). It is arguable, however, that this 'technocratic turn' is not as much the outcome of a conscious intent to constrain participation as it is the response to enormous institutional complexity. How much 'messiness' can the already overburdened system handle?

The focus on government, rather than governance, is likely to be reinforced by the idea of the developmental state, and by the ongoing concern with the technical performance of municipalities. In the current context, there is a strong rationale for strengthening the focus on the workings of government at all scales, but there is also the risk that the focus on government may direct attention away from the real challenges and opportunities presented by the non-state and (largely) informal instruments of governance.

Simone (2001a) has, for example, drawn attention to the informal institutions, processes and networks that configure African cities, and has acknowledged the possible role for associational networks – such as faith-based organizations, stokvels (or community-based rotating credit schemes), and migrant networks – within developmental processes. Beall (2001: 365), for example, wrote of the potential for these networks to be 'scaled up or captured for more generalized goals, as has happened, for example, in the case of the South African Homeless People's Federation, while Winkler (2006) has explored the role of faith-based organizations in inner-city regeneration. In the end, however, what is required is a clear recognition of the importance of the state in planning and development, as well as an acceptance that the agents of civil society also have a key role to play.

Another form of governance, and one that is ambiguously situated between formal and informal structures, is traditional leadership (an institution of considerable importance in provinces such as KwaZulu-Natal, the Eastern Cape and Limpopo). The relationship between traditional and elected authorities, including within the planning process, remains complex and unresolved (Pycroft 2002: 105–126; Ntsebeza 2004).

CRISIS IN LOCAL GOVERNMENT?

By 2005, local government seemed to be floundering with the most visible evidence in the (sometimes violent) protests that erupted in local authorities from Harrismith in the Free State to Khutsong on the Gauteng/North West border. Although some of the unrest had to do with the redemarcation of provincial boundaries, the lack of service delivery appeared to underlie most of the agitation, although a fair amount of the unrest may have been about political contestation around positions on municipal councils.[3]

The irony of the Mbeki era was that despite the emphasis given to good governance (see, for example, the 2004 State of the Nation Address), the everyday reality in many municipalities was of patronage in appointments and tendering, institutional conflict, poor delivery records and financial crisis. The state of crisis was acknowledged in a government audit of municipalities which revealed that 136 of South Africa's 284 municipalities did not have the capacity to fulfil their basic functions; a sobering finding that led to the April 2005 launch of Project Consolidate, a national government programme designed to fill the capacity gaps within local government.

While national leaders have fingered local government for the crisis, observers have suggested that South Africa's programme of decentralization has simply overwhelmed the capacities of new and fragile local governments. For Kulipossa (2004), for example, South Africa tried too much too quickly – there should have been a more gradual strengthening of the fragile institutional forms at local level through a careful, pragmatic and gradual process of decentralization, rather than lumbering local government so suddenly with such onerous responsibilities. Atkinson (2003: 2) asks the critical question, 'are local governments and their administrations actually capable of fulfilling their developmental mandate [as enshrined in the Constitution, the Municipal Structures Act, and the Municipal Systems Act]?'.

For planners, the question must be extended: 'to what extent have IDPs alleviated or even contributed to the apparent crisis in local government?'. It is possible that the preparation of IDPs (and the preparation of other plans and strategies required by national legislation) has been a considerable short-term burden for authorities where high-level skills are scarce, and has absorbed energies that may have been placed productively elsewhere. In this sense, planning may be complicit in the current crisis. The critical question, however, is whether, from a longer-term perspective, integrated development planning is building local capacity for the strategic and integrated decision-making and action that will lead (eventually) to better outcomes.

The critical issue is the relationship between the planning system and the differential capacity of municipal government. Arguably, one of the key problems with the development of post-apartheid planning was the lack of attention that was given to the huge diversity among municipalities and, as a result, the one-size-fits-all system was too sophisticated for many weaker authorities, and too limited for the larger

and better-capacitated authorities. Also, the uniform nature, and national determination, of the system meant that local planning in post-apartheid South Africa lacked
the open, experimental nature of planning in countries such as Brazil and the United
States, for example.

In the better-capacitated municipalities, the strategic and longer-term perspectives provided by a GDS or CDS are beginning to inform an increasingly
sophisticated array of short- and medium-term plans. In the City of Johannesburg,
for example, the GDS informs the five-year IDP, the Spatial Development
Framework (SDF), 7 Regional Spatial Development Frameworks (RSDFs), Regional
Urban Management Plans (RUMPs), Sector Plans, and may, in the future, also provide guidance to Ward-Based Plans.[4] Many other municipalities continue to
struggle with the preparation of an IDP, which suggests that planning will become
increasingly differentiated across the country, with a growing variance in the level
and scale of planning that happens.

OUTCOMES

It remains very difficult to evaluate the real effect of IDPs on the functioning of South
Africa's still very new local authorities. Harrison (2006b) asks whether 'the integrated development planning process has produced more integrated and
participatory ways of working – more joined-up government – and whether this integration (if it has occurred) has led to more effective delivery of services, and to more
effective responses to problems such as poverty, HIV/AIDS, crime, and spatial fragmentation'. He argues that it will take a while before we are able to provide answers
to these questions but does point to recent evaluations (admittedly commissioned
by national government and the GTZ) that suggest modest success for IDPs (or
some IDPs at least).

As an instrument of integration the IDP has been limited by the difficulty in
securing the participation and commitment of departments and agencies outside
the municipal sphere of government. This was a major concern identified in the
2005 National IDP Hearings and, at the time of writing, was being addressed by the
DPLG through a legislative review process. The emergent idea was of district- and
metropolitan-scale IDPs providing the instrument for intergovernmental agreement
around local development plans.

As an instrument of participatory governance the IDP has been constrained by
the increasing complexity of planning systems in South Africa and by a managerialist approach to governance. The untidy, unpredictable, often time-consuming
processes of citizen engagement cannot easily be accommodated within a process
that also emphasizes performance management and mainly technical solutions to

coordination across and between spheres of government (Pieterse 2004a). At the same time, however, planning has also been constrained by the politicization of local bureaucracies. One of the intentions of the managerialist approach is to depoliticize administrative (including planning) processes by increasing the independence and discretionary space available to senior managers in the civil service. However, as a number of writers now point out (for example, Hood and Peters 2004), the introduction of a performance management regime has had the unintended effect of politicizing bureaucracies as politicians are able to use performance contracts to exert their control over officials. In South Africa, IDP processes are almost always deeply imbued with the political struggles that inhabit local bureaucracies. In regions such as the Western Cape, where internal strife within the ruling party is especially severe, planning and other governance processes are bitterly contested from within the bureaucracy.

The IDP has had partial success as an instrument of transformation. IDPs, with their links to budgeting, have assisted in directing resources towards areas of disadvantage and deprivation, while participatory processes have alerted local councils to areas of special need. It is difficult, methodologically speaking, to show the relationship between integrated development planning and improved outcomes in terms of the scale and quality of delivery, but it is reasonable to hypothesize that the existence of a planning framework, such as an IDP, leads to more effective deployment of resources. This point was made by Cashdan (2002: 164) who argued that the existence of an IDP 'makes it harder to perpetuate old expenditure patterns'.

However, while the IDPs may have had a significant impact on the distribution of municipal resources, there is no real evidence to suggest that IDP processes have tackled the *structural* sources of inequality and fragmentation within localities. It is true, of course, that there are huge constraints on what may be achieved through local action, as many of the problems require intervention at a higher level (land reform being an example), but few, if any, IDPs offer more than a redirecting of financial resources towards areas of need. The SDFs, for example, generally reflect existing spatial patterns, rather than offering a real alternative to the legacies of colonialism and apartheid. For Pieterse (2004a), the managerialist rather than mobilizing orientation of the new planning system may be blamed for its failure to effect deep-rooted transformation as the participatory aspect of the IDP process is insufficient to pose a real challenge to the structures that sustain social inequality.

CONCLUSION

This chapter has shown the close link between local planning and systems of governance, and has illustrated both the successes and limitations of local planning after apartheid. The system of governance, and therefore of planning, however, continues to evolve. As indicated, government is giving close attention to the intergovernmental dimensions of planning, and legislative amendments are expected that would allow integrated development planning to be better aligned across the spheres of government.

However, considerable challenges remain. For example, South Africa's constitutional system is enormously complex, and without fundamental rationalization of government structures, the planning system will remain overly complicated. Also, without resolving matters relating to areas such as land-use management, and the duplication between planning and environmental management processes, serious points of weakness in the post-apartheid planning system will persist. One of the greatest challenges is the institutional and capacity weakness within the municipal sphere of government, and the future of local government is closely linked to the way in which government responds to this crisis.

The relationship between the state and its citizens is also evolving, and the nature of planning in the future will partly depend on the direction that this takes. On the one hand, the pressures for delivery and the goal of 6 per cent annual growth in GDP – expressed in the ASGI-SA programme, for example – is pulling planning in an increasingly technocratic direction, but, on the other hand, there is also a growing demand within the ANC-led alliance for more responsive forms of planning and policy-making. There is a danger that local planning will be caught between polarizing approaches towards participatory democracy and managerialism (increasingly expressed in terms of the idea of a developmental state) but the planning system also holds the potential for bringing these tendencies together in a creative and transformative combination, a possibility to which we will return in the concluding chapter of the book.

PLANNING AS GOVERNANCE BEYOND THE LOCAL: THE REGIONAL QUESTION, NATIONAL AND PROVINCIAL PLANNING

INTRODUCTION

Although the main focus of planning has been at the local level, there have been sev-eral important initiatives beyond this sphere. Indeed, it is possible to argue that since the late 1990s, forms of regional planning have become increasingly impor-tant, mirroring, in some respects, the rise of regionalist projects and forms of planning at a regional scale internationally (Brenner 1998; Frisken and Norris 2001; Swanstrom 2001; Soderbaum and Taylor 2003). Brenner (2002) links these initia-tives *inter alia* to contemporary trends in economic restructuring, which are creating new spatial relationships and pressures for new forms of governance at various spa-tial scales. In the South African context, regional planning was first used as a way of supporting homeland development in the apartheid era (Chapter 1). Weak forms of regional government and regional plans cross-cutting homeland boundaries were however instituted, as the reality of integration across boundaries became apparent in the 1980s. As Chapter 3 has shown, there has been a rescaling of government in the post-apartheid period with the establishment of new provinces and the system of district and local government. This has gone along with initiatives to introduce new forms of planning at these scales.

The demarcation of provinces and district/local government has explicitly attempted to create functional units incorporating contemporary economic and sociospatial relationships, although boundaries are contested in some cases and inevitably some key relationships spill over them. The result however has been very large units of district and local government so that regional planning has become a significant practice in South Africa. Thus, integrated development plans (IDPs) might be seen as forms of regional plans. Yet municipal IDPs are insufficient to coor-dinate across municipalities or to promote regional economic development; thus there are pressures for stronger regional plans at district and provincial level. New regionalist concepts from the global North are being deployed in this context. Planning for the Gauteng global city-region and debates over governance in this context provide the most important example of this tendency.

The primary orientation of regional planning has been as a way of coordinat-ing development between spheres and sectors of government over space. This has taken some time to be realized. In the early years of government, the main focus was at a more basic level – on dealing with administrative reorganization, on

getting systems to work, and on delivery (Pieterse 2004a). Thus, while both planning and policy discourse stressed a coordinated approach to development, in
reality, such 'joined-up' government remained hard to achieve, silo-based delivery
dominated, and efforts were relatively fragmented. From the mid-1990s, however,
there were various initiatives to improve coordination between and within spheres
of government, and planning played a prominent role in these processes. These
have included forms of 'area-based' management at a regional scale (see Chapter
3), initiatives to introduce forms of national spatial planning, and most recently, to
develop an intergovernmental system of planning, linking planning cycles within
and across spheres of government, creating spatial frameworks at all scales, and
linking fiscal transfers to integrated development plans, in response to the problems noted in Chapter 4. While the intention in these planning processes has
been to incorporate a range of actors, seeing them as a form of governance, in
practice, as Chapter 4 noted, a more managerialist, government-centred
approach has often operated, even more so at the regional than at the local level.

Planning at regional and national scale has had to confront the national spatial
legacy of apartheid and capitalist development: the sharp regional inequalities linked
to both patterns of resource endowment and accumulation and the way these were
overlaid by apartheid and the 'homeland' system; the complex urbanization and settlement patterns associated with influx control and forced removals; the economic
dominance of the Gauteng region; the declining agrarian base of rural areas; extensive poverty in the previous 'homelands'; and the persistence of places created by
apartheid policies with weak economic bases, such as resettlement areas, industrial
decentralization points and homeland capitals. In the late apartheid era, many critics
of the apartheid government assumed that the new government would wish to facilitate urbanization, given the history of influx control and the way spatial marginalization
was embedded in apartheid. Although government has never sought to reinstate any
form of influx control, it has been ambivalent about the extent to which expenditure
and development should focus on urban versus rural areas (Atkinson and Marais
2006), and on the question of growth versus spatial equity. This ambivalence is evident in policy, as well as in several of the regional development approaches used.
Initiatives to create a national spatial framework or perspective have attempted to
resolve these questions, but differences run deep, and both frameworks and concepts appear to be evolving in the context of these debates.

Chapter 5 considers these forms of planning within South Africa, focusing on
the themes of governance, spatial equity and regional development. It also examines
the experience of spatial development initiatives (SDIs), pioneering forms of regional
development centred on anchor projects in areas of potential. Although they were
short-lived, they have gone on to be used in the context of transnational planning
within the Southern African Development Community. Seen as a way of focusing

and coordinating development, their importance lies both in the model of governance they piloted, and in the approach to regional development used. The
experience of SDIs embodies several of the tensions within policy, and raises important questions about the power and limits of planning in South Africa.

CREATING AN INTERGOVERNMENTAL PLANNING SYSTEM

Under apartheid, government was hierarchical, with provincial and local government
subordinate to national government, and local government under the control of
provinces in several respects. Under the 1996 constitution, a system of 'spheres' of
government was created, moving away from the previous hierarchical system. Thus
each sphere was autonomous, but was required to cooperate with other spheres of
government. Functions are divided between spheres, but there are several overlapping areas. Provinces however largely have responsibility for functions linked to the
development of human capital, while local government functions are more strongly
linked to the 'delivery of infrastructure, the underpinning of economic activity, and
the myriad of public activities which support co-existence within communities' (van
Ryneveld 2005: 17), i.e. service delivery, land-use planning and the like. However
several functions cross-cut spheres, or exist in some form in all three spheres. Poor
coordination and confusion around responsibilities is common. In practice, national
government is dominated by strong line departments, each with their own agenda. A
system of government clusters has been set up to improve coordination, but the
problem of departments working as silos remains.

The lion's share of taxation (mainly income tax and value added tax) occurs at
national level (93 per cent), while local government accounts for most of the remainder (mainly property taxes and user charges). Monies however are allocated to the
provinces using a formula based on population, with an additional weighting for the
rural population, building in a form of spatial equity. A grant to local government on
the basis of population living under conditions of poverty provides a level of equal-
ization, although the reliance on own funding and grants tied to particular projects is
far greater. Overall, provincial governments accounted for 39.5 per cent of expenditure in 2002, while local government accounted for only 17.7 per cent (van Ryneveld
2005). Thus, while there is considerable emphasis on decentralization (Chapter 3),
the share of funding directly controlled by local government is relatively small. In this
context, considerable emphasis is being placed on planning processes and forms of
intergovernmental coordination to enable cooperation. This challenge, however, has
been particularly difficult to address.

In the early days, much of the development funding on offer was application-
based, leading to a scattering of development efforts, and poor coordination

between projects. The first spatial development initiatives and some of the other area-based programmes were in part initiatives to create more coordinated development, at least in limited areas (Platzky 1998). The Reconstruction and Development Programme (RDP) Office, established in 1994, was intended to enable more systematic intersectoral coordination, but was unable to withstand resistance by other departments, and was subsequently closed (see Chapter 3). The first initiative to create a spatially informed national growth and development strategy in 1996 used a bottom-up process of generating locally produced provincial growth and development strategies. These multisectoral plans were intended to include a spatial component that could be incorporated into the national strategy. Very few provincial plans however included a developed spatial component, and since most did not go beyond very broad statements of strategic direction, they were insufficient as a basis for the national strategy. A further attempt to produce a national spatial development framework that would have provided a visual perspective on spatial priorities also failed in the face of resistance by national departments and fears that it would overstep the boundaries of cooperative government (Harrison and Todes 2001a).

From 1998 there was a new drive to develop a national spatial plan, this time in the Office of the Deputy President (now the Office of the President). The renewed interest in spatial planning at this scale reflected concerns that limited government funds for capital investment were being wasted by poorly coordinated investments, and that there were major differences in the spatial investment patterns and visions of some national departments. For instance, there were differences between the Departments of Transport and Trade and Industry regarding future plans for the ports, and for infrastructure linking them to the main centres. In addition, there was a concern that government was not confronting the spatial consequences of policy. A consultation process with senior managers in several national departments and some of the provinces highlighted a common concern with a lack of clear spatial priorities. For many departments, investment decisions were not informed by explicit spatial criteria, and the implicit choices could be contradictory. Decisions were often made on the basis of communities that attracted most attention (Presidency 2003). Further, there were concerns that expenditure patterns were simply reinforcing apartheid spatial patterns (ODP 1998; DOT 1998). In contrast to earlier initiatives, which attempted to develop a framework, this time the focus was on developing indicative guidelines. As the process evolved, it was cast as a National Spatial Development Perspective (NSDP), drawing on the European experience. The document included a spatial narrative, a set of analytical maps and a strategic response based on setting priorities, principles and visions.

By mid-2005, the NSDP was being drawn into a broader process of intergovernmental planning. As Chapter 4 showed, with the failure of initiatives towards

alignment from the centre in the mid-1990s, more emphasis was placed on coordination through the local integrated development plans. However these planning
processes experienced severe difficulty in achieving the buy-in of agencies at
provincial and national level. Further, coordination between plans at regional level
was lacking, and there were poor links to both the NSDP and provincial plans
(DPLG 2005b). In response to these limitations, a series of initiatives has been put
in place to improve alignment between spheres of government.

First, new legislation and procedures were introduced to improve coordination
between the spheres of government. With the introduction of legislation determining
financial arrangements (Division of Revenue Act, Provincial Financial Management
Act and Municipal Financial Management Act), national and provincial departments
are being forced to participate in municipal budgeting processes. In addition,
medium-term expenditure frameworks and budgets are intended to link to planning
frameworks in each sphere. Further, the recent 2005 Intergovernmental Relations
Act formalizes systems of cooperative governance and strengthens relationships of
collaboration, although it does so through requiring consultation and cooperation,
and by establishing intergovernmental forums at different levels.

Second, there are initiatives to link planning from national level to provincial and
local level more strongly. Processes are being put in place to assess IDPs to ensure
that they are consistent with the NSDP. Greater emphasis is being placed on provin-
cial- and district-metropolitan-level plans as a way of aligning planning (Presidency
2004). Guidelines for Provincial Growth and Development Strategies are being
developed in order to strengthen these plans and to ensure closer alignment with the
NSDP. Peer-review and assessment processes are also being mooted to improve
plans. Although Provincial Growth and Development Strategies have been produced
since 1996, they did not receive the attention accorded to IDPs. Assessments of
these plans suggested that many were not sufficiently focused and strategic, nor did
they provide an appropriate framework for provincial development or an adequate
long-term agenda and direction for local level planning (DPLG 2005b).

Harmonization and alignment are intended to occur through interactive
processes, where agreement is reached between various spheres on the nature of
conditions in particular areas, the development potentials, and how policy and
implementation should address them. Planning, and particularly forms of regional
planning, is therefore coming to the fore in initiatives to improve cooperative government. Planning in this context is based on developing a common understanding, and
becomes a discursive process. Conceptually, this is not very different from the way
IDPs were viewed, and it will be interesting to see whether these mainly voluntary
forms of cooperation are able to overcome the problems experienced in the past.

Increased attention given to provincial planning however is also opening up
new dimensions. Provincial Growth and Development Strategies have to be more

than just an amalgamation of IDPs, and bring to bear their own dynamics and politics. Differences in the agendas and visions of provincial and local government – and particularly metropolitan government – have to be addressed, as do differences between provincial departments. For instance, provincial planning in the Western Cape is attempting to draw together sectoral and infrastructural planning in the province, and is having to confront the aspatial and often mutually contradictory way in which planning of this sort is being carried out. Planning at this scale is also becoming a space in which the interrelationship between areas is being addressed, and where common development agendas can be forged across municipal boundaries. This is most important in the Gauteng province, the country's economic heartland, where economic activities and commuting patterns cut across the three metropolitan areas and other local authorities, and there is an attempt to drive a common economic agenda. As the following section shows, the Gauteng initiatives have cohered around the concept of the global city-region. The drive for a regionalist agenda in this context is throwing up debates over the form of governance in the province, recalling, to some extent, international debates.

THE GAUTENG GLOBAL CITY-REGION AND NEW REGIONALISM

A number of international writers have identified the rise of a 'new regionalism' or a 'new regional politics' (e.g. Brenner 1998, 2002; Frisken and Norris 2001; Swanstrom 2001; Dreier et al. 2001). Although most commonly used with reference to supranational governance, the idea of a new regionalism is also associated with subnational governance, and especially with governance coalitions and networks within the city-region. The new regionalism, with its focus on the collaborative arrangements required to support economic competitiveness, may be distinguished from the traditional approach to regional or metropolitan government, which was concerned largely with creating structures that would improve the delivery of services and infrastructure (Swanstrom 2001).

Neil Brenner has written of the 're-territorialization' of the state at both supra- and subnational levels, and of the rise of multi-actor institutions at global city scale as a form of state territorial power, while Allen Scott (2002) has extended the established concepts of 'world cities' and 'global cities' (developed by Hall, Friedmann and Sassen, among others) in his theorizing on 'global city-regions'. Scott's work is also important for the extent to which it embraces city-regions centred on places such as Sao Paulo, Shanghai, Jakarta, Lagos and Johannesburg.

'New regionalism' as a concept has been widely debated in the literature, with some writers questioning its value (e.g. Lovering 1999; MacLeod 2001). Whatever its objective usefulness, the idea or discourse of the global city-region is highly sig-nificant for planning in South Africa, as it is increasingly framing debates on urban policy and planning, especially in the enormously important Gauteng region.

The genealogy of the global city-region debate in Gauteng goes back at least to 1999 when Ketso Gordhan, the then Chief Executive Officer of the Johannesburg Metropolitan Council, participated in the Global City-Regions Conference in Los Angeles which also involved key thinkers such as Allen Scott, Saskia Sassen, Peter Hall, John Friedmann and James Wolfensohn (then President of the World Bank). The idea of the global city-region was taken back to South Africa where it gradually gathered momentum until it emerged in about 2005 as the dominant official dis-course within the Gauteng region, with strong support from provincial and metropolitan governments. The South African Cities Network (SACN), linked to the World Bank-funded Cities Alliance, and especially the SACN chairperson, Andrew Borraine, have provided robust backing for the notion of a global city-region. The SACN's 2004 State of the Cities Report, for example, predicted that the Gauteng region (which includes the Johannesburg, Tshwane and Ekhuruleni metropolitan areas) would emerge as the twelfth largest city in the world by 2015, making it a city-region larger in size than Los Angeles.

In 2005, the premier of Gauteng and the metropolitan mayors and city man-agers embarked on a grand tour of global city-regions internationally – Tokyo, the Randstad in the Netherlands, London and Sao Paulo – to explore ways in which the provincial and metropolitan government could coordinate planning and administra-tive efforts across jurisdictional boundaries to promote the global city-region ideal. The construction of the controversial high-speed rail link between Johannesburg, Pretoria and the Johannesburg International Airport (the Gautrain) was justified in terms of the needs of a global city-region, while the 2010 Soccer World Cup was identified as an opportunity to showcase the city-region to the rest of the world.

In 2006, the global city-region ideal was officially adopted as policy of the Gauteng provincial government. The desire to build Gauteng into 'an integrated and globally competitive city-region' was the key theme in Premier Mbhazima Shilowa's budget speech of that year. The key elements of the global city-region initiative were identified as: creating a system of integrated metropolitan governance; building terri-torial and political cohesion in the province; developing strategic economic infrastructure (including, for example, the Gautrain); and growing the economy and economic competitiveness (see www.joburg.org and www.gautengonline.gov.za). There was also talk of economic cooperation with cities such as Durban and Maputo, suggesting an emergent concept of a global city-region which is not necessarily spa-tially contiguous (as argued in the international literature by Amin 2004).

The global city-region has emerged rapidly and forcefully as a framing concept for planning within Gauteng. For example, in his 2006 budget speech,

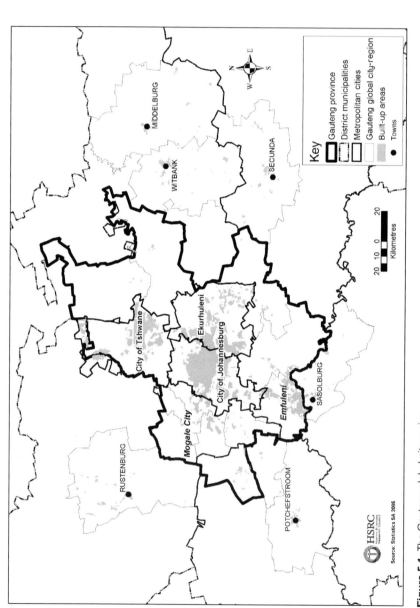

Figure 5.1 The Gauteng global city-region
Source: Statistics SA (2005)

Johannesburg's executive mayor, Amos Masondo, argued that the city's new Growth and Development Strategy and five-year Integrated Development Plan support efforts to create a globally competitive city-region. Yet the global city-region concept is also leading to debates over the relative powers and roles of metropolitan and provincial government, and over the nature and form of planning at this scale. These debates are beginning to raise questions about the notions of cooperative government, and the division in responsibilities between spheres more generally.

THE POST-APARTHEID SPATIAL LANDSCAPE

While the management of city-regions is a new focus for South African planning, debates over how to respond to the legacy of the highly unequal spatial landscape created by apartheid have been under way for much longer. Under apartheid, African people were expected to live in largely peripheral homeland areas, and movement to the cities was highly controlled. However, economic activity was concentrated in the metropolitan areas, and particularly in the Gauteng province (Table 5.1) – a pattern that was not significantly changed by decades of industrial decentralization policies (Bloch 1993). Although homeland areas were predominantly rural, urban settlements and dense semi-urban settlements were created through policies of forced resettlement from 'white' areas, as well as through the creation of administrative homeland capitals and industrial decentralization policies. The economic base of many of these areas was often weak. By the end of apartheid, some 75 per cent of households living in poverty were in rural areas, and 85 per cent of incomes in homelands derived from public expenditure (pensions, public sector employment and public works schemes), compared with 25 per cent in metropolitan areas (ODP 1998).

The post-apartheid era has not seen a major correction of apartheid spatial disjunctures, although spatial trends are increasingly shaped by an economic logic. The overwhelming concentration of poor African people in what were historically the homelands is still evident, but poverty is increasingly becoming an urban phenomenon as well (Parnell 2004). By 1998, resettlement areas created under apartheid did not seem to be disappearing (CDE 1998), although some had experienced out-migration (Krige 1996). The ending of homelands and industrial decentralization policy meant that many places which had depended on their status as capitals or on industrial incentives experienced economic decline, but some found new roles. Not all places which benefitted from industrial decentralization incentives declined once incentives disappeared. In the more successful industrial decentralization points, incentives underpinned decentralization trends based on competitive pressures towards low-wage peripheral locations in industries such as clothing (Hart and Todes 1997; Platzky 1995). Decentralization continued to occur in these industries

ten years after apartheid, but South Africa's increasing economic openness, combined with a strong rand, led to a sharp decline in employment even in peripheral
areas (Robbins *et al.* 2004).

Perhaps the most notable trend has been a movement of people to cities
experiencing economic growth, particularly the Gauteng metropolitan areas (Table
5.1).[1] Secondary cities experiencing high rates of economic growth also confronted
rapid in-migration. Both economic growth rates and population growth rates have
been variable in other metropolitan areas and secondary cities: while both have
been faster than average in the Cape Town and eThekwini metros, as well as in
some secondary cities, others have seen net or absolute decline (SACN 2004;
DBSA 2005). Similarly, there has been a net move away from the economically
declining Eastern Cape and Northern Cape regions to the Western Cape, and to
the north-east of the country (Tomlinson *et al.* 2003; Figure 5.2).

Not all movement follows economic growth however. Tomlinson *et al.* (2003)
and Cross (2001) argue that there are significant rural–rural movements, and census

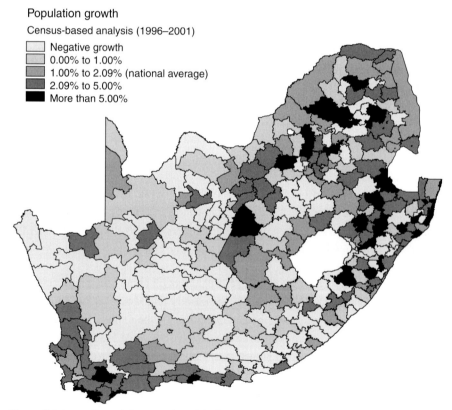

Population growth

Census-based analysis (1996–2001)

- Negative growth
- 0.00% to 1.00%
- 1.00% to 2.09% (national average)
- 2.09% to 5.00%
- More than 5.00%

Figure 5.2 Areas of population growth and decline
Source: Pillay *et al.* (2006)

figures for the 1996–2001 period show movements into some predominantly rural districts. In addition, the period since 1994 has seen a significant push off commercial farming areas. As many as a million farm workers and their families have been displaced by farmers who are fearful of the rights new tenure security laws might accord them. Many of these people have moved to small towns, where housing is sometimes more easily available than in the cities. For instance, in the Free State, a combination of available, already-serviced sites and a high minimum house size required by provincial housing policy, meant that housing built through the government subsidies was concentrated largely in small towns (Marais and Krige 2000).

In the context of continuing poverty, past patterns of fragmented and circular migration are perpetuated, although in somewhat different forms. Previous patterns of migrancy dominated by male mine workers have been displaced by both men and women (Posel 2003) – circular migrants working in a range of low-skill, insecure forms of work, such as domestic work, transport, security work, informal trade and the like (Cox *et al.* 2004). Migrancy has not declined (Posel 2003), but the sharp drop in employment on the mines has significantly affected rural incomes. Patterns of movement to concentrated rural settlements along roads, and to places on the metropolitan periphery, seem to reflect attempts to secure survival through combining partial access to urban centres with lower-cost locations, and partial reliance on natural resources (Cross *et al.* 1996: 173–214). Tomlinson *et al.* (2003) show a rapid growth of population just beyond the borders of some metropolitan areas, and on the metropolitan periphery. The extensive patterns of commuting into Gauteng from surrounding areas (DOT 1998) seem to be continuing as households keep peripherally located, but larger and better houses than could be acquired through the housing subsidy system in metropolitan areas (CDE 1998).

Economic growth remains highly concentrated in Gauteng and in the major cities. Gauteng itself accounted for 38 per cent of geographic value added (GVA) in 2003 (Table 5.1) and some 63 per cent of GVA was concentrated in the metropoles. Gauteng grew more rapidly than the rest of the country over the 1996–2003 period, and increased its dominance in the space economy (Figure 5.3). A recentralization of economic activity is evident in this period, compared with trends towards decentralization from the 1970s to the early 1990s. As Table 5.1 shows, regional inequalities are sharply defined, with strong disjunctures between the location of economic activity and where many people live, even if these are beginning to narrow as people move to cities.

It is perhaps not surprising then that debates over the 'regional question' – whether and how policy should attempt to shape the spatial distribution of development – are so contested. Despite rapid urbanization, many people continue to live in conditions of poverty in rural areas and in peripheral regions. For poor African people, the urban experience has been a harsh one and there is something of an

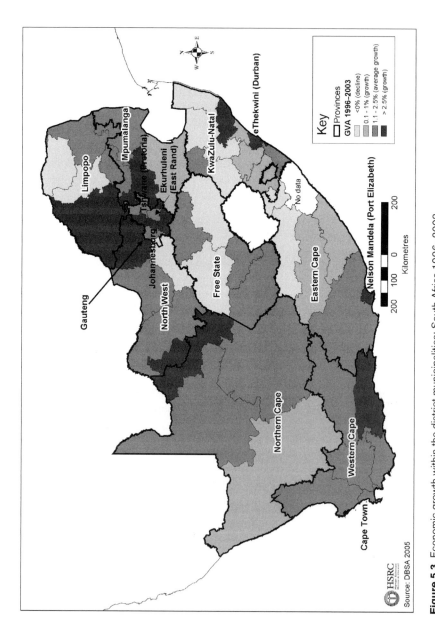

Figure 5.3 Economic growth within the district municipalities: South Africa 1996–2003

Source: DBSA (2005)

anti-urban sentiment at a popular and political level. At the same time, sharply declining household sizes coupled with urbanization has meant that despite relatively high levels of delivery of housing and services, most cities have been unable to dent the backlog, and informal settlements are growing. There are fears that cities are unable to cope with urbanization. Ironically then, while many expected a strongly pro-urban policy given the history of apartheid, state policy towards cities and urbanization has been ambivalent and internally contested. Thus initiatives to develop national spatial and/or urban policies of various sorts have been drawn out, and are frequently inconclusive, as the following section demonstrates.

RECONSIDERING THE REGIONAL QUESTION

In the early post-apartheid period, the regional question was not explicitly considered. Atkinson and Marais (2006) argue that policy statements were contradictory, and that implicit spatial policies often went in different directions. Spatial equity was nevertheless an important element of the fiscal system, and the constitution guaranteed a basic level of services as a right, wherever people were located. Some policies stressed rural development, and rural land reform and restitution were seen as important parts of government policy, given the history of dispossession under apartheid. Rural and urban development frameworks were developed in parallel in the mid-1990s, and took somewhat different views on urbanization and migration to cities (Atkinson and Marais 2006). Tensions between an emphasis on growth versus spatial equity, and on urban versus rural development, continued to be present in policy.

New thinking on regional development reacted to the legacy of industrial decentralization under apartheid, in which industrial subsidies were used to encourage firms to locate in peripheral places mainly in or close to homeland areas. Industrial decentralization as a policy was dropped in 1996, although for a few years after that, a programme of tax holidays for new industries contained a weak spatial element, this time focusing on areas experiencing industrial restructuring, or with an emerging industrial base. Thus, policy attempted to marry growth with a level of spatial equity, building on the way in which more successful industrial decentralization points had developed. The policy however had little effect, and by 1999 had been discontinued (Harrison and Todes 1999). The spatial development initiatives programme also attempted to combine growth with equity in a particular way. Following the logic of new approaches to regional development in Europe, it was based on promoting underdeveloped areas which had potential. Thus, while it sought to enable development in previously marginal areas, it did so on the basis of regional advantages. In practice, however, political pressure meant that SDIs were created on a more widespread basis than intended, including in areas with very limited potential.

Table 5.1 Changing regional and spatial inequalities in South Africa: selected indicators

Place	Population 2001	Population 2001 %	Population growth rate 1996–2001 %	Geographic value added (GVA) 2003 %	GGVA per capita 2003	GGVA growth rate 1996–2003 %
Metropolitan areas						
Cape Town	2893479	6.5	2.5	12.3	23123	1.4
Nelson Mandela Metro	1005804	2.2	0.8	2.8	14835	2.9
eThekwini	3089842	6.9	2.4	9.8	15946	2.8
Johannesburg	3225921	7.2	4.1	17.3	23601	4.2
Tshwane	1986078	4.4	3.4	8.8	19298	4.8
Ekurhuleni	2480459	5.5	4.1	7.4	14928	2.3
Gauteng and other metropolitan areas	15826447	34.8	3.5	62.7	19142	3.1
Provinces						
Western Cape	4524855	10.1	2.7	16.6	19611	1.6
Northern Cape	822820	1.8	-0.4	1.8	12114	2.6
Eastern Cape	6438762	14.4	0.4	6.4	5532	1.7
Free State	2706627	6.0	0.5	4.8	10990	-0.2
KwaZulu-Natal	9423923	21.0	2.3	15.0	8095	2.5
North West	3669633	8.2	1.9	–	–	–
Mpumalanga	3123415	7.0	2.1	6.9	11664	2.2
Limpopo	5272394	11.8	1.4	4.2	4016	1.3
Gauteng	8837322	19.7	3.7	37.8	19446	3.7
South Africa	44819751	100.0	2.0	100.0	11207	2.5

Source: derived from data in DBSA (2005)
Note: no gross geographic product (GGP) figures have been collected since 1991. Gross geographic value added is based on estimates derived from various data. It is similar to GGP, but does not include taxes.
This table provides data for four kinds of area and, as such, figures for each column do not add up. Data is given for each of the six metropolitan areas plus the economically dominant Gauteng province, which includes non-metropolitan municipalities in addition to the the metropolitan areas of Johannesburg, Tshwane, and Ekurhurleni; and the nine provinces, the sum of which is South Africa. It should also be noted that no GVA figures were available for North-West province, but provincial percentages come directly from DBSA (2005).

The National Spatial Development Perspective took on the question of the 'where' of development much more directly. Developed soon after the shift from the RDP to GEAR, and reflecting concerns that scarce capital investment in economic infrastructure was being wasted, it took a strongly pro-growth stance. The NSDP was developed at a time when Johannesburg as a city was facing financial crisis, and its ageing infrastructure threatened to undermine its core role in the national economy. The underlying text of the NSDP is a recognition of the role of major urban agglomerations (particularly Gauteng) in economic development, although other areas with economic 'potential' are also recognized. In contrast to some of the earlier policy processes, the NSDP avoided engaging with the urban–rural debate directly, and also desisted from developing a singular map showing areas of emphasis. Rather, it argued for a focus on areas of 'potential', and developed several categories of potential, around which expenditure on economic infrastructure should centre. It provided a series of maps which were indicative of various potentials, a basis for interaction between spheres on actual local and provincial potentials.

In its principles, the NSDP argued for a focus on 'people not places':

in localities with low development potential, government spending, beyond basic services, should focus on providing social transfer, human resource development and labour market intelligence … [to] enable people to … migrate … to localities that are more likely to provide sustainable employment or other economic opportunities … Infrastructure investment and development spending should primarily support localities that will become major growth nodes.

(Presidency 2003: 22–3)

While its focus on potential meant that only 20 per cent of magisterial districts would be included, they account for 89 per cent of GVA, and 57 per cent of poor households – and 75 per cent of poor households if immediately adjacent districts are included.

Although written largely in 1999, the NSDP took until 2003 to be accepted as policy, while de facto practice went in different directions. The Integrated Sustainable Rural Development Programme (ISRDP) dating from 2001 suggested a rather different emphasis on poor rural areas. In terms of this policy, a set of poverty nodes (district council areas) received preference in terms of expenditure. The intention here was not to increase expenditure, but to improve coordination, although with a greater focus on these areas. Critics however argued that the criteria for choice of nodes were not clear and that nodes were not necessarily the poorest areas. In addition, the policy contradicted the NSDP (DBSA 2005).

Attempts to set in place an Urban Development Framework faced similar problems. Begun as a strategy, it was later transformed into a broad framework in 1997, essentially encompassing a range of other policies. It was largely ignored, however, due to its institutional location, its cross-cutting orientation and its lack of a political champion (Pieterse 2004a). The NSDP and its arguments on the importance of cities in development was an important point of departure in initiatives to create a new urban policy/strategy/perspective/framework after 2002, but by mid-2006, several versions of the document had been produced, with no finality. Seemingly, the urban–rural debate, concerns about rapid urbanization, and questions of spatial equity were again surfacing. In 2005, a 'Geographic Spread' Programme was insti-tuted in the government's Programme of Action, which appeared to contradict the NSDP. Although the notion of geographic spread was used here as a way of encompassing a range of spatial programmes, some departments gave consider-able attention to ways of generating development on the periphery. Economic inequalities and differentiation between core and peripheral areas were equated to divides between the so-called 'first' and 'second' economies (or formal and informal: see Chapter 14) – a rather emotive analysis, given the significance of informal eco-nomic activities in urban areas.

By the time of writing in mid-2006, the debate had evolved further, with some accommodation between the different sides. The NSDP was under review, and was being modified to include a commitment to securing some 24 urban nodes (some of which were declining), which were important in terms of servicing a rural hinterland as well as their own populations. Plans to restore the rural integrity of historically homeland areas were also under consideration, particularly given the persistence of large numbers of people in these areas. The Department of Trade and Industry – which had pushed the idea of geographic spread – had published a draft Regional Industrial Development Strategy (DTI 2006), which sought ways of promoting devel-opment in peripheral areas with 'potential'. It drew on the language of the NSDP and committed itself to European Union-style regional development strategies, empha-sizing development on the basis of regional strengths and potentials, and focused on supply-side support such as infrastructure development. It explicitly contrasted its orientation with apartheid-style industrial decentralization strategy and incentives; it proposed to work through regional growth coalitions and with strategic partners. Yet aspects of the detail of strategy, including the production of factory buildings, cash grants to relocating firms or ones providing employment in areas of 'significant market failure' (DTI 2006: 78) do seem to hark back to past policy and seem to con-tradict the main aim of the NSDP – to avoid investment in economic infrastructure in low-growth areas.

It seems likely that policy in this arena will continue to evolve, reflecting real tensions in policy. Tensions over these issues are complex and are linked to both dif-ferences among technocrats and policy analysts within government and its advisers, as well as to contradictory pressures from various interests including politicians rep-resenting ANC's large constituency in rural areas and marginal regions, and voices representing the large cities, such as the South African Cities Network and policy groupings linked to business, such as the Centre for Development and Enterprise.

SPATIAL DEVELOPMENT INITIATIVES

Although the spatial development initiatives programme was relatively short-lived (1996–2000/1), it has been subject to several assessments and considerable atten- tion in the literature (e.g. Development South Africa 1998; Altman 2001; Adebayo and Todes 2003; Bond 2002; Soderbaum and Taylor 2003; de Beer and Arkwright 2003; SAGJ 2001; Rogerson 2001). It has also been the basis for a broader process of transcontinental planning (Figure 5.4), with the establishment of the Regional SDI Programme stretching into the SADC region, and has been explored by the UN- Habitat as a mechanism for regional development (Adebayo and Todes 2003).

SDIs were conceived in 1996 as a way of generating growth and investment in regions where there is significant potential for growth which had not previously been realized for historical and political reasons. The intention was to 'unlock' this potential through targeted interventions in improving infrastructure, and in facilitat- ing new investment, leading to sustainable job creation and the generation of new wealth in the area (Jourdan 1998). The SDI concept was based on the experience of the Maputo Development Corridor, which had begun in 1995, and was centred on the reconstruction of the Maputo harbour and the restoration of the transport axis between Maputo and Gauteng (Crush and Rogerson 2001).

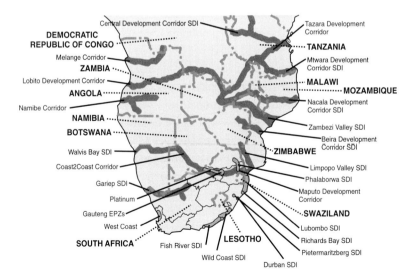

Figure 5.4 Spatial Development Initiatives

SDIs were seen as ways of 'fast-tracking' development in particular locations through the removal of bottlenecks to investment (usually the absence of infrastructure and the presence of institutional barriers to investment), and the identification of major anchor projects which would result in large-scale private-sector investment in the area. Linked to the GEAR strategy, they were intended to promote export-led, internationally competitive growth, drawing on and further beneficiating underused local resources (Platzky 2000). Both the construction phase, and the downstream effect of anchor projects, were expected to create significant employment opportunities, as well as spaces for small firms to develop through linkages or as a consequence of the multiplier process.

SDIs were as much about new forms of integrated governance as about regional development (Platzky 2000). In the original conception, a special project team would be set up for some 12 to 18 months, after which the project would be handed over to provincial or local government. This project team would have considerable flexibility and could move across and beyond bureaucratic boundaries. Support structures were also created at national level to enable SDIs to be effective. These included a political champion (usually a provincial or national government minister); a coordinating committee linked to a cabinet cluster (comprising project managers, senior government and parastatal officials); and a special unit in the Department of Trade and Industry and later in the Development Bank of Southern Africa.

Some 11 SDIs were identified throughout South Africa (Figure 5.4): the Maputo Development Corridor, the Phalaborwa SDI, the West Coast Investment Initiative, the Fish River SDI, the Wild Coast SDI, the Richards Bay SDI, Durban and Pietermaritzburg, the Lubombo SDI, Platinum SDI and the Gauteng Special Zones. Both Lubombo and Maputo Development Corridor SDIs were conceived as cross-border initiatives, linking to neighbouring countries. Most SDIs were in rural areas or smaller towns, but SDIs were also used in cities, at times as a way of modernizing their industrial base (Altman 2001). The focus on SDIs varied, depending on their perceived regional strengths and potentials. In the original thinking on SDIs, attention was given to manufacturing investment, but was later broadened to include other economic activities, particularly agriculture and tourism, in response to criticisms that SDIs did little to alleviate poverty (Crush and Rogerson 2001).

The impact of SDIs has been uneven. While several SDIs were successful in developing infrastructure and in dealing with other 'blockages', private sector development was slow to follow. Overall, growth and private-sector investment were disappointing, with estimates of employment growth of 100,000 and an investment of R164,777million by 2000 (Crush and Rogerson 2001) – most of it in the Maputo Development Corridor. Platzky (2000) attributes slow growth to the macroeconomic environment of the time and the impact of global economic crises. Not all SDIs had potential – some were chosen for political reasons. Nor did the SDI model fit well with the development conditions in all SDIs. In some places, such as Durban, differences between local, provincial and national conceptions of the SDI meant that it never got off the ground. In many rural SDIs, it took several years to address blockages, and in some cases these remain – a reflection of the complexity of local politics and contestation (Kepe *et al.* 2001). Nevertheless some SDIs grew at rates significantly faster than that of the national economy. Compared with many other SDIs, the Maputo Development Corridor stands out as a significant success, with the creation of some 65,000 temporary and permanent jobs and growth rates of 7 per cent per annum (de Beer 2001).

The dominance of resource-based industrialization, the high cost of investment relative to jobs, the temporary and low-skilled nature of jobs, and the limited local linkages created, are common criticisms of the SDI experience (Bond 2002; Taylor 2001; Pretorius 2001; Walker 2001). Thus in contrast to European-style 'bottom-up' regional development, South African SDIs might seem closer to traditional 'growth pole' regional development strategies (Soderbaum and Taylor 2003), or even to traditional colonial extractive models. In fact Jourdan (2003), one of the main architects of the programme, argued that this was the original conception, although local linkages and spin-offs might need to be planned to improve political acceptance of projects. Most private-sector investment has been minerals-based (Altman 2001), reflecting the historical strength of this sector in the South African economy and its international competitiveness (Walker 2001). Most SDIs however initiated programmes to develop local linkages, promote downstream activities, and to encourage more labour-intensive and high-skill activities (Altman 2001). Several SDIs also initiated broader development programmes, including training and skills upgrading, development of small-scale programmes, and promotion of small firms. The Lubombo SDI, for example, was successful in eradicating malaria in its area, providing infrastructure in a remote area, generating small-scale economic activities and local employment, and in establishing a nature reserve which combines conservation with development that benefits, rather than excludes, communities. In contrast to 'growth pole' policies, SDIs have worked largely with regional strengths, although some SDIs such as Coega and Maputo are closer to this model with their imported aluminium and potential steel plants. Even here, however, they link to the development of local resources in the form of harbours.

From an institutional perspective, SDIs as special agencies were generally highly effective. Although they were seen as a short-term measure, most were in place for much longer than intended. For the most part, SDIs attracted a dedicated and committed staff, who were prepared to push for development in their areas. They added capacity at a time when provincial and local governments were still being established, and were often weak. They had the flexibility to link to a range of stakeholders, to different levels of government, and to communities. Nevertheless, insufficient support was given to SDIs at national level, and poor integration between departments and unresolved policy conflicts impeded development. SDIs were also vulnerable to politics and individuals, and in some cases, relationships with provincial and local government were poor. Thus successes were not necessarily sustained as political leadership changed, or once the programme ended. Nevertheless, some projects managed to create a longer-term institutional base, or to carry their work forward in new institutional forms (Adebayo and Todes 2003).

The experience of SDIs in South Africa shows the tensions between growth and equity in spatial policy, and between a narrowly focused emphasis on 'delivery' versus a more holistic approach. Thus, while there is an acknowledgement of the need to move beyond the 'mineral energy complex' that has historically dominated the South African economy, most SDIs have remained relatively narrowly based in their economic focus. Nevertheless, the area-based approach in many cases attracted energetic planners who attempted to generate more integrated and wide-ranging development. The short-term focus of SDIs however appears to have constrained longer-term development potentials, and it is not clear that they will necessarily be realized in future.

CONCLUSION

Planning has occupied an important place in initiatives to promote regional development and to establish more coordinated ways of governing. Spatial planning in particular has increasingly come to the fore as a way of making decisions on key directions for development and in promoting 'joined-up government'. Spatial planners or urban and regional planners have been present in many of these processes, but they have not always led them, nor have they occupied singular positions in these contexts. Rather, they have been part of a more general grouping with skills in the broader field, and individuals have often been drawn on as a consequence of their particular history or knowledge base.

Although forms of regional planning appear to be on the rise, planning confronts tremendous difficulties at this scale. The 'regional question' is a profoundly political one and initiatives to make decisions through spatial planning processes have been difficult to carry through. Similarly, integrated planning contributions to 'joined-up government' confront the power of line departments, while special initiatives, such as SDIs, are often short-lived. Nevertheless, the appeal of these ideas does appear to be growing, and in the coming years, it will be interesting to see how much 'decentralized centralism' comes to depend on these forms of planning.

PART 3

DISCOURSES OF PLANNING

INTRODUCTION: INTERNATIONAL DEBATES

Debates and positions within planning internationally and in South Africa are being shaped and reshaped by an intersecting network of shifting discourses on big issues such as social transformation, the economy, the environment and space.

The origins of modern planning are to be found in the ideals of social reform and, despite planning's frequent tendency towards the technocratic, the idea of a link between planning and the broader cause of social change has persisted. Ideas of social change are, however, contested and changing, and so the relationship between planning and discourses of social transformation is a complex one. The 'cultural turn', for example, has had a significant recent impact on the ways in which the social goals of planning have been conceptualized. The work of Leonie Sandercock in particular represents the contemporary challenge as that of building the new multicultural city (referred to metaphorically as 'cosmopolis'). It is work that draws on current debates around citizenship, identity, gender, race and sexuality. This 'progressive postmodernism' has a substantive normative concern – that of supporting and promoting difference – which differentiates it, at least partly, from the so-called 'collaborative' approach which directs attention to procedural equity, and which is premised on a faith in the power of dialogue, open debate and deliberative democracy to produce just outcomes. The cultural turn has not entirely displaced a political economy or post-/neo-Marxist perspective – there are still voices within the planning debate that direct attention back to the material basis of inequality and injustice, and that challenge the privileging of identity politics and/or procedural equity (see especially the work of Susan Fainstein which argues for the conscious creation of a materially constituted 'just city').

The 'multicultural', 'collaborative' and 'just city' perspectives are three influential streams of contemporary planning thought that are derived from very different positions on what a good society or a good city would look like. The importance of these positions to planning practice is, however, secondary to the influence of shifting 'political ideology'. In the 1980s, the harsh logic of economic rationality eroded the connection between planning and hopes of social justice but, in the 1990s, and the early years of the new millennium, 'a softer form of neo-liberalism' (Tont 2005: 198) emerged in many parts of the world that has supported the re-emergence of concerns for social justice and transformation, albeit in muted tones. 'Third way' leaders such as Clinton, Blair and Schröder have, for example, claimed a social agenda which they have expressed in the use of terms such as 'community', 'part-nerships', 'choice', 'social capital', 'social cohesion' and 'inclusion'.

The one big idea of the 'third way' is of 'integration', or 'joining up' (to use Tony Blair's term). At its most progressive, this idea is concerned with strengthening the bonds of community but, in practice, it has had to do mainly with the managerial and technical task of providing more coordinated action by government. The notion of integration resonates with a longstanding leitmotif within planning (traditionally cap-tured in ideas such as holism, comprehensiveness and integrated systems) and so has been enthusiastically taken up by planners. The South African notion of inte-grated development planning is but one example of a new wave of international practices built around the idea of integration. Increasingly, planning internationally is seen as an instrument of governance that builds the linkages and coordination among the multiple agents (within and outside the state) that are involved in policy-making and coordination.

While the literature on planning (almost entirely produced in the global North) is strong on themes such as diversity, dialogue and integration, there is scarce ref-erence to the 'big social issues' of our time such as poverty, HIV/AIDS, and safety and security. The exceptions are mainly in the few contributions from the South. Hsu (2005), for example, argues that the link between social vulnerability and mobility is key to understanding the spread of HIV/AIDS, while Landman (2004) writes from South Africa of the relationship between gated communities, social exclusion, citi-zenship and democracy, and de Souza (2005) provides a Brazilian perspective on the vexed problem of planning in a city where millions of citizens live in settlements controlled by drug barons.

Discourses on social transformation are closely linked (and usually led by) dis-courses on the economy. The world economy of the late twentieth and early twenty-first centuries is framed largely within the discourse on globalization. As Soja (2000: 190) put it, globalization is the 'millennium metaphor for practically every-thing that has been happening almost everywhere'. Neo-liberalism is the ideology that rationalizes or naturalizes globalization (and especially the role and power of global capital). It is concerned with limiting the role of the state and of state planning to that of supporting the conditions for accumulation by global capital. The idea of neo-liberalism provides a potent analysis and critique of the contemporary super-structure of global power, and of the limitations of planning, but is sometimes used too crudely, and in ways that obscure the shifts in ideology and policy that are hap-pening within the broad framework of global capitalism, and that may provide opportunities for progressive action by the state and civil society.

From about the mid-1990s there has been a discernible reaction to the extremes of 1980s neo-liberalism. The 'third way' may have been a muted response, but its focus on rebuilding community and collaborative networks (in response to the atomism of the 80s) has, for example, supported the partnership-based regeneration of previously declining cities. It might be premature to talk of a 'post-Washington consensus' – as the previous Vice President of the World Bank, Joseph Stiglitz, has done – but there has been a shift away from the traditional stabilization policies of the World Bank and the IMF towards a more transformative focus on institutional development and poverty mitigation. The (at least partial) reframing of mainstream ideology has, arguably, opened the way for the return of governments with an overtly progressive agenda – in Latin America, most notably – and for the open use of ideas such as the 'developmental state' which ascribes to government a leading role in development.

These recent shifts may provide a reprieve for planning (or, at least, for *state-led* planning) but the relationship between planning and concerns for the economy remains ambiguous. The perception of planning as a constraint on economic growth persists in many places. In a context such as South Africa, for example, where the government is strongly committed to accelerated economic growth (a target of 6 per cent per annum in this instance), planning, and planning systems, will be criticized. However, planning is also seen as an instrument that may actively support and promote growth and development. A strong link has emerged, for example, between the ideas of long-range strategic planning for cities (an idea originally borrowed from the corporate sector) and the promotion of global competitiveness. In large cities especially, planning is increasingly viewed as an instrument to deliver both the hard infrastructure and the social consensus needed for successfully positioning a city within the world economy. Planning also supports the current focus on urban mega-projects to attract foreign investment and tourism, and the use of heritage and cultural uniqueness for the same reason.

There are trade-offs between global city or competitiveness agendas, and concerns for equity and justice, and the way in which these trade-offs are played are hugely important for the future development of cities, and often very controversial (as in the case of cities such as Johannesburg and Mumbai, for example). In contexts such as the European Union spatial concepts such as polycentricity and territorial cohesion represent an attempt to balance goals of equity and competitiveness (Faludi 2004).

Another constraint on a purely economic agenda is the contemporary discourse on the natural environment. The Brundtland Commission's famous 1987 report, *Our Common Future* (WCED 1987), brought together discourses on social justice, the economy and the environment within the framing idea of sustainability. In the 1990s 'planning for sustainability' (and the derivative 'planning for sustainable cities') became a powerful new rationality for planning (Rydin 1999; Murdoch 2004). The 1992 United Nations Conference on Development and the Environment, held in Rio de Janeiro, produced Local Agenda 21 which made the connection between the abstract ideals of sustainability and concrete concerns with planning and implementation at the local level. This connection, and also the link between social and temporal justice on the one hand, and economic growth on the other, was reaffirmed at the World Summit on Sustainable Development (WSSD) held in Johannesburg in September 2002.

The idea of sustainability has fed into the planning discourse on integration by shifting the environmental debate from its previously narrow focus on natural process towards an understanding of the interrelatedness of environment, economy and society (Pieterse 2004b). The connection between sustainability and institutional integration (so important in the case of South African planning) is clear in the emergent discourse of the World Bank, for example, which places local institutional development at the centre of the sustainability debate. Sustainability has, however, also connected with traditions of spatial planning, providing the rationale for ideals such as the compact city and the new urbanism. Since becoming a widely accepted political objective, sustainability has given planning a more technocratic and depoliticized appearance – the sustainability ideal is increasingly discussed in relation to objective measurement, indicators and appraisals, rather than in terms of social values and mobilization.

Discourses on space, and on spatial planning, are largely derivative of the broader discourses on society, economy and the environment. As indicated, the discourse on sustainability has been translated into conceptions of city form which has restored a strong normative conception to spatial planning. Coming from a very different perspective is the collaborative planning movement which has also shown a renewed interest in spatial planning (e.g. Vigar et al. 2000). For Healey (2005: 5), 'the core of a planning focus is the interconnection of people and place, of activities and territories' – an interconnection that is sharply revealed in the collaborative, multi-actor processes that are involved in producing the new generation of strategic spatial plans. Healey (2004: 45) identified the new spatial practices in Europe (framed by ideas such as polycentricity, territorial cohesion and hypermobility) as 'exemplars of new ways of thinking about place and space'. There are, however, also more critical perspectives on the new spatial practices that show how concepts of space and place are produced within particular configurations of power and also how 'new spatial ideas are becoming the source of new struggles at different spatial scales' (Dabinett and Richardson 2005).

As shown above, the international planning debate is vibrant and continually shifting in response to broader discursive movement. A key issue, however, is how the international discourse is translated into specific and concrete contexts such as South Africa at particular moments in time. The chapters that follow focus therefore on the global–local link in the formation and evolution of discourse.

CHAPTER 6

DISCOURSES OF THE SPATIAL

INTRODUCTION

By 1994, decades of urban spatial planning informed by goals of racial segregation had left their particular imprint on the cities and towns of South Africa (see Chapter 1). Well before the change of government in 1994 there had been a growing critique of these spatial outcomes by progressive planners, and the development of an alternative set of spatial ideas which were intended to integrate cities which had been segregated and fragmented by apartheid planning (see Chapter 2). This chapter will review attempts in the 1990s and beyond to develop and implement 'post-apartheid' spatial plans in a number of South Africa's larger cities. It will argue that in a context in which the 'hard infrastructure' (Healey 1997; Vigar *et al.* 2000) of the new planning system has been slow in the making, spatial plans have been shaped largely by the 'soft infra-structure' of planning discourses and the initiatives of particular individuals and groups, but also by the increasingly dominant demands of private investors. The chapter will further argue that the incorporation of spatial planning into the new integrated development planning process, while potentially improving the effectiveness of these plans, has in fact resulted in a dilution of the concept of spatial planning such that, as in other parts of the world (Vigar and Healey 1999), it is now seen more as the spatial coordinator of other sectoral plans rather than one of the informants of these plans.

This chapter will first describe the debates that gave rise to the emergence of particular forms of urban spatial planning in post-apartheid South Africa and the shifts that have occurred in this thinking in the years since 1994. It will then consider some of the factors that have bedevilled the implementation of these plans.

RESPONDING TO THE SPATIAL IMPRINT OF THE APARTHEID CITY

Todes (2006) has argued that although apartheid-style urban segregation is not unique to South Africa (see Abu-Lughod 1980), and several studies have shown the local origins of urban segregation (McCarthy 1991), the violence of state policy after 1948 meant that considerable academic work was devoted to analyses and critiques of the apartheid city (see collections by Lemon 1991; Smith 1992). Research on Group Areas removals (Hart and Pirie 1984; Western 1981) showed

the way in which they fragmented communities, marginalized their economic activities and undermined their participation in the economy. These removals located
people in newly planned suburbs (termed 'townships'), which allowed them poor
access to urban services and facilities, raised their transport costs, and sharply
increased levels of crime. Later research further documented the effects of urban
apartheid (Mabin and Smit 1997; Swilling *et al.* 1991; Turok 1994a), and demonstrated the disadvantages faced by the poor on the periphery, especially women,
who were forced to travel long distances to work, while also being responsible for
housework and childcare (Cook 1987).

During the 1980s a small group of University of Cape Town (UCT) planning
academics, operating through the Urban Problems Research Unit, played a central
role in developing alternative spatial proposals for restructuring South African cities.
Their arguments proved to be highly influential in shaping post-apartheid urban spatial policy, initially through the local and national policy forums which were established
after 1994, and in the mid-1990s through the Development Planning Commission
and its various products (see Chapter 3). Other strong influences on post-apartheid
planning, in particular the more process-oriented 'urban management' approach, are
less evident in the spatial thinking which emerged, but have had an important impact
on the functioning of spatial planning within government (Chapters 3 and 4).

Influenced by the urbanist critique of modern town planning by writers such as
Christopher Alexander, Lewis Mumford, Jane Jacobs, Leon Krier and David Crane, the
UCT-based academics criticized South African planning not only for its racial informants, but also for its application of inappropriate modernist planning ideas (Todes
2006; Watson 2002a). In the latter half of the 1980s these academics produced a
number of publications which framed the planning problem of metropolitan Cape
Town, and other South African cities, as lying in its inequitable and inefficient spatial
structure (Dewar and Uytenbogaardt 1991). This, they argued, not only exacerbated
problems such as poverty and unemployment, but also impacted negatively on the use
of valuable natural resources, particularly agricultural land on the urban edge. Largely
through the influence of this group of academics, but often interpreted in ways not
intended by them, a set of spatial concepts came to dominate plans prepared for most
of the major South African cities in the years after 1994 (Turok 1994b).

The central concepts of corridors (systems of public-transport-based movement flanked by high residential densities and mixed use), urban edges to contain
sprawl and encourage densification, new nodes or centres in areas deprived of
commerce and services, and open space systems, were not entirely new. They are
present in earlier spatial planning ideas which had evolved almost entirely in the
global North. The idea of containing urban development through the holding of open
space on the urban edge had appeared long before in Abercrombie's 1944 plan for
London and its green belt, and before that in the ideas of Ebenezer Howard and

Raymond Unwin (see Hall 1988). It is compatible with the classic Abercrombie tradition of viewing the city as a self-contained object set within the 'container' of the landscape (Graham and Healey 1999: 636–37). The strategy of concentrating development along public-transit corridors had featured in early plans for cities such as Copenhagen and Vienna. The design tradition of new urbanism (Box 6.1), with its emphasis on defined edges, pedestrian movement systems, formative public

Box 6.1 New urbanism influences in South African planning

Jill Grant's (2006) book, *Planning the Good Community: New Urbanism in Theory and Practice,* describes how, in the 1970s, a particular group of writers and planning practitioners based in the United States and in Europe developed a critique of modernist planning. They argued that post-war planning approaches had produced cities which suffered from sprawl, monofunctional and monotonous 'bedroom' suburbs, car dependence and the erosion of public space. Instead they promoted a vision of cities with fine-grained mixed-use, mixed housing types, compact form, an attractive public realm, pedestrian-friendly streetscapes, defined centres and edges and varying transport options (page 8). The South African critique of modernist planning identified the same problems as having emerged in South African cities, and drew as well on the writings of Mumford, Jacobs, Krier and Alexander to argue for urban environments with the same qualities promoted by the new urbanists. However, during the 1970s South Africa was experiencing a high degree of intellectual isolation, and this, together with the obviously different context characterized by poverty, led to a particularly South African brand of new urbanism (see Dewar and Uytenbogaardt 1991). Moreover the precedent which inspired South African new urbanism lay in part in an admiration of European and medieval towns, but more directly in an appreciation of the positive urban qualities found in the older (nineteenth-century) parts of Cape Town.

As a result there are some subtle differences between local and international versions. The South African urban vision is particularly concerned about the integration of local areas into larger city systems. Public transport systems are one means of integration, and in this sense the local vision is closer to the transit-oriented development (TOD) variant of international new urbanism, than to the spatially more 'closed' versions such as traditional neighbourhood design (TND) and the urban village concept. But local areas can also be tied into city systems through hierarchies of 'lines' and 'points', which can take the form of grids spanning the whole city. The objective here is to create equitable access to 'urban opportunities' for a poor population moving around largely on foot. A further important difference lies in the local concept of 'minimalism', which suggests that the role of the planner is to indicate the minimum 'clues' to urban development (usually through elements of public space) to which individuals and groups respond by providing their own shelter requirements and spaces. This is very different from the tendency in America for new urbanism to produce fully designed and built neighbourhoods and/or detailed design codes controlling all aspects of the built environment.

spaces, higher densities and mixed land use (see Calthorpe 1994) can be traced from the work of Leon Krier in the mid-1970s (Mandanipour 1996) and manifests itself in the increasing number of plans for 'neo-traditional' environments. Toronto, for example, in the period 1989 to 1992, adopted metropolitan plans dominated by the concept of the 'intensified city'. High-density development was proposed in order to reduce car use and the urbanization of rural land, and car-oriented retail strips were to be transformed into pedestrian and transit-conducive 'main streets' with continuous store facades and upper floor apartments (Filion 1999). These ideas had much in common with what was becoming known in the 1980s international literature as the 'compact city' approach (see Breheny 1992) which was also rationalized as a more environmentally sustainable way of planning cities. The fact that these ideas were also emerging in the international literature in the late 1980s and early 1990s served to lend legitimacy to the UCT planning academics' ideas (Todes 2006; Watson 2002a).

The notion of spatial integration found easy alliance with the new political goals of racial integration (although to assume a causative connection between the two was highly simplistic) and the administrative uniting of racially based government institutions, and hence the new spatial model quickly found its way into post-apartheid city plans and into national level policy documents and legislation. The 1994 Reconstruction and Development Programme (RDP) of the new government called for the 'need to break down the apartheid geography through land reform, more compact cities, decent public transport' (page 83), promoting 'densification and unification of the urban fabric' (page 86), redressing imbalances, promoting housing close to work and 'access to employment and urban resources'. It is perhaps not surprising then that these ideas were also evident in the 1994 Housing White Paper and in the principles of the first new, but interim, planning legislation, the 1995 Development Facilitation Act.[1]

The 1996 Metropolitan Spatial Development Framework for Cape Town (see Figure 6.1) reflected the influence of these national policy statements, but also of UCT planning graduates who had moved into Cape Town local government and consulting firms. The use of the term 'framework' in the title was intended to bring the plan more in line with the supposedly more flexible and facilitative structure plans of the UK, but in practice it retained elements of blueprint planning. It contained four spatial strategies: an urban edge, a metropolitan open space system, a new node (or CBD) located centrally to the residential areas which had been created during apartheid, and a set of demarcated corridors following the main metropolitan movement routes.[2] The plan claimed that this would achieve social and physical goals of equity and access (through the more even distribution of nodes across the city) and integration (through the corridors which were to link the richer and poorer parts of the city, and which would concentrate people from physically divided residential areas

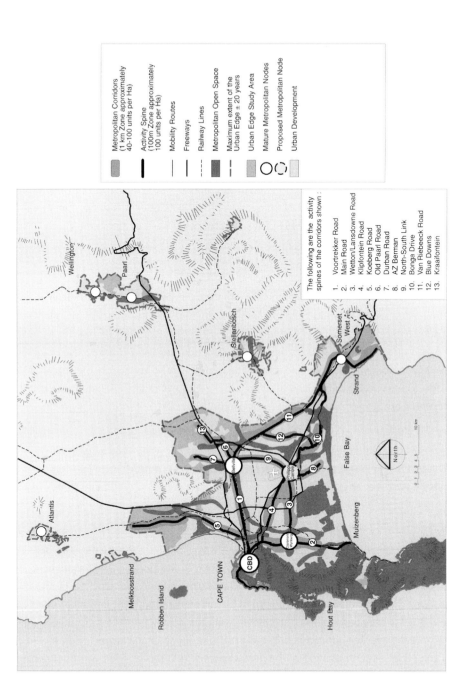

Figure 6.1 The Cape Town Metropolitan Spatial Development Framework

The following are the activity spines of the corridors shown :

1. Voortrekker Road
2. Main Road
3. Wetton/Lansdowne Road
4. Klipfontein Road
5. Koeberg Road
6. Old Paarl Road
7. Durban Road
8. AZ Berman
9. North-South Link
10. Bonga Drive
11. Van Riebeeck Road
12. Blue Downs
13. Kraaifontein

Metropolitan Corridors
(1 km Zone approximately
40-100 units per Ha)

Activity Spine
(100m Zone approximately
100 units per Ha)

Mobility Routes

Freeways

Railway Lines

Metropolitan Open Space

Maximum extent of the
Urban Edge ± 20 years

Urban Edge Study Area

Mature Metropolitan Nodes

Proposed Metropolitan Node

Urban Development

onto a commercial and public transport 'seam'). The concept of the integrated city was thus counterpoised to the segregated city of apartheid.

In Durban, the earliest attempt at countering apartheid planning emerged from a private-sector-led initiative (the Tongaat Hullett Planning Forum) in 1989. The spatial concepts of corridors, nodes and densification (presented as 'beads on a string' rather than as a continuous intense corridor) were evident in this plan and were applied to restructuring the wealthier north coast area of Durban and the poorer industrial corridor to the south of the city (Todes 2002). These ideas found their way into subsequent municipal planning for the whole Durban metropolitan area in the form of the 1997 Durban Spatial Development Framework and the subsequent Metropolitan Spatial Development Framework of 1999. These spatial plans were similar to the Cape Town one in their adoption of the strategies of nodes, corridors, open space systems and densification. They were also similar to early 1990s plans in Gauteng: the Interim Strategic Framework for the Central Witwatersrand also used ideas of corridors, nodes and compaction. There was less emphasis in the earlier Durban plans on an urban edge as the extended ring of informal settlements on the metropolitan periphery made such definition difficult. However, the more recent (2002) SDF defines such an edge in order to guide service investment: the edge defines the point beyond which density is so low that investment in infrastructure would be unduly expensive. The edge is also used to define land as either urban or rural and different categories of service level are linked to each of these categorizations.

SHIFTS IN SPATIAL PLANNING DISCOURSE AFTER THE MID-1990S

The switch to the market-friendly macroeconomic strategy termed Growth, Employment and Redistribution (or GEAR) in 1996 (Chapter 3) influenced spatial planning frameworks in subtle but important ways. In brief, the arguments for strong state intervention to restructure cities in favour of the poor, and to allocate well-located public land – often situated near wealthy residential and commercial areas – to lower-income housing developments, became less prominent in the late 1990s, and greater attention was paid to working with the spatial trends set by private capital investment. The tendencies in the 1990s in many of the larger cities towards commercial decentralization and multinodalism was often at odds with the idea of encouraging high-density, mixed-use environments along public transport corridors and led to competing notions of corridors as freeways with gated shopping malls and industrial estates alongside, but separated, from them. As Todes (2006) argues, the ideal of urban integration began to recede, although much of the language of compaction remained.

At the national level the development, during the 1990s, of various policy documents and draft legislation showed the tension between the older spatial discourse of compaction, reintegration, restructuring and redistribution and the newer spatial discourse which, in part, responds to the needs of private investors, urban competitiveness and the need by municipalities to balance their budgets. These two positions came to co-exist uneasily in policy documents as well as in the second generation of city-wide spatial plans.

The first major national statement on a new urban policy was the 1995 Urban Development Strategy, which broadly embraced the idea of urban integration but did not address inequalities in urban land markets or the need to locate lower-income people in more accessible urban locations (Bond et al. 1996). It broadly endorsed the compaction–integration model, but moved away from it to some extent. It refers to the 'end of the monocentric city', and argues that planners can only harness urban development, not completely change its spatial form. Reference is made to the polycentric nature of Johannesburg and other metropolitan areas. This position was strengthened by a concern to establish financially sustainable and effective local government, capable of service delivery. An unwillingness to challenge vested property interests, and thus the source of rates income and economic growth more generally, went along with this approach.

The Urban Development Strategy, which had initially been driven by the RDP Office, was subsequently given over to the Department of Housing (see Chapter 3). This Department's focus on housing delivery, under a new and inexperienced Minister of Housing, meant that it was not given priority. Moreover, the closure of the RDP Office meant that it was difficult to impose a cross-cutting spatial logic on other national departments. When the Urban Development Strategy was replaced by the Urban Development Framework in 1997, the language of urban spatial restructuring remained, but no measures were put in place to implement it or to direct the spatial outcomes of national spending departments. In fact, the form of post-1994 housing policy, which promoted the low-density distribution of low-income housing on urban peripheries and reinforced older apartheid patterns of development, made the implementation of the compaction model almost impossible (Royston 2003; Todes 2006).

The next attempt to direct urban spatial planning from the national level emerged through a process which had been provided for in the 1995 interim planning legislation, the Development Facilitation Act (DFA). The two policy discussion documents (a Green Paper in 1999 and a White Paper in 2001) produced by the DFA's Development Planning Commission (Chapter 3) promoted the spatial principles of the urban compaction and restructuring models, as well as the concepts of 'minimalist' rather than comprehensive planning, and planning led by values (or normative principles). These Papers were intended to form the basis for new planning legislation, but the draft Bill which was later produced in the Department of Land Affairs departed in many important ways from the proposals of the Commission. This draft legislation (the Land Use Management Bill) has since been through several iterations but has come under fire from other government departments concerned with urban and land development for reflecting a top-down, over-detailed and blueprint-style approach to planning.

The set of normative spatial principles in Chapter 1 of the 1995 DFA thus remains as the legal source to guide the spatial content of planning. However, research aimed at assessing the impact of these principles suggests that their effect has been limited (Todes 2006). They have been interpreted as only applying in special cases (such as RDP projects) rather than to more general plans and decisions. Moreover, they are so generally stated that they are often misunderstood by local public professionals and decision-makers and are used inappropriately. The establishment by the DFA of legalistically based planning bodies such as the Development Tribunals, intended to fast-track post-apartheid urban change, has in some cases backfired: where many Tribunal members are non-planners then there is little understanding of the spatial principles of the DFA and a tendency to use these bodies to push through large development projects.

A lack of capacity at the local level, and particularly outside of the metropolitan areas, has meant that planners have tended to look for simple 'rule-book' prescriptions rather than trying to apply the normative values set out in the DFA to develop local spatial frameworks. Furthermore, frustration by provincial governments and other national government departments at the lack of progress in producing final national planning policy and legislation has resulted in some provinces developing their own planning legislation, and the national Department of Provincial and Local Government has produced its own set of requirements for spatial plans which form part of integrated development plans.

SECOND GENERATION CITY-WIDE SPATIAL PLANS

Within the metropolitan areas, newly created as single-tier 'unicities' in 2000, a second generation of spatial frameworks has begun to emerge which reflects the tension between the first generation of spatial ideas and the more contemporary concerns of accommodating private investors and addressing the upgrade requirements of at least some of the existing poorer areas, all within a macroeconomic policy which continues to lean towards neo-liberalism. The newer plans refer to the persistence of the apartheid spatial forms in cities and the continued marginalization of the poor in remote locations on the urban edge as a result of the form of the housing subsidy. Proposals to integrate and compact the major cities, using ideas such as corridors, nodes and growth boundaries, remain in these plans but they are less radical in terms of attempting to move the poor into central locations or direct business to the poorer parts of the cities, and some of them are explicit about the need to focus public investment in those parts of the city which have potential for economic growth and the generation of a better rates income. New terms such as 'sustainability' and 'being globally competitive' appear in the plans. Generally, however, there is a tendency to apply what has become the accepted wisdom of urban spatial planning (corridors, nodes, edges) in unthinking and often inappropriate ways and often in the almost complete absence of an understanding of socio-economic and spatial trends on the ground.

The 2005 Metropolitan Spatial Development Framework for the metropolitan area of Tshwane, part of the Gauteng urban region, is an example of this second generation of spatial plans. The plan was prepared by internal planning staff of the municipality in coordination with other line-function departments and seemingly, as well, with political support. It was approved by the Tshwane Council in November 2005. The long-term spatial strategy is cast in the language of reintegration and restructuring and the spatial elements are the familiar corridors, nodes, open space system and urban edge. Emphasis is given to the need to develop and integrate the poor northern part of the metropolitan area which consists largely of informal settlements with few economic opportunities and inadequate infrastructure and social facilities. There is also an emphasis on the need to address the problems of the declining CBD which has been affected by decentralization and blight. Part 2 of the plan refers to 'the spatial alignment of priorities within the municipality'. Here it becomes clear that the focus of expenditure in the initial period will be on three parts of the city: the economically strong and wealthy south (the 'New Urban Region') where the promotion of growth, it is claimed, will benefit the city as a whole; the 'Capital Core', or CBD, to enhance the natural, cultural and tourist assets of the metro; and the 'Zone of Choice' which is that part of the poor north immediately north of the CBD – a low-density, formally developed area with well-developed nodes of economic activity. The view is that promoting economic development and investing heavily in services in the rest of the poor north is unwise as households will not be able to afford these services and non-payment will bankrupt the municipality. Essentially this is a strategy that builds on the economically stronger parts of the metropolitan area and defers the issue of redistribution to a later date. Where it differs from some of the earlier plans is in its emphasis on the strategic nature of spatial intervention and its shift towards accepting the spatial logic of the market rather than a strongly welfarist approach.

Another example of the second generation of spatial development frameworks is the new Johannesburg SDF, which takes a step beyond the broad and conceptual spatial framework to more detailed local plans and projects. The SDF has been used

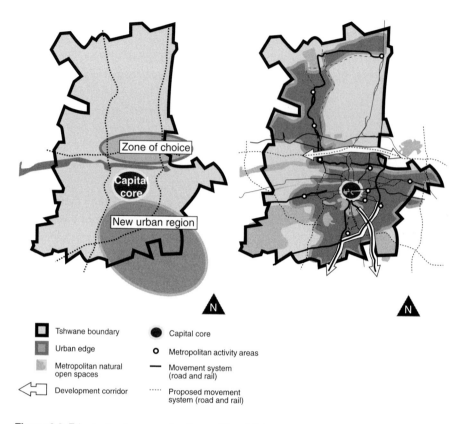

Figure 6.2 Tshwane's urban opportunities and Spatial Development Framework

to guide 11 regional spatial development frameworks and a number of precinct plans, particularly around the stations which will serve the new Gautrain rail system. These plans have provided a level of detail which allows spatial frameworks to be used far more effectively to guide decision-making around public-sector investments and private-sector development applications. The broad concepts of edge, node and corridor remain in the SDF, but the focus is now on developing and implementing very specific density policies across the city, in the form of graded densities around nodes and along movement corridors. In this way both the Gautrain system and the 2010 World Cup have had an important impact on thinking about urban form.

LOCAL SPATIAL PLANS AND PROJECTS

While it is still difficult to evaluate the impact of city-wide spatial plans on urban development,[3] numerous local development projects, usually unrelated to city-wide

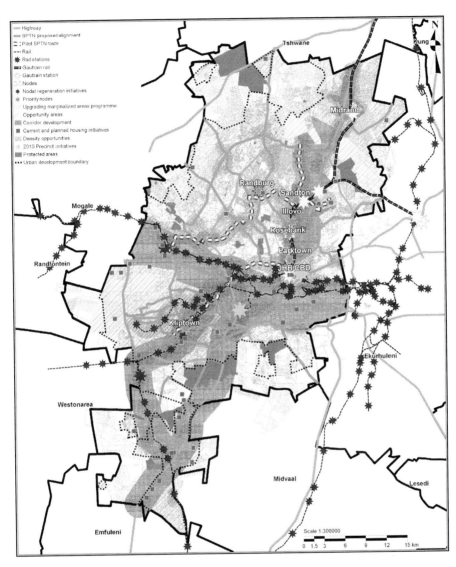

Figure 6.3 Johannesburg Spatial Development Framework

plans, have been shaping cities from within. Some public-sector-led projects began soon after 1994 as part of targeting particularly deprived or war-torn urban areas (what were termed 'Presidential Projects' such as Kathorus in Gauteng, Marconi Beam informal settlement in Cape Town, and Cato Manor in Durban); as part of developing sites previously cleared by Group Areas removals (such as the 2000-hectare development of Cato Manor in Durban – see Box 6.2 – and District Six in Cape Town); and more recently as part of the new national Urban Renewal

Programme (Chapter 3) which targets older township areas or informal 'nodes' within cities (such as Alexandra township in Gauteng, Khayelitsha and Mitchell's Plain in Cape Town and Inanda–KwaMashu–Ntuzuma [INK] in Durban). Significantly, the initiative for many of these projects, and for all of the urban renewal nodes, came from national government which also saw fit to decide on the location of these projects, usually with little regard for municipal spatial plans. Some of these projects have been largely infrastructure driven with the aim of providing basic services as quickly as possible, and the rationality of engineering efficiency tends to have prevailed over that of planning liveable environments.

Box 6.2 The redevelopment of Cato Manor (also see Chapter 8)

During the 1930s and 1940s Cato Manor was a thriving, mixed-race, working-class area some 5 km from the centre of Durban. In 1958 it was declared a White Group Area under apartheid laws, tens of thousands of families were removed, and the area became one of the largest vacant sites in urban South Africa. In the early 1990s, as land invasions onto the site began to occur, the Cato Manor Development Forum, working with a local planning NGO, adopted a policy framework to guide the redevelopment of Cato Manor. In 1995 it was declared a Special Presidential Lead Project and received national, and later European Union, funding. By 2003 the Cato Manor Development Project, restructured as part of the Durban municipality, could claim that bulk infrastructure had been installed, the target of accommodating 150,000 low-income people was in sight, and social and economic facilities had been provided.

In spatial planning terms, the 'compact city', and DFA, principles were followed. The intention was to achieve an intense and integrated environment, containing a full mix of uses. The area was to be structured by activity corridors (carrying public transport) and mixed-use nodes, with densities of 50–200 units per hectare net. Quality public space, to encourage social and informal economic activity, was an important element in the plan. While the project has been generally acclaimed and labelled an international best practice by the UN Commission on Human Settlements, it appears that the spatial vision was not fully achieved. Dewar and Kaplan (2004: 136) note that it is not an intensive mixed-use area, the vibrant nodes and corridors do not exist, densities are lower than planned (primarily due to constraints within the housing subsidy system), and few buses penetrate the area. Reasons are complex and many lie outside of the control of the development agency. For example, it has been difficult to establish intense, mixed-use corridors within the development when there are competing commercial nodes nearby. However, the spatial planning framework has proved useful in terms of achieving the spatial alignment and integration of the various line-function departments in the municipality. Thus the development of the engineering services and housing was able to proceed in a fairly seamless way in the project.

A second type of local project, also public sector driven, has been low-income housing projects funded by the national Department of Housing (Chapters 3 and 9). While South Africa has been much lauded for delivering 1.7 million houses (tiny units on single plots) since 1994, there is also now growing criticism of the location and spatial planning of these projects. Their location on cheaper land on the urban edge, and the low-density, car-oriented and 'dormitory' nature of their layouts, has attracted the accusation that they perpetuate the spatial form of the apartheid city together with the spatial and social marginalization of the poor that this implies, and that the form of delivery and layouts directly contradict the DFA principles. In 2004 the Department of Housing issued a new policy (*Breaking New Ground*) which aimed to produce 'sustainable human settlements'. In spatial terms this quite explicitly states that new developments should be 'compact, mixed land-use, diverse, life-enhancing environments with maximum possibilities for pedestrian movement and transit via safe and efficient public transport in cases where motorized means of movement is imperative' (DOH 2004: 12). Compliance with this directive would bring housing projects more closely in line with the DFA principles, but the first pilot project, the N2 Gateway Project in Cape Town, falls far short of meeting these criteria.

A third type, and the most prevalent form of local plan or project that has been shaping South African cities (as well as those in other parts of the world), is the private-sector-driven, upmarket, commercial and residential developments. Growing economic confidence in South Africa has fuelled a rapid rise in property prices and extensive new investment in property in the major cities. These developments tend to follow the logic of market demand in terms of location: they avoid 'crime and grime' locations and link closely with existing higher-income areas which also have good access and good amenities. As such they have tended to reinforce the older spatial divides between wealthier and poorer parts of cities. Many have adopted the architectural design principles of new urbanism and the semi-privatized spaces inside shopping malls, golf estates, town-house complexes, leisure complexes and commodified 'heritage' sites, echo some of these ideas but depart entirely from the underlying values of sustainability and urban integration in the 'compact city' approach, and the (purported) social agenda of the new urbanism movement. Hence most tend to be highly insular in terms of their relationship to surrounding urban areas, with controlled access points, set in high walls, and fences being the norm. Much of the justification for this spatial form lies in references to high crime rates in South African cities and the need to protect wealthier residents and investors, but the overall impact is one of increasing spatial fragmentation of cities.

An important question is why public-sector planning and the principles expressed in the DFA have had so little impact on these kinds of developments (Chapter 8). Significantly, many of these commercial mega-projects were granted

Figure 6.4 Gated upmarket residential areas

planning permission during the 1990s when the larger cities were governed by several municipalities. It was at the time quite common for developers to 'play off' different local authorities in a city, arguing that their investments would boost the rates income of local governments and make them more 'competitive' than their neighbours or other cities: this was, for example, an important argument put forward in the application for permission to build the huge new Gateway shopping mall (the largest in the southern hemisphere) to the north of Durban. Some of the newer or more laissez-faire municipalities were easily taken in by the lure of large-scale commercial development and smoothed the way for developers (planning permission for the Century City retail, office and residential complex in Cape Town, one of the largest property developments in South Africa, was reportedly processed in a week), but many subsequently found themselves having to pay for large additional infrastructural costs (access roads, water and sanitation) that had not been predicted. Significantly, the DFA principles give little guidance on how to handle large commercial developments such as these.

THE WEAKENING OF SPATIAL PLANNING AND LIMITS TO IMPLEMENTATION

In 1994 planning professionals were in a potentially strong position. They claimed to be able to offer an alternative future for South African cities and some had engaged (even if in a limited way) with communities and political parties about this future. As such they had managed to position themselves as the custodians of urban change in post-apartheid South Africa. Twelve years on there are probably few planners who would make this claim, yet there is no one simple reason for this.

An overarching reason has to do with the changing institutional context within which planners have operated, as well as the failure at national government level to put in place a clearly reformed planning system. This failure of the 'hard infrastructure' of planning could, from one perspective, be interpreted as an advantage: it might have allowed for the emergence of a 'bottom-up' and regionally differentiated approach to planning, or innovative collaborative efforts of the relational kind referred to by Healey (2004). Had there been a strong cadre of well-trained spatial planners in South Africa at the time, this might have been a preferred and possible outcome. But in fact this strength was highly uneven and was largely lacking outside the largest metropolitan areas.

Even today, many of the non-metropolitan municipalities have no more than two or three planners (some have none at all) who have to deal with land-use management and forward planning across very large areas, as well as having to play a role in formulating IDPs. Many of these planners are also young and inexperienced and quickly resort to old rule-book methods or the inappropriate use of spatial concepts when under pressure. Most of the municipalities have expended their efforts on trying to rationalize complex and fragmented land-use management systems from the past, but have been unable to develop innovative approaches which might impact on the rights of landowners, in the absence of a national framework which tackles this constitutional issue. Thinking in the early 1990s about the spatial restructuring of cities paid little attention to the issue of urban land-use management systems and hence a central planning tool has so far been unavailable to support spatial restructuring.

The IDP process, introduced into municipalities in the 1990s (see Chapter 4), has had a 'double-edged' impact on spatial planning. On the one hand, and as discussed elsewhere in this book, it has instituted planning as a central methodology to guide the functioning of municipalities, thus opening up new positions within the IDP process for those trained as planners. On the other hand, the particular methodology adopted for IDPs, largely introduced by the German Aid Agency GTZ, cast spatial plans in the weaker role as simply a mechanism for the spatial coordination of the plans and priorities of other line-function departments, rather than as an input in its own right. Vigar and Healey (1999) point to similar problems in the past for planning in the UK. The statement in 1997 that the IDPs are intended as a process, not a product, and that they are not physical plans but business plans, meant that spatial planning no longer had a potential role as the nexus of spatial integration. The concept of integrated planning implies that a common discourse is adopted by all professionals and departments, and this directly confronts the issue of discursive hegemony. Moreover, any process of integration requires a merging of positions in relation to the dominance of one particular discourse. Early conceptions of the IDP had proposed that the spatial plan act as the 'synthesizing element' (placing spatial planners in an advantageous position), but later conceptions put the budget in this position, thus offering opportunities (to exercise power) to a different set of professionals (Watson 2002a). It could be argued that through the IDP process the urban managerial (or process) approach to planning finally secured dominance over the outcomes-based or urban restructuring approach to planning.

Other reasons as well can be found to explain the fact that South African cities remain spatially unrestructured. A weakened and unreformed spatial planning system has also had to engage with urban areas increasingly shaped by the actions of local and international property developers. The first generation of spatial plans, such as the Cape Town Metropolitan Spatial Development Framework (MSDF), thus proved to be hopelessly naive in their assumption that formal business and upmarket investors would agree to locate in or near poor and marginalized township areas. Turok and Watson (2001) indicate how formal investors in Cape Town have largely avoided such areas and have located instead in those parts of the city that are historically wealthier and better serviced, thus exacerbating the apartheid divide between rich and poor Cape Town. It may be that the second generation of spatial plans, such as that of Tshwane which argues for the support of areas of higher economic potential, are more realistic in this sense but the problem of social and spatial marginalization remains unresolved.

It could also be argued that both earlier and later spatial plans tend to 'drop' spatial concepts such as corridors and nodes onto an urban reality which is highly complex and fluid. As such they fail to engage sufficiently with conditions of everyday life and the survival strategies of the poor in cities, and have promoted spatial strategies which are often at odds with the strategies of marginalized groups. Healey (2004), writing in the global North, has criticized approaches to planning which assume that they can order the dynamic and inherently disorderly nature of cities. This is even more relevant in cities of the global South which are increasingly characterized by informality (Box 6.3) (see also Chapter 14).

Box 6.3 Planned informality?

Yonn Dierwechter (2004) draws on the work of Amin and Thrift to map emerging geographies of the post-apartheid city and the multiple but connected spaces that are emerging relationally in Cape Town. He maps the daily routine of Mama J. who survives by selling cooked maize in one of Cape Town's informal settlements. Her day starts at 2.00 a.m. when she catches a taxi to a farm 150 km away to pick maize and returns by noon to cook and sell it to people coming home from work in the afternoon and evening. Her day ends at 7.00 p.m., having made about R20 profit. Reflecting on the MSDF and its proposal for new economic 'nodes', Dierwechter asks how people such as Mama J. fit in to this? He asks if to enter and trade in the new nodes requires particular subjectivities, bodies and performances? Are the nodes to be peopled by those on their way to an 'economic mainstream', to paying taxes, to being formal and competitive, and to a particular imagination of modernity (page 975). The non-trained, non-disciplined, non-tax-paying, non-entrepreneurial trader simply will not do, argues Dierwechter (Mama J.'s highly variable time schedule and income stream would make it very difficult for her to occupy administered space in the node), and therefore to enter the space of urban development (and the spatial plan) is to be disciplined and produced as a particular kind of human being (page 977). Dierwechter points to the conflict between the 'diagram of power that projects a plan-led vision of the post-apartheid city' (page 978) and the real worlds of informal sellers and their complex time and space geographies.

CONCLUSION

Efforts to spatially restructure the apartheid cities have now been in progress for a decade. South African cities have certainly changed during this period, but many of the characteristics that planners (and government) intended to change through a different spatial vision have persisted (see Turok and Watson 2001). Social and spatial disparities implemented under the apartheid government have essentially been reinforced by market forces, and while the disparities no longer entirely follow racial fault lines, this is still largely the case (Christopher 2005).

CHAPTER 7

DISCOURSES OF SOCIAL TRANSFORMATION

INTRODUCTION

This chapter explores the relationship between post-apartheid planning and discourses on social transformation. As is evident in almost every policy and piece of legislation relating to planning produced after April 1994, the new government has (more or less) consistently seen planning as an integral part of its (evolving) programme of social transformation. The nature of the link between planning and social transformation has, however, been complex and elusive, tempting many planners to fall back into a largely technocratic practice. The chapter deals broadly with the idea of social transformation, but it gives specific attention to the idea of integration, which may be regarded as a key contribution of post-apartheid planning to the wider discourse on transformation. This chapter should therefore be read in conjunction with Chapter 4 which deals with the institutional aspects of integrated development planning.

The ANC came to power in 1994, committed to the ideal of social transformation. It was an ideal described in the opening words of the ANC's election manifesto, known as the RDP Base Document, as 'the building of a democratic, non-racial and non-sexist future' (ANC 1994, paragraph 1.1.1). However, although these words captured a seemingly consensual vision of a transformed society, they glossed over considerable differences within the ANC-led alliance over the desired form and extent of social transformation. The socialist wing of the alliance – represented largely by the Congress of South African Trade Unions (COSATU) and the South African Communist Party (SACP) – looked towards a fundamental restructuring of the relations of production, while the Africanist and business-oriented wings of the movement found common ground in promoting the development of a black bourgeoisie. While the nature of the transformation ideal was contested from the outset, the mode or style of transformation was also a point of divide – a tendency towards 'democratic centralism' (or top-down command) competed with a tradition of grassroots participatory democracy.

The contested nature of transformation, and also the difficulties in tracking a direct link between planning and transformative outcome, makes the subject of this chapter a complex one. Even the more narrowly conceptualized ideal of integration is open to ambiguity and contest, as integration, like transformation, is a slippery concept.

RECONSTRUCTION AND DEVELOPMENT

The RDP was centred around four major objectives: meeting the basic needs of the people; developing human resources; building the economy; and, democratizing the state and society (ANC 1994; RSA 1994). As indicated in Chapter 3, the RDP represented a compromise position within the ANC-led alliance – it was a neo-Keynesian programme of state-led delivery rather than the manifesto for radical social transformation that the left wing of the alliance may have desired. The RDP Base Document made an explicit connection between planning and this fairly modest transformation agenda, but did so largely in relation to the technicalities of *implementing* the RDP. There were none of the grand objectives of planning that had been part of state socialism, for example. The final chapter of the Base Document provided, in embryonic form, many of the themes that were eventually to frame the new system of post-apartheid planning: the importance of a coordinated and coherent strategy that would guide public and private investment; the link between plan-making and budgeting; and the value of performance indicators, among others. Although democratization was one of the major planks of the RDP, little was said about planning and participatory government, suggesting that the RDP, despite its high ideals, contained a fairly technocratic and limited conception of planning.

The RDP White Paper, which followed the Base Document, maintained the link between planning and transformation but provided a more structured and detailed proposal for an integrated hierarchy of plans and planning process. The White Paper illustrated the tensions emerging between the decentralizing and centralizing aspects of ANC policy – the apex of the largely top-down planning system was to be a ten-year *National* Strategic Framework, but this framework was to be prepared through a 'bottom-up process'. Also, while the White Paper incorporated the classic development planning ideas of a national hierarchy of plans, it also drew on the language of the new public management (NPM) – of business planning, frameworks, performance reviews and the linking of planning and budgets (RSA 1994).

The Development Facilitation Act (DFA) of 1995 was the first piece of planning legislation and illustrated both the significance and limitations of planning under the RDP. The Act did not provide for a comprehensive planning system – focusing mainly on technical procedures and instruments for facilitating the release and use of land – but it did tie planning to normative objectives through a statement of guiding principles.

Despite the reasonably circumscribed role given to planning in the RDP (and the DFA), many planners eagerly latched onto the RDP to secure their continued legitimacy and there was a tendency at the time to overestimate the significance given to the planning profession by the RDP. There were, for example, calls for the 'massification of planning education' (Muller 2003) to prepare the huge cadre of planners that would be required for the task of reconstruction and development which, in the end, proved to be misguided (see Chapter 11). Larger ambitions for planning did surface within the new government subsequent to the release of the White Paper, informed by the development planning experience of countries such as Malaysia, Indonesia, India, Brazil and Botswana. The RDP Office, especially, had a vision of a national system of integrated planning, and defined development planning rather grandly as

> a participatory approach to integrate economic, sectoral, spatial, social, institu-
> tional, environmental and fiscal strategies in order to support the optimal
> allocation of scarce resources between sectors and geographical areas and
> across the population in a manner that provides sustainable growth, equity, and
> the empowerment of the poor and the marginalized.
>
> (FEPD 1995, Vol. 1)

This statement tied planning to the normative objectives of 'sustainable growth, equity, and the empowerment of the poor and the marginalized' and also pointed to 'integration' as the means to achieve this.

The abolition of the RDP Office in April 1996, and the introduction of the GEAR policy in July of the same year, put an end to the more ambitious hopes for planning but some elements of the thinking were carried through into the next phase of state policy.

DEVELOPMENTAL LOCAL GOVERNMENT

The idea of planning did not feature within the GEAR strategy – which was concerned mainly with macroeconomic strategy rather than local development – but it did feature prominently within government's efforts to establish viable, developmental local government (see Chapters 3 and 4). From 1996 onwards, the link between planning and social transformation was contained mainly in the concept of *developmental local government* (which was described in the 1998 White Paper on Local Government as meaning 'local government committed to working with citizens and groups within the community to find sustainable ways to meet their social, economic and material needs and improve the quality of their lives') (RSA 1994, Section B1).

As indicated in Chapter 4, the IDP became the key planning response to developmental local government. The IDP very clearly had a developmental objective, but because of the limited powers of local government, its focus was on building the capacity of local government to improve the *material* conditions of disadvantaged citizens, rather than on addressing broader objectives of social transformation such as, for example, black economic empowerment (BEE). IDPs did incorporate dimensions such as local economic development, and some IDPs dealt with cross-cutting dimensions such as gender empowerment and tackling the HIV/AIDS crisis, but these proved to be difficult issues to address in this context. The reasons for these gaps are complex, relating in some cases to the lack of instruments to deal with them and the long-term horizon required, and in others, such as gender, to the weak organization of women within and outside of municipal councils, the lack of support for action outside of councils, and a lack of analysis and understanding of the meaning of gender empowerment at a programme level (Todes *et al.* 2006). Predictably, very few municipalities have moved from rhetoric to real strategy in these areas. Participatory governance was also one of the objectives of IDPs, and there was some progress in this area, but over time the planning system tended towards a technocratic rather than a mobilizing approach. The one area where planning was expected to drive transformation was around spatial development. However, IDPs (and their component spatial development framework) have done little fundamentally to restructure the spatial forms inherited from colonialism and apartheid (Pieterse 2004a).

The IDP experience points to both the possibilities and limitations of state-directed planning. On the positive side, a strong link has been forged between budgetary and planning processes, and IDPs have contributed to a redirection of budgets towards areas of need. IDPs have also brought into the decision-making process concerns with matters such as gender empowerment and the development of local economy, and have promoted a more strategic approach to service and infrastructural delivery. However, it is not clear that IDPs are a very effective instrument in dealing with the big transformational issues such as spatial restructuring, social (including gender) empowerment, and economic growth and transformation.

THE DISCOURSE ON INTEGRATION

The special contribution of post-apartheid planning to the transformation agenda has been captured in the term 'integration'. The most prominent use of the language of integration is in the notions of integrated development planning and integrated development plans, but there are also integrated transport plans, integrated spatial frameworks, integrated sustainable rural development strategies, integrated environmental management plans, and more. There were and still are, high hopes surrounding integration, with a senior planning official in national government, for example, describing integrated development planning as the 'chief instrument of democracy at the local level' and as 'the key instrument for establishing a new governance paradigm' (Patel 2005). As Pieterse (2004b: 1) put it, 'one can be forgiven for thinking [integration] is the magic bullet that will resolve the many intractable problems that mark South Africa's cities'.

However, although integration is the leitmotif of post-apartheid planning, it remains an elusive concept. The term is used to refer, for example, to social integration, spatial integration, institutional integration, policy coherence, and the integration of planning and other governance processes (Harrison 2003b:13–25; Pieterse 2003a: 122–39, 2004a, 2004b; Wilkinson 2002). For Pieterse (2003a: 122), 'integration is burdened with multiple meanings and connotations and is therefore profoundly contested'.

Perhaps surprisingly, *social integration* has not been a major objective of the post-apartheid government, with post-apartheid settlement policy, arguably, even perpetuating racially segregated urban forms (Todes 2000: 617–29; Pieterse 2004b). It is only very recently with the Ministry of Housing's support for a form of inclusive zoning – which would require developers of middle- and high-income housing to incorporate a percentage of low-income housing within their housing schemes – that social integration has been given explicit attention in policy. Considerable attention has, however, been given to *spatial integration* (see Chapter 6 for a detailed discussion) and to the *institutional, intersectoral, programmatic* and *procedural integration* (see Chapter 4), and it is in these areas that planning is largely focused.

The key question is to what degree these forms of integration – to the extent that they are achieved in South Africa's complex spatial and institutional environment – have real and positive effects in people's daily lives. As Harrison (2003b: 23) put it,

> the language of contemporary planning is the language of synoptic thinking, policy coherence, compact cities, and spatial integration. It is a language that is unfortunately prone to a level of abstraction in which the issues of everyday life are translated into plans and policies that often bear little resemblance to the real concerns of people. It is a language that should be related far more concretely to lived experience, for there clearly *are* forms of fragmentation that add extra burdens to people's lives, and that detract from the possibility of safe, liveable, sustainable urban environments ... we need to understand more clearly what forms of integration make a real difference in everyday lives, and how we can achieve this integration.

CONTESTED FUTURES

By 2000, the economic and social consequences of ANC rule were becoming increasingly apparent. Prudent macroeconomic management had led to economic stability and improved rates of growth – the budget deficit had declined to less than 3 per cent of GDP, inflation was lower, competitiveness had improved, public-sector debt had fallen, and state finances were robust.

The government's Ten Year Review (in 2004) could also point to a number of achievements in service delivery: more than 1.6 million houses had been delivered, 15 million people had been provided with basic water infrastructure and 3.5 million homes had been electrified since 1994 (RSA 2005). In 2005, the presidency was able to report that the percentage of poor households with access to electricity had increased from 34.9 per cent in 1995 to 58.4 per cent in 2000, while the percentage with access to piped water had increased from 59.3 per cent to 77.2 per cent, and to telecommunications from 5.9 per cent to 16.1 per cent (PCAS 2005).

There were, however, some deep and persisting problems. Until 2000 employment was growing only in the informal sector, and the numbers of unemployed actually increased. Democracy had brought considerable opportunities for the upward mobility of the black middle classes but poverty remained stubbornly entrenched, and the gap between the rich and the poor may be widening – the presidency itself reported that the proportion of people considered to be below the poverty line had increased from 28 per cent of households in 1995 to 33 per cent in 2000 (PCAS 2005). While the government gave strong emphasis to the delivery of services to the poor, it was resisting more radical measures to promote redistribution such as the widely recommended Basic Income Grant. More seriously, perhaps, were the soaring rates of HIV/AIDS infection that threatened to undermine all progress that was being made in terms of social development, with the government's erratic, sometimes even eccentric, response to the epidemic attracting derision internationally.

The political Left has labelled Mbeki's moderate centrist or liberal social democratic policies as neo-liberal (e.g. Bond 2000) and within the ANC-led alliance itself there has been growing discontent which had fed into the bitter contest for the presidential succession. The trade union federation, COSATU (2006: 3), summarized the post-apartheid experience in the following words:

> In short, the post-apartheid socio-economic order can be characterized as one in which there is positive economic growth and opportunities for amassing wealth for a few. The growth is not equitably shared and does not trickle down much to the many that are desperately poor. While there is a formal break with the apartheid racial ordering of society, the dualistic development path continues, albeit with new features ...

There were, however, subtle but important shifts in the government's approach from about 2000. The one area of considerable criticism was BEE initiatives supported by the state. In Mbeki's pro-business government, BEE, or Africanization, was understood to mean the increasing ownership of the economy by the black popula-tion but, in practice, it appeared to represent the rapid enrichment of a small elite of politically connected black entrepreneurs. In December 2002, however, the National Conference of the ANC adopted a broader definition of BEE which was incorpo-rated in the Broad-Based Black Economic Empowerment Act of 2004.

Government's major response to the Ten Year Review was to focus on the bet-ter performance of the state, and it is here that planning has an important point of contact with the government's development agendas into the 'Second Decade of Freedom'. These agendas have been framed largely within the discourse of the 'developmental state', and have been given expression in the new Accelerated and Shared Growth Initiative for South Africa (ASGI-SA) (see Chapter 3). Although there is a strong focus on making local government work better, the emphasis is also on making government as a whole work better by ensuring that objectives and pro-grammes are aligned across the spheres. The key role given to planning is the coordination and integration of interventions. Although the response has been largely technocratic – with the focus on the functioning of government – there is also some indication of renewed attention to the concerns of social and economic inclusion, although Mbeki's administration remains very vulnerable to criticisms that its style is overly technocratic, and that its policies benefit the black middle classes at the expense of the working class and unemployed.

CONCLUSION

Planning in post-apartheid South Africa had a strong normative agenda, and must be assessed against this agenda. Planning was intended to promote the ideals of social transformation spelt out in policies and frameworks of the new government, although the possibilities and limitations of planning were understood differently at various times and by different segments of the ruling alliance, and the idea of trans-formation was itself contested.

In the final event, the relationship between planning and social transformation is difficult to untangle. The link between planning and the macro objectives of gov-ernment, such as BEE, io at best oblique. Planning's contribution to economic growth and employment creation is also uncertain – for example, there is little evi-dence to suggest that the local economic development strategies outlined in IDPs have had any measurable impact on economic fortunes, while delays in processing development applications, and the outdated nature of the land-use management system, may be impeding growth (see Chapter 8).

The relationship between planning and service delivery is more direct. There is evidence to suggest that IDPs have contributed meaningfully to the redirection of budgets to areas of need (Cashdan 2002: 159–80), and that IDPs may also have helped in the alignment of projects to strategic objectives and the prioritization of interventions. It remains, however, very difficult to show the relationship between planning input and the effectiveness of outcomes, and it remains to be seen whether the energy that the government is currently spending on developing harmonized and aligned systems across the spheres will result in the more effective operation of the state and, therefore, better delivery.

The extent to which planning has supported the democratization process is also debatable. There is little doubt that planning is more participatory now than ever before but there are critics who have warned of the 'technocratic creep' within planning (Heller 2001; Friedman 2001: 31–68; Pieterse 2004a, 2004b). As Pieterse (2004a: 101) put it,

> the biggest danger for discourses in support of urban integration is slipping into a technocratic mode, fixated on coordination, alignment, indicators, reporting, and the like ... it would be a grave error to think that the struggle for urban integration is not fundamentally about altering the balance of power between opposing interests in the city. For this reason, if urban integration is reduced to a particular multi-sectoral, or area based, or spatial planning model, it will have missed both the point and the political bus. The central political challenge is to empower insurgent interests in the city to claim their rights, entitlements and interests through the available participatory democratic forums.

Finally, in exploring the planning–transformation link it is necessary to interrogate the major promise that planning has made to nation-building in post-apartheid South Africa, that of *integration*. Is integration leading to more effective government, and is this effectiveness (if happening) being translated into transformative outcomes? Again, an answer partly depends on what is meant by transformation. It is fairly easy to show how IDP processes are leading to a redistribution of resources towards areas of need but it is far more difficult to show that the sort of integration promoted by planning is having any real impact on the underlying structures (social and spatial) of South Africa's towns, cities and rural areas.

CHAPTER 8

DISCOURSES OF THE ECONOMY AND THE MARKET

INTRODUCTION

Relationships between planning and the market are contested internationally. One important strand has seen planning as a way of containing the excesses of the market, of managing the anarchy and contradictions of capitalist development (Dear and Scott 1981). A related strand – present in the ideas of the early utopian planners – saw planning as enabling a social order alternative to the horrors of the industrial city produced by rampant and unchecked capitalism. Other perspectives however have seen planning as operating in capital's interests, and at the expense of other sectors of society. In these terms, economic interests have de facto dominated the outcomes of planning (e.g. see Flyvbjerg 1998a).

This chapter explores the main ways in which planning relates to the economy and the market post-apartheid. It begins by outlining planning–market relationships, and then focuses on planning and local economic development; initiatives to regenerate marginal or declining areas; the relationship between spatial planning, economic development and the market; and the system of land-use management and the market. The chapter concludes by arguing that planners have still to engage with the limits and potentials of planning and the market in South Africa.

PLANNING–MARKET RELATIONSHIPS

In the post-war era, the political compromise represented by the welfare state in developed countries allowed planning to take on the roles of producing cities with necessary infrastructure and spaces for economic development, but also of managing and mediating between various economic and social interests (Roweis 1983), as well as producing 'better' housing and urban environments for the working classes. Planning in this context to some extent acted as a brake on the market, and with the collapse of the welfare state, and the rise of neo-liberalism, planning was initially rolled back, with arguments that it was undermining growth. Under 'third way' capitalism, however, strategic planning has come to play new roles in fostering the growth of cities and regions (see introduction to Part 3). Planning is increasingly seen as a partner of the market, although critiques of the regulatory role of planning in constraining and slowing development periodically resurface, such as is occurring currently in the United Kingdom. In many developing countries, planning in the post-war era was imported, and a similar, but much watered-down logic to that in developed countries applied – particularly with regard to its social objectives. Its focus on regulation and control was subject to major critique by the World Bank and other agencies from the 1980s, which argued instead for planning to 'facilitate' development. This position was consistent with the neo-liberal attack on planning, but it also drew support from a wide range of socially oriented commentators (e.g. Harris 1990), since regulatory planning had often undermined the survival strategies of the poor.

In South Africa under apartheid, planning played roles in relation to the market that were similar to those of other countries in the post-war era, but strategic planning was far weaker, and planning activity was coloured by an apartheid logic. A key aspect of the apartheid state's use of planning was in constraining and promoting the location of economic activity, linked to the project of spatial segregation. Black residential townships were located, designed and regulated in ways which limited economic activity there (Dewar and Watson 1981; Todes 1998). Policies of industrial decentralization also sought to contain the growth of manufacturing in cities, while encouraging development on the periphery. Yet state regional policies remained marginal to the overall logic of an import-substitution-led economic policy, which continued to encourage growth in the Pretoria–Witwatersrand–Vereeniging area and the major cities.

In the immediate post-apartheid years, assumptions that the state and planning could direct economic activity continued. The Reconstruction and Development Programme (RDP) and policy documents of the time assumed that the state should act to create integrated cities, and to redress apartheid spatial inequalities. But in practice, the extent to which government and planning can and does influence the location of economic activity has been limited. The opening up of the economy to the global market, the rise of an increasingly market-driven discourse of development, and the privileging of global interactions have all been critical here. The recent turn towards greater state interventionism and the concern to redress inequalities associated with the pattern of growth is turning attention back towards spatial inequalities within cities and across national space, but the real effect of these expressed concerns remains to be seen.

Planning in South Africa post-apartheid has worked with several notions of its link to the economy and the market. One key strand draws from the World Bank and UN-Habitat position that planning should move away from regulation and focus on 'facilitating' development. This position however has meant that less attention has been given to land-use management, and de facto, a relatively laissez-faire approach has been adopted to the market and major private-sector-driven developments. A second strand – partially linked to the first – sees local economic development

(LED) as a key element of developmental local government, and of planning, although as an activity, it is often separated from spatial planning and is not the sole preserve of planners. The direction of LED however is contested, with debates over a pro-poor approach versus a focus on growth and competitiveness. In the big cities the emphasis on competitiveness has been more significant, and has gone along with a relatively laissez-faire approach to the market, a tendency to pay greater attention to the demands of the business, and a privileging of global interactions. Discourses of globalization and arguments that planning can only 'ride the wave' rather than changing its course, have played into this approach. In practice this has meant that spatial planning goals are often subordinate to economic imperatives.

A third strand however assumes that the state can and should direct economic activity – in the interests of creating more integrated cities, redressing the effects of apartheid, and countering economic decline. Thus attention has been paid to urban regeneration in declining inner cities, apartheid-created townships and in peripheral towns and regions. For the most part, these strategies have attempted to work with inherent economic 'potentials', and in concert with the private sector, rather than through regulation or incentives, and in this sense are different from the types of strategies used under apartheid. A fourth strand of planning works with an approach to design and strategic spatial planning that focuses on creating a network of defined routes and centres, creating 'nodes' and 'corridors', on the assumption that economic activity will accumulate there. Although these concepts might be useful for addressing the spatial needs of the informal economy, they do not seriously engage with the contemporary dynamics of urban space economies, and thus are ineffective in responding to the spatial patterns of wealthy residents and large business which are structuring much new development in cities. The privileging of this approach to spatial planning has also meant that planners' understanding of the space–economy relationships is weak, and thus the emphasis on LED ironically goes along with a limited ability to engage with the real economy in space.

PLANNING AND LOCAL ECONOMIC DEVELOPMENT

In the post-apartheid period, LED has become an important focus for planners (Faling 2002; Todes *et al.* 2003), although it is by no means the preserve of the planning profession. Under apartheid, some towns and cities undertook their own LED strategies – usually based on forms of place marketing and property development (Rogerson 2006: 227–53), but in the post-apartheid period, it has come to be seen as a significant part of 'developmental local government' (Nel and John 2006). In terms of the 1997 White Paper on Local Government, it is part of the mandate for local government, although as Nel and John (2006) point out, the main focus there is on making the links between an efficient governance and local economic development. Nevertheless, considerable work has gone into developing policy frameworks, guideline documents, accessible manuals and case studies which can be used in more proactive approaches. Both international donors and government have supported this thrust.

For several years, government policy on LED supported a 'pro-poor' approach, with a strong focus on small towns and rural areas. A few cities such as Cape Town (Parnell et al. 2005) developed systematic approaches to poverty, working through this concern across several sectors, and developing an integrated approach to the problem. In practice, in most cases, a pro-poor approach meant support for small poverty alleviation projects. A study by Williamson et al. (2004) of integrated development plans (IDPs) in the KwaZulu-Natal Province, for example, showed that economic development strategies were generally weak, focused largely on poverty alleviation. Projects included activities such as poultry, community gardens, sewing, bread-making and the like. Projects were not always sustainable (Nel and John 2006), and incomes generated were often tiny and irregular, as several studies showed (e.g. see Buthelezi 2004; Somtunzi 2002). The failure to emphasize the creation of sustainable economic activities and viable local economies, the weak capacity in local government, and the lack of engagement with the real economic potentials in particular areas, are common criticisms. The expectation that LED could generate economic development anywhere, and that it might be seen as a cure-all for the problems of marginal and declining areas, was also severely criticized (e.g. see Bloch 2000).

In response to these sorts of criticisms, LED policy has shifted to a more moderate approach – more strongly focused on growth, but including pro-poor elements (Nel and John 2006). No official policy document has been released to date, but working documents towards a framework and official guidelines include an emphasis on small business and the 'second economy' (discussed in Chapter 14), promoting comparative and competitive advantages, as well as pro-poor approaches. Documents also emphasize a deeper understanding of local economies and the development of strategies on this basis – linking to growing movements on the part of several provincial authorities to generate economic development strategies based on more systematic economic analysis of, for example, industrial clusters, value chains and the like. Links between LED and the policies of related programmes, particularly of the Department of Trade and Industry (DTI), are also being made. This shift in part reflects initiatives to create forms of 'joined-up government' (Chapters 3 and 5), but can also be tied to a more interventionist stance on the part of government (Nel and John 2006; Tomlinson 2003a).

While LED policy emphasized a pro-poor approach until recently, Nel and Rogerson (2005: 19) comment that 'pro-poor LED is upheld more in policy than in practice', with the mainstream 'still dominated by market-led activities that are geared towards achieving sustainable, high economic growth rates' (Rogerson 2006: 230). Discourses of competitiveness have been significant here. As Rogerson notes, 'several variants of "place entrepreneurialism" can be identified, with the most important relating to promoting localities as competitive spaces for production, consumption and knowledge-based activities' (2006: 230). Yet there are considerable variations across localities, and between cities, with some cities mixing pro-poor and pro-growth strategies. For instance, Durban has combined upmarket flagship projects (such as a waterfront development and convention centre) with a strongly pro-poor approach to service delivery and some innovative projects such as Warwick Junction, supporting informal trade linked to a major transport node (Robbins 2005).

As might be expected, property development and place marketing remain significant parts of LED. The development of marinas, convention centres, theme parks and the like have all been strong elements of LED in the large cities, but particularly in cities outside of Gauteng where growth rates have been lower and the tourist

Box 8.1 LED focus areas in cities

A survey of the nine largest cities (SACN 2006) showed the following focus areas, in order of importance:

- Regeneration of economic zones
- Property development
- Manufacturing sectors
- Small business development
- Partnership building
- Regeneration of townships
- Investment marketing and facilitation
- Institutional development
- Skills development
- Improving city administrative efficiency and effectiveness
- Development of new economic assets
- Black economic empowerment
- Urban agriculture
- Informal economy development
- Tourism marketing
- New bulk infrastructure
- Knowledge and service sectors
- Information provision

economy is more significant. Concerns to appeal to a global market and to promote city competitiveness are key elements of their rationale. Cape Town's economic development strategies from the mid-1980s were a response to long-term economic depression in the region, and sought to position the city as an international tourism destination. More recently, investment in 'flagship' projects subsidized by local government in Durban, such as the International Convention Centre and the Point waterfront redevelopment were rationalized on the basis that they would enable the city, which had lost a large part of its middle-class tourism market in the 1980s and 1990s, and had experienced some years of slow economic growth, to position itself in the global market. The development of a new stadium for the upcoming 2010 FIFA World Cup in the city (instead of upgrading an existing one at half the cost[1]) is similarly seen as helping the city to build itself as an 'event' city. Local government and planning are thus emerging as key players in initiatives to revitalize the city. In the case of Durban, local government is backed by both a 'growth coalition' of large business with significant local bases, and by local and provincial politicians who have sought to promote visible local development.

Concerns for promoting city competitiveness however are in part underpinning continuing spatial divides across the city, with new upmarket developments occurring largely in areas disconnected from the poor, often in contradiction to spatial plans. Location of these activities is driven by the market, with little consideration for how they affect overall city functioning. Plans for the 2010 FIFA World Cup seem to be reinforcing this tendency. For instance, the new Cape Town stadium will be built in Green Point, far from the bulk of the soccer-supporting public on the Cape Flats. One persuasive factor was reportedly the good views of Table Mountain for promotional pictures.

As the international literature suggests, the benefits of these strategies are ambiguous (e.g. see Metropolis 2002). Most cities hosting the 2010 World Cup are aware of the potential negative effects of mega-events, and are attempting to use it to accelerate their plans for urban restructuring and infrastructural improvements (such as the Gautrain, a high-speed rail system in Gauteng, and improvements to the public transport system in the inner city in Durban). But FIFA requirements constrain what can be done and place considerable demands on cities and the national fiscus. For instance, significant capital funding is going towards stadiums, potentially skewing investment away from more basic infrastructural needs, such as bulk water and sewerage capacity and maintenance of infrastructure, all of which are sorely needed after years of focusing on increasing delivery. While initial proposals suggested a massive positive impact on jobs and growth – and have shaped similar expectations on the part of the public (Pillay 2006) – recent assessments by the National Treasury are far more circumspect. As is the case with many flagship projects and event-oriented developments, initial proposals and assumptions were poorly interrogated. For instance, contrary to expectations, the impact of the World Summit for Sustainable Development on township tourism in Johannesburg was negligible, as most delegates stayed in more conventional upmarket areas. Similarly the usage of facilities at Durban's Point redevelopment has been much lower than expected – in part the result of poorly interrogated projections, but also because the major upmarket development is occurring in the northern part of the city, following proactive planning, development and promotion by a major landowner and property developer in the area. These experiences raise questions about the extent to which government planning is able to shift spatial development patterns, particularly in a context where levels of inequality and crime are high.

Regenerating marginal and declining areas

An important theme in South African planning has been an attempt to redress apartheid inequalities, and to develop marginal and declining areas. The assumption has been that planning by the state can help to unleash economic development in places neglected or deserted by the market, particularly rural areas, marginal regions, declining inner-city areas and townships historically reserved for African people. In some of these areas, planning has sought to redress the active suppression of the market under apartheid.

Debates over whether the state can and should reshape the space–economy were discussed in Chapter 5. On one hand, the (implicit) argument in the National Spatial Development Perspective is that planning cannot contradict market tendencies towards spatial concentration, that it should avoid attempting to generate economic activity in no-hope areas, and should instead support development in existing growth areas or places with real potential. In addition, arguments on the importance of big cities in economic growth are made by some sections of government, urban policy analysts, the South African Cities Network representing the major municipalities, and the Centre for Development and Enterprise linked to big business. On the other hand, some pro-poor advocates have identified spatial marginality with poverty, and argue that the state can and should use its policies to redress spatial inequalities at a national level. Elements of these arguments are implicit in the Integrated Sustainable Rural Development Programme (ISRDP), in the earlier versions of LED policy discussed above, and in the recent draft Regional Industrial Development Strategy (RIDS). Proponents for approaches emphasizing spatial equity include both policy analysts concerned about rural poverty, sections of government, and politicians representing the ANC's large political base in rural areas and marginal regions – as well as those in some other political parties. While policy is still evolving and being debated, the state and planning are, for the most part, seen as facilitators – enabling the development of inherent local or regional strengths and 'potentials', rather than generating these *de novo*. This notion of 'riding the wave' of the market – of developing through unexploited or underexploited potentials – is also evident in the motivation for spatial development initiatives (SDIs), as noted in Chapter 5. The key issue is how 'potential' is established, who defines it, and what is required for it to be realized. These issues remain unresolved. The conceptualization of 'potential' is also rather static, not taking into account economic restructuring and the changing nature of the market (such as the shifting fortunes of the coal industry and its implications for coal towns). Nor is it clear that the market will respond in ways assumed by planners – as the story of several SDIs has demonstrated (Chapter 5).

Even if real potential exists, the experience of regional development in South Africa and internationally is that sustained, long-term support is required if development is to succeed (Platzky 2000). Similar points can be made with regard to development in marginal areas more generally. For instance, in the Cato Manor urban renewal project in Durban, expected investment by the private sector occurred only after considerable public investment had been made: it did not occur at the beginning. The short-term focus of many development programmes in South Africa (such as SDIs) is problematic from this perspective.

Support for sustained development programmes has been more evident in the inner cities, where private property interests have converged with municipal initiatives to respond to inner-city restructuring. Forms of inner-city revitalization programmes have been under way since the 1970s, when shops and later offices began to decentralize, and new nodes emerged to compete with city centres. Trends towards decentralization, initially based on demand for new types of space, were accelerated by an oligopolistic financial sector with surplus capital and few alternative outlets for investment (Goga 2003). Dedicated urban renewal units were set up in several cities in the 1980s and 1990s as the pace of change in city centres accelerated. In many cities, retail activity shifted towards a lower-income, and predominantly black population, but remained vibrant. Informal trade grew rapidly in old CBDs as old controls broke down. As white residents moved from inner cities, they were replaced by middle-income black residents, and later by the urban poor living in crowded conditions in buildings which were poorly serviced or even abandoned by owners. Occupation took various forms – rental, doss houses, illegal occupation in 'hijacked'[2] buildings. Although office decentralization provided space for new small black-owned business in the CBD (Rogerson 1997), vacancies far exceeded demand, and vacated office buildings have sometimes been recycled to low-end residential use as well. High levels of crime became a recurrent and defining problem. Patterns varied between cities, with trends being most extreme and advanced in Johannesburg. Strategies adopted by urban renewal programmes to address these issues have been wide-ranging, and in several cases, agencies have attempted to chart a course of inclusive growth.

The private sector has been a key driving force in inner-city revitalization initiatives in several cities, and a number of municipalities have established programmes in partnership with the private sector, such as the Cape Town Partnership, a non-profit renewal and management agency representing the interests of local government and a range of private-sector interests. The establishment of Business or City Improvement Districts (BIDs and CIDs), in which additional security and cleaning services are paid for by property owners, are common, either as part of these partnerships, or as independent initiatives. Concerns have been raised that these initiatives represent a privatization of urban planning and management and serve to exclude the interests of the poor, such as informal traders and the homeless. In addition, critics argue that they create islands of safety, displacing crime to other areas (Pirie 2006).

Whether inner-city regeneration can occur in an inclusive way is open to debate. eThekwini's iTrump, a local government inner-city regeneration programme, and its previous Warwick Junction project, has put considerable emphasis on working with and improving conditions for informal traders in the inner city, creating a vibrant market area linked to commuter rail. Social housing has also been created in the inner city, and innovative projects providing informal traders with housing have been created. Cape Town's inner-city revitalization incorporates programmes aimed at street children, the homeless, and the development of inclusive public spaces and cultural programmes (Pirie 2006). Cultural and urban redevelopment programmes are attempting to generate more lively cities, and new creative industries and service-sector activities are being created. In all metropolitan areas, inner-city regeneration programmes coupled with strong economic growth have meant that office vacancies in CBDs have declined (SACN 2006), but declines have been sharpest in Cape Town, where the city centre has been recaptured by the market. The effects of regeneration and the long-term trajectory for CBDs are less clear in other major cities. Pirie (2006) notes that some R11.5 billion of private investment has gone into Cape Town's city centre since 1999. New developments are occurring, old buildings have been upgraded, and conversions to upmarket residential and mixed-use developments are underway. 'Urbanism' as imagined by South African planners is beginning to occur in Cape Town, but

> it appears as if apartheid red-lining on racial grounds has been replaced by a
> financially exclusive property market that entrenches white prosperity and privi-
> lege, and extends it to foreign investors, business entrepreneurs, and
> vacationers ... soaring residential property prices ... dashed hopes for a mixed-
> use, mixed-income, socially inclusive city centre.

(Pirie 2006: 10)

The rising tide of economic growth and the property boom of the past few years has finally begun to reach the townships – marginalized spaces where economic activity was constrained under apartheid. Both the spatial organization of townships reserved for black people – characteristically with one entrance and exit and few places where economic activity could agglomerate – and the regulations governing them, limited the extent of economic activity. For instance, in the Madadeni township, created to accommodate African people relocated from parts of Newcastle in the 1960s, entrepreneurs were limited to one shop only, even if they had owned several before. The state vetted and controlled the enterprises that could be established, limiting certain types of activity (such as cinemas), the number of businesses owned by individuals and the numbers of particular kinds of shops (Todes 1998). In the late apartheid years, when the state wished to accommodate black aspirations within the confines of these areas, and in homelands, the development of shopping centres and other economic activities were encouraged. The township shopping centres that were established in this period however largely failed (Kgara 1998), since they were treated as second-class outlets by the white-owned retail corporations, and were bypassed by residents. The physical design of the townships and established transport and shopping patterns focused on the CBD also served to undermine them. For many years, economic activity in townships comprised a sprinkling of formal businesses and a far larger number of informal low-order retail and service activities: *spaza* shops (cafes), *shebeens* (bars), panel beaters, block-makers and the like.

Initiatives to redress this situation – to enable them to offer the range of service functions, economic activities and employment opportunities that might be expected in a 'normal' low-income neighbourhood (Harrison *et al.* 1997) – have been an important focus of planning, particularly in the urban renewal nodes. Strategies used include the creation of high-access, public-transport-oriented nodes and corridors to create good market access for business. The co-location of public services on these and smaller nodes (in contrast to the previous dispersal of services to wherever sites were available) has also been used to create more convenient access, and to generate thresholds for business. These ideas draw on concepts put forward by the UCT planning school, but also bear similarities to traditional service hierarchy ideas. Other approaches include the creation of markets and facilities for small industries, small business support, vocational training, facilitation of township tourism, public works and urban agriculture. Strategies to respond to crime are also key elements of township development strategies.

Although a wide range of strategies have been adopted, it can be argued that while emphasis has been placed on physical design and facilities, such as markets, business hives, community halls, and the like, too little attention has been given to the development and ongoing support for programmes to build human capital. There are many examples of facilities that remain un- or under-used. In some cases, this is due to a lack of analysis or a poor understanding of how space is used by local entrepreneurs. There has also been less attention paid to the ongoing management of these places, so that some have become dysfunctional. For example, Cape Town's Dignified Spaces Programme, winner of an urban design award, created public facilities and marketplaces in some of the most impoverished areas of the Cape Flats. A new community bathhouse and washing facility costing R5 million was never opened as the municipality had not budgeted for management staff, and it was eventually dismantled by local residents.

Despite limitations, some of these strategies are starting to bear fruit. One example is the growth of shopping malls as the corporate retail sector finally recognizes the huge consumer markets that exist in townships. For instance, consumer incomes in Durban's Inanda–KwaMashu–Ntuzuma (INK) area are of the order of R3 billion. Despite widespread poverty, there are also pockets of wealth and stable incomes in parts of these areas. The townships are becoming more differentiated and property markets are developing, although they are still limited (FinMark Trust 2004). Their sheer size is also a factor (e.g. INK comprises around 500,000 people). In the last two years, township malls have been some of the most profitable in the country, although this trend appears to have reached its limit for the moment (Viruly Consulting 2006). The growth of township malls has not been a straightforward solution however. Shopping centres and retail outlets are owned largely by the highly monopolized retail and property industry, and in some areas established small businesses have reacted negatively to this perceived threat to their markets.

As might be expected, the new investment in townships is also not evenly distributed between areas, with better-off and more established areas attracting greater investment. The bulk of investment in the new township boom is going to Soweto, which is quite suddenly attracting massive public and private investments. Historically, a dormitory township, it is rapidly becoming a centre of commercial and even office development. Public investments include the R1 billion Orlando Ekhaya mixed-use development around the old power station, the R100 million Walter Sisulu Square of Dedication, the new Baragwanath taxi rank with 1600 trader stalls, and various developments in the Soweto Business Empowerment Zone. These developments are more than matched by the private sector. Within a couple of years, five shopping malls have been built, with a value greater than R1.2 billion, including the R450 million black-owned Maponya Mall, which is Soweto's first upmarket mega shopping complex. There has also been considerable vibrancy in the residential market, including the middle to upper-middle categories.

SPATIAL PLANNING, ECONOMIC DEVELOPMENT AND THE MARKET

Despite planners' foray into LED, South African spatial planning has, for the most part, worked with a weak understanding of economic development and markets. Strategic spatial plans rarely provide a systematic analysis of the economic spaces of cities and regions and how they are changing. Little attention is paid to how the city economy works spatially, and what kinds of spaces, infrastructure and forms of regulation are required to make it work. Harris's (1990) criticism of comprehensive metropolitan spatial plans in developing countries as devoid of an analysis of the real economy is apt here, although the style of spatial planning is rather different from the plans he considers.

The reliance on a 'design' approach, using abstract concepts of nodes and corridors (Chapter 6) to structure strategic spatial plans has in effect marginalized the significance of these kinds of analyses. The basic premise of the design approach used is that the creation of an appropriate spatial structure will lead business to locate in desired ways. In effect, the argument is that business is attracted to points of high accessibility which are created through a system of nodes and corridors. This more flexible approach moves away from the kind of prediction and control of land for particular use types required by traditional structure planning and master planning. It is based implicitly on a conception of small-scale competitive markets, and works well as a way of describing the spatial organization of informal trading, and for designing spaces in ways that support these activities. As Dierwechter (2002) points out, research by Dewar and Watson (1981, 1990) and the University of Cape Town planning school provides some of the only spatial analyses of informal economic activity. Nevertheless, it does not engage with the quantum of particular kinds of economic space which are likely to be used, nor with larger and more monopolized economic activity.

Strategic spatial plans are intended to address long-term development directions, and in this sense, must remain broadly based. However in several planning processes, concepts of nodes and corridors are used without engaging with the real prospects for development even over the long term. There are many instances of plans with corridors promising development in places with limited existing or likely long-term economic potential. Planners have also often found it difficult to move from this broad, abstract level to more immediate development, and in some cases the nodes/corridors concept is used in a literal way in this context, without assessment against economic dynamics and potentials. For instance, in the Cato Manor urban renewal project, the use of nodes and corridors was useful in concentrating markets and in providing space for informal traders. The spatial framework provided a long-term view of the development of the area. However an initial design concept for the main corridor through the area translated the idea literally to a road with a series of buildings with business use on the ground floor, and with residential occupation on top. In keeping with both the design approach used and the emphasis on planning as facilitating, rather than regulating the market, no attempt was made to assess the likely extent of demand for business space. A later evaluation found that the space made available for business along this route was way beyond what could be supported at the time. A recent assessment found that levels of business development are far lower than had been originally expected (Dewar and Kaplan 2004). The fact that the development managed to accommodate only about half of the anticipated population, and that they were very low-income, as opposed to being more mixed in income as initially anticipated, were contributing factors. Similarly the proximity of the CBD (7 km away) and a large regional shopping centre, and the fact that the transport routes used by taxis bypassed the local shopping areas, all served to limit what was possible in the area. The failure to engage with the realities of economic space however meant that planners did not confront these limits.

The nodes/corridors approach and the emphasis on broad design to facilitate development also does not come to grips with the way large-scale capital is structuring space. South Africa's property and retail industry is highly concentrated in terms of ownership and control, and its development patterns are similar across cities. It is largely focused on middle-income consumers, and favours the development of car-oriented shopping centres and decentralized offices, which locate along highways, distant from areas of poverty. As Chapter 6 showed, these patterns are often contrary to the logic of metropolitan spatial plans. Yet few metropolitan spatial plans have policies which respond to these processes or comment on whether these developments are acceptable and what form they might take. Of course, permissions for these and other activities are required through the land-use regulatory system, but as indicated in Chapter 6, there is often little reference to the metropolitan spatial plans in decision-making of this sort, although this is starting to change.

LAND-USE MANAGEMENT AND THE MARKET

There are few instances where business is actively using long-term or strategic planning to influence the development of particular areas. One exception is the Tongaat Hullett company, a large landowner in the north of Durban, and its property development company, Morelands, which as Chapter 6 noted, undertook metropolitan spatial planning with the aim of influencing the way development in its area would be considered by planning authorities. In effect, it has used a variant of the nodes/corridors concept to rationalize extensive upmarket development on its own land (mainly gated residential communities, office parks and retail complexes), and actively engages with local-government-led planning to shape outcomes in its interests. For the most part, property developers engage with planning through the land-use regulation system, or attempt to influence planning outcomes in more informal ways.

In practice, decision-making through the land-use management system has been far more laissez-faire than might be expected, and the market has tended to dominate outcomes. Despite the many ways in which South African municipalities have attempted to give voice to the poor, the privileging of economic development and urban competitiveness as discourses and the uneasiness with planning as control, have given greater effective power to business interests. In addition, the perpetuation of dated land-use regulation systems which do not embody contemporary ideas of urban restructuring has meant that old discourses have continued to dominate land-use decision-making as Chapter 6 noted. Nevertheless, the land-use regulation system does make demands on developers. Not all applications are accepted and modifications to proposals may be required. The slow processing of development applications is a major source of complaint. Thus South African land-use management sits in a rather ambiguous position in relation to the market: there are claims of too much control, but outcomes are largely in accordance with the market.

Major concerns are being raised around the processing of land-development applications, which, many argue, is slow, and is holding up development. At national level, claims are made that some R80 billion of investment is being held up by slow land-development processes. The slow turnaround time for development applications is being raised as a specific problem area in the Accelerated and Shared Growth Initiative for South Africa (ASGI-SA), which aims to accelerate economic growth through infrastructure delivery. This issue, among others, is now the focus of a high-level interdepartmental committee chaired by a senior committee within the Treasury.

The reasons for slow processing are complex. The long reorganization of local government, administrative systems and lack of capacity in both planning departments and in others which are expected to comment on development applications, are contributing factors. Approval by councillor committees is sometimes cited as a factor in slowing the process (Sim *et al.* 2004). Since 2005, some municipalities, including the City of Johannesburg, have moved development applications out of the political arena – in these cases applications are now adjudicated entirely by officials. The consequence for Johannesburg was the quicker processing of the more than 6000 development applications received annually, but this move may have also contributed to the more technocratic direction that planning appears to be taking.

In many cities, staffing capacity is too limited to cope with the volume of applications, and backlogs have grown in the context of a booming property market. For instance, Sim *et al.*'s study (2004) of the processing of development applications showed that an average of 827 planning applications (including transfers) per month were received in Cape Town in 2003, and only 718 could be processed, leaving a monthly backlog of 109 applications. The Cape Town situation was exacerbated by a decline in staff in the Planning and Environment Directorate from 2000. Numbers employed dropped from 779 (as against 1108 establishment posts) to 568 in 2004. A similar situation existed in Johannesburg. Municipalities are beginning to address these issues, but as is the case in some other countries, such as the UK, there are calls to roll back the system. Similar (and perhaps even stronger) arguments are being made about the system of environmental impact assessment, and as Chapter 9 shows, the combination of duplicating environmental and planning regulations has been a particular concern.

CONCLUSION

This chapter has shown that planning has had an uneasy and often contradictory relationship to economic development and the market. Approaches to planning–market relationships are implicit, and there is an absence of direct debate among planners about how they should relate to the market. The emphasis on planning as facilitation implicitly accepts a market-driven approach, but attempts to shape the market through physical plans. Yet planning visions are very different from patterns produced by the market, and this form of spatial planning has largely been ineffective in this context. As Chapter 6 showed, the recent more 'realistic' spatial plans largely accept market-driven patterns, and land-use management does little to challenge the dominance of the market. Several initiatives in marginal and declining areas have attempted to enable the market through sustained public-sector-led development efforts, and the reduction of constraints to investment. 'Pro-poor' LED was an attempt to move beyond a market-driven approach to development, but did not take on the workings of the larger economy, and for the most part, was confined to poverty-alleviation projects.

While planners have become more engaged in LED, the more traditional work of planning remains devoid of an engagement with economic dynamics and relationships. The design approach used has meant that planners have not spent much effort on understanding the relationships between markets, economic activity and space. This is a critical lacuna if planners are to manage cities in more effective ways.

At a national level, something of a 'spatial turn' is emerging in economic policy. Local and regional development, and space-development relationships, are being given greater attention. Analyses of the 'first/second economy' (Chapter 14) dichotomy frequently construct this relationship in spatial terms (urban/rural; core/periphery). The National Spatial Development Perspective, and voices representing the big cities, are drawing attention to the role of cities in economic development, and the place selectivity of economic activity (see also Chapter 5).

Attention to space foregrounds concerns which are at the heart of planning, but it is questionable whether generalist planners have the skills to play a central role here. This new field may in practice move out of the realm of planners, to newly trained local and regional development economists. If planners are to maintain their position in this regard, and if they are to be effective in more traditional realms of planning, they will need to take economic dynamics and development much more seriously.

CHAPTER 9

DISCOURSES OF SUSTAINABILITY

INTRODUCTION

Concepts of sustainability have become central to planning thought internationally, and in several countries the focus on sustainability has given new life to the planning profession. Nevertheless, parallel institutional systems of planning and environmental management frequently exist (Voghera 2003) and notions of sustainability are taken up unevenly within planning systems, with debates over how the concept is to be understood and applied (Owens and Cowell 2002). South Africa is similar in several respects, but the divide between planning and environmental management is perhaps greater, although there are now initiatives towards forms of integration.

Although planning systems in South Africa prior to 1994 included some space for environmental concerns (Claasens 2003), and some planners and planning bodies paid considerable attention to these issues (Mabin and Harrison 1996; Todes *et al.* 2005), the new emphasis on environmental management and sustainability emerged largely outside of planning. In effect, environmental management has emerged as a separate discipline, and a parallel set of legal processes has been institutionalized, particularly around assessments of applications to change land use. Planning and environmental management are in different institutional locations at national level, and frequently at provincial and local levels. In addition, important initiatives to infuse notions of sustainability within the realm of urban and regional development have emerged largely from outside of planning or national departments in control of planning.

This chapter explores how and why environmental management emerged as a separate set of processes from planning, and its consequences for planning as a transformative activity.[1] In particular, it examines the influence of sustainability as a discourse within planning, and the extent to which its principles have been taken up in the main forms of planning: in land-use planning, settlement planning and strategic planning. Sustainability as a concept is embodied in post-1994 planning legislation, and definitions are compatible with those in environmental legislation (Berrisford 2005). However, as Patel (2004: 282–92) points out, the South African government has tended to use all-encompassing definitions of sustainability, and has avoided making clear choices about which values are supported, and what sustainability might really mean in a South African context. Thus the often inevitable conflicts between the economic, social and biophysical dimensions of sustainability (see Haughton and Counsell 2004) and between the different meanings attached to the concept in various policies are played out on the ground. Furthermore, despite the inclusion of sustainability in legislation, its intentions are often contradicted by other more powerful policies and intentions, particularly with regard to economic development (Bond 2002). Policy contradictions are often played out in conflicts between planning and environmental management (but also within them), although there is growing mutual interest and understanding. The recent draft National Strategy for Sustainable Development (DEAT 2006) moves towards a more coherent statement of sustainability and its meaning for a range of policy areas, but it remains to be seen whether it will be adopted and how it will affect current policy contradictions.

PLANNING AND ENVIRONMENTAL MANAGEMENT

It is often argued that the holistic planning approaches of early twentieth-century writers such as MacKaye, Mumford and Geddes, with their emphasis on natural resource management and territorial planning for 'place–work–folk' were early forms of environmentally oriented planning, which was later lost with the impetus towards modernist planning (e.g. Roberts and Colwell 2001; Gasson and Todeschini 1997). In the South African context, this impetus was perhaps weaker, with a greater emphasis on physical and spatial planning. Nevertheless, the provincial Town Planning Ordinances from the 1920s and 1930s did include provision for consideration of environmental issues in town planning schemes and in assessment of site-level development applications, although these concerns were not given much priority in practice (Claasens 2003). A common argument in South Africa is that traditional town planning did not take environmental concerns into account, necessitating an alternative set of environmental regulations to address these issues (Fuggle and Rabie 1992).

This argument may be overstated. For example, from the 1940s to the 1970s, planning by the Town and Regional Planning Commission, in what was then the Natal province, was influenced by the early holistic planners. Considerable effort went into a series of studies around the province's Tugela River Basin, much of it documenting its natural resource base, and the activities that could be supported there (Mabin and Harrison 1996). Indeed in the subsequent work of the Commission, environmental concerns received considerable attention. At this stage, however, environment was seen quite narrowly, and fell short of the developmental and social concerns embodied in current definitions of sustainability.

From the 1970s, environmental issues began to receive greater attention from national government. A permanent cabinet committee on environmental conservation was established, and the national Department of Planning became the Department of Environment and Planning, mandated to address pollution control and conservation of natural resources, in addition to its previous functions. The Physical Planning Act was amended to include consideration of environmental issues in land-use planning, and a Habitat Council was created to promote integration of environmental issues within planning and design of projects (Fuggle and Rabie 1992). Although the new environmentalism emerged within a planning department, it nevertheless led to a plethora of overlapping structures and legislation (Jordi *et al.* 1998). In 1989, the Environmental Conservation Act was promulgated, which laid the basis for Environmental Impact Assessments (EIAs), although regulations were only put in place in 1997.

Prior to 1994, the main orientation of government environmental policy (like planning policy) was towards management and control. A conservative approach focused on biophysical concerns dominated – often at the expense of social considerations. It emphasized conservation of wilderness areas and particular species, and saw people and their use of the environment as the main problem. Thus forced removals of African people were often associated with conservation projects (Ngobese and Cock 1997).

A progressive environmental movement, focused on development, environmental justice and broader questions of sustainability, began to emerge from the late 1970s, although it remained relatively small and fragmented until the 1990s. Some organizations linked to the worker and political struggles of the time attempted to move beyond notions of environment as essentially a white middle-class concern (Ngobese and Cock 1997). The larger environmental movement, however, remained a mixture of organizations with very different interests and orientations. Progressive environmentalists linked into emerging international agendas around sustainability which increasingly defined it as a holistic approach addressing economic, social and biophysical dimensions, rather than as a narrowly 'green' agenda. The 1987 Brundtland Report, and the 1992 Rio Earth Summit with its Agenda 21 principles were important in shaping South African agendas. The Brundtland Report famously defined sustainable development as 'development which meets the needs of the present without compromising the ability of future generations to meet their own needs' (WCED 1987: 43). This definition is central to the 1998 National Environmental Management Act, which lays the basis for a holistic approach to environmental management in South Africa, although it also stresses the importance of ecological sustainability as a bottom line (Todes *et al.* 2005). The Act, *inter alia*, provides a set of principles which apply to all development in South Africa.

The relationship between progressive planning (see Chapter 2) and environmental management in the 1980s and early 1990s is a curious one. It might have been expected that there would have been considerable common ground between the two groupings, and that this would have infused planning with a strong sustainability orientation. Certainly, some planners and planning academics have always taken environmental concerns as being at the heart of planning, and some planning schools have long emphasized a broad definition of sustainability as core to planning. Further, a few planners were involved in progressive environmental movements, and documents from this era do include attention to issues such as the spatial form of the city, transportation, the quality of local environments, and informal settlements (EMG 1992). Similarly, a few environmentalists were involved in the built environment NGOs, and progressive environmentalists were well aware of the need to marry the 'brown' with the 'green' agendas. The importance of the sustainability discourse meant that it is contained in all legislation defining planning and its key guiding principles, such as the Development Facilitation Act of 1995, the 1997 Urban Development Framework, the White Paper on Spatial Planning and Land Use Management of 2000, as well as in the 1997 White Paper on Local Government, and the guidelines for integrated development planning.

Nevertheless, the conservative (and conservationist) orientation of mainstream environmental management, its technocratic approach, and its focus on site level assessments, jarred with initiatives to reformulate the identity of planning as a collaborative, developmentally oriented and facilitative practice, concerned particularly with redressing the apartheid heritage through delivering infrastructure and services and restructuring apartheid cities. The orientation of progressive planners reflected the predominant materialist and political focus of the left of the time. The South African urban studies literature that planners drew from similarly paid little attention to sustainability (Swilling 2004). While progressive planning was attempting to move sharply away from the past focus on land-use regulation towards a more forward-looking strategic approach, the dominant approach to environmental management was reactive, and centred on environmental protection through EIAs. Broader initiatives to attempt to infuse sustainability thinking within government and society came later, as did the shift towards a greater emphasis on strategic environmental management.

At the same time, the dominant practice of planning as land-use management was still relatively unreformed, with decision-making frequently based on old criteria defined by the Provincial Ordinances of the pre-1994 era, rather than by the new principles of planning legislation (Oakenfull 1998) or by sustainability criteria. For the environmentalists, and progressive environmentalists in particular, planning was often perceived as a narrow discipline, devoid of both social and ecological concerns (see Todes et al. 2005).

Thus planning and environmental management emerged as separate disciplines, with parallel sets of legislation, different institutional locations, and varying sets of networks, practices and discourses. While environmental management is the responsibility of the Department of Environment and Tourism, planning falls under the Department of Land Affairs, but much of the work of planners is carried out in terms of policy instruments located within the Department of Provincial and Local Government. The institutional positions of the two vary across provinces and local governments, but even where they are in single departments, there is not always a close relationship, let alone integration. There are also different policy communities, professional bodies and training. Although many planners have drawn sustainability concerns into their work, the drive towards the incorporation of sustainability thinking in policy has come largely from outside of planning. Initiatives such as Local Agenda 21 and Sustainable Cities have been driven mainly by environmentalists. The consequence of this divide has been a weak incorporation of sustainability concerns in planning, considerable duplication and a cumbersome system of planning and environmental assessment, placing severe pressure on limited capacity. The following sections explore these issues through an examination of the environment–planning relationships in land-use management, settlement planning, and in strategic planning at various scales.

LAND-USE MANAGEMENT

As noted in Chapters 3 and 6, the system of land-use management in South Africa still reflects colonial and apartheid history. There is an absence of national legislation providing a common framework for land-use management, and in many provinces, Planning Ordinances from the pre-1994 period remain in force. In addition, forms of land-use management are frequently fragmented along apartheid lines, with different levels of control, as well as forms of participation and decision-making around land-use decisions. For example, in the KwaZulu-Natal province, the 1949 Town Planning Ordinance remains, but largely covers historically white, coloured and Indian areas, with significant areas falling under the control of traditional authorities, or under systems of land-use management historically designed for 'black' areas, involving limited participation and a simplified system of zoning. However, since the formal property market in these latter areas is generally weakly developed, the bulk of applications for land-use change is concentrated in historically more advantaged areas. Fast-track systems to assess development applications have been created through the Development Facilitation Act of 1995, which in practice now makes decisions on large-scale developments in provinces where it is in force. In theory, all land-use change requires planning permission in terms of planning law (Berrisford 2005), although in many areas (such as informal settlements), no planning control exists de facto.

The formal system of land-use management exists alongside a system of environmental assessment, introduced through regulations in 1997. Unlike planning, the environmental assessment system is focused on activities which might have negative impacts, some of which go beyond the ambit of planning. Nevertheless, there are significant areas of overlap in the two processes. A new set of regulations was introduced in 2006, and while the intention was to narrow the range of activities which required assessment, and lighten the load of administrators, many commentators argued that they would place an even greater burden on administering authorities. In addition to environmental assessments, a third stream of Heritage Impact Assessments exists, with greater or lesser impacts in various areas.

The systems of planning applications and environmental assessments are governed through different pieces of legislation, occur through parallel processes (including participation), and are for the most part assessed by different authorities. Whereas environmental decisions are made by officials at provincial and national level, planning decisions are made at local level by politicians (although such decisions may be delegated to officials), and at provincial level by officials. Appeal bodies also differ, so that decisions on appeals may not be consistent. Applications that involve Heritage Impact Assessment can be even more complicated. The Development Facilitation Act provides a mechanism for coordinating all decisions, but even then has to await the outcome of the Environmental Impact Assessment (EIA), which can effectively veto development. While some provinces and municipalities are taking steps to enable better coordination between planning and environmental processes, there is considerable concern that this dual system is slowing development, but is not necessarily resulting in better decisions or ones that sufficiently reflect sustainability concerns (Todes *et al.* 2005).

As Chapter 8 showed, major concerns are being raised about the time taken to process land-development applications. The overlapping system of planning and environmental assessments is an important contributor to this problem. A study in Cape Town, where there is considerable development demand and no fast-track application system, showed how the triple processes of planning, environmental assessment and heritage assessment could result in decisions on development applications taking up to five years to complete (Townsend 2002). Concerns about these overlaps and delays have prompted a very recent revision of planning and environmental legislation and procedures in the Western Cape province. Sim *et al.*'s (2004) study of eThekwini municipality, which governs the Durban metropolitan area, showed that a minority of applications (11–20 per cent depending on the category) required both planning permission and environmental assessment, but where overlap occurred, processing times increased significantly from 3–6 months to 15 months. The eThekwini study however occurred in a period of relatively low growth, and in a situation where most larger and more complicated decisions which would require dual permissions were made through the tribunal created by the Development Facilitation Act. Although applications through the Development Facilitation Act are governed by strict time lines, the tribunal has to wait for decisions on the EIA before it can proceed. The dual process is also confusing and frustrating for developers and communities (Claasens 2003; Todes *et al.* 2005). In a study by Todes *et al.* (2005), environmental activists in Durban's polluted South Development Basin complained that they were constantly forced to chase after various applications, with very little effect.

It is not clear that the dual system is achieving its objectives in terms of sustainability. Although the intention of environmental assessments is to evaluate applications, such as planning applications, they are paid for by developers, and cannot necessarily be seen as an impartial assessment. There is presently no system of registration for environmentalists, and there is a concern that the quality of EIAs is frequently poor, and that no consistent set of values is being applied to EIAs (Patel 2004: 282–92). There is also overlap in the content of EIAs and planning applications, and in their assessment. Both planning and environmental authorities claim to assess applications on a holistic basis, and in this context, there is considerable potential for overlap. At the same time permissions in one sphere are often used to leverage permission in the other, so that decisions rest largely on either environmental or planning decision-making, rather than both (Todes *et al.* 2005). Berrisford (2005) argues that decision-makers may avoid making difficult decisions and leave hard choices to the other process, compromising the quality of the decision.

Further, there are indications that, despite the dual process, several issues frequently fall through the cracks, most notably social concerns (Sim *et al.* 2004; Todes *et al.* 2005). A narrow focus on biophysical dimensions is still common in EIAs, while in many provinces, the old logic of planning ordinances and dominant practice remains. For instance, in KwaZulu-Natal, the discourse of amenity, need and desirability, which was associated with the 1949 Ordinance, still prevails, despite the existence of a much broader set of principles in the Development Facilitation Act and the White Paper on Spatial Planning and Land Use Management. The establishment of an overlapping set of assessment processes can also be questioned in the light of severe capacity constraints in most municipalities and in provincial government. Further, dual processes of assessment in some areas co-exist with almost no assessment in others, linked to broader social divides.

Despite the difficulties associated with a parallel set of processes, the introduction of EIAs has at least provided a forum in which major land-use decisions are beginning to be debated. Thus in KwaZulu-Natal, an EIA played a major part in decisions on dune mining, with considerable implications for local livelihoods and the trajectory of development in a particular area. In the Eastern Cape, an EIA is the focus of debate over the potential impact of a major road development on both the

ecological integrity and economic prospects of the 'Wild Coast' – an impoverished, and hitherto relatively undeveloped area. More recently, a major debate has
ensued around the impact of the proliferation of golf estates in the Western Cape
on ecology, water supplies, farming, land values, access, design, communities and
their livelihoods, *inter alia*. This issue has emerged through the EIA system, and a
larger study (conducted by a planning firm) was undertaken to assess cumulative
impacts. In all of these cases a broader sustainability framework has been applied
to assess the range of potential impacts. By contrast, land-use decisions made
through the traditional planning system have rarely been a focus for such intense
social debate other than in the immediate locality. In part, the traditional planning
systems that still prevail invite more limited participation than do EIA processes.
Further, environmental groups have been active around EIAs, whereas planners
have not organized self-consciously around particular visions or ideas, in ways that
translate into activism around site-specific planning decisions. For instance, while
many planners subscribe to notions of compact, integrated cities, planners have
not lobbied against the shopping malls, gated communities and decentralized
office parks that are cutting across this vision, in the many planning processes
where site-specific decisions of this sort are made. Nor have the vague pro-
nouncements in academic papers and policy documents been taken forward into
concerted campaigns for alternative urban visions. Nevertheless, questions about
how land is used and its social implications – gated communities, divided cities,
and the like – are beginning to attract considerable debate, and it may be time for
planners to take land-use decision-making and the way it shapes life in cities much
more seriously. In this process, stronger engagement with environmentalists and
sustainability ideas could be important.

SETTLEMENT PLANNING

A common planning criticism of the apartheid city was the creation of monotonous
'black' townships and a poor environmental quality. As Chapter 6 noted, several
South African planners developed principles and guidelines for settlement planning
and layout which were intended to result in very different sorts of environments
(Dewar *et al.* 1979; Behrens and Watson 1996). Although not always articulated in
the language of sustainability, these concerns are present in the design concepts
developed. Texts of this sort were supplemented by those developed by environmentalists, such as Sowman and Urquhart's (1998) *A Place Called Home*, by the
outputs of NGOs, such as the Built Environment Support Group's *Towards the
Right to Adequate Housing* (BESG 1999), which paid considerable attention to
sustainability concerns, and by the work of architects and planners exploring these

concepts (e.g. Irurah *et al.* 2002: 244–62; du Plessis 2002). The Department of Housing carries responsibility for the implementation of the Habitat Agenda, and has generated conferences, research and guidelines on the sustainable settlements. There has thus been no shortage of manuals, concepts and ideas exploring the implications of sustainability for settlement planning and layout in South Africa, although it could be argued that these concepts have been developed on too abstract a basis, without sufficient consideration for the real constraints shaping the design of human settlements in South Africa.

As noted in Chapters 3 and 6, despite these efforts, the most striking visual feature of South Africa's post-apartheid urban development is the perpetuation of past settlement patterns. Several sustainability assessments of low-cost housing projects (Irurah *et al.* 2002; du Plessis 2002; Irurah and Boshoff 2003; Oelofse 1999) are highly critical of the architecture, design and layout of these projects. Oelofse (1999) argues that planners have not taken environment and sustainability seriously in the design and layout of low-cost housing schemes. Planners however frequently argue that their designs are highly constrained by the funding model and level of funding available (see also Chapter 6). For many authors, the key culprit is the housing policy itself, which has emphasized mass delivery of housing through the use of a housing subsidy which privileges 'greenfields' development based on a set of minimum standards: a stand size of 250 m^2, a minimum house size of 30 m^2, and a minimum set of services. Subsidies are for the production of the unit (which then cedes to ownership), and are graded by income. The subsidy is an uneasy compromise of considerations of 'width' (low-level to reach as many people as possible) versus depth (greater expenditure per unit). The effects of this policy in terms of sustainability are captured by Irurah and Boshoff:

> Through this programme, hundreds of thousands of houses have been developed on cheap land located on urban peripheries and with minimal levels of shelter and services. The typical product of the programme is the so-called matchbox typology replicated over tens or hundreds of hectares in a single project with minimal regard to sense of identity, pedestrian circulation, urban design and density, open spaces, integration of social services … Even though minimum service standards are set for sanitation, electricity and water, the overall shelter performance and standards of design and construction are only marginally better than the 'shack', which the so-called matchbox seeks to replace. Loss of community coherence and social networks creates further deficiencies in such settlements when compared to informal settlements …The above factors, coupled with others …, contribute to the perpetuation of poverty, segregation and environmental degradation.
>
> (Irurah and Boshoff 2003: 254)

The poor environments created by housing policy – which is ostensibly intended to further sustainability – is evidence of the policy contradictions and lack of resolution about the meaning of sustainability in South Africa noted by Patel (2004: 282–92). A National Strategy for Sustainable Development has been in the making for several years, and a draft document for discussion was published in 2006 (DEAT 2006). It remains to be seen whether some of its relatively radical recommendations will be taken up and carried through, and how it will affect these kinds of contradictions. Within settlement planning, stand-offs between planners and environmentalists frequently occur over the need for land for well-located low-cost housing development versus conservation. At one level, this might be seen as a classic brown versus green agenda conflict – and between planners focused on delivering development versus environmentalists attempting to conserve biodiversity. At another level, however, it can also be seen as a conflict between different emphases within a sustainability approach. Such trade-offs are inevitable, but there is as yet little guidance at national level on these issues, nor are they usually addressed in integrated development plans and spatial frameworks which could reflect local conditions.

There is a growing recognition of the limits of the past delivery approach within housing policy. NGOs have been active in developing approaches to more sustainable housing development, although generally at a project level (Irurah and Boshoff 2003). Recent policy shifts (DOH 2004) push more strongly towards a sustainability approach, and to taking environment into account in new housing schemes. It will be interesting to see whether the research and experience in this field inform the planning that is done, and whether the new policy does in fact provide the space in which more sustainable settlements can be developed.

Very little attention has been given to assessing whether sustainability concerns are being taken into account in the design of middle- and high-income areas, although there has been considerable debate over golf estates from this perspective. There is a growing fashion for eco-estates of various kinds, including golf estates, but it is doubtful that the construction of large gated estates, with poor access by workers, high levels of class separation, and which are dependent on transport by motor car, can be seen as a model of sustainable development.

STRATEGIC PLANNING

At national and provincial levels, strategic planning and strategic environmental management have occurred largely in parallel, although some strategic plans have reference to environmental concerns and sustainability issues. The system of Environmental Implementation Plans at national and provincial levels analyse environment and sustainability within sectoral departments, while State of Environment

Figure 9.1 Unsustainable settlements on the urban edge

Reporting provides an assessment of environment and sustainability at national and provincial levels, and for specific areas of environmental concern. The main forms of planning at these levels are the National Spatial Development Perspective (NSDP) and the Provincial Growth and Development Strategies (PGDS), which are expected to include a spatial component or framework. Findings of the State of Environment Report, and environment as a resource base, are considered in the NSDP, but the major concern is to argue for support for development in areas of economic potential. Environment and sustainability appear rather unevenly in PGDS documents, which focus largely on economic and social development, infrastructure, and on questions of governance.

Integrated development plans (IDPs) have been the most important form of strategic planning for local government in South Africa. In theory, IDPs provide an important space for integrating environment and sustainability in IDPs. According to

Coetzee (2002), IDPs can be seen as South Africa's version of Local Agenda 21 since they integrate social, economic and environmental issues into future-oriented plans with a multisectoral focus, and are based on a strong participatory process. In guide documents which were written to support the production of IDPs, environment and sustainability are seen as cross-cutting issues, and suggestions are made as to how they might be incorporated at various stages of the process. Nevertheless, plans which take sustainability as a starting point and central focus are rare, and where environment is included, it is often only considered as a sector focused on 'green' issues (Sowman 2002; DEAT 2003). Even national policies such as coastal zone management are often poorly integrated into IDPs (Markewicz and Rushby 2003). The weaknesses of IDPs in this regard in part reflect the limitations of the guide documents where most attention has been given to process, rather than content (Harrison 2003a). This is now being addressed by the production of guidelines on integrating sustainability into IDPs (e.g. DEAT 2003), but the impact of these initiatives remains to be felt. The limits of sustainability thinking in IDPs reflect the more general lack of attention to cross-cutting issues noted in Chapter 4. In effect many IDPs do little more than guide service delivery.

More fundamentally, the lack of attention to environmental dimensions of sustainability and to the overall concept of sustainability in IDPs reflects the outcomes of a collaborative approach to planning in which social and economic concerns emerge as dominant. Plans reflect the perspective of planners and the power of the various stakeholder interests and politicians represented in making them. As Evans and Rydin (1997) argue, an open collaborative process cannot ensure a sustainable outcome, nor that environmental dimensions are adequately addressed. For many communities and councillors, environmental concerns are seen as 'green issues', of less relevance to their immediate concerns for infrastructure, jobs, etc. Some innovative IDP processes, such as that of the Ugu district municipality on the KwaZulu-Natal south coast, have worked hard to draw the links between 'green' and 'brown' agenda issues, and to present sustainability as a more integrated idea, embedded in the daily concerns of marginalized communities and their councillors (Todes 2004). This more integrated approach has been promoted in more recent environmental guides (e.g. DEAT 2003), and later rounds of IDPs might reflect sustainability ideas more fully. To date, however, the role of individual planners and environmentalists in promoting this approach has been critical.

It might be expected that spatial development frameworks (SDFs) as part of IDPs would contain a strong environmental dimension. Local government legislation on SDFs includes a requirement for the production of a Strategic Environmental Assessment (SEA), but this is rarely done. It could be argued that the SEA process is likely to duplicate parts of the IDP and its processes, as has occurred in some instances, and that it would be preferable to integrate environment and sustainability as a standard concern within IDPs. Nevertheless, environment and sustainability are taken up unevenly within SDFs, giving rise to the production of a flurry of guides on these matters in some provinces.

The early proponents of the concept of spatial frameworks in South Africa were in part guided by concerns to create more sustainable cities (Dewar 2000). The critique of the sprawling apartheid city, and calls to compact and integrate the city, *inter alia*, through a set of mixed-use activity routes along which public transport would concentrate, can be seen in this light. Considerable attention was also given to the definition and protection of areas for conservation, and to the creation of urban edge. Critics of this approach however argue that the sustainability arguments against sprawl are overstated in the South African context where unemployment is high. The decentralization of employment in cities, and the reliance of the poor on domestic work and on local informal activities, has meant that the energy costs associated with the growth of peripheral low-income housing settlements are low, since few people travel to work in distant employment centres, and travel occurs through high-occupancy mini-bus taxis (Biermann 2003). Yet the energy costs of the growing pattern of car-oriented residential, office and retail development for the better-off on the edge of cities are likely to be more significant. A relatively laissez-faire approach to these developments was adopted in many cities, sometimes in contradiction to the spatial framework (see Chapter 6). Many spatial frameworks however did not directly consider the sustainability of property development patterns generated by the wealthy.

Some recent spatial frameworks have begun to consider these issues more explicitly. For instance, plans for the eThekwini's growing northern and western areas explicitly consider the carrying capacity of catchments and the health of rivers which offer environmental services to the city. Questions of landscape quality and quality of place are also considered (Sim 2005). In the case of eThekwini, attention to sustainability in current planning has built on several initiatives over the past decade, including major LA21 and State of Environment projects. Although the outcomes of individual initiatives have sometimes been disappointing (Roberts and Diederichs 2002), sustainability as a discourse is becoming far more prevalent in planning, as well as in other sectors. Environmental initiatives have also provided an information base upon which more environmentally sensitive planning can occur. Nevertheless, sustainability is understood in different ways by various actors (Sim 2005), so the meaning of policy and its implications for implementation are inevitably contested. Thus inclusion of these ideas within strategic planning is not a straightforward process.

CONCLUSION

The incorporation of environment and sustainability in planning has been uneven, although there is a growing interest by planners in these concerns. The dominance of political approaches to progressive planning and a history of conservative environmentalism under apartheid underpinned a divide between planning and environmental management as different, and sometimes competing sets of practices. Whereas planning focused on delivery and on strategic future-oriented planning, much of the focus on environmental management has been at site level, where planning remains largely unreconstructed. With some exceptions, strategic planning has not included a strong focus on sustainability, but there are several initiatives to strengthen these dimensions in contemporary planning.

There is a growing interest in initiatives to move beyond a divide between planning and environmental management in South Africa. The dysfunctionality of duplicating systems is being recognized and there are moves towards rationalization at national level, and in some provinces. Further, as both planners and environmentalists move to embrace more holistic approaches, traditional 'brown' versus 'green' agenda divides begin to be transcended. Nevertheless, as Owens and Cowell (2002) point out, there are real tensions between different aspects of sustainability, which will be played out however systems are structured. In South Africa, these tensions are exacerbated by policy contradictions at national level. There are also likely to be continuing differences between collaborative forms of planning, which require a balancing of interests, and environmental management, which demands an ecological bottom line. Yet there is considerable scope for strengthening attention to environment and sustainability as standard practices in planning. It can be argued that the failure of South African planning to embrace these dimensions sufficiently has meant that it has remained relatively marginal to one of the major agendas underpinning the resurgence of planning internationally.

PART 4

PLANNING AND SOCIETY

INTRODUCTION: INTERNATIONAL DEBATES

Debate about what might be the 'boundaries' of planning as a set of activities and a profession is ongoing, but there have been detectable shifts in these boundaries over time largely in response to changes in broader political and institutional contexts. Defining such boundaries has been of particular significance for those engaged in the education of planners and for those concerned with the definition and regularization of the planning profession. It has also become a central concern for those involved in producing planning 'theory', and it is here that the most intensive debates on this issue have occurred.

In most parts of the world planning has moved away from its post-war conception as the 'physical planning and design of human settlements' (Taylor 1998: 4), although this emphasis remains to a degree in European planning as well as in certain post-colonial planning systems. This conception tied planning firmly to a concern with physical space, making clear the belief that intervention in social, economic and political matters was the responsibility of other disciplines and professions. It also encapsulated the view of planning as a technical activity, carried out by trained experts within specialized bureaucratic structures, and preferably isolated from the parochial and immediate demands of citizens and politicians. The perceived relationship between planners and society thus remained a distant one, although it did not dissuade planners of the time of a belief in the ability of planned environments to deterministically shape social and economic life.

In more recent decades the context within which planners work has changed significantly, forcing planners to reconsider earlier descriptions of their discipline and focus of activity. In particular, the changing role of local government from service delivery and administration to one of orchestrating and facilitating development, in partnership with other organs of civil society (or the shift from government to governance), has recast the role of planners. Thomas's (2004) argument that in the UK departmental and professional boundaries have been destroyed and planning functions unbundled into other locations both within and outside of government, is true of South Africa as well. As local governments are required to become 'developmental', so planning has become a function of the whole institution and not just the spatial planning and development control sections. Moreover, the recent concern with integrating the sectoral actions of government (Chapter 7) has required planners to interact far more with other departments and professionals – often in strategic and project teams – thus further challenging the strictly spatial notion of planning. The same is true of planners working in a wide variety of roles within civil society.

The changing role of government and its new relationship with civil society have also presented a challenge to the notion of the planner as technical expert with an assumed mandate from the public to pursue a self-defined concept of 'the public good'. This challenge has been clearly reflected in debates in planning theory, where current mainstream writings focus on the communicative and collaborative role of planning, and where some authors (Innes 1995) claim that a 'paradigm shift' in planning has occurred. In terms of this position, the relationship between planners and society has changed completely: interaction (with stakeholders or interest groups), communicating ideas, forming arguments, debating differences in understandings, and finally reaching consensus on a course of action replaces detached, expert-driven plan-making as the primary activity of planners. The additional advantage of this approach, it is argued, is that it allows planners to benefit from 'local knowledge', referring to 'items of information that are mapped and interpreted within the sense-making frameworks and purposes of particular social networks' (Healey 1999: 116). This is different from 'expert' (or sometimes Western) knowledge: it consists of common sense and practical reason, proverbs and metaphors, practical skills and routines, and may be spoken or unspoken.

This new understanding of planning as socially constructed recognizes that it is also value driven (rather than being a technical and neutral activity). This in turn raises the question of whose values are driving it, or whose values emerge as dominant from the inevitable conflict that surrounds most planning decisions. The position of communicative action theorists, that consensus on shared values (or at least consensus on shared action) can be reached through dialogue, has been challenged by those who argue that power and domination are always present in such processes and cannot be so easily wished away (Flyvbjerg 1998a, 1998b). A faith in consensus-seeking processes to reflect agreed action based on shared values has also been challenged by those calling for a recognition of the increasingly multicultural nature of societies (Sandercock 1998) and by those who identify the deep and often fundamental differences that divide societies and render questionable certain of the assumptions on which mainstream planning theory is based (Watson 2002c, 2003a; Yiftachel 2003). Other authors (Connelly and Richardson 2004) have questioned the extent to which planning processes reliant on collaboration can deliver outcomes that achieve environmental and social justice, implying a possibly more active role for planners and experts and a refocusing on planning products as well as on decision-making processes.

Debates about the boundaries and focus of planning have found clearest expression in the attempts by professional planning bodies to define their areas of concern. The 2001 RTPI (Royal Town Planning Institute) document, *A New Vision for*

Planning, provides a stark contrast with the earlier view of planning as 'physical planning and design of human settlements'. The core concern of planning remains spatial: the document states that planning involves the twin activities of the management of competing uses for space, and the making of places that are valued and have identity. In addition, however, the need for integrated planning requires that spatial planning take account of a broader set of issues (such as 'inequalities in health and education, energy policy, the rural economy and urban design'), and bring together 'a wider range of professional skills and disciplines', such that 'professional planners facilitate, but do not own or monopolise [the activity]'. The boundaries of the profession are now blurred, both in terms of who engages in planning and the scope of planning knowledge and concerns. The idea of a profession based on disciplinary autonomy has gone, and there is recognition that the arenas of knowledge and action are sometimes shared. Furthermore, the role of the planner vis-à-vis society has changed: the vision statement calls for negotiated processes and a shared commitment to act, but within an equitable decision-making framework which recognizes that effective planning cannot always be achieved through consensus.

This section of the book traces the nature of these debates in South Africa as they have evolved over the past ten years. Both the planning profession and planning educators have had to come to grips with a rapidly changing context for planning, in which the role and definition of planning in South African society are continually challenged. Planning can no longer divorce itself, as it did in the past, from the pressing social issues of poverty, inequality and disease, and it has been forced as well to confront the reality of conflicting values and cultures in a context of scarce resources. These imperatives have lent a particularly sharp edge to debates in South Africa.

CHAPTER 10

THE PLANNING PROFESSION AND SOCIETY

INTRODUCTION

The focus of this chapter is on the work of planners and the organized planning profession in South Africa, and how both of these were affected by the process of transformation before and after 1994. It shows how the changing context within which planners work, and particularly change in the nature and role of government, has brought about tensions in the way planners conceive of their professional identity and the 'boundaries' of their work. In this respect there are commonalities between planners in South Africa and in many other parts of the world. But planners in this country have faced additional tensions involving the deep involvement of planning with the apartheid project of the past and the broader processes of societal and professional transformation which have taken place since 1994. The chapter[1] will show how planning professionals had great difficulty in maintaining both their jobs and status in the 1990s but that this position has changed in recent years with a growing recognition of the need for planners and a higher profile for an increasingly transformed planning profession.

Macdonald's (1995) notion of the 'professional project' provides a useful lens through which to understand aspects of the history of the South African planning profession. He argues that the primary goal of the professional project is to achieve and maintain a degree of 'social closure' that ensures adequate economic protection for members of the profession as well as status in the social order. This involves the need to carve out a jurisdiction for the profession, to define a social reality for the area in which the profession operates, to control the production of professional knowledge, to define the boundaries and relationships with other professions, and to gain and maintain the support and sponsorship of political elites. To achieve these goals a profession must establish a 'regulative bargain' with the state, which may need to be renegotiated in times of political change. Failure to secure a regulative bargain leaves the profession open to competition from related professions and raises the spectre of 'deprofessionalization'. In the context of South Africa planners were eventually able to secure such a relationship with the apartheid state, but this in turn has proved to be an undermining factor in the post-democracy period, and the negotiation of a satisfactory relationship with the (post-apartheid) state is still under way.

THE PLANNING PROFESSION AND APARTHEID

In South Africa, as elsewhere, the early part of the last century reflected a struggle to establish planning as a profession separate from those of land surveying, architecture and engineering, and to establish professional associations to represent the growing number of planners in the country. It involved as well the establishment of university-based programmes to train planning professionals – see Chapter 11. The first major milestone in the history of the organized profession was the establishment of the South African Institute of Town Planners in 1954, although a South African branch of the British Town Planning Institute had been set up in 1944, and professional bodies had been formed as early as 1919. The separation from the British profession was a difficult process. Muller (1993: 9) describes how 'much energy was expended in debate on the matter' and that 'after considerable hand wringing and head scratching, it was resolved that the time was appropriate for the formation of an independent South African Institute of Planners'. However, this newly formed independent body re-established ties with the British Town Planning Institute just four years later, through an Agreement of Affiliation, and these ties remained in place for 20 years until they were severed by the Royal Town Planning Institute (RTPI) as a gesture of protest against apartheid policies.

Throughout the 1960s planning remained a minor profession with relatively low status. The Secretary of the national Department of Planning observed in 1965, at the opening of a conference on planner training, that until very recently planning was a Cinderella of the professions. At universities it was an appendage to other faculties and in public organizations it was never more than a subsection in a big department (Oranje 1998). According to practitioners active at the time, clients did not regard town planners as professional people and often shopped around for the best price, resulting in unprofessional work and low fees for planners. Numerically, as well, they were a small grouping: a survey in 1967 found only 105 qualified planners engaged in planning work, compared with 9500 engineers and 1000 architects (Oranje 1998).

A rapid expansion in the demand for planning in the 1970s, particularly in the public sector, strengthened the ability of planning to establish its own identity and protect its domain. A regulative bargain between the profession and the state was eventually formalized by the Town and Regional Planners Act of 1984, which established a statutory South African Council for Town and Regional Planners (SACTRP). This allowed the registration of planners, the reservation of certain categories of work for planners (although job reservation was never actually implemented), disciplinary measures for 'improper conduct', the accreditation of educational programmes and the setting of tariffs and fees. But the process of establishing this regulative bargain had been highly contested. The Institute had promoted planning as an entirely technical and politically neutral profession, concerned only to rational-ize land development and management using the objectives and models internationally recognized at the time. This stance proved to be a useful source of legitimation for those involved in the implementation of the spatial goals of racial segregation, and in the process many planners had become deeply enmeshed in the project of apartheid. For some planners, the creation of a statutory body brought the profession far too closely into alignment with government, and they contested both the supposed neutrality of planning and the extension of state control over its work through the new Act.

Chapter 2 documents the split that began to emerge within the planning pro-fession and certain of the academic institutions over the political role of planning, and the emergence during the 1980s of a new generation of progressive planners who strongly challenged the dominant conservatism of the profession. In the then Natal Province, progressive planners formed a new association in 1986, the Planning and Development Association (PADA), 'to take an unequivocal stand against apartheid', but after political harassment of a number of its members, it dis-banded. At the 1985 congress of the South African Institute of Town and Regional Planning (SAITRP) a resolution was proposed which read that 'apartheid and all its statutory manifestations are antithetical to development and our planning ethic ...'. The resolution was defeated by 93 votes to 45 (Smit 1988). Yet only a few years later, the Institute began to question its earlier conservatism: in response to the 1990 announcement that the ANC would be unbanned and Nelson Mandela would be released from prison, it appointed a Planning Issues Committee to investigate 'those critical issues that need to be addressed by planners in the new South Africa' (in Harrison and Kahn 2002: 258). There appeared to be a realization within the Institute that its apparent collusion with the apartheid state would make it difficult to maintain a regulative bargain through a period of political transition.

THE PLANNING PROFESSION IN THE POST-APARTHEID PERIOD

During and after the transition to democracy, neither the ability of the profession to maintain its organizational unity nor the relationship between the profession and the state were guaranteed.

As it became clear that regime change was under way, the conservative lean-ings of the SAITRP were challenged again. At the 1992 AGM of the Institute a number of African members raised complaints that those with planning 'diplomas' (many of whom were African) rather than postgraduate degrees were not being fully recognized for Institute membership, that insufficient black planners were being trained, that Afrikaans was often used as the language medium of meetings and conferences and served to marginalize black people and international visitors, and that the constitution of the Institute needed review. When it became clear that the Institute was unwilling to address these concerns, a breakaway group of progressively minded planners, including a significant proportion of South Africa's black planners, organized themselves into the Planners' Forum. A committee under the convenorship of Professor John Muller of the University of Witwatersrand planning school drew up a list of 14 'points of concern' considered necessary to transform the Institute. The SAITRP, at a meeting with the Planners' Forum, was dismissive of the points of concern and claimed to be addressing them anyway. At this point the Forum members felt that negotiation with the Institute was unlikely to succeed and they formed the Development Planning Association of South Africa (DPASA) in January 1994.

The DPASA failed to gain any significant funding and struggled to extend its membership much beyond its Gauteng (Johannesburg region) base, but it was able to secure recognition from segments of the new political leadership that had withdrawn from the SAITRP. Thus it was not long before negotiations began between the institutionally weak DPASA and the politically illegitimate SAITRP. The SAITRP suggested a search for ways in which greater cohesion could be reached between the organizations, and in 1996 the two bodies amalgamated to form the new South African Planning Institution (SAPI), later amended to Institute. The profession had found a way to maintain a level of unity and also to secure continued recognition from the new government.

The issue of continued government recognition, however, was also not straightforward. Soon after coming into power the new government gave notice to the profession that the regulative bargain would have to be renegotiated. In 1995, the national Department of Land Affairs (under which the planning function had been placed) sponsored a workshop on the future of the planning profession, held at the resort of Club Mykonos in the Western Cape. Key progressive planners, now highly placed in the new state structures, pushed hard for the transformation of the profession. Dr Laurine Platzky, a senior planner in the Office for Reconstruction and Development, was particularly forthright about the need for change. She spoke of a credibility crisis in the profession and claimed that the 'profession is dominated by pedestrian planners who are poorly informed about the needs and aspirations of the majority of black planners' (Harrison and Kahn 2002: 259). The Club Mykonos Accord (see Box 10.1) committed the planning profession to support the principles of the ANC's Reconstruction and Development Programme, and to instituting a wide-reaching transformation within its structures and methods of operation. In 1996 the statutory Council (SACTRP) affirmed that 'the cornerstone of the code of ethics of planners should be to further the interests of the underprivileged and disadvantaged

Box 10.1 The Club Mykonos Accord (1995)

'Having noted the changed socio-political circumstances in South Africa, we the participants in the workshop on the future of the planning profession, resolve that:

1   We commit ourselves to the principles of the RDP.
2   Recognise the need to review the ethical base of the planning profession.
3   Recognise the need to restructure the provisions of the Act and to review the composition of the SACTRP so that it is more representative in terms of race and gender, and reflects the full spectrum of planning interests.
4   Mandate the restructured SACTRP to review the system of planning education at all levels (community, technical, professional and continuing education).
5   Mandate the restructured SACTRP to investigate the process of registration in order to improve access to the profession.
6   To devise a communication strategy to inform communities at large about the planning process and the profession.
7   The operations of the SACTRP be conducted in a fully participatory and transparent manner.
8   To establish ongoing co-operation with the Forum for Effective Planning and Development in order to contribute to policy debates pertaining to development.'

Source: (Muller 2003: 76)

communities' (Muller 1997: 55) and it set up a transition committee to rewrite the Town and Regional Planners Act of 1984. The new Planning Profession Act, passed in 2002, in fact did not depart significantly from the previous one. It provides for a Council located in the Department of Land Affairs, professional registration, the accreditation of planning training programmes, a set of ethics and procedures for dealing with disciplinary matters, and even allows for a measure of 'job reservation' for planning.

PLANNING PRACTICE IN THE POST-1994 PERIOD

It has been suggested a number of times in this book that for some planners the transition to democracy ushered in a period of great hope and euphoria: here at last was an opportunity to promote planning that was truly for the benefit of all and cities that met the goals of equity and sustainability, and to function in the international planning arena without the embarrassment that close links with the apartheid state had brought about. In the workplace, however, these hopes were rarely realized and planners found themselves negotiating new and difficult institutional and practical terrains. At the risk of some generalization, it is possible to identify a period of particular difficulty from the mid-1990s to the early 2000s, but with indications in the very recent period that certain aspects of the professional environment may be changing for the better.

The relationship between the profession and the state has been complicated by institutional restructuring and the fragmentation of the planning function across different line-function departments. While the Department of Land Affairs was given responsibility for the administration of the professional Act and for land management and physical planning, the Department of Provincial and Local Government was charged with the new system of integrated development planning at local level, of which spatial planning forms an important element. Emerging from this split are also competing definitions of planning: the DLA has tended to adopt a definition of planning as land-use control (evident in its still-pending Land Use Bill), while the DPLG has incorporated forward and strategic spatial planning, as a means of coordinating the actions of other line-function departments in space, into its system of integrated development planning. Confusion over where the responsibility for spatial planning lies, evident in two different and competing definitions from the two departments as to what should comprise a spatial development framework, led some planners to suggest that planning might more logically lie with Provincial and Local Government, and that stronger support for the profession could more likely be forthcoming from this department. Clearly the idea of a regulative bargain with the state can be nuanced by a consideration of which faction of the state it is best to strike that bargain with.

At the municipal level two rounds of restructuring, in 1995 and 2000, and efforts to 'streamline' the bureaucracies led to the freezing of many planning posts and a contraction of employment opportunities in the public sector. For example, in 2001 it was estimated that 45 per cent of posts in the various planning directorates in the Durban (eThekwini) Municipality were unfilled (Todes *et al.* 2003). While the demand for planners and the planning function remained high, the resources were simply not available to fill posts. The disruptions of restructuring and the resource squeeze similarly affected private planning firms. Firms had largely relied on the public sector for commissions, but during the 1990s this work became less predictable and secure, and payments were often delayed. At the same time the policy environment was in continual flux and became increasingly complex. Many larger firms downsized and chose to buy in specialized knowledge on a contract-by-contract basis. Private-sector planners interviewed during a survey in KwaZulu-Natal in 1999 (Harrison and Kahn 2002: 269) made the following comments: '... there is more institutional and legislative complexity at a time of reduced capacity ...'; '... consultants have to do the impossible and end up subsidising government ... this can't go on...'; '... I have high personal stress and related ill health...'.

Other workplace factors contributed to the difficulties faced by planners in both the public and private spheres. Planners complained of the low status of planning in the bureaucracy and the new role played by politicians in local government which in many places had largely removed delegated powers from planning officials. Planning decisions frequently became highly politicized issues in situations where the spatial allocation of resources or issues of racial integration were strongly contested. Harrison and Kahn (2002: 270) recorded the comments: '... there is little regard for planning which is seen as an obstacle to political initiative ...' and '... planners are being dictated to by people who have no knowledge of planning ...'.

Planners also complained of increasing workloads, the difficulties of keeping up with the constant stream of new policies and legislative requirements and the difficult and time-consuming nature of public participation in planning projects. The policy of affirmative action in government and in consultancies engaged by the public sector predictably had a negative effect on the sense of security and prospects of white planners (the bulk of the profession). It served to open up planning jobs for black planners, a process which might otherwise have taken many years to happen, but also resulted in young and inexperienced black planners being placed in positions of great responsibility, with little opportunity for mentoring or in-service learning. The pressure for affirmative action has been difficult for the private sector to respond to, as black planners have been largely moving into the better-paying public sector, and they are highly mobile in this context. Many white firms adopted the strategy of rapid promotion of new young black planners to director status, in order to meet state 'equity' requirements, but with these new young directors accorded little in the way of actual responsibilities or respect. For some this 'tokenism' has been a demoralizing and undermining experience. In the public sector affirmative action policies have been the cause of many resignations as white planners realized that promotion opportunities would be blocked, or found it impossible to work under new directors with much less experience than their own. Some comments from the KwaZulu-Natal survey (Harrison and Kahn 2002: 270) were: '... senior posts in the public sector have been filled with planners of little experience, or people not qualified ...'; '... promotion prospects are politically determined and are not based on relevant qualifications or experience ...' and '... morale is suffering as senior planners are passed over for promotion because of affirmative action criteria ...'.

By the end of the 1990s the organization of the profession was in bad shape. Membership of both the SAPI and the statutory Council (SACTRP) had fallen off and neither organization was strongly active. Seriously fraudulent activities on the part of an administrator of the SACTRP were uncovered at this time, and this led to financial loss and also the loss of the entire national database of planners.

Private planning consultancies across the country had downsized and many had diversified into areas such as environmental management, property management, housing, local economic development and geographic information systems (GIS) in order to survive. Planning firms also began to compete for work in the rest of the African continent to supplement domestic opportunities. As planning firms branched into other fields so firms in fields such as engineering, architecture, management and land surveying moved into territory that was traditionally delineated for planners. New turf disputes began to emerge between planners and the environmental profession which had expanded its scope to include impact assessment in relation to social and economic factors as well as biophysical ones, thus encroaching on planners' traditional territory. At the same time, and particularly in the Gauteng region, there was a decline in traditional forms of planning work such as land-use management, and layout and design. The competition in the job market faced by planners contributed to the declining profitability of planning firms, and tariffs increased at less than the inflation rate over a number of years. In the public sector as well, planners increasingly entered a range of professional areas other than planning and they were to be found in departments of environment, transport, housing, and economic development, and very often in charge of the overall integrated development planning process, where their generalized planning skills and understanding of a planning method stood them in good stead. The interpenetration of planning and other disciplines, and the related blurring of the identity of planning, was a significant trend of the 1990s.

PRESENT AMBIGUITIES

By 2006 this situation had largely changed for the better, although not in all respects. On the negative side, the regulative bargain between the profession and the state is in a state of tension. The passing of the Planning Profession Act in 2002 paved the way for the establishment of a new governing Council and new procedures to regulate and protect the profession. However, the planning function appears to have been of low priority in the DLA and the process of establishing the new structures has been slow and untransparent. Planning schools have complained that they have been sidelined in the process, as the three seats on the Council set aside for the education sector have been filled by just one planning academic and a law academic, with the third seat left unfilled. Four years after the passing of the Act, a new education subcommittee has been formed and one school has been newly accredited as at mid-2007. New legislation to govern the function and form of urban and regional planning has been in Bill form for a number of years, and planning remains the last unreformed area of national policy in the post-apartheid government. Tensions between the SAPI and the now-termed South African Council for Planners (SACPLAN) are still unresolved, and the SAPI continues to attempt to pressure the SACPLAN to carry out the functions it was set up to do.

Given the increasingly blurred boundaries, in practice, between the planning and other built environment professionals, and given the inability of the state to offer legal protection for planning work (both under the previous and current Act) it might be appropriate to ask what the real benefits are of a regulative bargain with state. The planning profession appears to have survived intact in South Africa despite the lack of a protective function from the state, as it has in other parts of the world (particularly Latin America) where less emphasis has been placed on the need for planning to assert and protect a particular identity. In the UK, anyone can call themselves a planner. In terms of a Royal Charter the Royal Town Planning Institute (RTPI) owns the title 'Chartered Town Planner', and the designatory letters MRTPI. The position of a spokesperson for the RTPI is that statutory protection would 'give the wrong message' and that 'the real effort should go into developing a competent and capable professional cadre (of planners) whose skills earn respect, and an educated and demanding clientele who are capable of recognizing what good spatial planning can do' (personal communication: Secretary-General RTPI 2006).

On the positive side, both the profile of planning and the level of organization of the profession have improved in the last few years. In the workplace, municipalities are recovering from the last round of restructuring and the larger ones, at least, are beginning to function more effectively. Departmental organograms have been drawn up and implemented and some frozen posts are being filled. This is particularly the case in the Gauteng region where jobs are being advertised and there is a substantial demand for planners, mainly in local government but also in the private sector as a result of the property boom. Currently planning schools in the region are struggling to meet this demand and there are indications of a growing shortage of planners. Consultancies are still battling with affirmative action policies and there are still many very small firms, but the number of black planning graduates (now numerically dominant in most planning schools) has increased steadily and these planners are finding their way into both public- and private-sector jobs. The number of planners carrying out spatial planning or land-use management work is probably quite limited, and planners continue to move into a wide range of related work areas.

Within the last couple of years there has been a renewed recognition at the national level that the benefits of economic growth do not automatically 'trickle down' to the poor. The recent shift in macroeconomic policy which adds on to the strongly neo-liberal GEAR a focus on infrastructure-led development (see Chapter 7) reflects a concern with the lack of delivery of local services and the continued inability of the poor to benefit from the fruits of economic growth, and represents a new focus on the ability of municipalities to deliver services and basic infrastructure. Debates about the need for a 'developmental state' are closely related to this concern, but the planning capacity of local government remains a constraining factor.

Very recently, questions have been asked at the national level (the Treasury) about the extent to which an unreformed planning system is constraining the achievement of economic growth targets (a similar concern in the UK has given rise to the Barker Commission). On all these issues the SAPI and individual planning professionals have had positive interactions with the Treasury and the President's Office where there seems to be growing recognition of the value of planning skills. This emerged most clearly in a recent statement by the Deputy President[2] who identified the scarcest skills in South Africa as city, urban and regional planning and engineering skills (see Chapter 7).

The SAPI has greatly strengthened as an organization in the last few years, now with 592 active members, largely due to the energetic efforts of twice-president Christine Platt (currently president of the Commonwealth Association of Planners). It organized two high-profile international planning conferences – Planning Africa 2002 in Durban and Planning Africa 2006 in Cape Town, which drew local academics and practitioners as well as delegates from the rest of Africa and other parts of the world. The organization is now well funded, national meetings are held regularly, and most of the nine provincial branches are functioning, if unevenly. An important issue for the organization has been the transformation of its leadership, which is now far less white than it used to be. Late in 2005, the SAPI's Gauteng branch committee hosted a workshop of mainly black planners in the province to debate transformation and the continued low level of black membership of the organization in the province. The outcome was the reconstitution of the branch committee into a majority black body, and significantly higher levels of black participation in the activities of the branch. Other regions, such as Limpopo and the Western Cape, have also succeeded in transforming the racial profile of their organization and, with the election of a black president and deputy president of the national body in 2006, the racial profile of leadership in the profession has finally shifted. There are, however, other dimensions of transformation that need serious attention. Currently, for example, the lack of mentoring of young professionals is a matter of concern, as is the need for ongoing upgrading of skills within a rapidly changing context.

Both the SAPI and individual South African planners have also been building an international profile, in parallel with the planning education sector in South Africa (see Chapter 11). The SAPI initiated the formation of an African Planning Association, and at the 2006 Planning Africa conference delegates from six countries outside of South Africa committed themselves to building an Africa-wide organization. The SAPI has also gained international recognition. It was invited to join the UN-Habitat Professionals Forum Steering Committee and was represented at the World Urban Forum in Vancouver in June 2006 where Christine Platt was elected president of the Commonwealth Association of Planners.

CONCLUSION

This chapter has discussed the changing fortunes of the organized planning profession in South Africa, using Macdonald's (1995) concept of a professional project.
This shows that planners have adopted strategies to promote and secure their professional status which are common to a wide range of professions. Significantly, in
the apartheid years this brought planning ethics into direct conflict with the ethics of
the segregationist project, only resolvable for the planning profession through the
claim that planning was a technical and politically neutral activity. Not only did this
claim serve to divide the profession during the apartheid years, but it placed it in a
difficult position when it came to renegotiating its regulative bargain with the state in
the period of political transition. While the terms of this bargain, for a variety of reasons, have not yet been satisfactorily resolved, the profession itself appears to have
weathered the difficult years of the 1990s and to be gaining in terms of profile and
organization. In the process planners have had to redefine the boundaries of their
expertise and their relationship to other professionals, very much as has been the
case in other parts of the world. Their ability to do this despite the weakened nature
of their formal and statutory relationship with the state raises the question of how
useful such a regulative bargain might be for the survival of the profession.

CHAPTER 11

EDUCATING PLANNERS

INTRODUCTION

Planning educators internationally are responding in various ways and to varying degrees to the changing nature and understanding of planning (e.g. see Friedmann 1996; Sandercock 1998; Poxon 2001; Oszawa and Salzer 1999; RTPI 2003). The diffusion of planning, its greater breadth and scope and the broader knowledge base required as a consequence of new technologies, the globalization of ideas, and significant shifts in the competencies required of planning, have sparked considerable debate over the appropriate orientation and focus of planning education. The blurring of boundaries between planning and other fields, and challenges to the notion of professionalism, have also been key concerns. In many countries, the relationship between planning education and planning practice has been at the heart of debates. The development of contextually 'relevant' planning education for the global South has also been widely debated as part of rethinking planning (Diaw *et al.* 2002; Rakodi 1996: 45–56; Hamza and Zetter 2000). While much of the literature has focused on what ought to be the orientation of planning education, in reality, the various pressures to rationalize higher education and to remould it in terms of the principles of the new public management, have been critical in shaping planning education (Hague 2002).

Planning education in South Africa has faced many similar challenges to those experienced internationally. In addition, planning educators are required to respond to the needs of a rapidly changing student body, a tertiary education system that is in considerable flux, and a transformed planning system that presents a huge demand in terms of new competencies. This chapter explores the challenges facing planning education in South Africa, and how educators have sought to respond. It begins by providing an overview of debates in planning education internationally, and then explores the changing context for planning education in South Africa. It considers the emergence and development of planning education under apartheid, and the major changes since 1994. It focuses in particular on the rapid shifts in the racial composition of students, the more nuanced gender shifts, and on the broadening and diversification of planning education as planning has extended beyond its traditional boundaries. The last section of the chapter discusses the way South African planning educators have constructed a broad set of planning competencies as a frame for planning education, in response to debates over the appropriate orientation and scope of planning education. It also considers the tensions and dilemmas in planning education between the need to provide a pragmatic practice-oriented training and the need to sustain a critical pedagogy that produces planners who are able to probe, challenge, think critically and pursue a transformative planning practice.

INTERNATIONAL DEBATES ON PLANNING EDUCATION

The decline of planning as a design-oriented technocratic field, and its growing diffusion and widening scope, have for some time posed considerable challenges for planning education internationally. In 1957, Perloff noted the tensions over whether planning education should focus on product or process skills, on technical versus humanistic concerns, and whether educators should aim to produce generalists or specialists. Several studies show the growing diversity of competencies and skills required by planners – for instance, Zehner's (1999) research in Australia showed that the number of skills required by planners almost doubled from 19 to 33 between 1979 and 1996. While planning schools have attempted to cope by adding courses and options, and rethinking what constitutes the 'core' of planning education, the work of the Royal Town Planning Institute's Education Commission (RTPI 2003) suggests a much deeper set of changes at work. It argues that in the future there will be an even greater diffusion of planning practices, and that disciplinary boundaries will continue to become more porous. From this perspective, a focus on a narrow set of skills and competencies is problematic, and planning education should instead produce critical and reflexive practitioners, operating with a strong sense and awareness of values – both their own, and those of other people.

The position of the RTPI's Education Commission is consistent with the work of Sandercock (1998) who critiques the notion of skills and competencies and argues instead for attention to literacies (technical, analytical, multicultural, ecological and design), and to encouraging critical thinking and self-reflection. Similarly Poxon argues that

> the role of the planner is so ill-defined now that it is difficult to claim that a planning course is providing training for a particular job. Instead, it should be exposing students to the complexity and intricacy of a planner's role, ... and equipping them with the knowledge, skills and attitudes upon which further training can be built

(Poxon 2001: 573)

A common theme in the literature is the split between planning education and planning practice. The divide is particularly acute in the USA context where the pressures on academia have resulted in a considerable distance between practice and the academy. For Poxon (2001), writing in the British context, the claimed split between planning education and planning practice is overstated, at least if planning education successfully encourages the development of 'reflexive practitioners'. Yet the degree of distance can be significant. Hamza and Zetter (2000) argue that planning education in developing countries does not engage with the dominance of informal urban processes, the weakness of the state, and the way in which development might occur in this context. Their work reflects the thinking of a broader set of writers (e.g. Rakodi 1996; Diaw *et al.* 2002) who find that planning education in developing countries is based on imported models and assumptions, and is thus unable to prepare graduates to confront a very different set of challenges.

Several of these tensions are evident in South Africa, where planning has broadened in scope, and where design and land-use management are being marginalized in favour of strategic and developmental planning, although they are still an important part of the work many planners do (Todes *et al.* 2003). Planning educators have experienced considerable dilemmas in addressing the varying demands of the marketplace, and in producing planners who are reflexive, but who also have sufficient skills to operate in a context where capacity and mentoring are limited, and demands on entry-level planners are high. These challenges underpin initiatives on the part of planning educators to develop more appropriate planning education, although there are questions as to whether they have sufficiently grasped the more pervasive realities of the South African context (Watson 2003b).

In exploring the appropriate directions for planning education, South African planners have drawn on both literature and links to planning schools internationally. Historically, links were largely to the colonial 'home' or to developed countries. For many years under apartheid, South African planning education was relatively isolated. In recent years, planning academics in South Africa have begun to build connections with those in the rest of Africa. At the first World Planning Schools Congress in Shanghai in 2001 a number of South African and other African planning academics were present, and the congress agreed to recognize an interim association of African Planning Schools. At this same congress eight other planning school associations from various parts of the world came together to form the GPEAN (Global Planning Education Association Network). In the subsequent two years the Association of African Planning Schools (AAPS) was formed and in 2003 it was accepted as a ninth member of the GPEAN.

THE CHANGING CONTEXT FOR PLANNING EDUCATION IN SOUTH AFRICA

Planning education in South Africa has undergone considerable change over the past decades. It has experienced a long-term shift from a limited set of diploma courses for people with technical qualifications in the built environment to offerings in 11 tertiary institutions of both stand-alone diploma and degree courses, as well as Master's courses, usually for people with backgrounds in the humanities. The types of courses offered under the name of planning have also changed significantly. Further, over the last decade and a half, a dramatic shift has been evident in the racial composition of planning students.

As was the case in many countries, planning education in South Africa began as a set of partial courses, then as a diploma on top of qualifications for architects, land surveyors or engineers (Chapter 10). Full degree courses began in the 1950s, with the University of Pretoria introducing a Master's degree in 1959, and the University of the Witwatersrand introducing the first undergraduate degree in 1962. From the 1970s, planning education expanded considerably. The growth of planning education followed international trends (Africa 1993), but also reflected the growing size and complexity of towns in South Africa, and the impact of apartheid planning (Oranje 1998). Several universities set up undergraduate or postgraduate courses, and technikons (now universities of technology) set up diploma courses. Planning education boomed in the 1980s as money trapped by exchange controls flowed into the built environment, and as homeland bureaucracies – and initiatives towards development there – expanded. At the same time, the progressive planning movement grew, attracting students who sought to use their skills to contribute to social transformation.

By 1994, there were six universities and three technikons offering planning courses. The 1984 Town and Regional Planners Act, set up to regulate planning, put in place a system of legal accreditation for planning education and registration for professional 'town and regional planners'. It replaced (and largely built on) the previous system of accreditation of university courses by the South African Institute of Town and Regional Planners. Technikon planning courses were originally set up to produce technicians, although many graduates went on to undertake postgraduate university courses, enabling professional registration. A BTech degree[1] was introduced at technikons in the mid-1990s, blurring the distinction between university and technikon education, and under the 2002 Planning Professions Act, BTech graduates qualify for professional registration.

While all planning courses were accredited in 1994, the period since then has seen a growth of non-accredited courses. In addition, several universities put in place new Master's courses that were not accredited. Some of these courses were initiatives to respond to a diversifying labour market, and the demand for graduates with a broader knowledge base. A study of the labour market for planning in 2001 (Todes *et al.* 2003) showed that the market for traditional fields of land use and physical planning had stagnated, while there had been a growth in the market for development-oriented planning. Thus work in areas such as integrated development planning, local economic development, housing and institutional development, had grown. Further, environmental management had emerged as a new specialism.

At the same time, new courses – in development studies, environmental management, housing, public policy and development management – had emerged. Although these courses seemed to draw on slightly different sets of students (Harrison and Todes 2001a), they were to some extent in competition with planning for students. Further, rather than planning graduates capturing the growth of these new fields of work, graduates from a variety of disciplines were employed. Several planning courses responded by diversifying their offerings and reworking courses to meet the needs of the changing market, but they were simply one source of education among others. With the diversification of the field, the value of accreditation specifically in planning declined. In addition, the pressure to employ black staff has often overridden concerns about accreditation. The 2002 Planning Professions Act reasserts the importance of accreditation, but it remains to be seen how it will be instituted, and how planning will be defined in practice. The new South African Council for Planners took some time to be established in 2005, and is still in the process of considering these issues (Chapter 10). It awaits the outcome of the recently established Standards Generating Body (SGB), which will define planning competencies. The SGB is set up under the South African Qualifications Association within the Department of Education, and includes representatives from both planning education and the profession.

Planning schools have also been discussing international benchmarking and accreditation through the RTPI since some planning graduates are seeking work in other parts of the world, and because education authorities are encouraging professions to seek international recognition and accreditation (Watson 2006a). The RTPI accreditation also represents a hallmark of quality, and a recognition that there are shared concerns, knowledge and practices. Since the RTPI emphasizes 'critical thinking about space and place as a basis for action or intervention', i.e. that it is critical thinking that makes spatial planning a transferable set of activities, which can be adapted to context, it avoids concerns that accreditation of this sort will reintroduce an inappropriate colonial agenda.

In part as a consequence of the declining importance of accreditation and the diffusion of the market, the numbers of students in accredited professional planning courses at universities had declined by 2003, although the numbers of those in planning education had grown in total (Todes and Harrison 2004: see Table 11.1). No consolidated figures are available since then, but patterns seem to have been volatile, with rapid growth in one year followed by decline the next, and shifting patterns across schools. By 2003, there had been a slight rise in the number of students in technikon courses, and a significant growth in the number of students in non-accredited courses. This shift may be overstated since the figures in Table 11.1

reflect students rather than graduates, and include both full-time and part-time students. By way of comparison, some 225 graduates were produced in 2005, 118 in university programmes and 107 in university of technology programmes. Some 72 per cent of university of technology graduates received diplomas (Watson 2006a) and would require a further BTech degree to qualify for registration as professional planners. Through-put rates for part-time students and in non-accredited courses are lower than in accredited courses. Todes and Harrison (2004) argue that the relative growth of students in non-accredited and university of technology courses reflects a demand for planning education that is more accessible in terms of costs and entry requirements to poorer black students, who will be able to enter the labour market more quickly. University of technology courses combine academic learning with practice, and enable students to begin earning from their second year. These patterns reflect more general trends in tertiary education in South Africa (Cooper and Subotzky 2001). For similar reasons, there was also a shift within accredited planning programmes from full-time undergraduate education to postgraduate education, which includes an increasing component of part-time students,[2] although patterns might now be changing.

While student numbers had not declined overall, numbers were far lower than had been expected in the early 1990s. Todes and Harrison (2004) explain slow growth in terms of the uncertain labour market for planners in the period compared with much more rapid growth in the demand for professionals in the business and scientific sectors, and the constraints on intake into tertiary education as a consequence of continuing poor performance in secondary education (DOE 2001). South Africa's history of extremely poor education for the majority of black people under apartheid has unfortunately not been rectified post-apartheid, despite various government initiatives. The number of school-leaving students with matriculation examination results of a sufficient standard to allow them to enter university, or even universities of technology, remains small, as does the number passing mathematics as a matriculation subject.

Student numbers over the longer term may however be expected to rise with a growing economy and a booming property market. In the important Gauteng region in particular, land development planning, and other forms of planning have been resurgent. The years of reorganizing local government are now over, and there is a drive to increase rates of delivery, but also to improve the quality of human settlements. There is a growing recognition that the focus on rapid delivery of low-cost housing produced poor quality environments (DOH 2004). At the same time the laissez-faire approach to high-income residential and commercial development exacerbated inequalities and often led to high unexpected costs for municipalities, which were forced to pay for bulk infrastructure. Spatial frameworks are becoming more refined and are beginning to relate to land-use management. The various roles of planning in development – in redeveloping declining inner-city and low-income township areas, in upgrading slums, and in guiding municipal development, *inter alia* – are beginning to be realized.

Recent calls by the Department of Provincial and Local Government for more empirically grounded and evidenced-based integrated development planning (Patel 2006) are also likely to lead to a growth in the demand for planners. Similar effects might be expected as a consequence of government's recent (2006) Accelerated and Shared Growth Initiative for South Africa (ASGI-SA), which places considerable emphasis on using infrastructure investment to accelerate growth. ASGI-SA in fact defines urban and regional planning as a 'scarce skill', and, along with other skills, it is the target of special intervention by the Joint Initiative on Priority Skills Acquisition (JIPSA). Thus the significance of planning is being recognized by government, and the demand for the range of services that planners offer appears to be on the rise again.

Perhaps the most dramatic shift in planning education has been in the racial composition of students (Table 11. 2). Planning schools were initially set up in universities and technikons that were reserved for whites under apartheid. A planning course was established in a technikon reserved for Indians in the 1980s. African students from the late 1970s could enter into planning programmes with a permit, but barriers to entry were dropped in the early 1980s. The first African planner graduated in 1982, and by 1993, only 74 black planners had graduated from planning schools (Badenhorst 1995). From the mid-1990s, the proportion of black students in planning schools rose dramatically, although numbers in English-speaking universities and technikons were already close to half by 1994. The proportion of black students in Afrikaans universities, which account for over half of university students, remains low, although there are significant variations between planning schools and between undergraduate and postgraduate education (Todes and Harrison 2004).

The changing racial composition of planning students reflects both the rise in the number of black students, and a sharp absolute decline in the number of white students. These trends are an important corrective to historical patterns, but also show the effects of at least perceptions of affirmative action on the employment prospects of white graduates (Todes and Harrison 2004). They are also linked to more rapid growth in other parts of the economy (HSRC 1999) and the movement of white students into better-paid commercial fields, which are less dependent on state employment.

The gender composition of planning students since 1994 has been more constant, although the proportion of women has risen since the 1980s (Todes and Harrison 2004). Women have remained at roughly a third of planning students since 1994 (Todes and Harrison 2004), but were close to half of all planning students in accredited university programmes. The proportion of women in universities of technology is relatively low at around 20 per cent, and around 30 per cent in non-accredited university programmes. Thus increasing 'access' has not benefitted women to the same extent as men.

Table 11.1 Changing number of planning students across planning programmes

Year	Total	Accredited professional programmes at university				Non-accredited university programmes			University of technology
		Total	Under-graduate	Post-graduate	% Afrikaans universities	Total	Under-graduate	Post-graduate	
1995	708	423	280	143	57				285
1997	674	376	237	139	55	24	23	1	274
1999	668	378	197	181	51	60	54	6	230
2001	698	337	163	174	51	133	97	36	228
2003	872	368	189	179	52	225	172	53	279

Source: After Todes and Harrison (2004)

Table 11.2 Racial composition of planning students by programme type

Year	Total % black	Accredited professional programmes at university % black			Non-accredited university programs % black	University of technology % black
		Total	Afrikaans universities	English universities		
1995	38	27	5	59		53
1997	48	32	7	62	96	67
1999	60	47	22	72	97	71
2001	70	53	27	81	89	83
2003	78	61	36	90	92	89

Source: After Todes and Harrison (2004)

One consequence of the historic biases in the racial and gender composition of planning students is that until fairly recently, planning educators were largely white and male. Although the gender composition of planning educators has changed relatively quickly over the past decade, there are still extremely few black planning educators, and hardly any local African planning educators. Reasons for this are complex and lie, *inter alia*, in the late entry of African people into planning as a consequence of apartheid, the high demand for African planners in practice, the pressure for very talented African planners to move into senior positions in government, and possibly, the relatively poor remuneration of academics in South Africa. Funding to support PhD students is also inadequate. These problems are mirrored elsewhere in South African academia, but are particularly sharp in planning, as in other applied disciplines from which African people have been historically excluded.

Planning education faces other challenges as well. In the context of financial pressures on tertiary education institutions, many institutions have been expected to take on larger numbers of students, but with declining staff and other resources. These conditions have put pressure on the ability of these institutions to offer quality education and to undertake research. As is the case in many parts of the world (Hague 2002), planning is increasingly part of larger multidisciplinary schools, and has less voice and autonomy in this context. Nor has the South African Council for Planning provided a platform for planning educators to express their concerns, as Chapter 10 demonstrated. It is hoped that JIPSA, with its link into high-level multi-departmental committees at national level will be a space in which these concerns can be addressed.

DEBATING THE CONTENT OF PLANNING EDUCATION

The growing scope of planning education in South Africa and the need to offer skills in both the traditional areas of land-use and spatial planning, as well as the new areas of development planning, have been a significant challenge for planning schools. This challenge is compounded by the fact that a large part of the student intake into planning schools comprises African students who come from educationally disadvantaged backgrounds, and are frequently studying in a second language. The rapid shift in the racial composition of planning students is of course an important corrective to the situation in the apartheid years, and promises to produce professionals whose living experience is far closer to that of the majority of communities they are likely to work in. Nevertheless, planning schools struggle to find sufficient students who have the educational background required, thus the broadening of the field presents particular challenges at the present time.

Planning education in most parts of South Africa followed the British model, and some planning courses were introduced by British academics (Faling 2002). Under apartheid, planning education was divided between Afrikaans- and English-speaking schools. Although both focused on physical planning, the former trained students to meet the immediate needs of practice and tended to accept the political status quo, while English schools more often saw themselves as providing a broader education, and expected graduates to learn the details of practice on the job. These divides no longer exist, and there are variations among both English- and Afrikaans-speaking schools. Most planning schools have embraced a broader developmental approach, and see physical planning as just one part of planning. In addition, there is ongoing debate within planning schools and between planning schools and the planning profession, as to how closely planning education should link to the immediate needs of planning practice (Africa 1993).

This is a particularly difficult question in the current context. In theory, planning education should provide a basic education in planning – a platform of skills, knowledge and critical thought that can be built on in practice. Inevitably, it provides only a fraction of the learning that will occur over the lifetime of a planner – through mentoring, experience and practice. However, despite an uncertain market for planners in South Africa, planners in practice are being called to take on high levels of responsibility at early stages of their careers. Due to pressures in the workplace, there is insufficient time and personnel to mentor new staff, and new staff are expected to 'come into the job running'. Research on employer perceptions of planning education[3] (Faling 2002) revealed a frustration among employers with what was sometimes perceived as an overly theoretical approach on the part of planning schools, and an inability of many graduates to apply theory to practice. Similarly, most employers called for a stronger link with practice, and argued for the incorporation of practice-based learning as part of the mainstream of planning education. Nevertheless, critical thinking and the development of creative reflective practitioners are valued, although some employers expressed doubts over whether planning education is producing these outcomes (Faling and Todes 2004).

Only a minority of employers felt that planning education is out of sync with contextual realities, and that planners should be replaced with 'urban development practitioners'. On balance, most employers felt that planning education is relevant, although there was a concern about declining standards, and about whether it is achieving its objectives. Thus, while planning education might be able to hold together a variety of fields of study, the increasingly poor educational backgrounds of students make it hard to achieve the intended outcomes. This is an ongoing dilemma for planning educators. It is likely to be exacerbated by expectations arising from the emerging emphasis on rapid and large-scale delivery that the 'hard' elements of planning – and thus planning education – should be strengthened.

In a context where the nature of planning is constantly evolving, continuing professional development (CPD) is critically important, as is the development of mechanisms to improve mentoring. Both of these areas have received too little attention in South Africa. While there is support for CPD in terms of the Planning Professions Act, there has been only limited response to it by planning schools, with only a few ad hoc initiatives. Staff shortages and space constraints are key limitations (Watson 2006a). Yet there is no special reason why planning schools should take responsibility for CPD. To date however, neither the South African Council for Planners nor the South African Institute for Planners has actively attempted to put in place CPD. Nonetheless, forms of CPD do occur through an array of workshops and training sessions available in the market and in some workplaces. The adequacy and effectiveness of this type of CPD however remains to be assessed.

Planning schools have responded in different ways to the broadening base of planning. Several planning schools now offer variations of the core-specialism model. Further, new specialisms and courses which mix planning with emerging disciplines (such as development planning and environmental planning) have been introduced, and in one university, planning is one option that students can undertake through assembling appropriate courses within a broader course on sustainability.

The amalgamation of planning schools with other disciplines has also affected planning education, although the extent to which these schools offer integrated teaching across old disciplines varies. Some planning schools have been combined with disciplines like geography or public management, but for the most part, combinations are traditional, with planning being combined with architecture. In some universities, planning students are taught along with other students, and lecturers are encouraged to offer their courses more widely to increase student numbers. Thus planning is becoming less of a stand-alone discipline. This follows international trends, and in part reflects the financial pressures on universities (Hague 2002).

The planning fraternity in South Africa has always accepted a high degree of variation in the curriculum between planning schools, although technikons were required to offer subjects which were defined nationally. From the late 1990s, however, all disciplines were required by the Department of Education to define their core competencies. This presented a particular problem for planning, given its breadth and the (increasing) variation in curricula. Following several earlier initiatives, planning schools met in Bloemfontein in 2000 to define a set of core competencies which could embrace the breadth of the field, and which would allow for variations. It was influenced by the work of the United Kingdom's RTPI Education Commission, which focused on a set of values and on broadly defined competencies as a basis for planning education. Interestingly, the South African work also subsequently fed into the work of that commission.

The Bloemfontein competencies attempt to capture the breadth of planning, without tying planning schools to a particular set of skill areas. They focus on learning outcomes, and avoid referring to specific theories or fields of knowledge, or even to the set of literacies required. In this way, they allow for flexibility and variation in the curriculum. They move beyond a priori assumptions that one or other body of work must be taught, and in this sense hopefully allow an avoidance of the 'layer cake' syndrome. The competencies are thus stated in a generic way, and focus largely on the development of conceptual skills. Box 11.1 provides a summary of these competencies, while the full list of competencies is contained in the appendix.

The Bloemfontein competencies outline six outcomes that should be the focus of planning education. These competencies are consistent with current thinking in the international literature, but also attempt to reflect local conditions. The first includes a set of moral and ethical orientations, and lays the basis for a strong focus on values in planning. It is an important element given South Africa's apartheid history, but refers to a set of broadly stated values, including an orientation to social justice and sustainability, embracing diversity, a human-centred approach, and an ethical position. Several of these values are included in the White Paper on Spatial Planning and Land Use Management (2001). There is thus consistency between national legislation and the work of planning educators – perhaps not surprising given the roles many planning academics have played in defining planning through the Planning and Development Commission, and in other forums.

The second and third groups of competencies focus on theoretical and contextual knowledge and its application, linking such knowledge to spatial planning at various scales. Reference is made to theory relating to planning, development, design and human settlements, and to understanding the complexity of diverse urban, rural and regional contexts. The political and institutional influences and processes linked to planning, and aesthetic and environmental dimensions, are

Box 11.1 The Bloemfontein competencies

- A knowledge and understanding of the moral and ethical issues in the public domain.
- Demonstrating a sound theoretical and contextual knowledge, and the ability to apply this in action.
- The ability to link knowledge to spatial plans and policies.
- Linking and synthesizing programmes and projects from various sectors and institutions within a framework of integrative development.
- Conducting academic research in order to develop critical thinking and problem-solving abilities.
- The application of managerial and communicative skills necessary for managing planning and development processes in the public and private sectors.

considered in this context. No specific theory is mentioned, giving planning schools the scope to teach what they see as most appropriate, to focus as they choose, and to change with shifting demands in the field.

The fourth group centres on the integrative dimensions of planning, attempting to capture the notion of integrated and synoptic thinking which has long been at the core of planning. It also focuses on a set of competencies necessary to achieve integrated development in practice in South Africa. The fifth group is concerned with research, critical thinking and problem-solving. The emphasis here is in part on academic research, but also includes creativity and critical reflection, which are valued in both the international and local literature. The final group of competencies brings together communicative aspects, and managerial and organizational elements. This area is frequently stressed as important in surveys of planning employers both locally and internationally, and is a common point in studies in developed and developing countries (e.g. Oszawa and Salzer 1999; Hamza and Zetter 2000). Although most planning schools do attempt to address it in various ways, it is often a weak element in planning courses. The need to strengthen skills in areas such as negotiation, mediation and communication is often noted in the international literature.

The Bloemfontein competencies offer an ambitious framework for planning education in South Africa, and will feed into the work of the recently revived Standards Generating Body for planning, which will define planning skills and competencies in a more formal way. While they encompass what most planning schools do, they also go beyond current educational practice in several ways, and it will be a challenge for planning schools to address all competencies. They are supported by employers interviewed by Faling (2002), and thus are a reasonable base for thinking about planning education. They lay considerable emphasis on critical thinking and reflection, and in several respects are closer to Sandercock's (1998) literacies than more formal definitions of skills and competencies. The development of reflective practitioners is thus seen as central to planning education. This may however continue to be in tension with demands for more immediate practical skills by planning employers, particularly if ASGI-SA leads to expectations for more 'hard skills' over the coming years. The way this tension plays out will be important to the future of the planning profession.

CONCLUSION

The past decade has presented considerable challenges for planning educators. Perhaps most difficult has been the instability and lack of growth in student numbers in many planning schools, against earlier expectations that planning would be in great demand, requiring even a 'massification' of planning education. However student numbers have not declined. Rather, where and how planning is taught has diversified, and planning schools are no longer the sole locus for the teaching of planning as it is currently constructed in South Africa. Nevertheless, there are indications that planning and the demand for planners is on the rise again. There is an increasing appreciation of the spatial dimensions of social problems at both an urban and a national scale, a call to move beyond a narrow focus on delivery, and a new interest in planning in the light of a shift towards an infrastructure-led development path.

The demand for planners who have a broad knowledge base and are able to shift across fields is likely to remain, but there are also likely to be increasing demands for 'hard' skills. Planning schools face difficult choices in deciding how to focus their efforts in this context. The Bloemfontein competencies provide space for a wide range of responses. Although they have no formal or legal status at present they are important as a way of thinking about planning education. They embrace a strong emphasis on critical thinking along with a definition of broad areas of knowledge which are significant for planning in contemporary South Africa. There are nevertheless questions as to how much they go beyond a modernist paradigm in which the state's ability to plan and to give effect to plans is taken for granted. This limitation however reflects the field of planning more generally, and despite limited capacity, these assumptions appear to be strengthening rather than weakening in the current context.

The core question in future years will be how to develop an appropriate planning education curriculum, but more importantly, how to do so with students from disadvantaged backgrounds who have limited access to funds. For many students, access to planning education that allows easy entry into the market, that combines paid work with studies, and reduces the costs of study, is critical to their ability to enter and remain in the field. Creative combinations of planning education and planning practice may help to provide a bridge between theory and practice, although there are dangers in the pressures to move towards a more skills-based approach, and in limiting the space and time for critical reflection. Planning educators will have to be innovative in the courses they develop, and the way they are packaged. They will also need to be sensitive to the range of students' backgrounds and experiences as well as to the more abstract demands of defining curricula that respond to the development context in South Africa.

CHAPTER 12

PLANNING, DEMOCRACY AND VALUES

INTRODUCTION

There has been a shift during the past decades in the way in which planners in South Africa have articulated their dominant values in order to justify or motivate their plans, although there are also strong continuities from the past to the present which can be related to the persistence of modernist thinking. Perhaps in response to planning in the apartheid years, when many planners were party to the implementation of racial segregation and forced removals (justified in terms of slum clearance, urban renewal or the creation of 'efficient' new residential areas), there has been a stronger emphasis, post-1994, on normatively driven planning and on the adoption of a clear ethical stance on planning matters. Given that a central element of apartheid was the recognition and entrenchment of (racial) difference, through technocratic and top-down planning approaches, it is perhaps not surprising that the emphasis in the post-apartheid years has been on planning for equity and justice, in order to overcome the inequities and injustices of apartheid. This emphasis has been more at the level of rhetoric than practice, with the latter continuing to be rather technocratic. More recently, there have been the beginnings of a critique of this position, partly on the grounds that material and cultural differences *are* important and need to be recognized and affirmed, and partly on the grounds that the often standardized policies which emerge from an equity position impact negatively on some people.

This chapter sets out the way in which modernist values have influenced planning in both the apartheid and post-apartheid era, and how these values are being brought into question by an emerging appreciation of difference: between regions of the global South and those of the North, and between the various and often conflicting groups (including the state) that shape the built environment.

VALUES AND MODERNITY

The values[1] that informed most planners in South Africa during the twentieth century were derived from a variety of sources, and were to a large extent implicit in planning practice. These values originated almost entirely from outside of South Africa and can be traced primarily to the influence of British colonial rule which brought with it particular attitudes to urban development in Africa and, later on, an approach to formal planning ideas and procedures (see Mabin and Smit 1997). From the post-war period onwards these values were shaped, in addition, by imported concepts informing the modernization and development of 'third world' countries, and by the broader government policy of racial segregation through spatial separation. Significantly, even though the form of apartheid planning was particular to the South African context, it was continually justified as being in keeping with accepted planning approaches in other parts of the world.

Central to the notion of modernization is a belief that the development of nations of the West has been achieved through promotion of the values of civilization, progress and liberal democracy, and that the development and modernization of countries outside of the West depends on the inculcation of these values. Underlying these values is, in turn, a set of beliefs which assumes a linear and upward path of development for all countries of the world towards the ideal of the West, characterized by increasing individual wealth and levels of consumption. Within the 'less developed' regions of the world a distinction is drawn between modern and traditional social systems with the former implying the scientific, the rational, the innovative, rising incomes, the urban–industrial and the universally relevant, and the latter implying backwardness, lack of ambition, religion, ethnicity, irrationality, the rural and the informal. The role of planning, it has been argued, is to diffuse modernist values throughout society in order to replace the traditional with the modern (Slater 2004).

The belief that planning in South Africa had a role to play in achieving modernization emerged clearly in the reports of the Social and Economic Planning Council of 1942 (Chapter 1). Against a backdrop of a commitment to rapid industrialization, the Council proposed to replace the pre-war fragmented and ineffectual planning system with a much stronger and state-directed system of spatial development at both urban and regional levels (Wilkinson 1996). In turning to the actual spatial approaches which it believed could achieve modernization, the Council was clearly influenced by the values underlying British planning of the time. Suggestions that development required balanced urban development and an avoidance of overconcentration in a few urban areas echoed similar sentiments voiced in the UK, where anti-urban sentiments (Taylor 1998) had inspired ideas of new towns, urban containment and green-belt development. Similarly, connections could be traced between the Council's insistence on the need for the state to gain control of urban land use, so as to achieve rational development of rapidly growing urban areas, and the recommendations of the British 1942 Uthwatt Committee which considered the possibility of land nationalization.

While the recommendations of the Council were received with little enthusiasm at the time, Wilkinson (1996) suggests that the real legacy of the Council emerged only later with the establishment by the apartheid government of a highly interventionist system of spatial planning. In this post-1948 period of apartheid planning, planners turned increasingly to the urban and regional spatial models of the UK and Europe. The values that were used to justify South African proposals for regional decentralization and constrained urban growth, and at the urban scale – slum clearance, urban renewal, new township development, and the restructuring of cities to improve car mobility – were all drawn from the modernist ideas of thinkers such as Le Corbusier as well as from British planners' concerns with protection of their countryside, the reconstruction of war-damaged cities and the accommodation of traffic in towns (Taylor 1998). In the South African case these imported values could all be used to underpin and reinforce the political ideology of racial segregation (see Chapter 1).

But contradictory tendencies were also evident. In South Africa, as in many other parts of Africa, the principle of indirect colonial rule involved the twinning of modernization with the conservation of 'traditional' or indigenous value systems. In parts of colonial South Africa (particularly present-day KwaZulu-Natal) this involved the British relying on traditional rulers, or chiefs, to administer and control the local population. In the apartheid years this system fitted well with the concept of separate development for African people and the object of instituting self-rule in those parts of the country termed homelands. Achieving the political viability and ultimate 'independence' of these homelands also required that they were economically viable, and modernist regional planning strategies aimed at less-developed regions (growth centre strategies involving the establishment of both industrial and agricultural 'nodes', in particular) became a central element of apartheid national and regional planning. The persistence, in contemporary South Africa, of these 'traditional' political systems and the implications which this has *inter alia* for the issue of gender, are discussed below.

Modernist influences on planning values were also regionally varied. In the 1930s, architectural academics Rex Martienssen and Leslie Thornton-White were instrumental in introducing the ideas of Le Corbusier and the Congrès International du Architecture Moderne (CIAM) to Johannesburg and Cape Town. At a student architectural conference in 1938 at the University of Witwatersrand, Johannesburg, there were discussions on the application of modernist ideas to a new business centre for Cape Town and a 'model native township' (Mabin and Smit 1997). Mabin and Smit (1997: 202) point to some of the ambiguities of modernism which emerged in this process, 'for example, in tension between the frequent pleas for radical social change which pepper the pages of the congress proceedings, and the acceptance of the prevailing order of segregation'. In KwaZulu-Natal, a somewhat different strand of modernism was evident through the Mumford-style holism which shaped regional planning in the province. The work of America's Tennessee Valley Authority (TVA) strongly influenced the work of the 1951 Natal Town and Regional

Planning Commission, particularly evident in the planning of the Thukela Basin as an attempt to promote the valley as South Africa's new industrial heartland (Harrison and Williamson 2001).

RADICAL AND PARTICIPATORY PLANNING VALUES

It is necessary to recognize the influence of other value-based subcurrents present in planning in the apartheid years, together with the sources that influenced them. The political economy approach to planning and geography, drawing largely on Marxist theory (and the 1970s work of Harvey, Poulantzas and Castells) and emerging as part of the critique of rational comprehensive planning (Taylor 1998), found resonance in South Africa in the work of two University of Natal academics (see McCarthy and Smit 1984). Their book drew attention to the political nature of planning in South Africa, and the usefulness of Marxist theory in analysing and explaining urban change under apartheid (Chapter 2). University of Natal planning students in the 1980s and early 1990s received an education that strongly emphasized the process-oriented and political nature of planning, together with values of social justice and equity. This differed from the more liberal, University of Cape Town position which focused on spatial and design outcomes with implications for the expert role of the planner, and the technically oriented and politically 'neutral' planning programmes at the more conservative Afrikaans-speaking universities, which tended to adhere to the rational comprehensive approach to planning.

A second important influence on planning values in South Africa emerged through the work of Professor John Muller, head of the planning programmes at the University of Witwatersrand from 1979 to 2002. His concern for participatory and inclusive planning processes ran directly counter to the official position on this at the time, which excluded people of colour from any form of democratic process in planning. As late as the mid-1980s, for example, planners in Cape Town's municipal government were instructed that they were *not allowed* to consult with African and coloured inhabitants of the city on spatial planning issues (Watson 2002a). Muller's focus on the procedural nature of planning influenced planning students at the University of the Witwatersrand throughout the 1980s and into the 1990s, and aligned closely with an evolving 'urban management' approach to planning, centred in that part of the country, in the 1990s. His notion of 'promotive planning' drew on the position that the way in which decisions are made is more important than their substantive content and that the role of the planner is essentially to formulate procedures and facilitate debate. His ethical motivation, based on a concern with the undemocratic and inappropriate nature of apartheid planning, was to promote democratic ideals, and to allow the surfacing of 'the priorities of the disadvantaged as defined by the disadvantaged' (Muller 1982: 255). His belief that this approach to planning was necessary for human development also led him to support the establishment of a new postgraduate planning programme at the University of Witwatersrand in the 1980s, called Development Planning. This programme still has a strongly procedural and management emphasis (now linked to teaching the integrated development planning process) rather than content on spatial outcomes.

VALUES AND POST-APARTHEID PLANNING

What is significant about planning in the post-1994 period is that while there is radical change in the values underlying official approaches to the planning process (and the acceptance of planning as part of broader processes of social democracy), as well as in the goals of planning (values of equity, justice and integration replace those of racial segregation), faith in the project of modernization remains largely unchallenged. Moreover, the values informing an outcomes-based approach to planning come into juxtaposition with those informing a procedural (urban management) approach to planning, in unresolved ways.

VALUES AND PLANNING OUTCOMES

Chapter 6 discussed the spatial forms which came to characterize the desired form of the post-apartheid city: compaction, densification, mixed use, integration around nodes and corridors, pedestrian scale, emphasis on the public realm and public space, and public transport-based, and the role of the University of Cape Town planning academics in this. This position is based on articulated values relating to human development and environmental sustainability, and on the assumption that spatial forms which give more equitable access to urban opportunities and which integrate elements of land use and infrastructure, will facilitate a more equitable and integrated society. This position says little about the procedural aspects of planning, and casts the planner as an expert acting in the long-term interests of a unified and consensual 'public good'. While the spatial outcomes promoted by this approach differ greatly from the modernist urban environments promoted in earlier years in South Africa, elements of modernism remain in the faith in expert-led planning intervention to achieve transformed urban environments and hence societies.

Chapter 6 also discussed how these spatial ideas came to be incorporated into the first, interim, planning legislation: the 1995 Development Facilitation Act (see Chapter 3). What was unique with regard to this legislation was that it set out (in Chapter 1 of the Act) normative principles intended to guide all planning decisions and override any specific law under which planning decisions were taken. In essence, then, it could be argued that values intended by the post-apartheid government to

guide future planning are captured in Chapter 1 of this Act. These values are reiter-
ated in the subsequent White Paper on Spatial Planning (2001) and appear in
slightly amended form in Chapter 3 of the (still draft) Land Use Management Bill.
However, the fact that a set of normative principles has found its way into both existing and draft legislation should not be interpreted as representing a national
consensus: a lack of a shared vision about the meaning of spatial planning was noted
by the Commission set up in 1997 to develop future planning legislation.

   While in practice there is yet little evidence of these principles being applied
in new planned developments, the intention to produce environments displaying
these spatial characteristics is still present. Chapter 6 discussed the new (2004)
low-income housing policy termed *Breaking New Ground*, which is critical of the
spatial qualities produced by public-sector developments to date, and recommits
itself to producing 'sustainable living environments' based on the spatial principles
in the Development Facilitation Act (DFA).

VALUES AND PLANNING PROCESSES

The norms that had guided planning processes in the apartheid years cast planning
as a technocratic and 'top-down' system. The role of public participation in planning
was minimal, even for the enfranchised white population, and the only critique of this
within the planning field came from the radical and proceduralist planning academics (see above) and the planning-related NGOs. During the years of political
transition, before and after 1994, organized civil society became centrally involved
in a wide range of planning processes and pressed for more inclusive processes,
but this occurred informally and outside of established legal procedures (see
Chapter 2). However, in the post-apartheid years, far greater attention has been
paid to the issue of decision-making processes. During the 1990s the proceduralist
emphasis of the Wits planning school was reinforced by an urban management
approach to planning (partly through academics linked to the School of Public and
Development Management at Wits), and by the growing influence of new public
management in the bureaucracies. This trend has also been reinforced by the reori-
entation of local government around the IDP decision-making process (see Chapter
4), but ironically it is in this process that the normative proceduralism of earlier planning academics (with its emphasis on participation and community involvement) has
been overtaken by the more technical and efficiency-driven proceduralism of new
public management, in which decision-making processes within and between levels
of government have become more important than community involvement.

   In the 1995 DFA the outcomes-based approach to planning found its way into
the Chapter 1 normative principles, while proceduralist concerns are evident in the
rest of the Act. There is thus an uneasy combination of the normative with the technical–managerialist approach. One of the tasks of the Act was to put in place a

more open and democratic planning system (in keeping with the normative principle in Chapter 1, Section 3d, that members of communities affected by land development should actively participate in the process of land development). To this end the Act allowed for provinces to create Development Tribunals to consider speedy approvals of development applications and suspend laws that would hinder the attainment of integration, equity, sustainability and efficiency. Half the membership of these tribunals comes from government and half from civil society. The Act further set out general principles for decision-making and conflict resolution (Chapter 1, Section 4) which puts in place requirements for public consultation in matters of planning. In a range of other national legislation affecting land development, principles of consultation and accountability were also enshrined. Consultation processes are now required in environmental impact assessments, heritage impact assessments, transport impact assessments and so on. The Municipal Systems Act of 2000, under which falls the process of integrated development planning, also has its own provisions for public participation.

But while at a level of principle the notion that planning should occur through open and democratic processes is clearly accepted in legislation, in reality the situation is not particularly democratic or participatory. The requirement for participation processes emanating from so many different government departments has given rise to a situation where these processes can duplicate and conflict with each other in relation to particular development initiatives at the local level. This has led to a greatly increased load on local and provincial government and to the creation of very lengthy approval processes for developments (see Chapter 9) which can take many months and sometimes years. In this situation, participation is seen as simply another factor prolonging decision-making and is often curtailed as far as is possible.

In addition, there is growing political pressure on government to speed up the delivery of infrastructure and services, particularly to those settlements which have been without basic services and shelter for many years. In the public housing field, earlier requirements for the establishment of a 'social compact' consisting of representatives of all major stakeholders, prior to the implementation of any major housing project, were relaxed in the late 1990s and made optional rather than mandatory. Experience showed that social compacts were frequently sites of deep and prolonged conflict between stakeholders with very different interests, and had become arenas in which local power dynamics played themselves out: attempting to achieve consensus in these committees greatly slowed and sometimes stalled the housing delivery process. Local authorities have sometimes taken advantage of this relaxation of the social compact requirement in the interests of speed of delivery, and in a recent major low-income housing project in Cape Town (the N2 Gateway Project), involving the resettlement of shack dwellers into new formal housing units, there was no participation process at all.

Here, as elsewhere in the world, the substantive and procedural aspects of planning, each driven by a different set of values, co-exist uneasily. An inability to bring them together has meant that the vision of a spatially integrated post-apartheid city remains without institutional and decision-making mechanisms to implement it (or to handle conflict around it), and the proceduralist aims of efficient and effective decision-making processes (still to be achieved in their own terms) have no clear way of debating or ensuring positive outcomes. It is possibly inevitable, therefore, that the nature of planning environments in post-apartheid South Africa reflects above all the norms and priorities of the market and of private developers, as well as strong continuities with modernist approaches of the past.

DEBATES ON EQUITY VERSUS DIFFERENCE

Both outcomes-based and proceduralist planning values are increasingly subject to a critique that begins to question some of the fundamental assumptions on which they are based. The issue of equity in planning as against a recognition of diversity and difference (see Chapter 13) links as well to international debates in planning theory and in particular to the work of Leonie Sandercock (1998) who argues that as planners we have to accept and accommodate different cultures in cities.

Apartheid policies were essentially based on a belief in the principle of human 'difference': that is, that different race groups should live and associate within their own groups, and should separately determine their own political futures. The achievement of this ideology also required that this difference was inscribed in space, and hence the demarcation of land at both national and urban levels, for different racial groups. The fact that this difference also translated into economic and political inequality between race groups was simply attributed, by adherents to a racist ideology, to the different levels of 'development' that had been achieved by different racial groups. It was assumed that over time processes of modernization would gradually uplift coloured and African people to a higher standard of living: the insistence in many older spatial plans that low-income residential areas should be planned to accommodate future high levels of car ownership illustrates this belief.

It is understandable, therefore, that the policies of the post-apartheid government have emphasized equity. This is particularly clear in the Constitution (Chapter 2) which sets out a Bill of Rights affirming the democratic values of equality, human dignity and freedom for all people. It is also then understandable that so many of the new policies that were put in place in the post-apartheid years have taken the principle of equity as a starting point. This has been the case in housing policy which has attempted to spread the available housing subsidy funds as 'equitably' as possible across the maximum possible number of poor households, but it has also been true for a wide range of other infrastructural and welfare policies. At provincial and city levels, as well, the principle is frequently used to justify policies and programmes.

Now however, some twelve years after the demise of apartheid, there are early indications that the equity principle is beginning to be questioned, and that a recognition of difference (not in racial terms, but in material, ethnic and gender terms) may be necessary to bringing about real improvements in people's lives. One source for this thinking has been in studies and policy critiques which argue that the application of standardized policies to a highly differentiated population will benefit some people but can also seriously disadvantage others. In other words, the principle of equity of opportunity, applied in a highly unequal context, often leads to greater inequalities.

In the case of housing policy, critiques (see for example Spiegel et al. 1996) have shown how the standard product of a tiny house on a freehold site has proved highly problematic for larger and extended families, for families who stretch their livelihoods between urban and rural areas and who do not consider their urban accommodation as the primary site for investment, and for families who are extremely poor and cannot meet the regular rate and service charge payments required by a formal dwelling. In the case of water delivery services, Jaglin (2004) shows how in Cape Town an insistence on a standardized approach to delivery (which she attributes both to an ethic of equality and to a modernization view within government) had an inequitable impact on consumers, particularly disadvantaging those who could not afford regular payments. Jaglin questions the assumption which the municipality appears to have made, that equal citizenship implies equal benefit by users.

A further instance has been in the arena of land-use management where those developing new and city-wide systems have had to consider if the same kind of land-use regulations should apply in all parts of the city. A major debate here has been around the issue of *shebeens* (informal bars) which are completely rejected as a possible consent use in wealthier parts of the city, and are both accepted and rejected by different groupings in lower-income areas. Those lower-income areas which have a predominantly Muslim population have demanded the exclusion of *shebeens*. As gradual racial mixing occurs in the formerly segregated residential areas, an increasing number of land-related intercultural disputes have been occurring. One issue that has emerged a number of times is that of the right to carry out animal sacrifices on a residential site, where those who wish to do this argue that it allows communication with ancestors and is a traditional right, while those who oppose it do so on the basis of the zoning scheme, as well as on the grounds of cruelty to animals.

In those parts of the KwaZulu-Natal province which are under traditional leadership, the extension of the land-use management system has been particularly difficult, and has been regarded with suspicion by those associating it with the expansion of municipal control, as well as the levying of rates and service charges where none exist at the moment. Research (Provincial Planning and Development Commission 2004) on the typical land uses mentioned in these rural areas yielded a list which included homesteads, burial sites, woodlots, thatching grass areas, sand and quarry areas, fields and grazing areas. This is land that is held under communal tenure and is open to use by individuals based on negotiation and agreements with traditional leaders. Land ownership, under freehold title, is regarded by some with suspicion as these resources would then be lost to those with a very vulnerable economic status. Land-use management in areas such as these obviously presents very different problems and issues to that of urban land management.

The extent to which value is placed on gender differences has been largely neglected in the planning field in South Africa to date. Although research pointed to the particular way in which the apartheid city disadvantaged black women (see Chapter 6), and some planners have argued for a gendered approach to planning (e.g. Gwagwa and Todes 1994; Todes 1995), in practice the issue has not been taken up systematically. No clear recognition is given to the fact that women's use of urban or rural space (linked usually to their childcare role) may differ from that of men, or that planning for the safer movement of women and children in public spaces or on public transport may require particular approaches and solutions. While the presence of women in political decision-making structures has progressed significantly in South Africa over the last ten years, ironically it is in those rural parts of the country where attempts to accommodate the specificity of 'traditional leadership' have come into direct conflict with national aims of promoting gender equity (and democracy more generally). In discussing the persistence of the institution of traditional chieftancy in parts of rural South Africa,[2] Beall et al. (2005) point to the fact that these traditional authorities entrench a system based on hereditary and male authority. They implement a practice of customary law that gives women curtailed rights to land, no access to communal resources outside of their relationship with their father or husband, and limited representation on traditional councils. Clearly the notion of 'acknowledging difference' in planning can become complex when recognition of one group implies the marginalization of another.

CONCLUSION

The values informing planning in South Africa have undergone a radical shift in the post-apartheid years, from values based on racial difference to those based on equality. What this chapter has argued, however, is that strong continuities are present from the apartheid to the post-apartheid period in terms of a belief in modernization and progress (defined in Western liberal terms), and that this belief informs planning, perhaps even more strongly, at the present time. What planning in

South Africa over the last ten years has shown is that implementing an ethical frame-work based on equity is not at all simple. At one level it is quite possible for equity goals emanating from different policy sources to contradict each other (as has been the case with housing policy and urban spatial policy); at another level it is becom-ing clear that an attempt to create equality of opportunity in a context of major inequalities, can worsen inequalities. Not everyone is in the same position to take advantage of opportunities and it cannot be assumed that the creation of equal citi-zenship translates into equity in dimensions such as income or employability.

There may thus be important reasons to pay attention to the emerging critique of a simple application of the equity principle. There is no doubt that it should be an aim of planning and policy to improve levels of shelter, health, security and welfare, but the instruments which are used to do this may be different, depending on mate-rial, cultural or other circumstances. The recognition of societal difference that has emerged in planning theory, together with its more specific applications in ideas about multicultural planning, are thus worth taking seriously, although as the contra-dictions between recognition of customary laws and authority and gender equity indicate, this issue is by no means simple.

CHAPTER 13

RESPONDING TO DIVERSITY: CONFLICTING RATIONALITIES

INTRODUCTION

Planning 'solutions' that have been promoted in South Africa tend to be almost entirely derived from countries elsewhere in the world, and usually from Western and developed economies. Furthermore, they are almost inevitably promoted as standardized solutions, relevant for any town or city or any part of a city. As such, they often take the form of abstract and idealized solutions which do not take account of how the South African context may differ from a 'first world' one, or the immense diversity that occurs within this context.

This chapter will draw on the case of South Africa's housing policy during the last ten years as an example of a policy arena in which attempts have been made to formalize and 'normalize' the conditions in which the poor in South African cities live. It draws attention to the gap that exists between the everyday lives and priorities of those living in informal settlements and the idea of what constitutes a proper living environment as seen from the perspective of policy-makers and those concerned with the technical and administrative management of cities. The chapter also draws attention to how the assumptions that are embedded in much planning and development theory simply do not hold in the highly differentiated contexts of cities of the global South.

UNIVERSALIZING TENDENCIES

In terms of both normative frameworks and substantive content, planning (as a factor in city building and city management) has long had universalizing tendencies. Forces such as colonialism, modernism, and more recently, globalization, have had the effect of diffusing planning ideas and practices across the globe. The vehicles for this diffusion have included consultants, donor and development agencies, and globe-trotting academics, but perhaps just as often they have been local agencies seeking a quick solution through a cut-and-paste from a 'best practices' website.

A growing volume of literature documents the spread of spatial concepts and urban forms: garden cities, green belts, new towns, and more recently waterfronts, mega-malls and new urbanist 'villages' have found their way into almost every city in the world, creating high levels of physical homogeneity. South African cities have all

Box 13.1 Rehousing families in Crossroads, Cape Town

In some recently completed anthropological research, Ngxabi (2003) relates how her Xhosa-speaking informants consistently refer to their Cape Town dwellings as *indlu* (a house) which is different from *ikhaya* (a home, usually to be found in the Eastern Cape). The term *indlu* has traditionally been used to refer to individual structures in a homestead which accommodate some members of the family (perhaps a wife and her children), but only together do the structures constitute *ikhaya* or *umzi* (a home). The term *ikhaya*, Ngxabi argues, suggests connectedness and it is a place where such connections can be made concrete through rituals which allow communication with deceased family members. *Ikhaya* is the place of graves, and this makes it sacred, giving the place power over the living. It is the place where rites of passage best take place, because here the child, becoming an adult, can be introduced to her ancestors who will then watch over her. It is the place where a child's umbilical cord is buried (it is dug into the wall of the great house of the home of the baby's father) and through this a strong connection is made between the soil of that place and the living human being. To be buried at this place is then a vital reconnection with home and with family members who have passed on.

The term *indlu,* by contrast, originally suggests separation within a family, but is also used to refer to formal urban dwellings because they serve physically to separate people from kin and from ancestors (Ngxabi 2003). The sense of separation from ancestors is attributed to the lack of yard space around urban dwellings, the difficulty of configuring the use of this space, and urban controls over space use. Contact with ancestors occurs primarily through the keeping of cattle and many rituals are based in the cattle byre. Without these, connection with deceased kin is difficult and an *indlu* cannot be considered *ikhaya.*

The unsatisfactory nature of urban dwellings is reflected again by Ngxabi's respondents in the term they use to refer to Cape Town: *esilungweni* (place of the white people's ways). One respondent (Ngxabi 2003: 53) describes the city as a place of *impangelo* (working for a wage, derived from the word *ukuphanga*, meaning to eat as fast as you can so that you can get more than others eating from the same plate). This conveys a sense of competition between people engendered by engagement in the urban economy, and is described as a form of moral degradation as it erodes values of reciprocity and mutual help. Thus Ngxabi's respondents see both living in the city and in urban dwellings as contributing to a process of individualization which is at odds with the communal nature of Xhosa culture.

Interestingly, not all urban dwellings are viewed in the same light. Dwellings in informal settlements are seen as approximating more closely a rural setting, and here Ngxabi found people who were attempting to keep cattle and to practise adapted forms of ritual in their cattle byres. Some of these households expressed strong resistance to moving to the new RDP houses in the nearby area of Crossroads (the scheme had been named *Veza*, meaning 'show foot' – suggesting that when a big man sleeps in these small houses, his feet will protrude outside), as the move implied a severance of communal ties: with extended family members who could not fit in to the tiny houses, with neighbours with whom reciprocal relations would be broken, and with ancestors with whom there could no longer be communication in the absence of space for even downscaled rituals. This gradual social isolation under conditions of economic marginality can be devastating for a household.

of these. In policy terms as well, international agencies such as the World Bank have been highly influential in spreading particular approaches to developing countries, and the low-income housing policy adopted by the South African government in 1994 was one such international model. Just as important, but more subtle, however, is the range of planning assumptions which underpins these physical forms and interventions. These are assumptions about the kinds of planning solutions which fit particular social or economic needs, assumptions about the nature of households and how they survive economically, assumptions about culture and cultural expression, and assumptions about the kinds of processes (consensus-seeking or otherwise) through which planning issues can be resolved. It is in these arenas that universalizing tendencies have been particularly strong, and have related to the assumed nature of the society with which planners interface.

The particular concept of society which, usually implicitly, shapes thinking and action in planning has been strongly shaped by post-Enlightenment and Western traditions. These ideas have shaped a dominant rationality which in turn sets standards of 'normality' regarding proper living environments, the proper conduct of citizens, the way in which individuals relate to society, notions of the public good, and so on. The notion of what is a proper living environment becomes stark in the context of developing countries where so often informal or shack settlements are regarded as unacceptable and in need of replacement by formal housing projects, as in the case of Ngxabi's story above. Extending the grid of formalized and regulated development over what is often termed the 'unruly' (or unrule-able) city (Pile *et al.* 1999) shapes the planning effort in many cities of the developing world.

This chapter argues that in many respects we are confronted by a situation of conflicting rationalities: on the one hand the rationality of the techno-infrastructural and managerial systems which are used to order urban environments, and on the other, the rationalities of those who are attempting to survive, materially and culturally, in what are often regarded as alien places (Watson 2003a; 2006b). From the perspective of mainstream urban planning theory, there has been a recent shift towards accepting, and responding to, the realities of social difference and multiculturalism, and yet planning still finds itself trapped by the liberal philosophical foundations that shape its thinking. The next sections consider how planning thought in South Africa has attempted to respond to these realities and how these attempts have reached their limitations in a particular context such as this one.

ACHIEVING 'PROPER COMMUNITIES'

It is first necessary to examine the thinking that underlies the notion of a 'proper' community and proper housing in the South African context because it is these ideas which informed the state-initiated, physical project of house-building in the Crossroads area in Cape Town (the building of *indlu* or RDP houses). The sources for these ideas of a 'proper' community lie, in part, in South African government policy documents and, in part, in broader theories of development and planning.

The notion that poor people should be provided, by the state, with formal housing structures in planned and serviced areas forms the cornerstone of current South African national housing policy. In many areas, including that of Crossroads, this has been interpreted to mean that informal structures do not constitute acceptable housing, and must be replaced. The desire on the part of governments almost everywhere to formalize informal, irregular or illegal settlement has a long history with its origins, as described by James Scott (1998: 4), lying in the early emergence of modern statecraft and its subsequent development into 'high-modernist ideology' aimed at 'the rational design of social order commensurate with the scientific understanding of natural laws'. These imperatives, in the first instance, shaped government action in Westernized societies but were applied as well, often with missionary zeal, in colonial and post-colonial territories where development and modernization came to mean the same thing. Ideals underlying this ideology have always been partly utopian (the creation of a better society and healthy, contented communities) but also partly bound up with the desire to administer, to control and to incorporate populations into municipal finance systems.

Implicit in this ideology are the assumptions that occupants of informal structures (usually assumed to be small, stable nuclear families) will accept the long-term, binding legal and financial obligations that accompany home ownership: adherence to various regulations regarding the use of the land and the conduct of the occupants (for example, respecting noise and health standards – with the keeping and slaughter of animals disallowed), and the payment of regular rates and service charges to the municipal authority. Also implicit is the assumption that shack-dwellers will be prepared to commit themselves to a particular piece of land or territory which they will come to regard as both their home (*ikhaya*) and as a marketable capital asset to be used for economic upliftment (the 'de Soto' thesis). Recent thinking on housing policy in the developing world (UN-Habitat 2002) ties the issue of shelter upgrade firmly to poverty reduction and sustainable urbanization, and argues particularly for the formalization of tenure systems: the link between these remains somewhat unclear.

The post-apartheid commitment to meeting basic housing needs in South Africa was extended significantly in the policy documents and legislation that accompanied the transformation of local government. The White Paper on local government (Ministry for Provincial Affairs and Constitutional Development 1998) demands that municipalities become 'developmental', i.e. that they work with citizens and groups within communities to find sustainable ways of meeting social and material needs. The White Paper explains that this assumes the establishment of democratic rule through elected councillors, that councillors should work with organs of civil society (seen as separate from the state), should foster community participation and (qualified[1]) consensus around development, and should work to build up 'social capital' to find local solutions to problems. What is involved in creating 'proper' communities is thus no longer a technical and managerial task, it is also a moral and political task (Chipkin 2003).

These ideas about state, citizenship and participation are not unique to South Africa: they are firmly rooted in current Western political and social theory, from which planning theory also takes its cue. Western traditions of liberal democracy, of which there are variations, influence much planning thought about individual rights and liberties, about ethical frameworks, and about planning processes. Liberalism takes the individual as the basic unit of society, able to be conceptualized and defined independently of society, and in a normative sense holding a distance from society as an autonomous and self-determining being (Parekh 1993). Morality then, or the notion of the good, is not a socially or collectively imposed construct, but rather an aggregation of individual choices or preferences. Much land-use policy, particularly in the US, has been driven by a utilitarian ethic which holds that the right decision is the one which creates the greatest aggregate level of social benefit, indicated by the price signals of a free-market economy in land. This view in turn sees land as an economic commodity, rather than (as in some other parts of the world) a communal resource with perhaps additional mystical or ancestral meanings. The British planning system, by contrast, follows a rather different form of utilitarianism. It has been far more accepting of a state interpretation of aggregated individual preferences, which sets the goals of amenity, convenience and efficiency as standards to define the best use of land (Campbell and Marshall 2002), and it has allowed for a greater measure of planning assessment to be applied to individual cases.

Planning theory, as well, has contributed to the conventional wisdom on the functioning of 'proper' communities, primarily through its ideas on decision-making processes in the context of urban and land development. Communicative action theory could be described as the current dominant approach in planning theory, although critiques of it have emerged (for example, see Tewdwr-Jones and

Allmendinger 1998). In brief (Watson 2002c), communicative action theory argues that planning decisions should be reached through collaborative processes involving all stakeholders, and conforming to particular rules which ensure that participation is fair, equal and empowering. Embedded in this approach are the assumptions that community divisions can be overcome and consensus reached on planning issues; that collaborative processes involving primarily civil-society-based groups can act to put pressure on the state to act more responsibly; and that collaboration can provide a learning environment and build social capital within communities.[2] Significantly, however, as the Crossroads case above shows, the splitting of extended families into individual, formal housing units is breaking social and family networks and probably doing a great deal to destroy social capital rather than to build it.

Certain planning theorists have attempted to move beyond the assumptions of universality contained in communicative action theory, which allows differences between actors to occur only at the level of speech or ideas, and which in turn can be overcome through the force of the better argument (Habermas 1984). Healey (1992: 152) acknowledges that communicating groups may operate within different 'systems of meaning', which means that 'we see things differently because words, phrases, expressions, objects, are interpreted differently according to our frame of reference'. The assumption that these differences can be overcome through debate in a consensus-seeking process remains, however.

Acknowledgement of diversity (and multiculturalism) is a central element in the work of Leonie Sandercock (1998). Her main point of departure is that citizenship is fragmented by identity, and that society is structured by culturally different group-ings based on sexuality, ethnicity, gender or race. This diversity should be celebrated rather than repressed, and the claims of different groups need to be rec-ognized and facilitated. It can be argued here that Sandercock is not simply interested in recognizing difference in procedural terms (in order to move towards a more homogenous or equal society); she is interested in 'substantive difference', or affirming a society made up of different groups. This is promoting difference for its own sake. The difference with Sandercock's work is that she is concerned to build consensus between groups, which affirms and valorizes difference rather than erases it, and which could take the form of resistance to the state. While this repre-sents an important shift away from assumptions of universal citizenship, a belief that culturally different groups can reach consensus is present here as well.

These concepts and assumptions regarding the role and functioning of state, society and citizens thus define one set of rationalities which are usually at play and which would have informed the Crossroads housing project. They could be described as closely linked to ideas of modernity and progress shaped by a Western experience, as well as to normative ideas about state, citizenship and recognition of identity which have also largely emanated from that context. They help

to define the notion of 'proper' citizens and communities which, at least at the level
of rhetoric, drives the policies and actions of local authorities in South Africa and in
other parts of Africa as well.

DEEP DIFFERENCE: CONFLICTING RATIONALITIES

Ngxabi's (2003) Crossroads story, which we are suggesting is far from unique in the
cities of South Africa, is telling us that a vast gap exists between the notion of
'proper' communities held by most planners and administrators (grounded in the
rationality of Western modernity and development), and the rationality which informs
the strategies and tactics of those who are attempting to survive, materially and culturally, in the harsh environment of South African cities.

The intention of the example above is not to romanticize cultural traditions, nor
to suggest they should be uncritically celebrated, as some positions on multiculturalism would have it. Communalist cultures can often disguise forms of
discrimination. For example, Ferguson (in Ngxabi 2003: 70) noted that in Lesotho
men keep cattle as a form of wealth as they are difficult for women to convert into
cash. The Crossroads example does, however, provide evidence of the co-existence
in South African cities of alternative rationalities or world views, which shape attitudes to land, its ownership and to the use of space, and which do not conform to
what is considered proper by city managers and most built-environment professionals. In fact, to some of Ngxabi's respondents, requirements linked to housing, tenure
and space use in *esilungweni* were contributing to moral degradation and were
directly undermining their own proper conduct.

The project, in Crossroads, of replacing informal shacks with formal structures
in a planned and serviced township, also reveals a significant lack of understanding
of the survival strategies of those who live in the informal settlements. In resource-
poor situations, marginalization in all its forms requires that individuals operate
within and through a dense web of personal networks, or sets of reciprocal relationships. The phenomenon of spatially 'stretched' households (Spiegel *et al.* 1996)
and kinship networks which allows access to resources in varying urban, peri-urban
and rural locations, as opportunity arises, has been well documented in South
Africa. Importantly, maintaining 'stretched' households or kinship networks produces frequent movement between urban and rural bases. Marginal economic and
political opportunities, as they arise in different locales, require physical presence
and hence movement. The population of South Africa and the wider continent is
highly mobile, ever shifting, ever searching for meagre sources of survival, or alter-
natively moving to escape warfare, persecution or natural disaster. There may well
be emotional ties to a piece of land somewhere – called, perhaps, home. But for

many of the poor in urban areas, there may be little commitment to a particular place or territory, particularly under freehold tenure. Such commitment comes with economic progress, and with the ability to loosen relational ties and invest in land and structure rather than in maintaining social networks. Most urban projects assume commitment to a particular piece of land or territory and a continuity of presence, but it cannot be assumed that individuals or households will meet the requirements of 'proper' community members – investing in their land or homes, contributing to rates and service charges, helping to build social capital and local democracy – when survival demands frequent movement.

Planning theories that attempt to recognize social difference and multicultural-ism represent an important advance. A multicultural approach would, in the Crossroads case above, directly draw attention to potential conflicts around the meaning and form of land and housing. But here again we have to be careful that the concept of identity which is embedded in the writings of largely Northern, developed-world theorists, is appropriate to the local context.

The point has been repeatedly made that political struggles in Africa, includ-ing South Africa, are far less like the identity/lifestyle politics that has become so visible in developed contexts and are far more likely to be reactive to material issues and the simple need for survival (Mohan 1997). This has led Mohan to argue that identity is not always a useful starting point in understanding political strug-gles, or at least it may require a more complete understanding of the relations between materiality and identity. Authors highlight the extremely complex and fluid nature of identity in poorer parts of the world. Social and economic turmoil leave many people with little sense of belonging (a process, some argue, which began with colonial penetration) or little idea of who represents them. One way out of this is to use identity in a highly opportunistic way:

> depending on the situation, sometimes religion, sometimes ethnicity may prove
> to be the determining factor in an individual's identity and behaviour. The organi-
> sational versatility of the orders that has made them the primary modes of
> organisation vis a vis the state lies in their capacity to adapt to this ambiguity,
> and even capitalise on it ...
>
> (Leonardo Villalon, cited in O'Brien 1996: 63)

Thus identity can often be a product of hybridization, fusion and cultural innovation. It is frequently self-generated and self-constructed, sometimes with a renewed stress on ethnic identity or 'retribalization', sometimes intertwined with global identi-ties (De Boeck 1996). Currently, religious commitment offers many young people a way of escaping from social marginalization, and Christian missions and pentacostal churches are forming a new focus for social organization in urban slum areas (Davis 2004), including in South Africa.

Thus the recognition and celebration of identity, as advocated by Sandercock, needs to be thought about differently, given the continued focus of political struggles in South Africa on material rather than lifestyle/identity politics. Nancy Fraser (2000) is concerned with identity politics more generally, but her arguments have relevance for operationalizing this approach in South Africa as well. Her concerns are first, that demands for recognition are eclipsing demands for redistribution (in a context of growing economic disparity), and second, that the reification of cultural difference is encouraging separatism and intolerance. The results, she argues, are growing inequalities and a sanctioning of the violation of human rights. Identity politics displaces struggles for redistribution in two ways. Some positions cast the roots of injustice at the level of discourse (for example, demeaning representations), rather than at the level of institutional significations and norms. This strips misrecognition of its social–structural underpinnings. Other positions, associated with cultural theory, assume that maldistribution is a secondary effect of misrecognition and that misrecognition should be considered prior to distributional issues. This appears to be Sandercock's position. Fraser (2000) argues that not only do these positions obscure the real roots of mis-recognition, which lie in institutionalized value patterns, but that reification of identity creates a moral pressure for group conformity, obscuring intragroup struggles, such as that around gender.

These ideas suggest that local planners, who may be keen to foreground identity issues, need to proceed with great care. To the extent that they sideline distributional issues, they may exacerbate central problems of poverty and dispar-ity. There is also the danger of failing to recognize that many expressions of identity are economically motivated and sometimes opportunistic. Assuming a pri-macy for identity may have economic consequences which are not entirely predictable or desirable.

Ngxabi's research in Crossroads is indicative of a clash of rationalities, or dif-ferences in world view, which are so great that it is difficult to believe that any amount of discussion or conflict resolution could overcome the divide and achieve consensus: differences go far beyond speech-level misunderstandings or an unwill-ingness to see the others' point of view. There are also indications that assumptions about the role of identity in multicultural planning need to be treated cautiously so that we do not again make the mistake of imposing inappropriate conceptions of planning and development. Finally, the central assumption underlying housing pro-jects in this context – that people will attach value to urban land as a marketable commodity – may hold for some, but clearly not for all.

RESPONDING TO CONFLICTING RATIONALITIES

Chabal and Daloz (1999) argue that it is a mistake to view Africa as a case of failed development; rather it is embracing modernity in a way that is highly particular to the economy and culture of the context. This argument has relevance for South Africa as well. The result is a fusion of the institutions and practices of Western modernity with local ways of coping in a situation of rapid change and economic crisis. Efforts to incorporate 'traditional authorities' into the formal legal framework of South Africa's democracy (see Chapter 12) are an example of this. In a similar vein, the post-development literature is now pointing to ways in which planning and development programmes are 'absorbed' selectively by target communities, and are mutated within local traditions and ways of doing things, giving rise to various combinations of what planners and urban managers regard as 'proper', and what communities might regard as more or less useful (see Arce and Long 2000). The term 'indigenous moder-nities' has been used to describe ways in which 'development packages are resisted, embraced, reshaped or accommodated depending on the specific content and con-text' (Robins 2003: 1). These writers are asking the question: how do people actually respond when confronted with attempts to impose particular forms of modernity? – especially programmes which impose change in the use and control of territory, often accompanied by the destruction of social networks and forms of survival.

What we need to understand about modernity in the African context, Chabal and Daloz (1999: 148) argue, is that politics cannot be separated from sociocultural considerations which govern everyday life. There is constant and dynamic interpretation of the different spheres of human experience, from the political to the religious. What this gives rise to is ways of operating in relation to the state and economy that are different, but nonetheless highly rational. They can only be defined as irrational when an attempt is made to hold them up against models of Western modernity which claim a monopoly on rationality.

CONCLUSION

This chapter has outlined the problems of universalism which have, for a long time, shaped the actions of those who intervene in the built environment. Liberalism, which has provided an overarching philosophy for planning thought, has itself always assumed universal relevance, and this in turn has inhibited a debate within the built-environment professions regarding the implications of social difference. In the field of planning theory, there has been some important questioning of this universalism, and the position broadly termed multiculturalism recognizes and affirms social difference and the role of identity.

This chapter has argued, however, that multicultural planning has its limitations in contexts which are significantly different from those of the developed world, and in situations where differences go beyond simple misunderstandings of words and meanings and where they take on the nature of rationality conflicts. Thus assumptions of people's relationships to land, shelter and to the city, and assumptions regarding the role and nature of identity and social networks, often do not hold in the cities of South Africa, and such differences often cannot be overcome through participatory or communicative processes, however well managed they may be.

CHAPTER 14

RESPONDING TO INFORMALITY

INTRODUCTION

Early international thinking about informality (or what is often termed the 'informal sector') was informed by a modernist perspective which defined it as small-scale economic activity, often characterized by illegality of some kind, relatively autonomous from the formal economic sector, and as a stop-gap or safety net form of income generation through which certain categories of people would pass on their way to formal jobs or more formal business establishment (Hart 1973). Subsequent policy positions and writings (see Sanyal 1988) pointed to the more varied nature of informal activity, as well as to the persistence of informal activities despite economic growth and change. Some writers linked their presence to structural economic forces shaped by capitalism and globalization (Wallerstein 1984). There has been a growing acceptance of the existence of informality as a response to poverty, especially in Africa (Rogerson 1997), but a tendency in South Africa to subsume this kind of activity within the ambit of local economic development (LED) policy, where the label SMMEs (small, medium and micro enterprises) has tended to replace 'informal' as a descriptor, and where the policy focus is on encouraging informal activities to take on, or adapt to, the characteristics of the modern or formal world.

Rather differently, arguments within some current literature suggest that the scope of what is termed informality is much wider than previously suggested (Hansen and Vaa 2004). Informality extends well beyond the realm of small businesses into state bureaucracies, public services and infrastructure provision, housing and land, and into all kinds of decision-making and political processes. There is also recognition of the important role that social and kinship networks have to play in shaping informality. There have been objections, as well, to the characterization of these activities as 'illegal' when the 'legality' of many of the laws (often of colonial origin) which marginalize these activities can be questioned, and when many of these practices represent a norm in resource-poor contexts such as South Africa, rather than a deviation from a norm. Put another way, it has been argued that informality cannot be understood as the object of state regulation, but rather as produced by the state itself (Roy 2005).

This chapter will document the growth and changing form of informality in post-apartheid South Africa and the ways in which this kind of activity has been recast in policy terms. It will indicate that despite stated policy claims that the informal is an important source of jobs, income and shelter for the poor, it is still subject to spatial marginalization and control at the level of the cities, and misrecognition in policy of its complex, fragile and fine-grained operational requirements.

INFORMALITY IN SOUTH AFRICA

Relative to Sub-Saharan Africa generally, where the ILO (International Labour Organization) estimated in 1992 that 63 per cent of the total urban labour force was in informal employment, and that this sector would generate 93 per cent of all additional urban jobs (Rogerson 1997), South Africa currently has a far stronger formal economy. The most recent labour force survey of Statistics South Africa (Statistics South Africa 2005) stated that the informal sector has not been showing signs of growth and remained at around three million people out of a total of 11.9 million employed (or 25 per cent of those employed). Formal employment had increased since 2000 (from 7.9 to 8.4 million) and those classified as not economically active had increased significantly over this period (from 11.4 to 13 million), suggesting that those who could not find formal employment were not turning to the informal sector but were dropping out of economic activity entirely, or were generating income in ways not captured by the census data. Thus illegal economic activity – crime, drug-trafficking, prostitution and scams of various kinds – would escape formal government statistics, but the size of this sector is known to be very large. Also in contrast to the official statistics are local studies, particularly of the larger urban areas, which suggest that the level of informal economic activity has been growing rapidly, both as a result of rapid population growth and the trend towards the informalization of formal activities (such as through the process of subcontracting) (SACN 2004). There are important gender dimensions as well to informality: women and women-headed households are strongly represented in the informal economy.

There is a range of other arenas in which informal practices are dominant. In terms of housing, it was estimated in 1994 that there were 3.7 million households in South Africa which required formal housing, and by 2005 there were still 2.4 million households in informal settlements, despite the large-scale roll-out by government of formal housing units. The numbers of households living under conditions of non-formal tenure are probably a great deal higher as it is not unusual in lower-income areas for formal housing to be bought and sold outside of official land registration processes, and the process of registering titles is inefficient.[1]

But informality is far more pervasive in South Africa than the narrowly defined categories above suggest. Simone (2004: 2) argues that African cities 'can be seen as a frontier for a wide range of diffuse experimentation with the reconfiguration of bodies, territories, and social arrangements necessary to recalibrate technologies of control'. In South Africa, the extent of informality is not nearly as great as elsewhere

in Africa, but there are elements in common: the evasion of formal or official mechanisms of regulation, or perhaps the use of these mechanisms in unintended ways,
gives rise here as well to a level of ungovernability which is also essential to the survival of those on the economic margins, and an easier route to wealth and power for
others. The forms which this takes are many: corruption by government officials; tax
and legal evasion; the use of informal and personal contacts to broker deals within
and across the boundaries between public and private sector; selling of professional services inside or outside of public-sector jobs; the making of informal water
and electricity connections, informal land and housing deals and so on.

Other studies have argued that the daily lives of many people in South Africa
are centred on searching for ways of survival (short and longer term), and that
understanding kinship and social networks and relations is the key to understanding
how livelihoods are structured. When these relations break down as a result of
crime or HIV/AIDS, as is increasingly the case in parts of South Africa, then the
impact is far-reaching as basic survival mechanisms are threatened. Samuels
(2000) argues that kinship relations almost always have a transactional rationale,
which is closely bound up with morality and social obligations. These relationships
are viewed in a long time frame and may be played out over generations, and also
span space: rural and urban areas function as a series of interlocking, intercon-
nected and interrelated livelihood locations. People 'cycle' in and out of a range of
different locations, combining different strategies in different ways at different times
in their life span. Informality thus permeates most aspects of the lives of the poor in
South Africa, as it does in the wider continent.

CHANGING DISCOURSES OF THE INFORMAL

The terms 'informal sector' and 'informality' have more or less disappeared from
South African economic policy discourse in the last ten years. And in the field of
housing policy discourse, the goal of replacing informal shelter and land occupation
with formal housing units has been a consistent theme since 1994, and is emphasized particularly strongly in recent policy shifts. The concept of informality, which
encompasses the bulk of practices and relationships which sustain the poor in South
Africa, has thus mysteriously vanished to be recategorized in alternative forms which
make them (supposedly) more susceptible to enumeration, regulation and 'development' into entities that conform more readily to a dominant modernist rationality.

INFORMAL ECONOMIC ACTIVITY

In the field of economic policy, informality has been recategorized as 'small business'; in other words it is seen as comprising entities which have the same

characteristics as formal businesses and are only distinguished by their smaller size. In the Reconstruction and Development Programme (ANC 1994), which set the basis of policy-making for the new post-1994 government, a section (4.4.7) is devoted to micro, small and medium-sized enterprise which is intended to include informal activities. This section categorizes small enterprises as part of the national economy and sees the prime developmental task as growing them into larger and more formal businesses: 'Micro producers should develop from a set of marginalized survival strategies into dynamic small enterprises that can provide a decent living for both employees and entrepreneurs' (ANC 1994: 94). The chapter goes on to identify four constraints that prevent these survival strategies from growing into dynamic enterprises: these are lack of access to credit, markets, skills and supportive institutional arrangements. This statement may accurately describe problems experienced by larger formal businesses, but ignores entirely the nature of informality and the often very different arrangements which survivalist operations have to make in order to function. For example, it is usually impossible for informal activities to access credit in the same way in which formal businesses do this, and they are far more reliant on social networks or informal savings and loan associations (*stokvels*) to do this.

Figure 14.1 Informal traders, Johannesburg

The notion that informal activities were simply 'too small' formal businesses persisted in subsequent economic policy in South Africa, where they have been incorporated into a policy framework labelled as LED. LED (see Chapter 8) has been described as a current alternative way of approaching development issues, originating in a number of key USA texts and in policies promoted by the World Bank and similar agencies. It has the benefit of being compatible with policies of decentralization and the promotion of the 'entrepreneurial' local state, as well as being highly non-specific in terms of the scale or context in which it is applied (Freund and Lootvoet 2004). Thus LED policies could be used to encourage large-scale businesses to locate in specific local areas (see Chapter 8), or small scale (medium and micro-) enterprises to develop in larger areas. It is also compatible with strategies related to 'place-entrepreneurialism' and with assumptions evident in a range of current policy approaches that action at the local level can address or ameliorate national and international structural inequalities (Watson 2002c).

In 2004 the first drafts of South Africa's new LED policy began to emerge. The prime motivation for the new policy is that while South Africa's macroeconomic policies have achieved stability and growth, the number of people unemployed and living in poverty has continued to grow. The draft then goes on to introduce a particular conception of the South African economy that has entered economic policy discourse in recent years, particularly via the President's 1998 'Two Nations speech'.

This speech described South Africa as having 'two nations' – a white, prosperous and well-serviced nation, and a poor, black and largely rural nation. This dualism has since been translated into a conception of two economies: a first-world and a third-world economy. The third-world economy in South Africa (now sometimes referred to as the 'second economy') is described as structurally disconnected from the first-world economy, and hence non-responsive to various attempts at development through macroeconomic policy. It would appear that this second economy is, in the minds of policy-makers, equal to the informal sector. Faull (2005) quotes the following from a document entitled *Towards a Ten Year Review*, issued by the President's Office in 2003: 'The first economy is an advanced, sophisticated economy, based on skilled labour, which is becoming more globally competitive. The second (economy) is a mainly informal, marginalized, unskilled economy, populated by the unemployed and those unemployable in the formal sector'.

In terms of intervention, the answer is seen to be one of directing capital and skills development to the 'second economy' so that it can function more like the 'first economy'. Thus the new LED policy refers to the need to create large and sustained human, financial and technological resource transfers from the first economy to the second economy, in order to 'integrate' the second economy into the first. There are interesting parallels here with much older international theorizing around the informal sector (Hart 1973), which referred to the problem of third-world 'dual economies' made up of a formal and informal (or traditional) sector, and which assumed that economic growth and modernization would ultimately eradicate the undesirable informal sector. This, of course, never happened and the growth of the informal sector has continued apace.

In a set of LED guidelines produced by the Department of Provincial and Local Government in 2005, it becomes clear that despite the definition of the 'second economy' as comprising primarily informal activities, and despite the primary motivation for LED being to develop and integrate the second economy, LED policy in South Africa is aimed at small (largely formal) business and fails to consider or understand the realities of informal activities. First, the LED guidelines identify micro-businesses (that is, employing fewer than five people) as just one category of activity which falls under the definition of LED. There is, therefore, no distinction between the very large number of formal businesses which fall into this category, and the fragile, intermittent, home or pavement-based activities which make up the vast majority of the informal sector. It could be argued that the latter require rather different approaches to small formal businesses.

Second, there are indications that the focus of LED is to be on productive businesses, that is, those involved in aspects of manufacture. Paragraph 11 of the guidelines directs municipalities to focus on: 'Enterprises that are job creating, promote environmental and ecological sustainability, promote social development, and broad-based black economic empowerment …'. And Paragraph 20 notes that

> in relation to growth sectors the focus will be on further enhancements in the well performing tourism and auto sectors and in sectors that need more attention such as clothing and textiles, the ICT industry, agriculture, and the services sector.

By contrast, most informal activities fall into the retail and services sectors.

Third, the overriding intention appears to be to formalize informal activities. Paragraph 102 of the guidelines directs municipalities to identify potential economic clusters and support these by

> providing land or assisting in its acquisition, assuring that the necessary skills training facilities are present, relevant and accessible in the territory; stimulating and facilitating PPPs (public–private partnerships) and the growth of co-operatives; assisting in access to loans and grants for small producers to participate in the value chain of the clusters; and facilitating the presence of BDS (business development services) and mentoring capacity to enable the small businesses and co-operatives to survive and grow; and promoting and marketing the area and its products.

These are all strategies that would have little meaning for much of the informal sector.

The point being made here is that while it is certainly necessary to institute policies and programmes aimed at developing small business, and while there will always be elements of informal activity (of the more entrepreneurial type) which can respond to these programmes and 'formalize' themselves, much informal activity is of the 'survivalist' type or is, for other reasons, not amenable to these kinds of interventions (Dewar and Watson 1991). It has long been recognized that the informal sector offers no universal panacea to problems of material deprivation, but that it is nonetheless important to facilitate it via generic strategies which aim at improving its operating environment and removing obvious obstacles to its presence. Such strategies would involve flexible land use and trading regulations, the making available of spaces and marketplaces where small trade can occur, the provision of land and housing in such a way that units can be used as a base for income generation and so on (Dewar and Watson 1991). Above all strategies would be based on a far more sensitive understanding of informality on the part of managerial institutions and a far greater tolerance to anti-hegemonic 'holes' in the 'meshwork' (Lefebvre 1991) of urban space.

INFORMAL HOUSING

Emerging housing policy discourse in South Africa over the last ten years mirrors, in many ways, that of LED policy. The constitutional right of all South Africans to 'adequate housing' (Constitution of the Republic of South Africa 1996: Section 26, 1) as well as the vision set out in the Housing Act No. 107 of 1997, that all citizens should have access to permanent residential structures with secure tenure, potable water, adequate sanitary facilities and domestic energy supply, laid the basis for a housing policy focused on the replacement of informal settlements with formal housing units. Policy goals were entirely quantitative (numbers of new units that could be produced each year) and existing informal settlements were ignored as it was assumed that they would soon be replaced with formal townships.

In the ten years following 1994, the Department of Housing did indeed manage an impressive roll-out of new housing units. An expenditure of R29.5 billion created 1.6 million 'housing opportunities' during this time. And yet by 2004 there was a realization that South Africa, like other developing countries, was not going to be able to build its way out of a housing backlog. Between 1996 and 2001 the number of households living in shacks in informal settlements and backyards had increased by 26 per cent (due to household splitting as well as population growth) and the annual rate of public housing delivery had, for a variety of reasons, begun to decline. Thus the housing backlog in 2004 was still 2.4 million households. Problematically, a proportion of these households are not eligible for housing subsidies as they had already received subsidies but had abandoned or sold their units and had found their way back into informal settlements.

These criticisms prompted a major review of housing policy in 2004 and the production of a new policy entitled *Breaking New Ground* (see Chapter 3). It indicates
some shift away from a standardized and quantity-driven approach: there is strong
emphasis on the need to provide sustainable human settlements in good locations in
order to achieve spatial restructuring, and the opening up of a more differentiated
approach to housing delivery which includes the in situ upgrade of informal settlements and the recognition of the role of informal rental (backyard shacks). However,
the previous negative attitude to informal settlements remains. Section 3.1 of the new
policy (DOH 2004) is entitled 'progressive informal settlement eradication', and it sets
out the aim of a phased in situ upgrade approach to be applied to informal settlements
in acceptable locations. Informality, in housing terms, is now recognized in the new
policy but is still regarded as inferior, and hence the new policy sets out ways in which
informal settlements can be changed so that they are no longer informal and approxi-
mate more closely the (officially held) formal housing ideal.

A related issue here has been the unquestioned assumption on the part of government that the provision of new housing should be linked to the provision of
freehold tenure for each household. The influence of the 'de Soto thesis', that ownership of land and property will allow poor people to use these as loan collateral in
order to start small businesses, thus activating 'dead capital' and solving the problem
of poverty (de Soto 2000), has been strong here and remains so. This despite growing evidence (FinMark Trust 2004) that there is great reluctance on the part of poor
people to do this and risk the loss of their basic shelter, an asset that can be used to
generate income directly (through informal rental), and an item that plays an important role in the rituals and practices of inheritance. The *Breaking New Ground* policy
takes a step forward here in recognizing the need for a range of tenure options and
rental options, but in practice there are few alternatives to freehold available.

It is not the intention here to suggest that informal settlements are necessarily
preferable places to live, although they vary greatly in this respect, or that their persistence should be used as an excuse to downscale the public provision of sturdy,
secure and serviced homes. Recent surveys (Zack and Charlton 2003) have shown
that many households have welcomed the move away from informal settlements and
feel that their quality of life has been improved in formal housing areas. Recent surveys (FinMark Trust 2004) have also shown, however, that for some households
informal settlements provide a level of flexibility and cheapness which cannot be
obtained in formal settlements. The survey showed that 73 per cent of households
interviewed in informal settlements regarded their location as good, 42 per cent had
carried out improvements on their homes, and a very high 92 per cent said that they
felt secure and not in danger of being moved or evicted, despite the lack of freehold
tenure. This percentage was higher than in the new site and service areas or in the
older township areas where 91 per cent and 89 per cent respectively felt secure.

Research in Africa more generally has also shown the important role played by informal settlements on the urban periphery which allow people access to a range of rural and urban employment opportunities (Bebbington and Bebbington 2001) not available in formal or more centrally located areas.

CONCLUSION

The official attitude to the informal in South Africa has been highly ambiguous. It has proved to be impossible for government to ignore its existence as growing income inequalities have plunged more households into poverty, making survival in informal settlements and in informal business activities the only option for them. Informality has thus been given prominence in policy terms, but described either as a 'second economy' which needs to be developed so that it can be integrated with the 'first economy', or as informal settlements which need to be 'eradicated' through upgrade processes which will turn them into formal settlements. The recently formulated LED policy and the new housing policy – *Breaking New Ground* – are the policy instruments that have been developed to achieve these transformations.

Within the municipalities this ambiguity has been evident as well. Informal settlements are rarely removed unless they are on prominent parcels of land or land required for other purposes, and most new housing projects (even those under the new housing policy) are new formal developments on greenfield sites. Legislation that was developed as an emergency measure under the apartheid government (the Less Formal Townships Establishment Act of 1991) is still used formally to recognize informal settlements and to suspend building regulations while the settlement is being upgraded. And the Western Cape Provincial government has made provision for an informal residential zone which can be included in all municipal zoning schemes. The assumption remains in both of these, however, that the provisions are temporary until the settlement has been upgraded.

The flagship pilot project of the new housing policy in Cape Town (the N2 Gateway Project) is replacing an informal settlement on the edge of the old Langa formal township with three-storey walk-up apartments, at a capital cost of some R120,000 per unit. It is no accident that the informal settlement is sited on the main route in from the international airport, and the adverse impression which this gives to tourists has, in the past, been the subject of ministerial comment. Very few of those previously in the informal settlement will be able to afford these units, and it would be difficult to counter the idea that such projects amount to little more than the 'aestheticization of poverty' (Roy 2005).

Ambiguity is also evident in local approaches to informal businesses. Generally these are tolerated in city locations where they can be regulated by formal

Figure 14.2 The N2 Gateway housing project, Cape Town

market infrastructure or sometimes painted squares on the ground, and an official 'blind eye' is usually turned to people running businesses from home, particularly in the poorer residential areas. At the same time there are moves to enforce the licensing of informal liquor outlets – termed *shebeens* – and some new land-use management schemes provide for the gradual upgrade of use restrictions in poorer areas as they become more 'developed'. This is a move which would directly impact on home businesses which are often the most fragile of survivalist strategies.

There appears therefore to be a failure to understand or accept the role that informality plays in survival strategies of the poor, and a failure to accept that it has a form and logic which may not conform to the norms of modernity, but is nonetheless a rational response to poverty and marginalization in its own terms. There is no existing precedent for the complete and successful formalization of informality, even in wealthier parts of the world, where informalization is now on the increase. In a context such as South Africa, where income inequalities and poverty are increasing it would appear to be far more sensible to adopt a policy of tolerance and support for informality, while at the same time opening up opportunities for growth and development for those activities or households that are willing and able to take advantage of them.

CONCLUSION: THE POWER OF PLANNING, AND THE LIMITS TO ITS POWER: LEARNING FROM THE SOUTH AFRICAN EXPERIENCE

INTRODUCTION

Planning theorists have questioned and debated the power of planning, and the limits to its power. As early as 1981 Shoukry Roweis argued that 'planners lack a systematic understanding of their discipline/profession: of the real constraints imposed on, and the objective opportunities open to, their practice' (Roweis 1981: 159). He went on to locate planning within the development of capitalism, and to argue that the power of planning is derived from the specific form that capitalist development takes within a concrete historical context. More recently questions around the power of planning have emerged in a spirited debate between theorists who direct attention to the power of communicative or deliberative processes to bring about positive change (e.g. Healey, Innes, Forester) and those who focus on the intersections of power and planning, and who direct attention to the ways in which planning is manipulated by the interests of power (e.g. Flyvbjerg, Yiftachel, Richardson). A very recent contribution by Ananya Roy has drawn on postcolonial theory to argue for an 'interrogation of planning's innocence' (2006: 23).

Positions in the debate have, invariably, been strongly influenced by context. For example, Flyvbjerg's forceful critique of the rationalities of planning was inspired by an experience of planning in Aalborg, a small city in Denmark, while Yiftachel's account of the use of planning as an instrument for the control of minority groups is situated in Israel–Palestine (Flyvbjerg 1998a; Yiftachel 2001). Theorists of the Communicative School have generally written in the context of the stable democracies in Western Europe (e.g. Healey 1997) and North America (e.g. Innes 1995) where civil society is relatively strong and the instruments of governance are mainly stable.

Contemporary South Africa offers an interesting and revealing context – albeit a very particular one – in which to consider the power of planning. It is a post-conflict society where a remarkable social and political settlement, or concordat, was reached in the early 1990s, but where divides are still deep-rooted. It is a democratic society, but one where institutions of democracy are new and still fragile. Significantly, it is a country where the current government has accepted planning as an important instrument of transformation, and has incorporated planning within its new policy and legislative frameworks.

It has been more than a decade since the arrival of democracy and, with the huge benefit of hindsight, we may have sufficient perspective to *begin* a process of critical appraisal. What has planning in South Africa achieved, what has it failed to achieve, and what does this tell us of the power of planning (to do good) and the limits to this power? In the pages below, this chapter explores these questions under the headings 'The innocence of planning?' and 'The efficacy of planning?' but, before doing this, we give brief consideration to the question 'what do we mean by planning?'.

THE BOUNDARIES OF PLANNING

To a very large extent the answer to the question on the efficacy of planning depends on what is meant by the term 'planning'. In the introduction to this book we stated that we find it impossibly limiting to work within a narrowly defined conception of town and regional planning which saw planning being solely about land-use management and the design of human settlements. We also indicated that planning should not be considered as the sole preserve of the state. Although the state has had a large part to play in planning – arguably the dominant part in the apartheid and post-apartheid history of South Africa – planning has involved multiple activities carried out by multiple agents and actors with a multiplicity of values. We have shown, for example, how various forms of oppositional planning practice, driven by different ideologies and values, emerged outside the boundaries of the state, especially in the latter days of the apartheid era. Even in terms of state-directed planning we can identify this multiplicity, as the state is itself a fractious and complex structure where human agency and human values play a strong role. In the apartheid and post-apartheid eras there have been significant, albeit sometimes subtle, differences between planning within different spheres and departments of government.

The way in which we choose to delineate planning is important for how we understand the relationships between planning and apartheid, and between planning and the transformative goals of the post-apartheid era. Under apartheid, the narrowly defined discipline of town and regional planning was, arguably, a very limited instrument for achieving ideological objectives. While town and regional planning clearly happened within the framework of apartheid, and there were planners, especially within national government, who were directly involved in the apartheid project, town and regional planning was, for most of its history, a fairly marginal profession. The real power lay elsewhere (except, perhaps, during P.W. Botha's era of reform when planning seemed to have an elevated position within government). However, in terms of an extended definition, which incorporates all forms of territorial reorganization, we must accept that planning was powerfully, directly and centrally involved with apartheid, an ideology that had as one of its main objectives the racial ordering of space. If, for example, we recognize the Group Areas Act – a potent mechanism for racial spatial ordering – to have been an instrument of planning, then the relationship between planning and apartheid must be regarded as having been deeply intimate. But, at the same time, we must also recognize the diversity of values that informed planning in the apartheid era. While many planners (using both a restricted and extended definition) were driven by the values that underpinned the ideology of apartheid (e.g. a commitment to Afrikaner nationalism or, more broadly, to preserving white supremacy and culture), there were, arguably, many others whose professional norms were strongly influenced by the then internationally dominant modernist values and approaches.

In the post-apartheid period, perceptions of the boundary of the professional activity of planning have shifted, and so it is now easier to speak of planning in the broader sense. Particularly important has been the expansion of planning to incorporate the fields of development and governance (especially in relation to institutional strategy and integration). It is significant, for example, that even the term 'town and regional planning' is gradually falling into disuse – the Town and Regional Planners Act of 1984, for example, was repealed by the Planning Professions Act of 2002, while the South African Institute of Town and Regional Planners has been replaced by the South African Planning Institute. As early as 1995 the RDP Office and the Forum for Effective Planning and Development offered a wide definition of planning as 'a participatory process aimed at integrating sectoral strategies, in order to support the optimal allocation of scarce resources between sectors and geographic areas and across the population in a manner that promotes sustainable growth, equity and the empowerment of the poor and marginalized' (FEPD 1995). In the 2002 Act, the term 'planner' is defined broadly as meaning a 'person who exercises skills and competencies in initiating and managing change in the built and natural environment in order to further human development and environmental sustainability' (RSA 2002a: Chapter 1). The 2002 definition could however still be seen as relatively constrained, compared with notions of integrated development in particular places as envisaged in integrated development planning, or as we defined planning in our introduction.

For us these expanded definitions are to be welcomed but we realize that as the socially defined activity of planning stretches, so more is expected of planning, and yet what is expected is less definable. Methodologically speaking, it becomes increasingly difficult to track the efficacy of planning, and to make the links between planning and its outcomes. Planning can no longer be considered only in terms of its impacts on spatial transformation (which is, admittedly, still important), but must also be evaluated in terms of its contribution to the processes and outcomes of governance across a wide area of concern, and also in terms of its contribution to addressing the big social concerns of the day which in South Africa include the HIV/AIDS epidemic, safety and security, poverty, gender empowerment and persisting racial divides.

THE INNOCENCE OF PLANNING?

As we have shown, planning and apartheid (an ideology and practice declared by the United Nations in 1973 as a 'crime against humanity') were linked in multiple ways, and this complicity has left a deep stain on planning in South Africa. Even using the restricted definition of planning, many planners working in state bureaucracies, or as consultants to these bureaucracies, had a role to play in the implementation of the Group Areas Act, in the design of segregated townships, in forced removals and resettlement, in the delineation of homeland boundaries, and in the implementation of the 'border industries policy', although, admittedly, more empirical work is required before we fully understand the extent and nature of this role.

In many cases the link between planning and apartheid was direct but there were also ambiguities. Many planners, for example, worked in the private sector or for 'white' local authorities and, as Mabin and Smit (1997) put it, 'the kinds of activities that busied these planners were not markedly dissimilar to those being pursued by their professional counterparts in other national contexts', and many of these planners, despite working within the general framework of racial separation, may have seen themselves 'largely as technical-built-environment professionals' (Mabin and Smit 1997: 208). However, even for the planners most removed from the institutions of apartheid, there was constant compromise and, at least, indirectly, complicity. As a perceptive commentator put it in relation to planners working in the province of Natal – where the United Party remained in control of the administration, and also where British-trained planners advised the Town and Regional Planning Commission – 'their dilemma is that in order to be able to plan at all they must say less than they know and plan less well than they can' (Scott-Brown 1964: 165).

From about the mid-1970s onwards, however, the situation became more complex and ambiguous, with forms of planning (within both the state and civil society) being informed by an increasingly differentiated set of values. The apartheid state was fracturing and in decline, with the earlier ideals of apartheid being questioned, even from within the heartland of Afrikaner nationalism. While a strong conservatism persisted, and was even reinforced, in places, there were also planners in government bureaucracies, supportive of the ruling party, who saw in the new reform agendas an opportunity for a more liberal practice. There were also planners within state structures opposed to the ruling party who saw themselves (perhaps naively) as *guerrillas within the bureaucracy*. Outside the state, resistance was becoming more vocal, with planners of very different value orientations (from classical liberal to radical socialist) being drawn into diverse circles of opposition. Internationally, as we know, the post-war modernist ideals of planning were being confronted by a set of oppositions – labelled variously as neo-Marxist, neo-liberal, postmodernist, and so on. This too had its impact on South African planning. In the

dying days of apartheid, the role of state-directed planning was increasingly to medi-
ate and mitigate the excesses of apartheid-induced fragmentation. Outside the
state, planning offered an alternative vision of a post-apartheid spatial order, or a
means to mobilize political resistance.

After 1994, planning was tied directly to the progressive agendas of a new
government committed to 'the building of a democratic, non-racial and non-sexist
future' (ANC 1994). Post-apartheid planning gradually took shape through the mid-
to late 1990s, and is still continuing to evolve. In this process various traditions,
inspired by progressive normative ideals, have intersected – sometimes uncomfortably so – to produce the current system of planning.

First, there was a spatial planning tradition – most strongly represented locally
in the University of Cape Town (UCT) school of planning but which was also connected to the broad international movement that has given us such ideals as the
compact city and new urbanism. Even before the dawn of democracy, this tradition
offered South Africa the possibility of more integrated, compact, sustainable and liv-
able urban spaces. Then, there was an urban management tradition, only partially
located within planning, but which connected to a process-oriented approach to
planning. This tradition was closely connected to the idea of governance and, in the
South African context, is most strongly represented in the IDP. This tradition
promised to make local government more developmental, integrated, strategic and
participatory. There was also, however, a tradition which focused very strongly on
human settlements which had as its concern such matters as informal settlement
upgrading, participatory housing processes and urban regeneration. It is an
approach which was linked to the UN-Habitat Human Settlements agenda, and
which was associated with the early work and advocacy of progressive agencies
such as BESG, DAG and Planact. The strong theme in this tradition was creating
better places for (especially poor) people to live. Unfortunately, however, the influence of this approach was far less than it could have been, as the housing sector
separated from the more integrative field of planning, and as the focus of this sector
was, until very recently, on the quantity of houses provided rather than on the quality
of living environments.

Through the admittedly uneven influence of these traditions, planning in South
Africa has played a positive role in what Forester (2004) has called the 'organization
of hope', and post-apartheid planning may be regarded as a heartening exemplar of
the benevolence of planning and, specifically, of *state-sponsored* planning.
However, even in democratic South Africa, the 'goodness of planning' cannot be
assumed and continued vigilance is necessary.

The state, at all levels, is an arena of contestation – some ideological and
some purely personal – and planning is used and abused by competing groups. In
many areas also the ethics of planning are blurred. Planning in post-apartheid South

Africa has, for example, become implicated in the construction of new forms of modernism – such as the global city ideal with its urban renewal projects – which are, at times, insensitive and disruptive to the livelihoods and lives of marginalized people. Roy points out that 'to destroy a city in order to renew it ... is planning's modernity, its dialectic of progress' (Roy 2006: 14). She uses Walter Benjamin's discussion of Klee's painting, *Angelus Novus*, which 'calls into question the liberal ruse of progress and rejects the liberal consolations of creative destruction' (Roy 2006: 15). On the ground, however, the moral dilemmas are complex and considerable. In inner-city Johannesburg, for example, cleaning up the city has involved the eviction of residents from 'bad buildings', a practice which has disrupted many lives and attracted considerable criticism (e.g. Chenwi 2006), but, even in this instance, it is not simply the case of (poor people) good and (government) bad, as the occupation of buildings in inner-city Johannesburg commonly involves hijacking of buildings, exploitation, severe health and safety hazards, and control by criminal gangs.

However, whatever the moral complexities of particular cases, the hard lesson is that even in post-apartheid South Africa – with its enviable reputation for social transformation, and one of the world's most progressive national constitutions – there are limits to what Roy termed the 'liberal moral order'. Even if we assume that the norms and values of actors and agents in post-apartheid South Africa are mainly positive, it is crucial that we have an understanding of what is *actually* going on – analytical rigour remains the necessary condition for normative prescription.

THE EFFICACY OF PLANNING?

South Africa's statutory commitment to value-led or norm-driven planning is a considerable achievement of a history of struggle, but the sobering question remains: to what extent has post-apartheid planning succeeded in meeting its transformative and progressive goals?

It is difficult to isolate the outcomes of planning from the consequences of many other policy influences, and also from the impact of a multitude of intervening and contingent factors, but there are areas where preliminary conclusions about the efficacy of post-apartheid planning can be drawn.

As will be shown below these include the impacts of planning on: spatial transformations, dealing with the big social issues of our time (especially HIV/AIDS, safety and security, poverty and gender empowerment), and the effectiveness and functioning of government (and, especially, local government). Before dealing with each of these impacts in turn, the chapter compares the efficacy of apartheid-era planning and post-apartheid planning.

COMPARING APARTHEID AND POST-APARTHEID PLANNING

One of the frequent assumptions in debate on the efficacy of planning is that the impact of post-apartheid planning has been very muted in comparison with apartheid-era planning which has left us with a considerable, albeit odious, legacy. The apparent limits of post-apartheid planning have been explained in terms of the enormous complexities of planning in a diverse, changing, globalizing world. Mabin (1995b: 196) wrote, for example, of the problems the ANC has had in 'waking up in a postmodern era while equipped only with the politics and practices of a modernist past'. This idea mirrors Beauregard's (1989: 389) observation of 'modernist planners in the grip of postmodern helplessness'.[1]

Post-apartheid planning is indeed happening in the context of extraordinarily difficult local and international circumstances. One of the enormous difficulties that post-apartheid planning encountered was its fragile institutional basis. After 1994, the hugely difficult process of creating and consolidating new institutions within all spheres of government commenced and, in the local sphere (most closely connected to planning) the transitional phase formally ended only in December 2000, although the reality of weak and struggling municipal authorities remains. In a sense it is remarkable what post-apartheid planning has achieved given this context. It should also be remembered that the 'achievements' of apartheid planning were ultimately not sustainable, and were never as certain as may now be supposed. After all, the apartheid rule of National Party leaders Vorster, Botha and de Klerk – which spanned more than two-and-a-half decades – was associated with the decay, rather than the success, of apartheid.

Even a comparison with the early years of apartheid is not unambiguous. In 2006, after twelve years of post-apartheid rule, there is a new system of planning in place (or, at least, partially in place as the land-use management system is still largely unreformed), but one that can only claim very modest success. In 1960, twelve years after the apartheid government had come to power, the major instrument of spatial restructuring, the Group Areas Act (GAA), had been on the books for ten years, but the outlines of the broader spatial vision of apartheid, connected to the development of homelands, had still to be fully expounded, and the implementation of the GAA, with its forced removals, was only beginning. Also, in 1960, there was an urban crisis – most famously represented by the Sharpeville shootings – that threatened to unravel the entire system. Admittedly, in the 1960s, the apartheid regime regained control, consolidated its position and, in the context of rapid economic growth, was able to implement a large part of its vision for racial spatial ordering. But this also was a brief era of progress for the apartheid planners – by the early 1970s the apartheid model was faltering and, after the Soweto uprising in 1976, the gradual dismantling of the awful edifice began.

Will post-apartheid planning ever achieve the level of effectiveness that apartheid planning attained for the short time in the 1960s? Perhaps not, but there are indications that post-apartheid South Africa is emerging from a long period of institutional transition and that, with the benefit of sustained economic growth, the state may be in a stronger position to use planning more effectively in pursuit of social and spatial reconstruction.

Is there anything to learn from apartheid in the 1960s? Perhaps. The successes of apartheid planning had to do with such factors as: strong instruments of spatial restructuring (including the GAA), high levels of institutional integration (especially within the Department of Native Affairs which dealt with almost all aspects of the lives of black South Africans), a growing resource base, a willingness to enforce controls, an ideological coherence (for a while, at least) and a ruthlessness evident, for example, in a large-scale and brutal programme of forced removals.

Post-apartheid South Africa could learn lessons from the policy and institutional coherence of the apartheid programme, and from the effectiveness of some of the tools used by the apartheid state but, in defining what is meant by the effectiveness of planning in the current context, we are not looking at the ability of the state to impose a top-down blueprint for transformation, but rather for the ability of the state, and governance more broadly, to generate and guide processes that will deliver equitable and sustainable outcomes, while promoting inclusive participation and deepening democracy. Perhaps the single most important lesson has to do with the importance of values to the practice of planning – there is no point in having effective tools and practices (and apartheid had many of these) if the outcomes of planning are unjust. In post-apartheid South Africa, state action will (hopefully) always be constrained by democratic process and a respect for human rights.

In terms of the latter definition of effectiveness it is clear that the apartheid state failed dismally, but more difficult to determine is whether the post-apartheid state performs better. The ideals and underlying values of (the mainly state-directed) post-apartheid planning would be almost universally accepted as positive and progressive (albeit somewhat 'modernist', as illustrated by the lack of acceptance of informality, as discussed in Chapter 14), but how effective has it been in delivering outcomes? As we argue below, the story here is very mixed – in terms of spatial transformation and addressing the big social questions the performance of planning has been disappointing but planning has contributed to the performance and development of a new system of local government.

PLANNING AND SPATIAL TRANSFORMATIONS

The promise of post-apartheid planning to address the spatial fragmentations and inefficiencies of apartheid is largely unfulfilled. Pieterse put it bluntly:

> we are confronted with the harrowing fact that South African cities may be as
> segregated, fragmented and unequal as they were at the dawn of political libera-
> tion. Given the amount of intellectual capital, institutional resources and political
> will we have thrown at the problem of the apartheid city, how can this be?
>
> (Pieterse 2004a: 82)

Of course, this failure cannot be laid only at the feet of planning as space is produced at the intersection of multiple rationalities, and there are considerable limits to the power that planning has to shape spatial outcomes. In South African cities also, the efficacy of planning is constrained by informality, while the conflicting and diverse spatial rationalities of government policies and programmes outside the realm of planning have made it very difficult for planners to achieve their spatial objectives.

The truth, however, is that planning frameworks have been simply too weak to force the necessary spatial coordination within government and, until the creation of consolidated metropolitan authorities at the end of 2000, the institutional basis for coherent spatial policy within South Africa's large cities was missing. The develop- ment of planning systems has also failed to bring together processes such as land-use management, transportation planning, and environmental management and, despite recent efforts to achieve this in provinces such as the Western Cape, these disjunctures remain and continue to undermine attempts at integration.

For these and other reasons, post-1994 frameworks and systems have struggled to substantively influence private-sector decision-making and invest- ment. In many places the interests and decisions of private developers have overwhelmed the intellectual and practical capacity of public authorities, and growth patterns have thus been largely dictated to planners. A large part of the problem is that spatial plans and frameworks have been poorly related to the actual mechanisms of implementation. A new generation of metropolitan scale spatial plans (or, rather, frameworks and perspectives) emerged in the 1990s and early 2000s which reflected new and progressive approaches to spatial gover- nance, but a significant component of the old rule-based regulatory system of planning remained in place – by 2006, a decade after IDPs had been introduced into local government legislation, the long promised new land-use management legislation was still ponding, and most municipalities were still using town-planning schemes that had been prepared in the apartheid era.

Also undermining the efficacy of spatial planning was the poor grounding of many plans and frameworks in a real understanding of development processes and imperatives. The gap between spatial visions and plans, and real patterns of invest- ment in the urban environment, grew quickly, and the credibility of plans was called into question. The most powerful trends in urban development, for example, were towards decentralization, multinodal growth and locational flexibility, at a time when planners were attempting to fix urban boundaries and channel development into urban corridors that often had very little appeal to risk-averse private-sector investors.

The one area where there was some success was in inner-city regeneration. The flight of capital from CBDs accelerated in the 1990s, and there was rapid visible deterioration in many central areas. By the early 2000s, however, there was a turnaround: in Johannesburg, for example, crime rates dropped, there was heavy public-sector expenditure in regeneration projects, renewed interest by private investors, and the development of economic precincts such as the new Jewel City and Fashion District. Planning strategies and frameworks did play a role but much of the success may be ascribed to the role of public–private partnerships and instruments such as the City Improvement District (which has partially privatized the management of urban space).

In South Africa, planning has also attempted to reshape space at a regional scale. Under apartheid, the industrial decentralization programme was intended to reinforce the racial ordering of space which involved removals, resettlements and the redrawing of regional (i.e. homeland) boundaries. Territorial restructuring for apartheid was attempted on a grand scale with more than two million people removed and resettled, and there can be little doubt that these interventions had a huge impact on spatial reorganization. The outcomes of the industrial decentralization programme are however more ambiguous. The programme was associated with a shift of production from metropolitan to rural homeland areas but this shift was not as large as the government may have intended, and it is not clear to what extent the decentralization was a consequence of market-led processes (i.e. the search for cheap non-unionized labour) rather than of policy.

In post-apartheid South Africa, the old national spatial divides still remain, although they may be eroding in places. Dealing effectively with the 'regional question' has been hindered by the lack of a clear, strongly supported regional or national spatial policy. The ambivalence around regional policy has to do with a set of complex cultural and sociopolitical issues, including constructions of culture and identity, people's memories of life in the city and their continued ties to rural areas, and the intricate and changing relationship between notions of tradition and modernity. While there has been a strong push from city-based academics and policy-makers for a greater focus on urban development (and, to some extent, also on other areas where clear economic potentials may be identified) anti-urban sentiment remains a strong factor in South Africa's spatial politics. The role of the National Spatial Development Perspective (NSDP) – which directs major investments very firmly towards areas of identified potential – in directing patterns of growth, has yet to be shown. Although the NSDP has recently been given more prominence in government, there are also indications that it is being systematically ignored in places where this policy does not offer clear benefits.

In many respects the story of post-apartheid spatial planning is disappointing. It is a story of high hopes and strong ideals, but, at least partially, failed practice. It is a story that may provoke scepticism. However, there are indications that a less ambitious and more pragmatic practice of spatial planning is emerging that may ultimately have a stronger influence on spatial outcomes than the bold visions of urban reconstruction will ever have. Rather than seeking to 'buck the trends' by imposing a new urban form, the more pragmatic approach is to 'bend the trends' towards outcomes that would be more sustainable and equitable than if left entirely to the market, and to take a longer-term view of the restructuring of cities and regions.

PLANNING AND THE BIG SOCIAL PROBLEMS

The other area where planning has struggled to make the connections is around the key societal issues of contemporary South Africa, including, most importantly, HIV/AIDS, crime prevention, poverty alleviation and gender empowerment. Planning has been enthusiastically embraced and promoted as an agent of social transformation, but in practice it has been exceedingly difficult to use the instruments of planning to address the great social concerns of our time.

HIV/AIDS is a pandemic of disastrous proportions. In December 2005 the UN estimated (perhaps somewhat conservatively) that there are 40.3 million people worldwide living with HIV, and that there were some 3.1 million AIDS deaths in 2005 alone.[2] Sub-Saharan Africa, with just 10 per cent of the world's population, accounts for more than 60 per cent of these HIV infections, with Southern Africa remaining the global epicentre of this epidemic. It is difficult to ascertain exact figures for HIV infection in South Africa but it is known, for example, that 29.5 per cent of women attending ante-natal clinics in 2004 were HIV-positive (with a figure of 40 per cent for KwaZulu-Natal).

Despite the enormity of the problem, there have been few attempts to make the link between planning and HIV, the exceptions including Thomas and Crewe (2000), van Donk (2002), Tomlinson (2001, 2003b: 76–87). As van Donk put it, 'HIV/AIDS is one of the most – if not, in some areas, the most – important urban development issues in developing countries, especially Sub-Saharan Africa. Yet, urban development planning is largely silent on the issue' (van Donk 2002: 9). She challenges the conceptual framing of the epidemic as a medical issue, and demands that planning's failure to incorporate HIV/AIDS be remedied. In policy terms, there has been some attention to HIV/AIDS in terms of housing and HIV/AIDS has been recognized as an important cross-cutting theme in integrated development planning, but local authorities have been slow to find effective ways to address the epidemic (Thomas and Crewe 2000). Nevertheless, despite the late start, there are new signs of more proactive local initiative – including the setting up of local HIV/AIDS councils – and of a stronger link between the planning of HIV/AIDS interventions, as reflected in IDPs, and implementation.

Crime remains one of the greatest challenges of South African society, with crime rates in South Africa being extraordinarily high when compared with those of Europe and North America. The statistics provided by the United Nation's Office on Drugs and Crime (UNODC) show, for example, that South Africa's homicide rates are over 13 times higher than in the USA, and 32 times higher than in England and Wales (UNODC 2003). Crime and fear of crime are constant realities in South Africa's large cities especially, and have had a profound effect on urban spatial form – as evidenced, for example, in gated communities, security villages, enclosed malls and confined business parks. It is surprising, however, how little impact the public concern for safety and security has had on the discourse and practice of planning. A recent exception is the controversy around gated communities that has entered the planning debate. Planners and urban policy-makers have had to confront the contradictions posed by this particular response to urban fear – that is, the need for secure living environments versus the rights of movement and the desire to protect public space (Landman 2004; Harrison and Mabin 2006; Lemanski 2006). The 'Safer Cities' approach promoted through the UN-Habitat Agenda is beginning to influence planning discourse and approaches in South Africa with some work on 'planning for crime prevention' having been undertaken under the auspices of the NGO, Safer Cities (e.g. Van Huyssteen and Oranje 2003).

Poverty remains an enormous challenge for South African society. Although South Africa may be a middle-income country in per capita terms, there are huge levels of inequality, and a large section of the population does not have a socially acceptable standard of living. In 2004 the Human Sciences Research Council estimated that 57 per cent of South Africans (or about 26 million people) were living below the poverty line at the time of the 2001 Census, unchanged from 1996, with levels varying from 32 per cent in the Western Cape to 77 per cent in Limpopo province (HSRC 2006). A direct link has been made between integrated development planning and the concern with poverty reduction, with IDPs seen as providing the framework for municipal-level responses to problems of poverty (Cole and Parnell 2000; RSA 2002b). This link was expressed in a government report in the following words:

> South African government objectives of poverty reduction are unambiguous and are reliant on a multiplicity of local planning tools … Underpinning these efforts is a conviction that a focus on participative integrated development planning, cost effective infrastructural and service delivery, and local economic development strategies, will lead to beneficial effects, in the sense that they will lead to the creation of livable conditions for residents, stimulate job creation and business confidence that automatically impact on poverty levels.

(RSA 2002b: 27)

There are a number of assumptions in this statement that are largely untested. Reviews of integrated development planning have suggested that many IDPs do incorporate strategies for dealing with poverty (UNDP 2002) – many of these being about better service delivery and LED strategies – but it is difficult to determine the extent of real impacts. There are also indications that attempting to deal with poverty obliquely through service delivery does not necessarily work – recent critiques of housing policy, for example, reveal that the provision of formal shelter may, in fact, have worsened the financial position of households which now face additional expenses (Charlton and Kihato 2006).

The other big issue that the post-apartheid state has taken on board is gender empowerment. South Africa's constitution provides for legal equality between men and women, while the first ANC government committed itself to building a non-sexist society (ANC 1994). Among the institutions and programmes of state are a Commission on Gender Equality, a Women's Charter and a National Policy for Women's Empowerment, while many other policies and programmes have been at least partly framed using a gendered lens. However, as Beall (2003: 18) has reminded us, 'the realities of women's experience in South Africa have been much more complex and paradoxical than the country's celebrated status suggests'.

A similar point may be made in relation to *gender and planning*. The gendered approach to spatial analysis and planning in the international debate and literature (e.g. Moser 1993) has had an influence on thinking about planning and development in South Africa (e.g. Todes and Posel 1994; Sadie and Loots 1998; Cole and Parnell 2000; Beall and Todes 2004; Beall 2003, 2005), and gender-based analysis and methodologies have been incorporated into the requirements for IDPs (Cole and Parnell 2000; Beall 2005). However, it is doubtful whether this new emphasis on gender awareness in planning has yet been translated into substantive progress in implementation. In 1998, Sadie and Loots identified a large number of government policies that had incorporated some degree of gender analysis and sensitivity but nevertheless concluded that 'women's particular needs are not prioritized in the planning and execution of projects' (page 12). There may have been some progress since then but it is likely to have been slow. Todes *et al.* (2006), for example, point to the ambiguous outcomes of gender empowerment through planning. They show that, in a project such as Cato Manor, there is a high level of project-related participation by women, and also clear benefits for women who take much of the responsibility for families and livelihoods, but that women are poorly represented at the strategic level, and while they may participate in IDP processes, the separation of real decision-making from participation negates their influence.

A final and enormously challenging big social issue is the abiding racial divide in South African society. To a very large extent South African society remains racially segregated, with only limited integration happening within some of the older working-class suburbs, in the residential and working environments of the middle classes, and in sub-urban schools. There is little to suggest that planning has facilitated even the limited social integration that has occurred post-apartheid. In the few cases where planners have succeeded in overcoming the resistance of the (mainly white) middle classes to the location of (mainly black-occupied) low-income housing there is no indication that geographic proximity has translated into meaningful social contact. The impact of the Department of Housing's *Breaking New Ground*, which may support a greater mix of income groups, has yet to be shown.

The conclusion in relation to all the big social issues is that there have been considerable, albeit uneven, advances in terms of rhetoric and policy, but that there is no evidence yet to suggest that the various concerns have been translated into practice at any significant scale. The one area, however, where planning may have made a direct and significant impact is in the functioning of local government, and it is to this that we now turn.

PLANNING AND PROCESSES OF GOVERNANCE

The impact of integrated development planning on the functioning of local govern-ment, and on broader processes of governance, is still far from clear, but preliminary evidence does suggest that municipalities are increasingly using IDPs as the pri-mary strategic instrument for structuring and coordinating activities, and that IDPs are influencing budgetary processes (Harrison 2003a; Western Cape 2005). Although empirical evidence is still thin, it does seem that municipalities may be working in more integrated, participatory and strategic ways because of IDPs, although in the case of some poorly capacitated municipalities, the preparation of IDPs may have been a burden that deflected energy away from more basic delivery functions (Atkinson 2003).

A report on the IDP Hearings of 2005 concluded optimistically that, 'in the four years since the establishment of new municipalities on 5 December 2000, government has made significant progress in both planning and service delivery in a more inclusive and targeted manner', and IDPs were identified as an important contributor to this success (Western Cape 2005: 2). However, these findings have to be interpreted against the deep unease, and even unrest, around levels of service delivery that marked the run-up to the 2006 municipal elections, and also against the important qualifier in the report on the hearings that 'the capability of the state is uneven [and] even where capacity is evident, the integrated impact of government on communities needs to improve considerably' (Western Cape 2005: 5).

The stated ideal was 'to have municipalities which are highly capacitated and have geared their institutional structures to the achievement of strategic priorities outlined in their integrated development plans and long-term city strategies'

(Western Cape 2005: 16). However, stated the report, 'it was clear from the IDP hearings that an extremely limited number of municipalities have reached this point'. Indeed, in the case of 33 of South Africa's 56 metropolitan and district municipalities (i.e. 60 per cent of the total), institutional capacity for planning was judged to be a matter of serious concern, and it is thus clear that post-apartheid planning is seriously constrained by the limits of the local state.

However, despite the unevenness of success, the strongest achievement of post-apartheid planning has been its impact on the processes of governance. Largely through the introduction of the IDP – but also through the arrival of other instruments such as city development strategies – processes of planning have diffused through bureaucracies of government, and into civil society. As we argued in the introductory chapter, there has been a transformation in the practice of planning within government, which has permeated beyond traditional departments of planning, into a wide range of state organizations, and beyond. It is still difficult to measure the impact of this change but the hope, at least, is that planning is gradually leading to stronger capacity for strategic decision-making and implementation.

To the future

In the introductory chapter we indicated that the book would explore the outcome of the window of opportunity for planning that South Africa's transition to democracy has provided. We have shown that the outcomes have been mixed and, in many instances, disappointing. The window has, however, not yet closed. There is no sign, for example, of a waning commitment by government to the idea of planning, although there is some indication of a growing frustration within some key agencies such as the National Treasury and presidency at the constraints that weak planning and land-use management systems pose on growth initiatives. The continued, even enhanced, recognition given to planning was evident, for example, in a keynote speech by South Africa's Deputy President, Phumzile Mlambo-Ngcuka, at the launch of the Joint Initiative on Priority Skills Acquisition (JIPSA), in which she identified 'city, urban, and regional planning' as 'skills desperately needed by our municipalities' (JIPSA 2006: 1–2).

Government itself is giving strategic thought to the future direction of planning. Coming out of the nationwide 2005 IDP Hearings, for example, are five strategic thrusts which have been approved by cabinet: developing a shared paradigm for sustainable development; improving government's connectivity with communities; improving intergovernmental investment in localities; strengthening the strategic developmental role of provincial government; and improving the credibility of municipal IDPs.

The link between planning and the directions of the 'developmental state' is clear: 'looking ahead, IDPs need to be improved within a clear longer-term development trajectory to respond to national development objectives and build sustainable human settlements and viable local economies' (Western Cape 2005: 5).

The intention, it would seem, is to 'harden' or 'firm up' planning so that it can play a stronger role in delivering government's ambitious investment programme (Patel 2006). This offers the opportunity to deepen and extend the contribution of planning, and enhance its image. However, it also presents significant challenges and possible threats. It puts an enormous burden on the education and training system to produce graduates competent to do this work and, with the difficulties planning currently has in attracting high-calibre entrants, and the limited number of experienced educators, the planning profession may struggle to deliver what is required.

It is possible that planners – with their generally softer skills than other built-environment professionals – may become marginalized as the delivery programme takes hold, and the challenges of delivery may overwhelm the capacity of planners to deliver. Another real danger, however, is that the emphasis on infrastructural development and investment will erode participatory, collaborative and empowering types of planning. Over the past few years, the trend has been towards more technocratic styles of planning – the legal requirement to be participatory notwithstanding – and this may be reinforced with the implementation of ASGI-SA.

In responding to the challenges, there are clearly identified areas where improvement and reform are necessary. The need to build capacity in the planning field is an urgent and obvious task, with mentoring, continued professional development, and the expansion and improvement of planning in tertiary education, all requiring attention. In terms of systems and processes, the continued divide between planning and environmental management needs to be resolved, while the neglected practice of land-use management needs to be strengthened and reformed. Even existing forms of strategic-level planning which provide a now widely accepted framework for spatial government – such as the IDP, the SDF and City Development Strategies – must be improved so that they become stronger instruments for decision-making, while more work is needed in developing an effective system of *inter-governmental* planning and coordination. The relative weakness of the organized planning profession makes it difficult to respond effectively to these many challenges, although there has been some recent improvement in the profile of the South African Planning Institute, at least.

The relative weakness of planning outside the boundaries of the state is also an area for attention. International literature suggests an expanding role for non-state actors within planning internationally but, in South Africa, it is ironic that the role of non-state actors has declined after political liberation (following an era of relatively active engagement in planning by actors outside the state in the latter days of apartheid). It is, perhaps, understandable that the focus of attention post-1994 should have been on constructing and strengthening new structures and instruments of state, and it is arguable that this focus should continue into the foreseeable future, but far more effort is needed to build the capacity of non-state sectors both to engage in state-initiated planning processes, and to initiate processes of their own. For planning to be robust, and to respond to the diversity of South Africa's make-up, we need a multiplicity of planning practices within, outside, and cross-cutting, the boundaries between state and civil society.

All this is necessary for a more effective practice of planning in South Africa but far more may be needed. To a very large extent the discourse and practice of planning in South Africa remains a product of the intellectual hegemony of the global North. Although more attention is being given to context, the assumptions underlying planning practice in South Africa are largely still those derived from Western Europe and North America – assumptions of high levels of capacity, of adequate funding, of formal systems with a wide reach, of well-developed and independent structures of civil society, of clear mechanisms for adjudicating conflict, and of a relatively high level of social consensus. While borrowed thinking may provide valuable intellectual and practical resources, it cannot provide all that is needed to respond to contexts where, for example, large segments of the city operate outside formal regulatory systems, and where the lives of many urban citizens are lived through networks of association that have little connection to official arrangements of government. To intervene effectively in the shaping of spatial processes that are often elusive, complex and highly unpredictable requires new ways of thinking about space and society, and especially about the city.

Fortunately, a new literature is emerging that may provoke a rethinking of the role of, and possibilities for, planning in (South) African cities. This literature directs our attention towards: the associational networks that provide regularity to the lives of ordinary people in the tough environments of African cities (Gotz and Simone 2003: 123–47; Simone 2001a, 2004); the diverse, often conflicting rationalities of the city (Watson 2003a, 2006b); the creative hybridities of post-colonial cities (Bremner 2004; Mbembe and Nuttall 2004; Harrison 2006a); and, both the 'worldliness' and 'ordinariness' of African cities (Mbembe and Nuttall 2004; Robinson 2002, 2005).

Pieterse suggests, with hopeful anticipation, that 'we are on the threshold of an exciting era of indigenous theorizing that seeks to use innovative theoretical ideas to reimagine the horizon of pragmatic interventions into profoundly brutal, complex and challenging urban environments across Africa' (Pieterse 2006: 7). The challenge, however, is to translate this emergent consciousness of the African city into a real sense of how to plan more contextually, sensitively, intelligently and effectively within the African context. For Pieterse, the 'wave of recent scholarship on cities in the global South confirms [an] urban sensibility of ambiguity and possibility without really knowing what to do with it in planning terms' (Pieterse 2006: 1). Finding ways for planning to respond to a more contextually informed understanding may be the great intellectual and practical challenge for the medium term, at least.

CONCLUSION: SPEAKING TO A WIDER CONTEXT

In the introduction we expressed our hope that the book would speak to both South African and international audience. We hope that the critical policy perspective employed in our analysis will assist the South African audience in interpreting and understanding a complex period of its history, and in finding better ways to respond through planning to the huge and continuing challenges of development and nation-building. Planning may have been less than we had initially hoped for in 1994, and in some aspects post-apartheid planning may be regarded as a failure, but there have also been successes, especially on the process side, and planning continues to offer the prospect of better and more progressive governance. The revived inter-est in the developmental state – after a 'neo-liberal lapse' – strengthens this possibility, even if it brings its own pitfalls.

For the international audience, we hope that the South African case may pro-vide stronger insights into the possibilities for, and limits to, transformative planning practice. The central lesson from post-apartheid South Africa is that the idea of plan-ning may be appropriated in a positive and progressive way by the state but that there are significant limits to the power of planning – albeit limits that can be expanded, and that do change over time. A further lesson is that, to see real success, we need the commitment and patience to support sustained action and political will over an extended period. If the outcomes of planning in post-apartheid South Africa today were to be measured against the noble intentions of planning in 1994 there would be cause for disappointment. However, if expectations are adjusted, and more modest hopes are articulated for planning within the context of a gradually transform-ing spatial landscape and a progressively strengthening system of governance, then the performance of planning post-1994 may be viewed more positively.

South Africa had an unusual chance in 1994 to undertake planning that would make a difference, and so the contextuality of the South African case must be prop-erly recognized, but there are a growing number of reformist and progressively minded governments in other parts of the world – Latin America is a case in point – where the South African experience of success and failure may be helpful. One of the strongest lessons may simply be that in developing planning systems and processes, careful attention should be paid to context – to such issues as uneven capacities, the challenge of informalization, the nature of everyday life in the city, the limits of local government, and the real concerns of society that planning so often struggles to make a connection with. The South African experience may provide a resource for those elsewhere to use in coming to terms with cycles of hope, disappointment and restored hope, and in finding ways to expand the limits of planning to realize more socially just and sustainable cities and regions.

It may be possible to find in South Africa's post-apartheid planning a hopeful pointer towards a positive combination of a managerialism, which emphasizes performance, outcomes and efficiency, and a participatory approach, which deepens local democracy, and creates a voice for the marginalized. At the level of macropolicy Fakir (2005) saw the possibilities for a productive synthesis in the notion of the *democratic* developmental state, while Pieterse (2002: 5) saw these possibilities already existing in the IDP:

> the genius of the policy design [for IDPs] is that it reconciles the democratic aspirations of South Africans with the service-delivery imperative, which can only be addressed through systematic, incremental, collaborative effort over the long term. It nudges democratic aspirations in the direction of pragmatism and pulls institutional practice towards popular democratic control in a system with clear norms and rules and respect for financial durability.

This synthesis may be one of South Africa's contributions to the practice of planning internationally although much depends on the resolution to the current stand-off in South African politics between factions of the ruling alliance which are variously associated with managerialist and populist styles of governance.

The South African experience shows very clearly how the transformation of planning requires both the reform of the 'hard infrastructure' of planning – the laws, tools and procedures – and the 'soft infrastructure' which includes practices, actor networks, discourses and power arrangements. In South Africa, legislative changes (such as the introduction of the IDP) have been critical agents of transformation, and the lack of legislative reform (in the area of land-use management, for example) has constrained transformation, but changes within the soft infrastructure are as important. Here the transformation has been significant but not as clear-cut as in the world of legislation and regulation, and continued work is needed in areas such as building strong and progressive discourse coalitions, and reorienting the work and values of a profession that has deep roots in an era of racial ordering.

Finally, at a very practical level, post-apartheid planning must show that it is making a real and positive difference to the lives that people lead. At present much of the focus is on producing the institutional arrangements and frameworks for integrated planning, which may have important long-term consequences for strategic decision-making and the effectiveness of delivery, but which have immediate outcomes that are often indeterminate or, at least, extremely difficult to track. In addition to establishing these systems and processes, there is an urgent need to plan more directly for 'better places for people to live'. This means more attention to good design, but also to ensuring more effective local- and community-level participation, and better response to the livelihood strategies, and the real patterns of people's lives. As we argued in the introductory chapter, successful planning requires balanced attention to both the process and product of planning. In the South African case, the focus over the past decade or so has been directed more strongly towards developing the appropriate processes of planning, and the time may now be right for more targeted attention to the desired product of planning, as we continue to work towards the realization of socially just and sustainable cities and regions.

APPENDIX

THE BLOEMFONTEIN COMPETENCIES

1 A knowledge and understanding of the moral and ethical dimensions of acting in the public domain, and applying this in planning practice. The sub-outcomes showing evidence of this include:

- Orientation to social justice and equal opportunity
- An appreciation of the diversity of cultures and views
- A people-centred approach
- Promotion of efficiency in resource use
- An orientation towards sustainable development
- Respect for professional ethics.

2 Demonstration of a sound theoretical and contextual knowledge, and ability to apply this in action. The sub-outcomes showing evidence of this include an understanding of:

- The nature, purpose and methods of planning
- The histories, philosophies and theories of planning and of development
- The theories relating to the natural, social, economic, developmental and political environments
- The theories and principles relating to the design of urban environments
- The theories relating to urban, metropolitan, rural and regional development, and to these contexts and processes
- The South African context and its particular challenges
- An application of these theories to the design, management and implementation of planning interventions to bring about positive change and societal benefits within human settlements.

3 Linking knowledge to spatial plans and policies. The sub-outcomes showing evidence of this include an aptitude to:

- Collect, analyse and organize information to determine planning processes
- Use technologies to assist these processes
- Apply appropriate knowledge pertaining to political, policy and institutional contexts, and of planning legislation and procedures
- Prepare plans and formulate policies with spatial orientation at different scales

- Undertake planning with due appreciation of aesthetic dimensions, and with sensitivity to the links between human settlement and the natural environment
- Interpret and apply plans to ongoing decision-making and problem-solving
- Apply knowledge to the implementation of plans and to land management and development processes.

4   Linking and synthesizing programmes and projects from various sectors and institutions within a framework of integrative development. The sub-outcomes showing evidence of this include:

- An integrative understanding of development issues and processes
- An understanding of the management requirements of integrative development processes
- An ability to think creatively and synoptically
- An understanding of the legal, policy and institutional frameworks within which such planning and development occurs
- An understanding of key issues in relation to development in South Africa including local economic development, land reform, and urban restructuring and the development of integrated settlements.

5   Conducting academic research in order to develop critical thinking and problem-solving abilities. The sub-outcomes showing evidence of this include:

- An understanding of appropriate methodologies for different research requirements
- An ability to collect, analyse and evaluate information
- An ability to apply generated knowledge to planning problems, in a creative way.

6   Application of the managerial and communicative skills necessary for managing planning and development processes in the public and private sectors. The sub-outcomes showing evidence of this include:

- An understanding of social dynamics and power relations
- An understanding of political processes and governance
- Strategic thinking and management
- Financial management
- Organizational management
- Project management
- Decision-making skills
- Organizational skills
- An ability to relate to and work with people

- An ability to work in teams as well as individually
- An understanding of approaches, processes and techniques associated with participatory and collaborative forms of planning
- Negotiation, facilitation and mediation skills
- An ability to communicate effectively verbally, graphically and by electronic means.

NOTES

INTRODUCTION

1   In this book we use the terms 'black', 'coloured' and 'white' to refer to apartheid-legislated categories or 'population groups'. We prefer to use the term African to describe people who were legally classified as 'black', and to use the term 'black' to refer to African, coloured and Indian people together. We continue to make such distinctions because of the profound repercussions this classification still has on the lives of people in South Africa, and because of the continued use of these categories in official reports and census data. It does not imply agreement with the principles of that classification.

2   Bantustans were the regions within South Africa set aside for African occupation and were intended ultimately to be independent, self-governing states.

CHAPTER 1

1   The 51 stands for 1951 and the 6 and 9 refer to the drawing numbers in the work of one of the architects, Douglas Calderwood, who designed the houses.

2   Also referred to (sardonically) as Bantustans.

3   In August 1985 Foreign Minister Pik Botha assured the world that President P.W. Botha would announce radical policy shifts. The president's speech was, however, a terrible disappointment and followed by a massive capital outflow. Botha had failed to 'cross the Rubicon' but his address is nevertheless cynically known as the 'Rubicon speech'.

CHAPTER 2

1   A term used by some progressive planners at the time.

2   In South Africa at the time, the term 'progressive' was used to distinguish people who saw themselves as radicals, different from those espousing a more liberal or reformist approach.

3   The 'coloured labour preference policy', initiated with the so-called 'Eiselen Plan' of 1955, was progressively tightened up through the 1960s and only abandoned finally in 1985. It was aimed, originally, at the removal of all Africans from the Western Cape, which was to remain the 'natural' home region of the coloured people and an area in which they enjoyed a degree of protection in the labour market.

4   As noted in the introduction to this chapter, this term is used to encompass the two strands of planning (liberal and progressive) which were critical of apartheid planning, and developed new visions of and approaches to planning.

CHAPTER 4

1   The provincial Development Tribunals, however, remain in place, and there are tensions between municipalities and these tribunals with municipal authorities claiming that developers are bypassing municipalities by submitting their applications to tribunals which ignore the content of local plans.

2   Within the metropolitan areas – Johannesburg, Ekhuruleni (East Witwatersrand), Tshwane (Pretoria), eThekwini (Durban), Cape Town, Nelson Mandela (Port Elizabeth) – there is a single-tier municipal authority but in the rest of the country there is a two-tier system with district councils sharing power with local councils.

3   Significantly, the levels of agitation died down almost completely after the local government elections of March 2006.

4   For administrative and planning purposes the City Of Johannesburg was divided into 11 regions, now consolidated into seven. RSDFs were prepared for each of the original 11 regions. The RUMPs are in the course of preparation, and will provide detailed guidance on how to coordinate and monitor service delivery and day-to-day management in precincts across the city. The introduction of Ward-Based Plans for each of the city's 103 wards is currently under consideration.

CHAPTER 5

1   Population figures in Figure 5.2 and Table 5.1 are based on census data. A recent report by the South African Cities Network (2006) suggests that population growth rates in the cities from 1996 to 2005 are lower than might be expected from 2001 census figures. The 2001 figures were too high, and are likely to be revised downwards. The broad direction of trends is however consistent in the two sets of data.

CHAPTER 6

1   Chapter 1c of the 1995 Development Facilitation Act contains a set of eight normative planning principles giving spatial guidance: they refer to integration, mixed land use, curbing urban sprawl, correcting past spatial distortions and environmental sustainability. The principles were drafted by a group of planners in local government and NGOs, all trained at UCT, but also informed by the then Ontario planning Bill (personal communication: S. Berrisford).

2   There were also corridors indicated which followed movement routes of lesser importance. The reasons for this were largely political: each of the then municipalities which made up metropolitan Cape Town demanded a corridor within their area as they believed it might indicate expenditure of public resources.

3   The impact of the earlier plans does not appear to have been significant, and it is too early to judge the impact of the more recent plans.

CHAPTER 8

1   This stadium is privately owned, however, so this option is not straightforward.
2   Hijacked buildings are those that are effectively taken over by people who do not own them. Apartments or space within them are then illegally rented out to others. In some cases, hijackers force existing tenants or illegal occupants to pay rent to them.

CHAPTER 9

1   This chapter draws on research and thinking for a project exploring the relationship between environmental management and planning in KwaZulu-Natal, and reported in Todes *et al.* (2005). Although the report is extensively acknowledged in this chapter, the contribution of other authors, particularly Vicky Sim and Cathy Oelofse, and of the KwaZulu-Natal Provincial Planning and Development Commission, which commissioned the study, is noted.

CHAPTER 10

1   The first two sections of this chapter draw heavily from Harrison and Kahn (2002).
2   Address delivered by the Deputy President, Phumzile Mlambo-Ngcuka, at the launch of the Joint Initiative for Priority Skills Acquisition (JIPSA), Presidential Guest House, 27 March 2006.

CHAPTER 11

1   A one-year degree, which was studied on top of a three-year diploma (of which one year was practical training).
2   The number of part-time students however inflates figures for postgraduate education. In some planning schools, part-time postgraduate studies are done on a block basis, sometimes with as little as one week's contact time per semester. These courses verge on distance education.
3   Some 40 employers in senior positions in the public and private sectors in Cape Town, Gauteng and Johannesburg were interviewed.

CHAPTER 12

1   We recognize that there was no one coherent set of values that informed planners, that planners themselves no doubt regarded these values in different ways, and that there are almost always conflicts around which values should prevail.

2   The role of traditional authorities has been gradually formalized in post-apartheid South Africa. The 2004 Traditional Leadership and Governance Framework Act validates the role of chiefs in local government through their leadership of traditional councils.

CHAPTER 13

1   Ministry for Provincial Affairs and Constitutional Development (1998: 20): '... the participatory process should not become an obstacle to development ...'.
2   Consensus-seeking processes can have an added benefit in that the shared understanding, mutual trust and 'identity-creation' that are built up, linger on as new 'cultural resources' or 'cultural capital' (Healey 1999: 114).

CHAPTER 14

1   In 2004 there was a titling backlog of 53 per cent of the sites in older formal township areas, and of 11 per cent of RDP and site and service plots. Thirty-six per cent of three million existing title deeds in the country are considered unregisterable due to legal errors or other legal constraints (www.finmarktrust.org.za).

CHAPTER 15

1   It should be noted that the contextual use of terms such as 'modern' and 'postmodern' should be given careful consideration. In South Africa, for example, apartheid represented a peculiar form of modernism, but the majority of the population never got to live the modernist dream. There is thus no shared memory or experience of the modern to inform the construction of either a 'new form of modernism', or a more 'postmodern' social and physical landscape.
2   http://www.unaids.org

BIBLIOGRAPHY

Abu-Lughod, J. (1980) *Rabat: Urban Apartheid in Morocco*. New Jersey: Princeton University Press.

Adebayo, A. and Todes, A. (2003) 'The spatial development initiative in South Africa: an assessment of sustainable development and employment creation', report to the United Nations Habitat, Nairobi.

Adelzadeh, A. (1996) 'From the RDP to GEAR: the gradual embracing of neo-liberalism in economic policy', *National Institute for Economic Policy*, August.

Adelzadeh, A. and Padayachee, V. (1994) 'The RDP White Paper: reconstruction of a development vision?', *Transformation*, 25: 1–18.

Africa, E. (1993) 'A historical analysis of the relationship between planning education and planning practice: broken ties or suffocating embrace?', unpublished Master's dissertation, Durban: University of Natal.

Altman, M. (2001) 'Evaluation of spatial development initiatives', report to the Development Bank of Southern Africa, Midrand.

Amin, A. (2004) 'Regions unbound: towards a new politics of place', *Geografiska Annaler*, 86(1): 33–44.

ANC (African National Congress) (1994) *The Reconstruction and Development Programme: A Policy Programme*, Johannesburg: Umanyano Publications.

Arce, A. and Long, N. (eds) (2000) *Anthropology, Development and Modernities*, London: Routledge.

Atkinson, D. (2003) 'Post-apartheid local government reforms: a small town perspective', *Occasional Paper No. 4*, Johannesburg: Centre for Development and Enterprise.

Atkinson, D. and Marais, L. (2006) 'Urbanization and the future urban agenda in South Africa', in R. Tomlinson, U. Pillay and J. du Toit (eds) *Democracy and Delivery: Urban Policy in South Africa*, Pretoria: HSRC Press.

Bache, I. and Flinders, M. (eds) (2004) *Multi-Level Governances*, Oxford: Oxford University Press.

Badenhorst, M. (1995) 'The changing profile of town and regional planners in South Africa', *Town and Regional Planning*, 38: 13–22.

Beall, J. (2001) 'Valuing social resources or capitalizing on them? Limits to pro-poor urban governance in nine cities of the South', *International Planning Studies*, 6(4): 357–75.

–– (2003) 'Decentralizing government and centralizing gender in Southern Africa: lessons from the South African experience', *Occasional Paper No. 8*, Geneva: United Nations Research Institute for Social Development.

–– (2005) 'Decentralizing government and de-centering gender: lessons from local government reform in South Africa', *Politics and Society*, 33(2): 253–76.

Beall, J., Mkhize, S. and Vawda, S. (2005) 'Emergent democracy and "resurgent" tradition: institutions, chieftancy and transition in KwaZulu-Natal', *Journal of Southern African Studies*, 31(4): 755–71.

Beall, J. and Todes, A. (2004) 'Headlines and head-space: challenging gender planning orthodoxy in area-based urban development', *IDS Bulletin*, 35(4): 43–50.

Beauregard, R. (1989) 'Between modernity and postmodernity: the ambiguous position of US planning', *Environment and Planning D: Society and Space*, 7, 381–95.

–– (1995) 'Challenges to progressive service organizations: Planact of South Africa', *Community Development Journal*, 30(4): 364–71.

Beavon, K. (2004) *Johannesburg: The Making and Shaping of a City*, Pretoria: University of South Africa Press.

Bebbington, A. and Bebbington, D. (2001) 'Development alternatives: practices, dilemmas and theory', *Area*, 33(1): 7–17.

Behrens, R. and Watson, V. (1996) *Making Urban Places: Principles and Guidelines for Layout Planning*, Cape Town: University of Cape Town Press.

Beriatos, E. and Gospodini, A. (2004) '"Glocalising" urban landscapes: Athens and the 2004 Olympics', *Cities*, 21(3): 187–202.

Berrisford, S. (2005) 'Review of legal requirements relating to planning and environmental management in KwaZulu-Natal', in A. Todes, V. Sim, P. Singh, M. Hlubi and C. Oelofse (eds), 'Relationship between environment and planning in KwaZulu-Natal', *KwaZulu-Natal Provincial Planning and Development Commission – Main Series*, 78: 20–26.

BESG (Built Environment Support Group) (1986) 'St. Wendolins: building the community', unpublished manuscript, Durban: University of Natal.

–– (1988) *1987–88 Annual Report*, Durban: University of Natal.

–– (1999) *Towards the Right to Adequate Housing*, Durban: BESG.

Biermann, S. (2003) 'Investigation into the energy consumption implications of alternative locations for low-income housing development in South African urban areas', report to the Housing Finance Resource Programme, USAID, Pretoria.

Bloch, R. (1993) 'From dispersal to concentration. Regional industrial development policy in South Africa: past, present and future', unpublished Industrial Strategy Project Report, Johannesburg.

–– (2000) 'Sub-national economic development in present-day South Africa', *Urban Forum*, 11(2): 227–72.

Böhme, K., Richardson, T., Dabinett, G. and Jensen, O. (2004) 'Values in a vacuum? Towards an integrated multi-level analysis of the governance of European space', *European Planning Studies*, 12(8): 1175–88.

Bollens, S. (2004) 'Urban planning and intergroup conflict: confronting a fractured public interest', in B. Stiftel and V. Watson (eds) *Dialogues in Urban and Regional Planning*, London and New York: Routledge.

Bond, P. (2000) *Elite Transition: From Apartheid to Neoliberalism in South Africa*, London: Pluto Press.

—— (2002) *Unsustainable South Africa: Environment, Development and Social Protest*, Pietermaritzburg: University of Natal Press.

Bond, P., Bremner, L., Geldenhuys, O., Mayekiso, M. *et al.* (1996) 'Response to government's draft Urban Strategy document II', *Urban Forum*, 7(1): 101–20.

Breheny, M. (ed.) (1992) *Sustainable Development and Urban Form*, London: Pion.

Bremner, L. (2004) *Johannesburg: One City, Colliding Worlds*, Johannesburg: STE Publishers.

Brenner, N. (1998) 'Global cities, global states: global city formation and state territorial restructuring in contemporary Europe', *Review of International Political Economy*, 5(1): 1–37.

—— (1999) 'Globalization as re-territorialization: the re-scaling of urban governance in the European Union', *Urban Studies*, 36(3): 431–51.

—— (2002) 'Decoding the newest "metropolitan regionalism" in the USA: a critical overview', *Cities*, 19(1): 3–21.

Buthelezi, M. (2004) 'A critical evaluation of local level responses to mine closures in the Northwestern KwaZulu-Natal coal belt', unpublished Master's thesis, Grahamstown: Rhodes University.

Calthorpe, P. (1994) 'The region', in P. Katz (ed.) *The New Urbanism: Towards an Architecture of Community*, New York: McGraw Hill.

Campbell, H. and Marshall, R. (2002) 'Utilitarianism's bad breath? A re-evaluation of the public interest justification for planning', *Planning Theory*, 1(2): 163–87.

Cashdan, B. (2002) 'Local government and poverty in South Africa' in S. Parnell, E. Pieterse, M. Swilling and D. Wooldridge (eds) *Democratising Local Government: The South African Experiment*, Cape Town: University of Cape Town Press.

Castells, C. (1977) *The Urban Question*, Cambridge: MIT Press.

—— (1983) *The City and the Grassroots: A Cross-cultural Theory of Urban Social Movements*, Berkeley, CA: University of California Press.

CDE (Centre for Development and Enterprise) (1998) *South Africa's 'Discarded People': Survival, Adaptation and Current Changes*, Johannesburg: CDE.

Chabal, P. and Daloz, J. (1999) *Africa Works: Disorder as Political Instrument*, Oxford: International African Institute.

Charlton, S. and Kihato, C. (2006) 'Reaching the poor? An analysis of the influences on the evolution of South Africa's housing programme' in R. Tomlinson, U. Pillay, J. du Toit (eds) *Democracy and Delivery: Urban Policy in South Africa*, Pretoria: HSRC Press.

Charlton, S., Silverman, M. and Berrisford, S. (2003) 'Taking stock: a review of the Department of Housing's programmes, policies and practice 1994–2002', unpublished report to the National Department of Housing.

Chenwi, L. (2006) 'Advancing the right to adequate housing of desperately poor people: City of Johannesburg v. Rand Properties', *Human Rights Brief*, 14(1): 13–16.

Chipkin, I. (2003) '"Functional" and "dysfunctional" communities: the making of ethical citizens', *Journal of Southern African Studies*, 29(1): 63–82.

Christopher, A. (1990) 'Apartheid and urban segregation levels in South Africa', *Urban Studies*, 27(3): 421–40.

–– (2005) 'The slow pace of desegregation in South African cities, 1996–2001', *Urban Studies*, 42(12): 2305–20.

Claasens, P. (2003) 'The role of environmental management (spatial planning, development planning and conservation of the natural Environment) in promoting sustainable development in South Africa', report to the National Research Foundation, Pretoria.

Coetzee, M. (2002) 'Summary document on the IDP LA21 relationship', in 'Local pathway to sustainable development in South Africa', package presented to the World Summit on Sustainable Development, Department of Provincial and Local Government, Johannesburg.

Cole, J. and Parnell, S. (2000) 'Poverty, gender and integrated development planning in South African municipal practice', report to the Department of Provincial and Local Government, Pretoria.

Connelly, S. and Richardson, T. (2004) 'Value-driven SEA: time for an environmental justice perspective?' *Environmental Impact Assessment Review*, 25(4): 391–409.

Cook, G. (1987) 'Time budgets of working women in a disadvantaged society', *Bluestocking*, 37: 33–5.

Cooper, D. and Subotzky, G. (2001) *The Skewed Revolution: Trends in South African Higher Education: 1988–1998*, Cape Town: Education Policy Unit, University of the Western Cape.

COSATU (Congress of South African Trade Unions) (2006) 'Possibilities for fundamental change, a political discussion document'. Available online at http://www.cosatu.org.za (accessed 4 September 2006).

Cox, K., Hemson, D. and Todes, A. (2004) 'Urbanization in South Africa and the changing character of migrant labour in South Africa', *South African Geographical Journal*, 86(1): 7–16.

Cross, C. (2001) 'Why does South Africa need a spatial policy? Population, migration, infrastructure and development', *Journal of Contemporary Studies*, 19(1): 111–27.

Cross, C., Luckin, L., Mzimela, T. and Clark, C. (1996) 'On the edge: poverty, livelihoods and natural resources in rural KwaZulu-Natal', in M. Lipton and F. Ellis (eds) *Land, Labour and Livelihoods in Rural South Africa*, Durban: Indicator Press.

Crush, J. and Rogerson, C. (2001) 'New industrial spaces: evaluating South Africa's spatial development initiatives programme', *South African Geographical Journal*, 33(2): 85–92

Dabinett, G. and Richardson, T. (2005) 'The Europeanization of spatial strategy: shaping regions and spatial justice through governmental ideas', *International Planning Studies*, 10(3–4): 201–18.

Davis, M. (2004) 'Planet of slums', *New Left Review*, 26 (March/April): 1–23.

DBSA (Development Bank of South Africa) (2005) *Overcoming Underdevelopment in South Africa's Second Economy*, Midrand: DBSA.

De Beer, G. (2001) 'The Maputo Development Corridor', report to the Development Bank of Southern Africa, DBSA, Midrand.

De Beer, G. and Arkwright, D. (2003) 'The Maputo Corridor: progress achieved and lessons learnt', in F. Söderbaum and I. Taylor (eds) *Regionalism and Uneven Development in Southern Africa: The Case of the Maputo Development Corridor*, Aldershot: Ashgate.

De Boeck, F. (1996) 'Postcolonialism, power and identity: local and global perspectives from Zaire', in R. Werbner and T. Ranger (eds) *Postcolonial Identities in Africa*, London: Zed Books.

De Soto, H. (2000) *The Mystery of Capital*, New York: Basic Books.

De Souza, M. (2005) 'Urban planning in an age of fear', *International Development Planning Review*, 27(1): 1–20.

Dear, M. and Scott, A. (1981) *Urbanization and Urban Planning in Capitalist Society*, London: Methuen.

DEAT (Department of Environmental Affairs and Tourism) (2003) *Strengthening Environmental Sustainability in the Integrated Development Planning Process*, Pretoria: DEAT.

—— (2006) 'South Africa's strategy for sustainable development, draft integrated strategy for review', Pretoria: DEAT.

Desai, V. and Imrie, R. (1998) 'The new managerialism in local governance: north-south dimensions', *Third World Quarterly*, 19(4): 635–50.

Devas, N. and Rakodi, C. (1993) 'Planning and managing urban development', in N. Devas and C. Rakodi (eds) *Managing Fast-Growing Cities*, Harlow: Longman.

Development Southern Africa (1998) Special Issue on Spatial Development Initiatives, *Development Southern Africa*, 15(5): 717–26.

Development Works (2006) 'The Planact way', draft report to Planact, Johannesburg.

Dewar D. (2000) 'The relevance of the compact city approach: the management of growth in South African cities', in M. Jencks and R. Burgess R (eds) *Compact Cities: Sustainable Urban Forms for Developing Countries*, London: Spon Press.

Dewar, D. and Kaplan, M. (2004) 'Disjuncture between project design and realities on the ground', in P. Robinson, J. McCarthy and C. Foster (eds) *Urban Reconstruction in the Developing World: Learning Through an International Best Practice.*, Sandown: Heinemann.

Dewar, D. and Uytenbogaardt, R. (1991) 'South African Cities: a manifesto for change', Urban Problems Research Unit, project report 9, Cape Town: University of Cape Town.

Dewar, D. and Watson, V. (1981) *Unemployment and the Informal Sector*, Cape Town: University of Cape Town, Urban Problems Research Unit.

Dewar, D. and Watson, V. (1990) *Urban Markets: Developing Informal Retailing*, London: Routledge.

Dewar, D. and Watson, V. (1991) 'Urban planning and the informal sector', in E. Preston-Whyte and C. Rogerson (eds) *South Africa's Informal Economy*, Cape Town: Oxford University Press.

Dewar, D., Uytenbogaardt, R., Hutton-Squire, M., Levy, C. and Menidis, P. (1979) *Housing, Urbanism in Cape Town*, Cape Town: David Philip.

Diaw, K., Nkaya, T. and Watson, V. (2002) 'Planning education in Africa: responding to the demands of a changing context', *Planning Practice and Research*, 17: 337–48.

Dierwechter, Y. (2002) 'Six cities of the informal sector – and beyond', *International Development Planning Review*, 24(1): 21–40.

–– (2004) 'Dreams, bricks, and bodies: mapping "neglected spatialities" in African Cape Town', *Environment and Planning A*, 36(6): 959–81.

DOE (Department of Education) (2001) 'National plan for higher education', Pretoria: DOE.

DOH (Department of Housing) (2004) *Breaking New Ground: A Comprehensive Plan for the Development of Sustainable Human Settlements*, Pretoria: Government Printer.

DOT (Department of Transport) (1998) *Moving South Africa*, Pretoria: DOT.

DPLG (Department of Provincial and Local Government) (2005a) 'IDP hearings 2005: national report', departmental report, 30 August.

–– (2005b) 'Provincial growth and development strategy guidelines', draft report, Pretoria: DPLG and the Presidency.

Dreier, P., Mollenkopf, J. and Swanstrom, T. (2001) *Place Matters: Metropolitics for the Twenty-first Century*, Lawrence, Kans: Kansas University Press.

DTI (Department of Trade and Industry) (2006) 'Draft regional industrial development strategy'. Available online at: http//www.dti.gov.za (accessed 22 July 2006).

Du Plessis, C. (2002) 'Sustainability analysis of human settlements in South Africa', unpublished report, Department of Housing, Pretoria.

EMG (Environmental Monitoring Group) (1992) 'Towards sustainable development in South Africa: a discussion paper', unpublished manuscript, Cape Town.

Evans, B. and Rydin, Y. (1997) 'Planning, professionalism and sustainability', in A. Blowers and B. Evans (eds), *Town Planning into the Twenty-First Century*, London: Routledge.

Fainstein, S. (1997) 'Justice, politics, and the creation of urban space', in A. Merrifield and E. Swyngedouw (eds) *The Urbanization of Injustice*, New York: New York University Press.

——(1999) 'Can we make the cities we want?' in S. Body-Gendrot and R. Beauregard (eds) *The Urban Moment*, Thousand Oaks, CA: Sage.

Fainstein, N. and Fainstein, S. (1979) 'New debates in urban planning: the impact of Marxist theory within the United States', *International Journal of Urban and Regional Research*, 3(3): 309–32.

Fakir, E. (2005) 'The democratic state versus the developmental state: a false dichotomy', *Isandla Development Communiqué*, 2(6): 1–4.

Faling, W. (2002) 'The relevance of planning education in South Africa', unpublished Master's thesis, Durban: University of Natal.

Faling, W. and Todes, A. (2004) 'Employer perceptions of planning education in South Africa', *Town and Regional Planning*, 47: 32–43.

Faludi, A. (2004) 'Territorial cohesion: old (French) wine in new bottles?' *Urban Studies*, 41(7): 1349–65.

Faull, J. (2005) 'Tracing the "two economies": the politics, policy and practice of pragmatism', *ePoliticsSA*, 1.

FEPD (Forum for Effective Planning and Development) (1995) *Documentation*, Vols 1, 2 and 3.

Filion, P. (1999) 'Rupture or continuity? Modern and postmodern planning in Toronto', *International Journal for Urban and Regional Research*, 23(3): 421–44.

FinMark Trust (2004) 'Workings of the township residential property markets'. Available online at http://www.finmarktrust.org.za (accessed 1 November 2005).

Fischer, F. (2003) 'Beyond empiricism: policy analysis as deliberative practice', in M. Hajer and H. Wagenaar (eds) *Deliberative Policy Analysis: Understanding Governance in the Network Society*, Cambridge: Cambridge University Press.

Fischer, F. and Forester, J. (eds) (1993) *The Argumentative Turn in Policy Analysis and Planning*, Durham, NC: Duke University Press.

Flyvbjerg, B. (1998a) *Rationality and Power: Democracy in Practice*, Chicago, Ill: University of Chicago Press.

—— (1998b) 'Empowering civil society: Habermas, Foucault and the question of conflict', in M. Douglass and J. Friedmann (eds) *Cities for Citizens: Planning and the Rise of Civil Society in a Global Age*, Chichester: John Wiley & Sons.

Forester, J. (1999) *The Deliberative Practitioner: Encouraging Participatory Planning Processes*, Cambridge, MA: MIT Press.

—— (2004) 'Reflections on trying to teach planning theory', *Planning Theory and Practice*, 5(2): 242–51.

Forster, C. (2006) (previous director of the Built Environment Support Group), interview, Durban.

Fraser, N. (2000) 'Rethinking recognition', *New Left Review*, 3: 107–20.

Freund, B. and Lootvoet, B. (2004) 'Local economic development: utopia and reality in South Africa: the example of Durban, Kwa-Zulu Natal', paper presented at Reviewing the First Decade of Development and Democracy in South Africa, Durban.

Friedman, S. (2001) 'A quest for control: high modernism and its discontents in Johannesburg, South Africa', in B. Ruble, R. Stren and J. Tulchin (eds) *Urban Governance Around the World*, Washington, DC: Woodrow Wilson International Center for Scholars.

Friedmann, J. (1996) 'The core curriculum in planning revisited', *Journal of Planning Education and Research*, 15: 89–104.

Frisken, F. and Norris, D. (2001) 'Regionalism reconsidered', *Journal of Urban Affairs*, 23(5): 467–78.

Fuggle, R. and Rabie, M. (1992) *Environmental Management in South Africa*, Johannesburg: Juta.

Galvin, M. and Habib, A. (2003) 'The politics of decentralization and donor funding in South Africa's rural water sector', *Journal of Southern African Studies*, 29(4): 865–84.

Gasson, B. and Todeschini, F. (1997) 'Settlement planning and integrated environmental management compared: some lessons', paper presented to the International Association for Impact Assessment Conference, Cape Town.

Glaser, D. (1987) 'A periodization of South Africa's industrial dispersal policies', in R. Tomlinson and M. Addleson (eds) *Regional Restructuring under Apartheid: Urban and Regional Policies in Contemporary South Africa*, Braamfontein: Ravan Press.

Goga, S. (2003) 'Property investors and decentralization: a case of false competition?', in R. Tomlinson, R. Beauregard, L. Bremner and X. Mangcu (eds), *Emerging Johannesburg: Perspectives on the Post-apartheid City*, London and New York: Routledge.

Gonzalez, S. and Healey, P. (2005) 'A sociological institutionalist approach to the study of innovation in governance capacity', *Urban Studies*, 42(11): 2055–69.

Gotz, G. and Simone, A. (2003) 'On belonging and becoming in African cities', in R. Tomlinson, R. Beauregard, L. Bremner and X. Mangcu (eds) *Emerging Johannesburg: Perspectives on the Post-apartheid City*, London and New York: Routledge.

Graham, S. and Healey, P. (1999) 'Relational concepts of space and place: issues for planning theory and practice', *Regional Planning Studies*, 7(5): 623–46.

Grant, J. (2006) *Planning the Good Community: New Urbanism in Theory and Practice*, London and New York: Routledge.

Gumede, W. (2005) *Thabo Mbeki and the Battle for the Soul of the ANC*, Cape Town: Zebra Press.

Gwagwa, N. and Todes, A. (1994) 'Durban City Council urbanisation strategy: gender aspect', report to the Urbanisation Strategy Working Group, Durban City Council, Durban.

Habermas, J. (1984) *The Theory of Communicative Action Volume 1*, Boston, MA: Beacon Press.

Hague, C. (2002) 'Planning education and power: reflections from the UK experience', paper presented at the Rethinking Planning Education Conference, Istanbul, May.

Hajer, M. and Wagenaar, H. (eds) (2003) *Deliberative Policy Analysis: Understanding Governance in the Network Society*, Cambridge: Cambridge University Press.

Hall, M. (1987) *Farmers, Kings, and Traders: The People of Southern Africa, 200–1860*, Cape Town: David Philip.

Hall, P. (1988) *Cities of Tomorrow*, Oxford: Blackwell.

Hamza, M. and Zetter, R. (2000) 'Reconceiving the knowledge-base of planning education in the developing world', *Third World Planning Review*, 22: 433–55.

Hansen, K. and Vaa, M. (eds) (2004) *Reconsidering Informality: Perspectives from Urban Africa*, Oslo: Nordiska Afrikainstitutet.

Harris, N. (1990) *Urbanization, Economic Development and Policy in Developing Countries*, London: Development Planning Unit, London College University.

Harrison, P. (2001) 'The genealogy of South Africa's integrated development plan', *Third World Planning Review*, 23(2): 175–93.

–– (2003a) 'Towards integrated inter-governmental planning in South Africa: the IDP as a building block', report prepared for the Department of Provincial and Local Government and the Municipal Demarcations Board, Pretoria.

–– (2003b) 'Fragmentation and globalization as the new meta-narrative', in P. Harrison, M. Huchzermeyer and M. Mayekiso (eds) *Confronting Fragmentation: Housing and Urban Development in a Democratizing Society*, Cape Town: University of Cape Town Press.

–– (2006a) 'On the edge of reason: planning and urban futures in Africa', *Urban Studies*, 43(2): 319–35.

–– (2006b) 'Integrated development plans and third way politics', in U. Pillay, R. Tomlinson and J. du Toit (eds) *Democracy and Delivery: Urban Policy in South Africa*, Pretoria: HSRC Press.

Harrison, P. and Kahn, M. (2002) 'The ambiguities of change: the case of the planning profession in the province of KwaZulu-Natal, South Africa', in A. Thornley and Y. Rydin (eds) *Planning in a Global Era*, Aldershot: Ashgate.

Harrison, P. and Mabin, A. (1997) 'Ideas, philosophy and personality in the history of KwaZulu-Natal's Town and Regional Planning Commission', *South African Planning Journal*, 42: 25–44.

–– (2006) 'Security and space: managing the contradictions of access restriction in Johannesburg', *Environment and Planning B: Planning and Design*, 33: 3–20.

Harrison, P. and Todes, A. (1999) 'New forms of spatial planning for regional development in South Africa', paper presented at the Regional Studies Association Conference, Regional Potentials in an Integrating Europe, Bilbao, Spain, September.

—— (2001a) 'The use of spatial frameworks for regional development in South Africa', *Regional Studies*, 35(1): 65–85.

—— (2001b) 'The changing nature of planning, planning education and planning students in South Africa', paper presented at the World Planning School's Congress, Shanghai, July.

Harrison, P. and Williamson, A. (2001) 'The role of planners and planning in shaping urban space', *South African Geographical Journal*, 83(3): 240–48.

Harrison, P., Todes, A. and Watson, V. (1997) 'Transforming South Africa's cities: prospects for the economic development of urban townships', *Development Southern Africa*, 14(1): 43–60.

Hart, D. and Pirie, G. (1984) 'The sight and soul of Sophiatown', *Geographical Review*, 74(1): 38–47.

Hart, G. and Todes, A. (1997) 'Industrial decentralization revisited', *Transformation*, 32: 31–53.

Hart, K. (1973) 'Informal income opportunities and urban employment in Ghana', *Journal of Modern African Studies*, 11: 61–89.

Haughton, G. and Counsell, D. (2004) *Regions, Spatial Strategies and Sustainable Development*, London: Routledge.

Healey, P. (1992) 'Planning through debate: the communicative turn in planning theory', *Town Planning Review*, 63(2): 143–62.

—— (1997) *Collaborative Planning: Shaping Places in Fragmented Societies*, London: Macmillan.

—— (1999) 'Institutional analysis, communicative planning, and shaping places', *Journal of Planning Education and Research*, 19: 111–21.

—— (2004) 'The treatment of space and place in new strategic spatial planning in Europe', *International Journal of Urban and Regional Research*, 28(1): 45–67.

—— (2005) 'Editorial', *Planning Theory and Practice*, 6(1): 5–8.

Heller, P. (2001) 'Moving the state: the politics of democratic decentralization in Kerala, South Africa, and Porto Alegre', *Politics and Society*, 29(1): 131–63.

Hindson, D. (1987) 'Orderly urbanization and influx control: from territorial apartheid to regional spatial ordering in South Africa', in R. Tomlinson and M. Addleson (eds) *Regional Restructuring under Apartheid: Urban and Regional Policies in Contemporary South Africa*, Braamfontein: Ravan Press.

Hood, C. and Peters, G. (2004) 'The middle aging of new public management: into the age of paradox', *Journal of Public Administration and Theory*, 14(3): 267–82.

Horwitz, R. (1991) *Communication and Democratic Reform in South Africa*, Cambridge: Cambridge University Press.

HSRC (Human Sciences Research Council) (1999) *South African Labour Market Trends and Future Workforce Needs, 1998–2003*, Pretoria: HSRC.

—— (2006) 'The provincial indices for multiple deprivation in South Africa', report of the Human Sciences Research Council together with Statistics South Africa and Oxford University.

Hsu, L.-N. (2005) 'HIV epidemics in developing countries: looking beyond health dimensions to the role of development', *International Development Planning Review*, 27(1): i–xii.

Huchzermeyer, M. (2001) 'Housing for the poor? Negotiated housing policy in South Africa', *Habitat International*, 25(3): 303–31.

Huntington, S. (1991) *The Third Wave: Democratization in the Late Twentieth Century*, Norman: University of Oklahoma Press.

Hutton, T. (2004) 'Post-industrialism, post-modernism and the reproduction of Vancouver's central area: retheorising the 21st-century city', *Urban Studies*, 41(10): 1953–82.

Innes, J. (1995) 'Planning theory's emerging paradigm: communicative action and interactive practice', *Journal of Planning Education and Research*, 14(3): 183–9.

Irurah, D. and Boshoff, B. (2003) 'An interpretation of sustainable development and urban sustainability in low-cost housing and settlements in South Africa', in P. Harrison, M. Huchzermeyer and M. Mayekiso (eds) *Confronting Fragmentation: Housing and Urban Development in a Democratizing South Africa*, Cape Town: University of Cape Town.

Irurah, D., Bannister, S., Silverman, M. and Zack, T. (2002) *Towards Sustainable Settlements: Case Studies from South Africa*, Johannesburg: STE Publishers.

Jaglin, S. (2004) 'Water delivery and metropolitan institution building in Cape Town: the problems of integration', *Urban Forum*, 15(3): 231–53.

Jessop, B. (2005) 'The political economy of scale and European governance', *Tijdschrift voor Economische en Sociale Geografie*, 96(5): 225–30.

JIPSA (Joint Initiative on Priority Skills Acquisition) (2006) Address delivered by the Deputy President, Phumzile Mlambo-Ngcuka, at the launch of the Joint Initiative for Priority Skills Acquisition, Presidential Guest House, Pretoria, 27 March. Available online at http://www.skillsportal.co.za/asgisa/jipsa (accessed 2 September2006).

Jones, G. and Datta, K. (2000) 'Enabling markets to work? Housing policy in the "New" South Africa', *International Planning Studies*, 5(3): 393–416.

Jordan, A., Wurzel, K.W. and Zito, A.R. (2005) 'The rise of "new" policy instruments in comparative perspective: has governance eclipsed government?', *Political Studies*, 53(3): 477–96.

Jordi, R., Kingwill, J. and Scott, E. (1998) 'Integrating environmental evaluation into planning', paper presented to the International Association for Impact Assessment Conference, Johannesburg.

Jourdan, P. (1998) 'Spatial development initiatives – the official view', *Development Southern Africa*, 15(5): 717–26.

–– (2003), Personal communication (telephonic), Durban–Johannesburg.

Jourdan, P., Gordhan, K., Arkwright D. and de Beer, G. (1996) 'Spatial development initiatives (development corridors): their potential contribution to investment and employment creation', unpublished paper, Pretoria: Department of Trade and Industry.

Kepe, T., Ntsebeza, L., and Pithers, L. (2001) 'Agri-tourism spatial development initiatives in South Africa: are they enhancing rural livelihoods?', *Natural Resource Perspectives*, 65: 1–4.

Kgara, S. (1998) 'The emergence of major retail centres in the townships: case studies of Daveyton and Dobsonville', unpublished Town and Regional Planning Master's dissertation, Durban: University of Natal.

Khan, F. and Thring, P. (2003) *Housing Policy and Poverty in Post-Apartheid South Africa*, Sandown: Heinemann.

Krige, S. (1996) 'Botshabelo: former fastest-growing urban area in South Africa approaching zero population growth', *Urban and Regional Planning Occasional Paper*, 20, Free State: University of the Orange Free State.

Kulipossa, F. (2004) 'Decentralization and democracy in developing countries', *Development in Practice*, 14(6): 768–79.

Laburn-Peart, K. (1993) 'Pre-colonial towns of Southern Africa: integrating the teaching of planning history and urban morphology', proceedings of a symposium of the South African Planning History Study Group, Pietermaritzburg, 6–7 September.

Landman, K. (2004) 'Gated communities in South Africa: the challenge for spatial planning and land-use management', *Town Planning Review*, 75(2): 151–72.

Lefebvre, H. (1991) *The Production of Space*, Oxford: Blackwell.

Leftwich, A. (1993) 'Governance, democracy and development in the Third World', in *Third World Quarterly*, 14(3): 605–24.

Lemanski, C. (2006) 'Spaces of exclusivity or connection? Linkages between a gated community and its poorer neighbour in the Cape Town master plan', *Urban Studies*, 43(2): 397–420.

Lemon, A. (ed.) (1991) *Homes Apart: South Africa's Segregated Cities*, Cape Town: David Philip.

Long, E. and Franklin, A. (2004) 'The paradox of implementing the government's Performance and Results Act: top-down direction for bottom-up implementation', *Public Administration Review*, 64(3): 309–19.

Lovering, J. (1999) 'Theory led by policy? The inadequacies of the New Regionalism', *International Journal of Urban and Regional Research*, 23(2) 379–95.

Mabin A. (1986) 'Land, capital, class struggle, and the origins of residential segregation in Kimberley, 1880–1920', *Journal of Historical Geography*, 12: 7–13.

—— (1992) 'Comprehensive segregation: the origins of the Group Areas Act and its plan-
    ning apparatuses', *Journal of Southern African Studies*, 18(11): 405–32.

—— (1993) 'Conflict, continuity and change: locating "properly planned native townships"
    in the forties and fifties', proceedings of a symposium of the South African Planning
    History Study Group, Pietermaritzburg, 6–7 September 1993: 305–37.

—— (1995a) 'Reconstruction and the making of urban planning in twentieth-century
    South Africa', in H. Judin and I. Vladislavic (eds) *Blank – Architecture, Apartheid
    and Beyond*, Rotterdam: NAI Publishers; Cape Town: David Philip.

—— (1995b) 'On the problems and prospects of overcoming segregation, fragmentation
    and surveillance in southern Africa's cities in the post-modern era', in S. Watson
    and K. Gibson (eds) *Postmodern Cities and Spaces*, Oxford: Blackwell.

—— (2002) 'Local government in the emergent national planning context', in S. Parnell, E.
    Pieterse, M. Swilling and D. Wooldridge (eds) *Democratizing Local Government:
    The South African Experiment*, Cape Town: University of Cape Town Press.

Mabin A. and Harrison P. (1996) 'Imaginative planning with practical considerations?
    The contribution of the KwaZulu-Natal Town and Regional Planning Commission to
    planning and development', report to the KwaZulu-Natal Town and Regional
    Planning Commission.

Mabin, A. and Smit, D. (1997) 'Reconstructing South Africa's cities? The making of
    urban planning 1900–2000', *Planning Perspectives*, 12: 193–223.

McCarthy, J. (1991) 'Class, race and urban locational relationships', in M. Swilling, R.
    Humphries and K. Shubane (eds) *Apartheid City in Transition*, Cape Town: Oxford
    University Press.

McCarthy, J. and Smit, D. (1984) *South African City: Theory in Analysis and Planning*,
    Cape Town: Juta & Co.

Macdonald, K. (1995) *Sociology of the Professions*, London: Sage.

MacLeod, G. (2001) 'New regionalism reconsidered: globalization and the remaking of
    political economic space', *International Journal of Urban and Regional Research*,
    25(4): 804.

Mandanipour, A. (1996) *Design of Urban Space*, Chichester: John Wiley.

Manuel, T. 'Budgeting challenges in the developmental state', speech given at the Senior
    Management Service Conference, Cape Town, 20 September.

Marais, H. (1998) *South Africa: Limits to Change. The Political Economy of
    Transformation*, Cape Town: University of Cape Town Press.

Marais, L. and Krige, S. (2000) 'Who received what where in the Free State,
    1994–1998: an assessment of post-apartheid housing policy and delivery',
    Development Southern Africa, 17(4): 603–19.

Markewicz, T. and Rushby, J. (2003) 'KwaZulu-Natal coastal management programme:
    review of coastal IDPs', report to the Department of Agriculture and Environmental
    Affairs, Pietermaritzburg.

Maylam, P. (1990) 'The rise and decline of urban apartheid in South Africa', *African Affairs*, 89(354): 57–84.

—— (1995) 'Explaining the apartheid city: 20 years of South African urban historiography', *Journal of Southern African Studies*, 21(1): 19–29.

Mbembe, A. and Nuttall, S. (2004) 'Writing the world from an African metropolis', *Public Culture*, 16: 347–72.

Metropolis (2002) 'The impact of major events on the development of large cities', report of Commission 1, Metropolis 2002, Seoul, May.

Mhone, G. and Edigheji, O. (eds) (2003) *Governance in the New South Africa: The Challenges of Globalisation*, Cape Town: University of Cape Town Press.

Ministry for Provincial Affairs and Constitutional Development (1998) *The White Paper on Local Government*, Pretoria: Government Printer.

Miraftab, F. (2006) Presentation to the roundtable on Insurgence, Consurgence, Resurgence, Second World Planning Schools Congress, Global Planning Education Association Network and Universidad Nacional Autonoma de Mexico, Mexico City, July.

Mohan, G. (1997) 'Developing difference: post-structuralism and political economy in contemporary development studies', *Review of Radical Political Economy*, 73: 311–28.

Moser, C. (1993) *Gender Planning and Development: Theory, Practice and Training*, London: Routledge.

Muller, J. (1982) 'Promotive planning: towards an approach to planning for the disadvantaged', in P. Healey, G. McDougall and M. Thomas (eds) *Planning Theory: Prospects for the 1980s*, Oxford: Pergamon Press.

—— (1993) 'Parallel paths: the origins of planning education and the planning profession in South Africa', *Planning History*, 15(2): 5–11.

—— (1997) 'The planning profession', *South African Planning Journal*, 40: 54–6.

—— (2003) *Thought and Action: A Personal and Partial History of the South African Planning Profession*, Centrahill: QS Publications.

Murdoch, J. (2004) 'Putting discourse in its place: planning, sustainability and the urban capacity study', *Area*, 36(1): 50–58.

Napier, M. and Rust, K. (2002) 'Summary report of the SIPPs evaluation: key lessons learnt from five projects', Special Integrated Presidential Projects Evaluation for the South African Department of Housing by the Centre for Scientific and Industrial Research (CSIR), Pretoria, May.

Nel, E. and John, L. (2006) 'The evolution of local economic development policy in South Africa', in U. Pillay, R. Tomlinson and J. du Toit, *Democracy and Delivery: Urban Policy in South Africa*, Pretoria: HSRC Press.

Nel, E. and Rogerson, C. (2005) 'Pro-poor local economic development in South Africa's cities: policy and practice', *Africa Insight*, 35(4): 15–20.

Neuman, M. (forthcoming) 'Multi-scalar large institutional networks in regional planning', *Planning Theory and Practice.*

Ngobese, P. and Cock, J. (1997) 'Development and the environment', in P. Fitzgerald, A. McLennan and B. Munslow, B. (eds) *Managing Sustainable Development in South Africa*, Cape Town: Oxford University Press.

Ngxabi, N. (2003) 'Homes or houses? Strategies of home-making among some amaXhosa in the Western Cape', unpublished Master's thesis, Cape Town: University of Cape Town.

Ntsebeza, L. (2004) 'Democratic decentralization and traditional authority: dilemmas of land administration in rural South Africa', *The European Journal of Development Research*, 16(1): 71–89.

Oakenfull, L. (1998) 'The chapter 1 principles: practical experiences', *Development and Planning Commission Document 67/98*, Pretoria: Development and Planning Commission.

O'Brien, D. (1996) 'A lost generation? Youth identity and state decay in West Africa', in R. Werbner and T. Ranger (eds) *Postcolonial Identities in Africa*, London: Zed Books.

ODP (Office of the Deputy President) (1998) 'Poverty and inequality in South Africa', unpublished report, Pretoria: ODP.

Oelofse C. (1999) 'Environmental consideration and the right to housing', report to the Built Environment Support Group, Durban: University of Natal.

Oldfield, S. (2002) '"Embedded autonomy" and the challenge of developmental local government' in S. Parnell, E. Pieterse, M. Swilling, and D. Wooldridge (eds) *Democratizing Local Government: The South African Experiment*, Cape Town: University of Cape Town Press.

Oranje, M. (1998) 'The language game of South African urban and regional planning: a cognitive mapping from the past into the future', unpublished doctoral thesis, University of Pretoria.

—— (2002) 'Should provinces/regions have their own planning Acts? An exploration of the debate using the post-1994 South African experience', in A. Thornley and Y. Rydin (eds) *Planning in a Global Era*, London: Ashgate.

Oszawa, C. and Salzer, E. (1999) 'Taking our bearings: mapping a relationship among planning practice, theory and education', *Journal of Planning Education and Research*, 18: 257–66.

Owens, S. and Cowell, R. (2002) *Land and Limits: Interpreting Sustainability in the Planning Process*, London: Routledge.

Parekh, B. (1993) 'The cultural particularity of liberal democracy', in D. Held (ed.) *Prospects for Democracy: North, South, East, West*, Oxford: Polity Press, Cambridge and Blackwell Publishers.

Parnell, S. (1993) 'Creating racial privilege: the origins of South African public health and town planning legislation', *Journal of Southern African Studies*, 19(3): 471–88.

—— (1997) 'South African cities: perspectives from the ivory tower of urban studies', *Urban Studies*, 34(5): 891–906.

—— (2004) 'Constructing a developmental nation – the challenge of including the poor in the post apartheid city', paper presented at the Conference on Overcoming Underdevelopment in South Africa's Second Economy, Pretoria.

Parnell, S. and Mabin, A. (1995) 'Rethinking urban South Africa', *Journal of Southern African Studies*, 21(1): 39–62.

Parnell, S. and Pieterse, E. (2002) 'Developmental local government', in S. Parnell, E. Pieterse, M. Swilling and D. Wooldridge (eds) *Democratizing Local Government: The South African Experiment*, Cape Town: University of Cape Town Press.

Parnell, S., Douglas, S. and Boulle, J. (2005) 'Institutionalizing pro-poor local economic development through expanded public works in the urban environment of Cape Town', *Africa Insight*, 35(4): 53–61.

Parnell, S., Pieterse, E., Swilling, M. and D. Wooldridge (eds) (2002) *Democratizing Local Government: The South African Experiment*, Cape Town: University of Cape Town Press.

Patel, Y. (2005) 'Integrated planning is vital', *Cape Times*, 1 August.

—— (2006) 'Integrated development plans', paper presented at the South African Planning Institute Conference on Planning Africa 2006: Making the Connection, Cape Town, March.

Patel, Z. (2004) 'Environmental values and the building of sustainable communities,' in E. Pieterse and F. Meintjies (eds) *Voices of the Transition: Perspectives on the Politics, Poetics and Practices of Development*, Johannesburg: Heinemann.

PCAS (Policy Co-ordination and Advisory Services, the Presidency) (2005) 'A nation in the making: a discussion document on macro-social trends in South Africa', Pretoria.

Perales, J. (2004) 'Consensus, dissensus, confusion: the "Stiglitz debate" in perspective', *Development in Practice*, 14(3): 412–23.

Perloff, H. (1957) *Education for Planning: City, State and Regional*, Baltimore: John Hopkins.

Perri 6 (2004) 'Joined-up government in the Western World in comparative perspective: a preliminary literature review and exploration', *Journal of Public Administration Research and Theory*, 14(1): 103–38.

Pieterse, E. (2001) 'Delivering social services to the poor', *Dark Roast Occasional Paper Series*, 5, Cape Town: Cape Town Isandla Institute.

—— (2002) 'Participatory local governance in the making', in S. Parnell, E. Pieterse, M. Swilling and D. Wooldridge (eds) *Democratizing Local Government: The South African Experiment*, Cape Town: University of Cape Town Press.

—— (2003a) 'Unraveling the different meanings of integration: the urban development framework of the South African government', in P. Harrison, M. Huchzermeyer and

M. Mayekiso (eds) *Confronting Fragmentation: Housing and Urban Development in a Democratizing Society*, Cape Town: University of Cape Town Press.

–– (2003b) 'At the limits of possibility: working notes on a relational model of urban politics', *Dark Roast Occasional Paper Series*, 14: 1–26.

–– (2004a) 'Recasting urban integration and fragmentation in post-apartheid South Africa', *Development Update*, 5(1): 81–104.

–– (2004b) 'Untangling "integration" in urban development policy debates', *Urban Forum*, 15(1): 1–35.

–– (2006) 'Planning as translation', paper presented at the South African Planning Institute Conference on Planning Africa 2006: Making the Connection, Cape Town, March.

Pile, S., Brook, C. and Mooney, G. (1999) *Unruly Cities? Order/disorder*, London: Routledge.

Pillay, U. (2006) 'South Africans pin job creation hopes on 2010', Cape Town: *HSRC Review*, 2(4): 12–13.

Pillay, U., Tomlinson, R. and du Toit, J. (2006) (eds) *Democracy and Delivery: Urban Policy in South Africa*, Johannesburg: HSRC Press.

Pirie, G. (2006) 'Reanimating a comatose goddess: reconfiguring central Cape Town', unpublished paper, Cape Town: University of Cape Town.

Platzky, L. (1995) 'The development impact of South Africa's industrial location policies: an unforeseen legacy', doctoral thesis, The Hague: Institute for Social Studies.

–– (1998) 'Can South Africa's new spatial development initiatives turn cumulative disadvantages into competitive advantages?', paper presented at the Ruth First Memorial Seminar, Durham University.

–– (2000) 'Reconstructing and developing South Africa: the role of spatial development initiatives', paper presented to the International Conference on Sustainable Regional Development, University of Massachusetts, Lowell.

Posel, D. (2003) 'Have migration patterns in post-apartheid South Africa changed?', paper presented to the conference on African Migration and Urbanization in Comparative Perspective, Johannesburg.

Poxon, J. (2001) 'Shaping the planning profession of the future: the role of planning education', *Environment and Planning B: Planning and Design*, 28: 563–80.

Presidency (2003) *National Spatial Development Perspective*, Pretoria: Presidency.

–– (2004) 'Harmonising and aligning: the national spatial development perspective, provincial growth and development strategies and municipal integrated development plans, policy co-ordination and advisory services', unpublished report, Pretoria: Presidency.

Pretorius, L. (2001) 'Industrial free zones in Mozambique: a case study of the Mozal Aluminium Smelter', in *International Labour Resources and Information Group Occasional Paper*, Cape Town: ILRIG.

Provincial Planning and Development Commission (2004) *Land Use Management System (LUMS) KwaZulu-Natal Update: Phase 3 Final Research Report*, KwaZulu-Natal Provincial Government.

Pycroft, C. (2002) 'Addressing rural poverty: restructuring rural local government', in S. Parnell, E. Pieterse, M. Swilling and D. Wooldridge (eds) *Democratising Local Government: The South African Experiment*, Cape Town: University of Cape Town Press.

Rakodi, C. (1996) 'Educating urban planners', in N. Hamdi and A. El-Sherif (eds) *Educating for Real: The Training of Professionals for Development Practice*, London: Intermediate Technology Publications.

Robbins, G. (2005) 'eThekwini Municipality's economic development-related capital programmes: improving the prospects of the urban poor?' *Africa Insight*, 8(4): 63–71.

Robbins, G., Todes, A. and Velia, M. (2004) 'Firms at the crossroads: the Newcastle-Madadeni clothing sector and recommendations on policy responses', *School of Development Studies Research Report 61*, for the KwaZulu-Natal Department of Economic Development and Tourism.

Roberts, D. and Diederichs, N. (2002) *Durban's Local Agenda 21 Programme 1994–2001: Tackling Sustainable Development*, Durban: Institute for Environment and Development.

Roberts, P. and Colwell, A. (2001) 'Moving the environment to centre state: a new approach to planning and development at European and regional levels', *Local Environment*, 6(4): 421–37.

Robins, S. (2003) 'Whose modernity? Indigenous modernities and land claims after Apartheid', *Development and Change*, 34(2): 1–21.

Robinson, J. (1997) 'The geopolitics of South African cities – states, citizens, territory', *Political Geography*, 16(5): 365–86

—— (2002) 'Global and world cities: a view from off the map', *International Journal of Urban and Regional Research*, 26: 531–54.

—— (2005) *Ordinary Cities: Between Modernity and Development*, New York: Routledge.

Robinson, P., McCarthy, J. and Forster, C. (eds) (2004) *Urban Reconstruction in a Developing World*, Sandown: Heinemann.

Rogerson, C. (1997) 'Globalization or informalization? African urban economies in the 1990s', in C. Rakodi (ed.) *The Urban Challenge in Africa: Growth and the Management of Large Cities*, Tokyo: United Nations University Press.

—— (2001) 'Spatial development initiatives in Southern Africa: the Maputo Corridor', *Tijdschrift voor Economische en Sociale Geografie*, 92(3): 324–47.

—— (2006) 'Local economic development in post-apartheid South Africa: a ten-year review', in V. Padayachee (ed.) *The Development Decade? Economic and Social Change in South Africa, 1994–2004*, Pretoria: HSRC Press.

—— (1997) 'The central Witwatersrand: Post-elections investment outlook for the built environment', *Urban Forum*, 8(1): 93–108.

Roweis, S. (1981) 'Urban planning in early and late capitalist societies: outline of a theoretical perspective', in M. Dear and A. Scott (eds) *Urbanization and Urban Planning in Capitalist Society*, London and New York: Methuen.

—— (1983). 'Urban planning as professional mediation of territorial politics', *Environment and Planning D: Society and Space*, 1: 139–62.

Roy, A. (2005) 'Urban informality. Towards an epistemology of planning', *Journal of the American Planning Association*, 71(2): 147–58.

—— (2006) 'Praxis in the time of Empire', *Planning Theory*, 5(1): 7–29.

Royston, L. (2003) 'On the outskirts: access to well-located land and integration in post-Apartheid human settlement development', in F. Khan and P. Thring (eds) *Housing Policy and Practice in South Africa*, Cape Town: University of Cape Town Press.

RSA (Republic of South Africa) (1994) *White Paper on Reconstruction and Development*, Pretoria: RSA Government Printers.

—— (1995) 'Development Facilitation Act, No. 67 of 1995', Government Gazette, Vol. 364, No 1673', Pretoria: Government Printers.

—— (1996a) *Growth, Employment and Redistribution Strategy*, Pretoria: RSA Government Printers.

—— (1996b) *Constitution of the Republic of South Africa Act, 108 of 1996*, Pretoria: RSA Government Printers.

—— (2002a) 'Planning Profession Act, No. 36 of 2002', Government Gazette, Vol. 449, No. 24028.

—— (2002b) 'Local governance for poverty reduction: South Africa country report to the Fourth Africa Governance Forum', report prepared by the Department of Provincial and Local Government, 2002. Available online at: http://www.undp.org/rba/pubs/ agf5 (accessed 15 July 2006).

—— (2005) 'Towards ten years of freedom: progress in the first decade – challenges of the second decade', report. Available online at: http://www.gov.za (accessed 10 August 2006).

—— (2006) 'Accelerated and shared growth initiative for South Africa'. Available online at: http://www.info.gov.za/asgisa (accessed 2 September 2006).

—— 'Local governance for poverty reduction: South Africa country report to the Fourth Africa Governance Forum', report prepared by the Department of Provincial and Local Government, 2002. Available online at: http://www.undp.org/rba/pubs/agf5 (accessed 15 July 2006).

RTPI (Royal Town Planning Institute) (2001): 'A new vision for planning. Delivering sustainable communities, settlements and places', London: RTPI.

RTPI (Royal Town Planning Institute) (2003) 'RTPI Education Commission, final report', London: RTPI.

Rydin, Y. (1999) 'Can we talk ourselves into sustainability? The role of discourse in the environmental policy process', *Environmental Values*, 8(4): 467–84.

SACN (South African Cities Network) (2004) *State of the Cities Report*, Johannesburg: SACN.

–– (2006) *State of the Cities Report 2006*, Johannesburg: SACN.

Sadie, Y. and Loots, E. (1998) 'RDP projects in South Africa: a gender perspective analysis', *Security, Development and Gender in Africa*, ISS Monograph Series, No. 27, Johannesburg.

SAGJ (South African Geographical Journal) (2001) Special issue on spatial development initiatives, *South African Geographical Journal*, 33(2).

Samuels, F. (2000) 'What goes around come around, or does it? Kinship, networks and social obligations in Lusaka, Zambia', in *Reconsidering Informality: Perspectives from Urban Africa*, Copenhagen: Nordic-Afrika Institute.

Sandercock, L. (1998) *Towards Cosmopolis: Planning for Multicultural Cities*, Chichester: John Wiley.

Sanyal, B. (1988) 'The urban informal sector revisited: some notes on the relevance of the concept in the 1980s', *Third World Planning Review*, 10(1): 65–83.

Saul, J. (1991) 'South Africa between barbarism and structural reform', *New Left Review*, 188 (July–August): 3–44.

Schön, D. and Rein, M. (1994) *Frame Reflection: Towards the Resolution of Intractable Policy Controversies*, New York: Basic Books.

Scott, A. (2002) *Global City-Regions*, Oxford: Oxford University Press.

Scott, J.C. (1998) *Seeing Like a State*, New Haven and London: Yale University Press.

Scott-Brown, D. (1964) 'Natal plans', *Journal of the American Institute of Planners*, 30(2): 161–66.

Shaw, D. and Sykes, O. (2004) 'The concept of polycentricity in European spatial planning: reflections on its interpretation and application in the practice of spatial planning', *International Planning Studies*, 9(4): 283–306.

Silverman, M. and Zach, T. (2003) 'Urban Regeneration: lessons from the Kathorus Special Presidential Project', a report prepared for the Gauteng Provincial Government Department of Housing.

Sim, V. (2005) 'Case study 1: eThekwini municipality', in A. Todes, V. Sim, P. Singh, M. Hlubi and C. Oelofse, 'Relationship between environment and planning in KwaZulu-Natal', *KwaZulu-Natal Provincial Planning and Development Commission – Main Series*, 77: 148–72.

Sim, V., Oelofse, C. and Todes, A. (2004) 'eThekwini Municipality: assessment of the municipality's environmental and planning processes', report to the eThekwini municipality, Durban.

Simone, A. (2001a) 'Straddling the divides: remaking associational life in the informal African city', *International Journal of Urban and Regional Research*, 25(1): 102–17.

—— (2001b) 'On the worldling of African cities', *African Cities Review*, 44(2): 15–43.

—— (2004) *For the City Yet to Come: Changing African Life in Four Cities*, Durham and London: Duke University Press.

Slater, D. (2004) *Geopolitics and the Post-colonial: Rethinking North–South Relations*, Oxford: Blackwell.

Smit, D. (1984) 'Urban planning and progressive social change in South Africa', paper presented at the Association of Collegiate Schools of Planning Annual Conference, New York, October.

—— (1988) 'The political economy of urban and regional planning in South Africa', unpublished doctoral thesis, Durban: University of Natal.

Smith, D. (ed.) (1992) *The Apartheid City and Beyond: Urbanization and Social Change in South Africa*, London: Routledge.

Soderbaum, F. and Taylor, I. (eds) (2003) *Regionalism and Uneven Development in Southern Africa: The case of the Maputo Development Corridor*, Aldershot: Ashgate.

Soja, E. (2000) *Postmetropolis: Critical Studies of Cities and Regions*, Oxford: Blackwell.

Somtunzi, N. (2002) 'The role of local government in income-generating poverty alleviation projects in Amahlathi Municipality', unpublished Master's dissertation, Durban: University of Natal.

Sowman, M. (2002) 'Integrating environmental sustainability issues into local government decision-making processes', in S. Parnell, E. Pieterse, M. Swilling and D. Wooldridge (eds) *Democratizing Local Government: The South African Experiment*, Cape Town: University of Cape Town Press.

Sowman, M. and Urquhart, P. (1998) *A Place Called Home: Environmental Issues and Low-cost Housing*, Cape Town: University of Cape Town Press.

Spiegel, A., Watson, V. and Wilkinson, P. (1996) 'Domestic diversity and fluidity among some African households in Greater Cape Town', *Social Dynamics*, 21(2): 7–30.

SPP (Surplus People's Project) (1983) 'Forced removals in South Africa, Cape Town and Pietermaritzburg', Cape Town: Surplus People's Project.

Statistics South Africa (2005) *Labour Force Survey*, Pretoria: Government Printer.

Stiglitz, J. (2002) *Globalisation and its Discontents*, London and New York: W.W Norton & Co.

Suttner, R. (2004) 'The UDF period and its meaning for contemporary South Africa', *Journal of Southern African Studies*, 30(3): 691–701.

Swanson, M. (1976) 'The "Durban system": roots of urban apartheid in colonial Natal', *African Studies*, 35: 159–76.

Swanstrom, T. (2001) 'What we argue about when we argue about regionalism', *Journal of Urban Affairs*, 23(5): 479–96.

Swilling, M. (1995) 'Rival futures: struggle visions, post-apartheid choices', in H. Judin and L.Vladislavic (eds) *Blank – Architecture, Apartheid and Beyond*, Rotterdam: NAI Publishers; Cape Town: David Philip.

—— (1997) 'Building democratic local urban governance in Southern Africa', in M. Swilling (ed.) *Governing Africa's Cities*, Johannesburg: Witwatersrand University Press.

—— (2004) 'Rethinking the sustainability of the South African city', *Development Update*, 5(1): 215–42.

Swilling, M., Humphries, R. and Shubane, K. (eds) (1991) *Apartheid City in Transition*, Oxford: Oxford University Press.

Taylor, I. (2001) 'Methodology and application of resources in the spatial development initiatives', report to the Development Bank of Southern Africa, Midrand.

Taylor, N. (1998) *Urban Planning Theory Since 1945*, London: Sage Publications.

Tewdwr-Jones, M. and Allmendinger, P. (1998) 'Deconstructing communicative rationality: a critique of Habermasian collaborative planning', *Environment and Planning A*, 30(11): 1975–89.

Thomas, E. and Crewe, M. (2000) 'Local authority responses to HIV/AIDS: an overview of a few key cities', *Urban Health and Development Bulletin*, 3(2): 566–82.

Thomas, H. (2004) 'What future for British planning theory', *Planning Theory*, 3(3): 189–98.

Tibaijuka, A. (2006) 'The importance of urban planning in urban poverty reduction and sustainable development', paper presented at World Planners Congress, Vancouver.

Todes, A. (1995) 'Gender in metropolitan development strategies: the case of Durban', *Cities*, 12(5): 327–36.

—— (1998) 'Restructuring, migration and regional policy in South Africa: the case of Newcastle', unpublished doctoral thesis, Durban: University of Natal.

—— (2000) 'Reintegrating the apartheid city? Urban policy and urban restructuring in Durban', in S. Watson and G. Bridges (eds) *A Companion to the City*, London: Blackwell.

—— (2002) 'Spatial change and Durban's spatial framework', in A. Bouillon, B. Freund, D. Hindson and B. Lootvoet (eds) *Governance, Urban Dynamics and Economic Development: A Comparative Analysis of the Metropolitan Areas of Durban, Abidjan and Marseilles, Three Cities Project*, Durban: Plumbline Publishing.

—— (2004) 'Regional planning and sustainability: limits and potentials of South Africa's integrated development plans', *Journal of Environmental Planning and Management*, 47(6): 843–62.

—— (2006) 'Urban spatial policy', in U. Pillay, R. Tomlinson and J. du Toit (eds) *Democracy and Delivery: Urban Policy in South Africa*, Johannesburg: HSRC Press.

Todes, A. and Harrison, P. (2004) 'Education after apartheid: planning and planning students in transition, *International Development Planning Review*, 26(2): 187–208.

Todes, A. and Posel, D. (1994) 'What has happened to gender in regional development analysis?' *Transformation*, 25: 58–78.

Todes, A., Harrison, P. and Watson, V. (2003) 'The changing nature of the job market for planners: implications for planning education', *Town and Regional Planning*, 46: 21–32.

Todes, A., Sithole, P. and Williamson, A. (2006) 'Gender, decentralization and integrated development planning in South Africa', paper presented at the International Development Research Centre Workshop, Women's Rights and Decentralization, Buenos Aires, September 2006.

Todes, A., Sim, V., Singh, P., Hlubi, M. and Oelofse, C. (2005) 'Relationship between environment and planning in KwaZulu-Natal', *KwaZulu-Natal Provincial Planning and Development Commission – Main Series*, 77: 1–222.

Tomlinson, M. (1999) 'South Africa's housing policy: lessons from four years of the new housing subsidy scheme', *Third World Planning Review*, 21(3): 283–95.

Tomlinson R. (2001) 'Housing policy in a context of HIV/AIDS and globalization', *International Journal of Urban and Regional Research*, 25(3): 649–57.

—— (2002) 'International best practice, enabling frameworks and the policy process: a South African case study', *International Journal of Urban and Regional Research*, 26(2): 377–88.

—— (2003a) 'The local economic development mirage in South Africa', *Geoforum*, 34: 113–32.

—— (2003b) 'HIV/AIDS and urban disintegration in Johannesburg', in P. Harrison, M. Huchzermeyer and M. Mayekiso (eds) *Confronting Fragmentation: Housing and Urban Development in a Democratizing Society*, Cape Town: University of Cape Town Press.

Tomlinson, R. and Addleson, M. (eds) (1987) *Regional Restructuring under Apartheid: Urban and Regional Policies in Contemporary South Africa*, Braamfontein: Ravan Press.

Tomlinson, R. with Abrahams, G. and Gildenhuys, B. (2003) 'The changing nature of South African housing demand: element three of the Department of Housing's programme to develop a new policy', report to the Department of Housing, Pretoria.

Tomlinson, R. with Abrahams, G. and Rust, K. (2002) 'Evaluation: housing delivery, sustainable settlements and the consequences of apartheid', *Policy and Programme Review*, Department of Housing, Gauteng Province, Johannesburg.

Tont, M. (2005) 'Neoliberalism and changing regional policy in Australia', *International Planning Studies*, 10(3–4): 183–200.

Townsend, S. (2002) 'Towards sustainable management', paper presented to the South African Planning Institute Conference, Planning Africa Conference, Durban, September.

Turok, I. (1994a) 'Urban planning in the transition from apartheid. Part 2: towards recon-
    struction', *Town Planning Review*, 65(4): 355–74.
–– (1994b) 'Urban planning in the transition from apartheid. Part 1: the legacy of con-
    trol', *Town Planning Review*, 65(3): 243–58.
Turok, I. and Watson, V. (2001) 'Divergent development in South African cities: strategic
    challenges facing Cape Town', *Urban Forum*, 12(2): 119–38.
UNDP (United Nations Development Programme) (2002) 'Agenda 21 case studies'.
    Available online at: http://www.undp.org.za/agenda21 (accessed 17 May 2006).
UN-Habitat (2002) 'Urban development and shelter strategies favouring the urban poor',
    Nairobi: UN Governing Council of the United Nations Human Settlements
    Programme.
UNODC (United Nations Office on Drugs and Crime) (2003) 'Seventh UN survey of
    crime trends and operations of criminal justice system covering the period
    1998–2000', United Nations Office on Drugs and Crime. Available online at:
    http://www.unodc.ord/pdf/crime/seventh_survey/7sf.pdf (accessed 26 June
    2006).
Van Donk, M. (2002) '*The missing element: HIV/AIDS in urban development planning,
    reviewing the South African response to the epidemic*', Working Paper No. 1998,
    London: Development Planning Unit, University College, London.
Van Huyssteen, E. and Oranje, M. (2003) 'Planning for crime prevention: the case of the
    City of Tshwane', Pretoria: Safer Africa. Available online at: http://www.safer-
    africa.org/DocumentsCentre/Monographs (accessed 28 September 2006).
Van Ryneveld, P. (2005) 'The fiscal system and sub-national patterns of growth in South
    Africa', report for the Programme of Advisory Support for Rural Livelihoods,
    London: Department for International Development.
Vigar, G. and Healey, P. (1999) 'Territorial integration and "plan-led" planning', *Planning
    Practice and Research*, 14(2): 153–70.
Vigar, G., Healey, P., Hull, A. and Davoudi, S. (2000) *Planning, Governance and Spatial
    Strategy in Britain*, New York: St Martin's Press.
Viruly Consulting (2006) 'Property market trends in South Africa', report to the Human
    Sciences Research Council, as input to the report on Urban Trends and
    Performance, for the State of Cities report, South African Cities Network,
    Johannesburg.
Voghera, A. (2003) 'European planning systems at the front of sustainability', paper pre-
    sented to the ACSP-AESOP congress, Leuven, July.
Wade, R. (1990) *Governing the Market: Economic Theory and the Role of Government*,
    Princeton: Princeton University Press.
Walker, M. (2001) 'Resource-based industrialisation strategies: a comparative analysis
    of the South African and international experience', *South African Geographical
    Journal*, 33(2) 93–104.

Wallerstein, I. (1984) 'Household structures and labour force formation in the capitalist world economy', in J. Smith, I. Wallerstein and H. Evers (eds) *Household and the World Economy*, Beverley Hills, CA: Sage.

Watson, V. (1998) 'Planning under political transition: lessons from Cape Town's Metropolitan Planning Forum', *International Planning Studies*, 3(3): 335–50.

—— (2002a) *Change and Continuity in Spatial Planning: Metropolitan Planning in Cape Town under Political Transition,* London: Routledge.

—— (2002b) 'Do we learn from planning practice? The contribution of the practice movement to planning theory', *Journal of Planning Education and Research*, 22(2): 178–87.

—— (2002c) 'The usefulness of normative planning theories in the context of Sub-Saharan Africa', *Planning Theory*, 1(1): 27–52.

—— (2003a) 'Conflicting rationalities: implications for planning theory and ethics', *Planning Theory and Practice*, 4(4): 395–408.

—— (2003b) 'Taking informality into account in planning education in South Africa', paper presented at the Workshop on Planning Education, Durban, January.

—— (2004) 'Transforming the South African city: issues of culture', *Architecture SA*, 8 (Jan/Feb).

—— (2006a) 'Position paper on the role of the town and regional planning system in the growth and development of South Africa', report to the JIPSA Technical Working Group.

—— (2006b) 'Deep difference: diversity, planning and ethics', in *Planning Theory*, 5(1): 31–50.

WCED (World Commission on Environment and Development) (1987) *Our Common Future*, Oxford: Oxford University Press.

Webster, E. and Adler, G. (1999) 'Towards a class compromise in South Africa's "double transition": bargaining liberalization and the consolidation of democracy', *Politics and Society*, 27(3): 347–85.

Weiss, L. (2000) 'Developmental states in transition: adapting, dismantling, innovating, not normalizing', *Pacific Review*, 13(1): 21–55.

Weiss, T. (2000) 'Governance, good governance: conceptual and actual challenges', *Third World Quarterly*, 21(5): 785–814.

Western Cape (2005) 'IDP Hearings 2005', report prepared by Department of Local Government and Housing, Western Cape Provincial Government, 30 September 2005, Cape Town. Available online at: http://www.capegateway.gov.za/eng/publications/reports_research (accessed 18 July 2006).

Western, J. (1981) *Outcast Cape Town*, Cape Town, Pretoria and Johannesburg: Human & Rousseau.

Wilkinson, P. (1996) 'A discourse of modernity: the Social and Economic Planning Council's fifth report on regional and town planning, 1944', *African Studies*, 55(2): 141–81.

—— (2002) 'Integrated planning at the local level? The problematic intersection of integrated development planning and integrated transport planning in contemporary
South Africa', paper presented at Planning Africa 2002: Regenerating Africa
through Planning, Durban, September.

Williamson, A., Kitchin, F. and Vaughan, A. (2004) 'Analysis of the municipal (spatial)
interpretation of the KwaZulu-Natal Industrial Development Strategy', McIntosh
Xaba Associates, report to the KwaZulu-Natal Department of Economic
Development and Tourism.

Williamson, A., Ndlovu, F., Sithole, P. and Todes, A. (2005) 'Decentralization and voice:
women's participation in integrated development planning processes in KwaZulu-
Natal', paper presented at the Gender Research, Urban Planning and Everyday Life
IV Conference, Gender and Generation, University of Lesotho, Roma, November.

Winkler, T. (2006) 'Kwere kwere journeys into strangeness: alternative narratives of hope
and social transformation in the inner city neighbourhood of Hillbrow,
Johannesburg', unpublished doctoral thesis submitted to the University of British
Columbia, Vancouver, Canada.

Yiftachel, O. (2001) 'Introduction: outlining the power of planning', in O. Yiftachel, J.
Little, D. Hedgcock and I. Alexander (eds) The Power of Planning: Spaces of
Control and Transformation, Dordrecht and London: Kluwer Academic Publishers.

—— (2003) 'Relocating "the critical"? Reflections from Israel/Palestine', Environment and
Planning D: Society and Space, 21(2): 137–42.

Zack, T. and Charlton, S. (2003) 'Better off, but. Beneficiaries' perceptions of the government's housing subsidy scheme', Occasional paper No. 12, Pretoria:
Department of Housing.

Zehner, R. (1999) 'Tracking planners' activities as part of the education review process:
New South Wales from 1979 to 1996', paper presented at the Australia–New
Zealand Association of Planning Schools Conference in Darwin, NT, September
1999.

INDEX

246–7; and participatory governance
88–9; and problems in local government
87; struggles to prepare 70, 88; study of
economic development strategies 146
Integrated Sustainable Rural Development
Strategy (ISRDS) 67, 105, 149
'intensified city' 120
Intergovernmental Relations Framework Act
2005 70, 84, 95
international: debates on planning 113–16,
175–7; planning trends 30, 36, 40, 41,
85; tendencies 214–17
International Labour Organization 226
International Monetary Fund 115
investment: in Cato Manor, Durban 150; coordination of 81; foreign 115; private
sector 108, 109, 117, 123, 243; in
property 129, 131; public sector 126,
250; in townships 153
Irurah, D. 167, 168
iTrump programme 69, 151
Ivory Park, Midrand 34

Jewel City 244
Johannesburg: Central Johannesburg
Partnership (CJP) 68; City Development
Strategy 70; corridors 63; crime rate 150;
evictions 240; Growth and Development
Strategy (GDS) 88, 99; informal traders
228; Jo'burg 2030 85; Johannesburg
Development Agency (JDA) 69;
Johannesburg Housing Company 69;
Johannesburg Municipal Proclamation Act
1901 22; modernist ideas 205; National
Spatial Development Perspective (NSDP)
105; Native (Urban Areas) Act 1923 24;
processing of land development
applications 156, 157; regional and
spatial inequalities **104**; spatial
development framework 125–6, **127**;
urban regeneration in 68–9, **69**; World
Summit for Sustainable Development 149
John, L. 145, 146
'joined-up' government 82, 92, 110, 114, 146
Joint Initiative on Priority Skills Acquisition
(JIPSA) 195, 249
Jourdan, P. 107, 109
'just city' perspective 113

Kahn, Mike 44, 180, 183, 184
Kaplan, M. 128, 155
Kathorus, East Rand 26, 59–60, 127
Khayelitsha, Cape Town 34
kinship networks 220, 227

knowledge 176; transfer 4
Krier, Leon 120
Krige, S. 99, 101
Kulipossa, F. 77, 87
KwaMashu 26
KwaZulu-Natal: civil war 36; HIV/AIDS 245;
integrated development plans (IDPs)
146, 170; land-use management 163,
165, 211–12; planning legislation 65–6;
regional and spatial inequalities **104**;
survey of planners 183, 184; traditional
leadership 86, 205, 211–12

labour camps 21
labour supply 21, 22, 29, 33, 41–2
Land Act (1913) 21, 37
Land Act (1936) 25, 37
Land Development Objectives (LDOs) 62,
64–5, 80, 81
land, differing meanings of 218, 221, 222
land economy 218
land ownership 10, 212
Land Reform and Restitution 59
Land Tenure Advisory Board (LTAB) 26
land-use management 42, 53, 64, 131, 144,
154, 163–6; delays in implementing
legislation 65, 82, 124, 243; equity
principle 211–12; facilitating acquisition
42, 61–2; informal economic activity 231;
and integration with planning 243; and
the market 155–7; processing of land
development applications 156–7, 164–5,
209; reform 71–2
Latin America 115, 186, 251
Le Corbusier 23, 204–5
Leftwich, Adrian 76, 77
Legal Resource Centre 47–8
Less Formal Township Establishment Act 1991
37
liberal approach to planning 39, 40–3, 218,
223
'liberal moral order' 240
Limehill, Natal 28
Limpopo 86, **104**, 187, 246
literacies 190, 201
Local Agenda 21 62, 115–16, 161, 163, 170,
171
Local Economic Development (LED) 145–9,
225, 229, 230, 233, 246
local government: crisis in 70, 87–8;
developmental 79, 137–8, 145, 218,
239; elections 79, 83; forums 37, 52;
framework for democratic, non-racial
79–80; and planning 12, 66–7, 71, 80–3,

ALSO AVAILABLE FROM ROUTLEDGE...

DESIRE LINES

SPACE, MEMORY AND IDENTITY IN THE POST-APARTHEID CITY
EDITED BY NOËLEEN MURRAY, NICK SHEPHERD AND MARTIN HALL

This collection investigates cities as sites of memory and desire (and of fear and forgetting); as contested spaces given to plays of power and privilege, identity and difference. How have the profound social and political transformations and the release of energies in South Africa post-1994 been written into its cities and public spaces?

Desire Lines: Space, Memory and Identity in the Post-Apartheid City addresses the innovative strategies that have emerged in the sphere of public culture in post-apartheid South Africa. The case studies pay particular attention to how these strategies relate to contests over heritage practices in community museums, tourism and other memory projects.

Drawing together work by architects and planners, historians, archaeologists, social anthropologists and other scholars working in the fields of African Studies, Literary Studies, Heritage and Public Culture Studies and from the spatial disciplines, this selection of papers offers insight into the debates that have reconfigured the shape of city spaces, and of heritage and public culture, while posing new questions in the direction of scholarship.

ISBN: 978-0-415-70130-3 (Hb)
      978-0-415-70131-0 (Pb)
      978-0-203-79949-9 (eBook)

Available at all good bookshops
For ordering and further information please visit:
http://www.routledge.com/builtenvironment

THE FRIGHTENED LAND

LAND, LANDSCAPE AND POLITICS IN SOUTH AFRICA IN THE TWENTIETH CENTURY
JENNIFER BENINGFIELD

An investigation into the spatial politics of separation and division in South Africa, principally during the apartheid years, and the effects of these physical and conceptual barriers on the land.

In contrast to the weight of literature focusing on post-apartheid South Africa, the focus of this book includes the spatial, political and cultural landscape practices of the apartheid government and also refers to contemporary work done in Australia, England and the US. It probes the uncertainty and ambiguity of identities and cultures in post-apartheid society in order to gain a deep understanding of the history that individuals and society now confront.

Drawing on a wealth of research materials including literature, maps, newspapers, monuments, architectural drawings, government legislation, tourist brochures, political writing and oral histories, this book is well illustrated throughout and is a unique commentary on the spatial politics of a time of enormous change.

ISBN 978-0-415-36555-0 (Hb)
      978-0-415-36593-2 (Pb)
      978-0-203-01691-6 (eBook)

Available at all good bookshops
For ordering and further information please visit:
http://www.routledge.com/builtenvironment